Dramatic Character in the English Romantic Age

Edmund Kean as Macbeth

DRAMATIC CHARACTER IN THE ENGLISH ROMANTIC AGE

JOSEPH W. DONOHUE, JR.

PRINCETON UNIVERSITY PRESS
PRINCETON, NEW JERSEY
1970

L. C. Card: 71-112997

ISBN: 0-691-06187-4

This book has been composed in Linotype Baskerville

Printed in the United States of America

by Princeton University Press, Princeton, New Jersey

For

my mother and father

with gratitude

for their understanding

Acknowledgments

AN AUTHOR'S debts are in some ways beyond recording, but it is a pleasure still to name those friends and colleagues, scholars and library staffs, whose knowledge, advice, and assistance went far towards the making of this book.

The late Alan S. Downer awakened my interest in the drama and theater of post-Restoration England. Afterwards, with an understanding and engagement that gave character to all he undertook, he read each draft of this work from its inception as an essay on Hazlitt to its present form, and then, always generous, loaned his watercolor painting by George Cattermole of Edmund Kean as Macbeth for reproduction as a frontispiece. To him I had hoped to pay my fullest thanks in completing a study in which, through example and encouragement, he retained so large a share.

A. Walton Litz first drew my attention to Romantic critical theory and practice, and he, Gerald E. Bentley, and Carlos Baker read portions of the manuscript and gave much useful advice. The bibliographical note was composed at the suggestion of E.D.H. Johnson. Others who helped to shape this work include C. F. Burgess, Denis Donoghue, MacDonald Emslie, Attilio Favorini, Suzanne Gossett, Shirley S. Kenny, Arthur C. Kirsch, Peter Kline, Robert S. Knapp, John C. Pratt, C.J.L. Price, John H. Reibetanz, John W. Velz, John M. Wallace, Robert M. Wren, and the late John Crow, a mentor whose deep learning, amplitudinous wit, and tireless critical energies are unforgettable by all who knew him.

Research conducted over several years benefited from the timely aid and direction of Sybil Rosenfeld and the late I. K. Fletcher of the Society for Theater Research; George W. Nash, Curator, and the staff of the Enthoven Collection, Victoria and Albert Museum; Sir Julian Hall and Mrs. Dorothy Anderson, Librarian, of the Garrick Club; Jennifer Aylmer, Curator of the British Theater Museum; the staffs of the Reading Room, North Library, Department of Manuscripts, and Department of Prints and Drawings, the British Museum; Dr. Louis B. Wright, former Director, Dorothy E. Mason, Reference Librarian, and the staff of the Folger Shakespeare Library; Helen D. Willard, Curator, and the staff of the Harvard Theater Collection; Marguerite McAneny, former Curator, and Mary Ann Jensen, Curator of the William Seymour Theater Collection, Princeton University Library, and the staff of the Library.

The completion of this book was speeded by the award of a Frelinghuysen dissertation fellowship at Princeton; a Fulbright junior fellowship to King's College, University of London; a grant-in-aid from the American Council of Learned Societies; a fellowship at the Folger Shakespeare Library; the Henry E. Annan Bicentennial Preceptorship at Princeton; and funds in support of photography and typing from the Princeton University Research Council for the Humanities and Social Sciences. Except for some few products of my own camera, the photographs were made by John G. Peoples and Willard S. Starks of the Princeton University staff, Horace Groves of the Folger Shakespeare Library staff, and my colleague John G. Peck, whom I especially thank for photographing the frontispiece. Mrs. Helen S. Wright typed a long, difficult manuscript with flawless proficiency and endless good will. William M. Hamilton, my editor, laid expert snares for elusive errors and kept a trans-oceanic correspondence in constant control.

The editors of the *Keats-Shelley Journal, Studies in English Literature 1500-1900,* and *Theatre Notebook* have kindly permitted the publication of parts of this work which first appeared, with some differences, in their pages. Permission to reproduce graphic materials and to quote from sources in their possession has cordially been granted by Harry R. Beard, the British Museum, the Folger Shakespeare Library, the Galleria Nazionale d'Arte Antica, the Garrick Club, the Harvard Theater Collection, and the Princeton University Library.

To all these individuals and institutions I offer sincere and warmest thanks.

JOSEPH W. DONOHUE, JR.

London
May 1970

Contents

PART III. SHAKESPEAREAN CHARACTER IN THE ROMANTIC AGE

Illustrations

Dramatic Character
in the English Romantic Age

Abbreviations and Citations

Abbreviations of titles of journals follow those established by the Modern Language Association and printed in its annual bibliography.

For plays, all dates in parentheses accompanied by the name of a theater refer to the season of the first production, in London unless otherwise stated; unaccompanied dates are of the first edition. The place of publication of all works which appeared up to 1850 is London unless otherwise indicated.

The bibliographical citations in the notes, although sometimes full, are meant to be representative rather than exhaustive. Readers wishing more information may consult the Bibliographical Note.

Introduction

i. The Subject of Dramatic Character

THE EMBLEM of human nature on the stage and in the text of the play is a constantly engaging but problematic figure. Whether man remains in all ages the same or possesses no nature, only a history, his analogue in dramatic art has in the course of time undergone striking transformations. Andromache, Ophelia, Beatrice Cenci, and Blanche DuBois may all have a reference in distressed femininity; Agamemnon, Faustus, Cato, and Willy Loman may each epitomize inevitable human defeat. But if their common plight sometimes reassures us, it helps very little to explain the protean differences they exhibit. For this explanation we turn more to history than philosophy. Yet philosophy has its history too. One of the most stimulating aspects of the study of dramatic character is that its link with surrounding ideas and assumptions about human experience is close and sure. Players are the abstract and brief chronicles of the time. In the days of Garrick and Kean (as always) players unwittingly brought to their characters certain qualities common only to themselves and to their fellows opposite that quaint but practical rail of spikes that edged the sides of ornate proscenium stages. Few better ways exist of understanding the past than by studying its theater. The subjects, the conventions of art in a given time say much about that time as a whole—its delights and aversions, its shared attitudes and tacit preconceptions, its image of itself.

The present work is based on the premise that a study of the drama, the theater, and criticism in the English Romantic age and in the period leading up to it reveals innovations that mark it as "revolutionary" and so connect it meaningfully with our own day. Often we use the term *modern* to express this connection, and in doing so we suggest a break with the past. Significant cleavage begins to occur in the late eighteenth-century movement toward subjectivity in the arts—and in religion, philosophy, and even government, where a new sense of man's individuality contributed to revolutions (in France and America) and to a subsequent series of reforms (in England) that have determined to a great extent the history of nations since that time. But revolutions, as everyone knows, do not flower overnight. Continuity endures, valuable to weigh along with change but demanding an accurate balance. Surely the development of the novel from Defoe through Richardson to Sterne, of poetry from Pope through Johnson to Wordsworth, and of painting from Hogarth through Reynolds to Fuseli, must be weighed with such care, and has been. Yet no documentation of this movement toward subjectivity exists for the drama and theater of the period. Specifically, no study has been made of a phenomenon that emerged in the late eighteenth and early nineteenth centuries: a change in the concept of dramatic character. The plays of this age form a homogeneous group, as Allardyce Nicoll's comprehensive account of post-Commonwealth drama has shown.[1] A similar unity lies in the theatrical productions and actors' performances recorded in Arthur Colby Sprague's detailed syntheses.[2] A like wholeness reveals itself in the ideas of Romantic critics surveyed in René Wellek's imposing history.[3] But the area in which these interests overlap has not been explored. The point at which the actor converges with the dramatic character he interprets and portrays for his audience remains a fruitful subject.

The purpose of this book is to describe what occurs on that at once palpable and elusive place William Hazlitt called "the lofty but striking platform of the imagination." Not a comprehensive or even relatively brief history of English Romantic drama, nor an exhaustive or piecemeal account of the theater in which it developed (or against which it sometimes revolted), this study singles out a related special concern: the Romantic concept of dramatic character. The variety of its manifestations argues its importance. It is found with equal prominence in the new drama of the period and in the fresh treatment of plays inherited from past generations. It is similarly evident in actors' interpretations and in the tradition of character criticism developing independently. In addition, it makes its way into the graphic arts, particularly that class of ephemera known as the theatrical portrait. To treat such variety in full is plainly impossible in a single volume, and I

[1] *A History of English Drama 1660-1900*, 6 vols. (Cambridge, Eng., 1952-59).

[2] *Shakespeare and the Actors* (Cambridge, Mass., 1944); *Shakespearian Players and Performances* (Cambridge, Mass., 1953).

[3] *A History of Modern Criticism: 1750-1950*, 4 vols. (New Haven, 1955-65).

make no claim to completeness of this sort. My approach is frankly eclectic. Bearing in mind the wholeness and immediacy of theatrical performance, I propose to examine in detail a relatively small number of plays and productions, each representing an important facet of the concept of dramatic character that burgeoned in England in the eighteenth century and attained full growth in the time of Coleridge and Kean. Certain aspects of this development have been omitted, either because, like melodrama, they deserve and have received full length treatment on their own or because, like farce, pantomime, and opera, they involve specialized considerations irrelevant to the topic as a whole. This book concentrates on dramatic character in tragedy, on the stage and off, during the half-century up to 1820. One chapter on comedy is also included, since the issues raised by the development of this genre illuminate by analogy those of contemporary serious drama.

Because of the derivative nature of Romantic plays and the continuity of theatrical production behind them, it will be necessary to look back as far as the Jacobean drama and the Restoration theater for contexts adequate to an understanding of dramatic character in this later age. But despite my view that the fullest historical perspective comprehends almost three centuries beginning about 1600, I have chosen to focus on the half-century that falls about two-thirds of the way along in this period. I have done so for several reasons. One of these is simply that I do not think a work of manageable proportions could begin with Shakespeare and Fletcher and end with the emergence of "modern" British drama in the works of George Bernard Shaw. More important, the essential fact about the concept of dramatic character in this long period is its increasing emphasis on the character's subjective mental state. This preoccupation becomes evident in the Romantic age and then continues, more domesticated perhaps but largely unaltered, through succeeding years. The innovations in nineteenth-century theater and drama include the greater development of illusion and spectacle as qualities of production, technical advances in the capabilities of the stage, and adjustment of subject matter to a changing age and audience, but not any fundamental change in the concept of dramatic character itself. So I have concluded this study at about 1820, by which time Kemble and Mrs. Siddons had retired from the stage; Hazlitt had ended his career as a day-by-day reviewer; Kean had established himself as the foremost subjective actor of his day; and Macready had made his mark as the hero of Sheridan Knowles' *Virginius*—a drama so thoroughly Victorian, in spite of its early date, that to follow its tendencies would be to find no culmination short of the early plays of Shaw, the transplantation of Ibsen to England, and the growth of the independent theater movement throughout western Europe. Moreover, a study of the nineteenth-century drama and theater would ideally employ principles and emphases foreign to the present aims. And so I shall attempt to describe a phenomenon most characteristic of the era of Burke and Shelley, Siddons and Kean, Lamb and Hazlitt, in hope of setting in a clearer light the complex ties of dramatic character to the society and culture of that age.

ii. Methods and Assumptions

In the course of its development, modern scholarship has come to understand that the individual play may be illuminated by other works to which it bears similarity. This approach has been particularly successful in the case of Renaissance drama. While granting that each playwright brings to his subject a distinct personality and background, with all that these imply, readers have found that the uniqueness of the work holds greater meaning when seen to emerge from the conventions it embodies. Whether they explore craftsmen's guilds, midsummer revels, Christian tropes, baited bears, or pastoral romances, the best of such studies combine the skill to identify and define patterns with a sense that, far from existing in lifeless permanence, they undergo constant change. To cite an instance, the characteristic concern of Jacobean tragedy for moral order may be viewed as a heritage from the medieval belief in God's Providence and the Tudor fascination with the hero and his deserved or unmerited misfortunes. It is in fact true that, in dealing with theatrical and dramatic art, we must sometimes establish long temporal contexts to comprehend certain developments. While it is clearly significant to examine the period from 1580 to 1600, or from 1880 to 1900, a similar study of the two decades from 1780 to 1800 would prove thankless, if not futile. An investigation of Romantic drama—or even, let us say, Georgian drama—requires the adoption of a longer historical perspective.

To determine its limits, two basic facts must be taken into account. First, the traditional English repertory theater maintains a large number of plays, sometimes altered, sometimes withdrawn, sometimes revived, all to suit the changing capacities of the company and the shifting tastes of demanding audiences. Second, as a result, the author of a new play must compete not only with those of his contemporaries but with works of proven merit, some of them one hundred or one hundred-fifty years old. The theater of the age was emphatically not a playwright's theater but an actor's theater, and the successful playwright was one with the knack of tailoring his piece to the abilities and tastes of players who in turn depended for their livelihood on an almost instinctive responsiveness to the vagaries of tyrannical theatergoers. "The Drama's Laws the Drama's Patrons give," explained Doctor Johnson in his celebrated prologue of 1747; and they "who live to please, must please to live." In the situation Johnson describes, the "Playwright's Laws" were also clear. To win the approbation of a fiercely critical theater manager, he must write to satisfy the demonstrated preferences of the drama's patrons. And if wise he will include an exploitable role for each possessive actor and actress whose specialty falls within the scope of his play. By and large, audiences did not go to the theater to see *The Alchemist* or *The Chances;* they went to see Garrick as Abel Drugger [see Plate 1] or Don John. Indifferent toward *The Fair Penitent,* they risked the loss of shoes and limbs to view Mrs. Siddons as Calista. Kemble, not Addison, drew audiences to *Cato* long after its politically sensational subject had ceased to amuse. [see Plate 2] For Kean as Sir Giles Overreach and Eliza O'Neill as Juliet the conditions were the same. The play was chiefly a wagon for a star, and the sooner the playwright realized that his task was to fashion such vehicles, in a self-effacing and even self-degrading way, the sooner he achieved his goal of performance—and counted the proceeds of his benefit night.

Because of these circumstances, unfortunate as they were for the writer bent on becoming a dramatist, a study of the drama and theater of the Romantic age cannot be concerned with a series of brilliant examples of the playwright's art. It is in fact all too obvious that the autonomous artistic unity and vitality of individual Romantic plays cannot be the object of sustained pursuit. Yet if, however regretfully, we make this admission, there remains a subject to engage attention. The characters of Romantic drama manifest a concept whose radical departure from the notion of character in the age of Shakespeare marks the change from which grew the drama as we know it today. The emergence of this concept on the stage and in the study is one of the most important cultural manifestations of the Age of Revolution. Behind it, in the perspective presently sought, lie some two hundred years of dramatic writing and performance. Although an investigation of dramatic character in the Romantic age must naturally include the acting and theatrical production of its day as well as its corpus of dramatic literature, these several concerns are best explored as a culmination of trends in the drama that began as far back as the age of Beaumont and Fletcher, and of trends in the theater that appeared no later than the time of Davenant and Killigrew.

As I have explained, a conventional historical survey of this long tradition would exceed reasonable limits. Accordingly, the reader will find another approach, of which he is due some advance notice. In examining the conventional features of a given play, I do not regularly stop to establish conventionality by adducing forty-nine others like it. Such a task, admittedly important, has been done already in not a few areas relevant to this study by such scholars as Allardyce Nicoll, Alfred Harbage, Bertrand Evans, Arthur Sherbo, and Eric Rothstein.[4] Where it has not been done the reader is of course free to test my sense of conventionality by adducing whatever other plays he likes. No claim is made that the particular works discussed in detail are the only ones amenable to the purpose. A similar grouping that the reader prefers would doubtless do equally well. Where I plump for the importance of a certain work, I do so because it seems an unusually apt representative case, or simply because it raises in an especially convenient way issues that must in any case be raised.

The space "saved" by assuming a knowledge of dramatic convention and continuity on the part of the reader has been devoted to establishing other contexts which, except in the case of sentimental comedy, have been largely ignored. For example, to my knowledge no one has attempted to estimate the force of eight-

[4] In addition to Nicoll's *History,* see Harbage, *Cavalier Drama* (New York and London, 1936); Evans, *Gothic Drama from Walpole to Shelley* (Berkeley and Los Angeles, 1947); Sherbo, *English Sentimental Drama* (East Lansing, Mich., 1957); and Rothstein, *Restoration Tragedy: Form and the Process of Change* (Madison and Milwaukee, 1967).

eenth-century notions of "the sublime" on contemporary tragedy. Nor does any estimate exist of the *combined* effect of traditional comic form and eighteenth-century moral philosophy on the theatrical and cultural milieu in which both Cumberland and Goldsmith wrote. Admittedly it takes a certain temerity to link a tinseled commercial treasury-saver like Sheridan's *Pizarro* with contemporary notions of natural religion, but the risk is worth the possible gain in understanding at stake. These contexts provide backgrounds for detailed inspection of the characters and dramatic forms of some relatively few plays. The assumption throughout is that the presence of high literary quality (whatever that may be; to us and to the Romantics it is often a different thing) is not necessary to recommend a work for attention. A very bad play may well prove more instructive than a mediocre one, dead from inanition instead of apoplexy. Accordingly the reader may find treated in sometimes a dozen or more pages, or even in whole chapters, plays covered in a grudging half-paragraph or bludgeoning footnote in histories of the drama. Dealing with bad plays is the occupational hazard of any student of the drama, regardless of his period. The percentage of such in the Romantic age is not much higher than in other times; more, however, are hopelessly undistinguished by anything, positive or negative. I have sought out those with recognizable features, and where some quality, heretofore undiscerned, uncovers itself, I strive to do it justice.

But in many instances no effort of the sort is required. For this reason, and for others more important, material on contemporary drama is balanced with an equal emphasis on Shakespeare. Here again the purpose has not been to provide a history. Eighteenth- and nineteenth-century Shakespearean acting, production, and criticism have been extensively documented, and mere repetition is pointless. These subjects, however, are often inspected in germ-free wards, uncontaminated by air from other quarters. As in the case of the contemporary drama, the treatment of Shakespeare in this period is set in larger but nonetheless relevant contexts. At the same time, I have singled out two of Shakespeare's characters instead of surveying the fortunes of many. Because Richard III and Macbeth represent for the Romantic age two extremes within which human nature itself is encompassed, they hold a special attraction. But in concentrating on them I suggest that they are unusually significant, not exceptional, instances. The eighteenth-

and nineteenth-century treatment of Shakespeare's heroic characters is all of a piece. Any one will do to see what was happening; Richard and Macbeth do especially well.

Devoting half a book to a playwright of another and much different time will suggest Shakespeare's importance for the study of dramatic character in the period of Coleridge, Shelley, and Hazlitt. It should serve as well to test the conclusions of the first two parts of this study. Simply stated, my belief is that the reception accorded the plays of Shakespeare in ages after his own provides a valuable key, not only to contemporary drama, but to the very attitudes and assumptions that make any age recognizably itself.

PART I

Dramatic Character and Romantic Drama

CHAPTER I

The Affective Drama of Situation

> I tried to imitate [Shakespeare's] manner in the *Remorse*, and when I had done, I found I had been tracking Beaumont and Fletcher, and Massinger instead.
>
> —Coleridge, *Table Talk* (1835)

i. Shakespearean and Fletcherian Drama in the Seventeenth Century

AN AUTHOR who attempts to write for a repertory theater will naturally cast his eye about for successful models on which to base his own play. Because this is especially true of the English theater in the early nineteenth century, the great popularity of Shakespeare in that day is commonly taken as the key to the nature of Romantic drama. And the common conclusion is that the later playwright badly misinterpreted the poet whose works had inspired him. Not only in their language but in dramatic character and structure as well, the plays of Romantic writers have been seen largely as the inevitable product of Bardolatry. Surely, no playwright of that age or any other could equal the high esteem in which Shakespeare was held in both the theaters and closets of the late eighteenth and nineteenth centuries, and his influence on the period of Coleridge and Keats was undeniably extensive. Close echoes of *Macbeth*, for example, evident in plays as early as George Lillo's *Fatal Curiosity* (Haymarket, 1736), occur almost as a matter of course in Shelley's *The Cenci* (1819). Imitations of the diction and general tone of Shakespearean tragedy number in the hundreds, including Richard Lalor Sheil's *Evadne; or, The Statue* (Covent Garden, 1818-19), a work seemingly typical of the spawn of the pseudo-Shakespearean Muse. Notwithstanding his acknowledged debt to the plot of James Shirley's *The Traitor*, Sheil's tragedy appears to bear all the marks of an attempt to indite flowing dramatic verse, late-Tudor style, as a fitting ornament for the panoramic structure familiar to any reader of Shakespeare. It is easy to judge *Evadne*, along with its many fellows, as no more than an outrageous bastard claimant to the legacy of the great Elizabethan.[1]

Such a facile view of Sheil's play, however, omits a vital fact that, once considered, alters the entire context of discussion. We may come at this fact conveniently by simply looking again at Sheil's title. The name of the chief female character, by more than mere coincidence, repeats that of a prominent figure in Beaumont and Fletcher's *The Maid's Tragedy*. A comparison of the two plays suggests that Sheil knew the earlier well and drew on its basic situation, the unsuspecting marriage of a fine young man to Evadne, a woman supposedly virginal but in reality the king's debauched mistress. Nor is this an isolated example of Fletcherian influence. The age abounds with plays that pay lip service to Shakespeare but are basically Fletcherian in structure and in the presentation of dramatic character. That this is so may be understood by considering the long tradition of performance which lies behind them. In assuming that the Romantic playwright based his dramas on the successful characteristics of those around him, one must carefully distinguish between the general popularity of a playwright and the extent of his direct influence. For it is a fact that, while Shakespeare was easily the most popular of playwrights in the Romantic age, he was not so at an earlier time when a theatrical situation developed that ultimately conditioned the nature of Romantic drama.

In the early decades of the seventeenth century a schism took place in what had been up to that time a homogeneous popular stage.[2] An aristocratic, indoor theater developed to attract the more cultivated segments of audiences that before had frequented the popular houses. Here a new kind of drama was de-

[1] Arthur E. DuBois' defense of nineteenth-century drama against the supposed ravages of Shakespearean influence appeared as long ago as 1934, but little attention has been paid to it—"Shakespeare and 19th-Century Drama," *ELH*, I (1934), 163-196. Previously, Allardyce Nicoll had observed that Sheil's mind "was filled with images and ideas culled from Byron, Fletcher and Kotzebue," but Professor Nicoll views Renaissance dramatic influence largely in terms of language, and this he sees—rightly—as predominantly Shakespearean—*A History of Early Nineteenth Century Drama 1800-1850*, 2 vols. (Cambridge, Eng., 1930), I, 167, 88-91, 157-159.

[2] See G. E. Bentley's account of this well-known phenomenon in "Shakespeare and the Blackfriar's Theatre," *ShS*, I (1948), 38-50.

veloping, its most notable practitioners a team of "entertainers to the Jacobean gentry," Francis Beaumont and John Fletcher. Although other playwrights including Shakespeare and Massinger shared their success in these early years, the plays of Beaumont and Fletcher endured most successfully the ordeal of translation from their own period to that of the Restoration. In 1668, less than a decade after regular performances were available to Restoration playgoers, Dryden summarized the popularity of the two authors. "Their Playes," he observed, "are now the most pleasant and frequent entertainments of the Stage; two of theirs being acted through the year for one of *Shakespheare's* or *Johnsons. . . .*"[3]

Dryden's estimate of frequency of performance and general popularity presages the findings of modern scholars. Some thirty-nine plays by these writers were acted between 1660 and 1700, and three more may have been. Sixteen were mounted during the first season alone, fifteen in the next. Just as important, the majority appeared unaltered, and the approximate one-third revised were almost all produced later in the period.[4] During the same years the plays of Shakespeare followed a much less certain course. Although by 1700 twenty-six had found their way to the stage, no more than six appeared in a single season, some for perhaps only one or two performances. Introduced gradually over forty years, not immediately and in great numbers like those of Beaumont and Fletcher, Shakespeare's works were produced consistently as adaptations, many extensively rewritten and some even transmogrified into operatic spectacles.[5]

Clearly, Beaumont and Fletcher's plays were suitable to Restoration audiences in their pre-Commonwealth form, while

[3] *Of Dramatick Poesie, An Essay* (1668), Sig. H1.

[4] See John Harold Wilson, *The Influence of Beaumont and Fletcher on Restoration Drama* (Columbus, 1928); Eleanor Boswell, *The Restoration and Court Stage (1660-1702)* (Cambridge, Mass., 1932), pp. 105-107; and, especially, Arthur Colby Sprague, *Beaumont and Fletcher on the Restoration Stage* (Cambridge, Mass., 1926). Consult also *The London Stage 1660-1800*, Pt. I, ed. William Van Lennep, with a critical intro. by Emmett L. Avery and Arthur H. Scouten (Carbondale, Ill., 1965), Intro., p. cxxviii, and text, *passim.*

[5] *London Stage,* Pt. 1, Intro., pp. cxxviii-cxxix; see also Hazelton Spencer, *Shakespeare Improved* (Cambridge, Mass., 1927); Arthur H. Scouten, "The Increase in Popularity of Shakespeare's Plays in the Eighteenth Century," *SQ,* VII (1956), 189-202; and Christopher Spencer, ed., *Five Restoration Adaptations of Shakespeare* (Urbana, 1965), Intro., pp. 1-3.

Shakespeare's required often extreme alteration to accord with the changed tastes of this later generation of playgoers. Although Shakespeare's reputation as a playwright scaled unimagined heights in later years, his works were evidently not of considerable practical influence in the early days of the Restoration, when playwrights were seeking appropriate forms and techniques to reinvigorate the almost dormant Commonwealth theater. The fact that Beaumont and Fletcher's works achieved immediate and phenomenal success in the first decade of the Restoration, while certainly reflecting the understandable paucity of new plays, also suggests that Restoration playwrights found available to them, on the stages of their own theaters, models of successful performed drama which they might naturally attempt to emulate.[6]

Consequently, examination of the debt of Romantic drama to the plays of previous ages can hardly dwell primarily on Shakespeare or other dramatists whose plays either failed to survive the interregnum or did so predominantly in severely altered form. It must instead concern the two playwrights whose works above all others endured the widespread changes in theaters, companies, and plays that occurred during the seventeenth century. Study of the English drama leads to an awareness of continuity as its abiding characteristic. Most plays either openly or clandestinely derive from those that come before. This is particularly true of the early Restoration, when authors and theatrical managers almost systematically rifled the stores accumulated over the previous century for whatever might work as it stood or else be adapted or transformed entirely to satisfy changed but ever-demanding audiences.[7] The reputation of Beaumont and Fletcher declined during the closing years of the century and then fell into virtual eclipse during the next. The success of *The Chances* as a vehicle for David Garrick, the perennial popularity of *Rule A Wife and Have A Wife*, and the temporary revival of

[6] The classic example is the heroic play; see Arthur C. Kirsch, *Dryden's Heroic Drama* (Princeton, 1965). Consult also James W. Tupper, "The Relation of the Heroic Play to the Romances of Beaumont and Fletcher," *PMLA*, xx (1905), 584-621.

[7] Alfred Harbage established a firm idea of continuity in the development of seventeenth-century drama in *Cavalier Drama* (New York and London, 1936); see esp. pp. 255-256, as well as Harbage, "Elizabethan-Restoration Palimpsest," *MLR*, xxxv (1940), 287-319, and Leslie Hotson, *The Commonwealth and Restoration Stage* (Cambridge, Mass., 1928).

interest in *Philaster* and *Bonduca* spurred by George Colman the Elder are lonely exceptions to the obscurity that overtook their works.[8] Yet, phenomenally, the *pattern* of their plays persisted undeterred well into the nineteenth century.

To identify this influence and to chart the course it held through a series of important mutations are the purposes of this chapter and the three following. I propose to show that serious Fletcherian drama contains in essence or in embryo the characteristics manifested by Romantic tragedy. The development of the Fletcherian pattern, following a line through the temporary success of the heroic play and the more long-lived pathetic tragedies and "she-tragedies" that evolved from it, culminated in a form of drama still fundamentally Fletcherian, even though heavily influenced by empirical theories of psychological perception, notions of conduct inherited from eighteenth-century moral philosophy, and other equally profound cultural movements.[9]

ii. Character and Scene in Fletcherian Drama

Commenting on the ill-fated revival of *Philaster* at Drury Lane in 1722-23, the *St. James's Journal* viewed it as "an Attempt that deserv'd more Success than it met with: The natural Rise of the Distress in that Play, that Simplicity of Passion in the young Maid, with the many fine Passages throughout, pleas'd every one who has a just Taste of those Entertainments."[10] Similarly, a few years earlier, Charles Johnson summarized the qualities discriminating playgoers seek. "Expiring Tragedy," he observed, can "hope for Countenance and Patronage but from those few, very few elegant Spirits who are pleas'd with the Distress of a well wrought Scene, who with the utmost Indulgence to their Reason, behold the Conduct of our Passions on the Stage, and with a generous Sympathy feel alternate Joy and Pain, when Virtue either

[8] See Lawrence B. Wallis, *Fletcher, Beaumont & Company: Entertainers to the Jacobean Gentry* (New York, 1947), pp. 243-249, and Donald J. Rulfs, "Beaumont and Fletcher on the London Stage 1776-1833," *PMLA*, LXIII (1948), 1245-64.

[9] Following general critical precedent, I use the convenient form "Fletcherian" to refer to the dramatic mode under discussion, without meaning to slight the collaborative efforts of Beaumont or any other playwright, especially Massinger.

[10] 8 December 1722, quoted in *The London Stage 1660-1800*, Pt. II, ed. Emmett L. Avery (Carbondale, Ill., 1960), II, 697.

conquers, or is contending with adverse Fate."[11] A familiar aesthetic argument against older ideas of Aristotelian mimetic order, Johnson's comment pairs nicely with that of the *St. James's Journal* to indicate an important early eighteenth-century emphasis on the development of distress, "Simplicity" of passion, and rhetorical display. These observations are strikingly typical, not at all novel. With regard to Fletcherian drama, such ideas first found expression in Shirley's well-known eulogy of Beaumont and Fletcher in the First Folio (1647):

> You may here find passions raised to that excellent pitch and by such insinuating degrees that you shall not chuse but consent, & go along with them, finding your self at last grown insensibly the very same person you read, and then stand admiring the subtile Trackes of your engagement. Fall on a Scene of love and you will never believe the writers could have the least roome left in their soules for another passion, peruse a Scene of manly Rage, and you would sweare they cannot be exprest by the same hands, but both are so excellently wrought, you must confesse none, but the same hands, could worke them.
>
> . . . Thou shalt meete almost in every leafe a soft purling passion or *spring* of sorrow so powerfully wrought high by the teares of innocence, and *wronged Lovers*, it shall perswade thy eyes to weepe into the streame, and yet smile when they contribute to their owne ruines.[12]

[11] *The Force of Friendship. A Tragedy* (1710), Sigs. A2-A2ᵛ, quoted in Eric Rothstein, *Restoration Tragedy: Form and the Process of Change* (Madison and Milwaukee, 1967), p. 19; see also Rothstein, "English Tragic Theory in the Late Seventeenth Century," *ELH*, XXIX (1962), 306-323. I am indebted to Rothstein for ideas about late seventeenth-century Aristotelianism and other notions discussed below.

[12] *Comedies and Tragedies Written by Francis Beavmont and Iohn Fletcher Gentlemen* (1647), Sig. A4ᵛ. Because it is essential to my argument, I quote this passage despite its frequent appearance in previous scholarship and criticism. Among the works helpful in contributing ideas to the ensuing discussion are the following: George Darley, ed., *The Works of Beaumont and Fletcher*, 2 vols. (1840), Intro.; Arthur Mizener, "The High Design of *A King and No King*," *MP*, XXXVIII (1940), 133-154; Eugene M. Waith, *The Pattern of Tragicomedy in Beaumont and Fletcher*, Yale Stud. in English, Vol. 120 (New Haven, 1952); William W. Appleton, *Beaumont and Fletcher: A Critical Study* (London, 1956); Philip Edwards, "The Danger not the Death: The Art of John Fletcher," *Jacobean Theatre*, Stratford-Upon-Avon Studies, I (London, 1960), 159-177; Clifford Leech, *The John Fletcher Plays* (London,

1. David Garrick as Abel Drugger in Garrick's alteration of *The Alchemist*

2. John Philip Kemble as Cato in Addison's tragedy

After making some adjustment for Shirley's obvious purpose of enticing prospective buyers, we must still acknowledge the accuracy and comprehensiveness of his analysis. Shirley's point is that the playwrights aim to arouse extreme responsiveness in the audience, and their method is to raise passions gradually and deviously to such a height that the audience becomes completely involved, even identifying with the character who speaks. The rhetoric carries such a strong emotional imperative that it moves the speaker himself toward an absolute stance: because it is so extreme, the rhetorical position rules out, for the moment, any alternative emotion. And, since rhetoric is the language of persuasion, the reader becomes convinced of the reality of the emotion, while at the same time the pleasure of finely wrought language produces in him a corollary sense of wonder that he could be led so subtly to such a point. Yet Shirley also implies that the position of the speaker is only seemingly absolute. Where a "Scene of love" is followed by a "Scene of manly Rage," the first rhetorical position has nothing to do with the second. Although Shirley may well be inviting the interested buyer to sample the text here and there with the prospect of finding considerable variety, the implication remains that the reader need not be much concerned with continuity. There is no suggestion that he may miss some pervasive thematic concern, nor does even a hint appear that he will discover "fully developed" characters. Shirley's emphasis is on *the scene, taken by itself*.

Another writer for the Folio, Thomas Palmer, describes in his commendatory verses the experience of playgoers and emphasizes the degree of their involvement in Fletcher's quick succession of scenes. In attending a product of his "Tragicke Muse," Palmer recalls,

> Like Scenes, we shifted Passions, and that so,
> Who only came to see, turn'd Actors too.
> How didst thou sway the Theatre! make us feele
> The Players wounds were true, and their swords, steele!
> Nay, stranger yet, how often did I know
> When the Spectators ran to save the blow?

1962); John F. Danby, *Elizabethan and Jacobean Poets: Studies in Sidney, Shakespeare, Beaumont & Fletcher* (London, 1964); and Arthur Kirsch, "*Cymbeline* and Coterie Dramaturgy," *ELH*, XXXIV (1967), 285-306.

> Frozen with griefe we could not stir away
> Vntill the Epilogue told us 'twas a Play. (Sig. $f2^v$)

Palmer's description (extravagant as it is) of involvement in the pathos of the play juxtaposes a notion of the spectators' active commitment with a contrary notion of almost graphic stasis. Caught up by high-running emotions, the audience is impelled to involvement and yet transfixed, "Frozen with griefe," by its attraction to the scene. An analysis of *Philaster*—one of the best and most familiar examples of the genre—will serve to demonstrate that the emotional manipulation of the audience, well summarized by Shirley and Palmer, is carried out through the skillful alternation of tendencies toward action and counter-tendencies toward the graphic or even emblematic embodiment of impassioned stance.

In the opening situation Philaster, heir to the crown of Sicily, and Pharamond, Prince of Spain, appear as rivals for the hand of Arathusa, daughter of the King of Sicily and Calabria, and consequently claimants to the two kingdoms as well. Philaster enters and immediately takes a wholly uncompromising position. Having "my selfe about me, and my sword" (I.i.181), he offers open challenge to Pharamond's claim: "I tell thee *Pharamond,*/When thou art King, looke I be dead and rotten,/And my name ashes, as I . . ." (185-187).[13] His threat is couched in such extreme language that the bland, unheroic Pharamond takes him for a madman. Here, as often in the Beaumont and Fletcher canon, echoes of Shakespeare intrude. Philaster's impassioned reference to his dead father "Whose memory I bow to" (179) suggests Hamlet's reverence for the murdered Dane, and the situation supports this echo by making it clear that the King favors Pharamond over Philaster, who supposedly has prior right. There is in addition an implication in Pharamond's accusation of madness that Philaster is only mad "in craft." Fully aware, somewhat like Hamlet, that his stance is extreme, Philaster employs rhetorical devices to make it evident in his speech; at the same time his emotion is apparently genuine enough to convince his on-stage auditors (and perhaps the audience) that he is in truth mad. When the King chides him for his intemperate words, Philaster responds with

[13] All quotations of *Philaster* are from *The Dramatic Works in the Beaumont and Fletcher Canon,* ed. Fredson Bowers, I (Cambridge, Eng., 1966).

a hint of the Hamlet-like "motive" that has driven him to offend so egregiously:

> If you had my eyes sir, and sufferance,
> My griefes upon you, and my broken fortunes,
> My wants great, and now nothing hopes and feares,
> My wrongs would make ill riddles to be laught at.
> (241-244)

Fletcher presents a character who gives the initial impression of near-insane rage. In contrast to Shakespeare's technique of development, however, no preparation exists for Philaster's outburst, for he has entered only a moment before his challenge to Pharamond and takes the assembled company completely by surprise. Only after the shock has registered on the other characters and on the audience as well does Fletcher undercut this effect by having Philaster reveal that he is a deserving but wronged and unfortunate man and so the necessary object of compassion. Within less than a hundred lines a significant manipulation of audience interest has occurred. Fletcher goes on to exploit this newly won sympathy by having Philaster speak apart to the King in order to explain more fully the nature of his wrongs. These we do not discover; in fact, they are never fully revealed in the course of the play. Importance lies not in the exact nature of Philaster's grievance but in the fact that *as we see him now* he is a wronged man. Fletcher invites his audience to sympathize more fully by showing us the King's guilty reaction to Philaster's explanation. As Dion comments after the King and his entourage have left,

> What a dangerous traine
> Did he give fire to? How he shooke the King,
> Made his soule melt within him, and his blood,
> Run into whay: it stood upon his brow,
> Like a cold winter dew. (292-296)

So, in this scene of "manly Rage," Fletcher's purpose is manifestly to catch up his audience in the heat of the moment, and his method includes attention both to what the audience hears and sees. The King is silent while Philaster mimes speech to him as they stand apart, and Dion's subsequent description not only gives direction to the actor playing the King but reminds the audience of his sudden and impassioned reaction. Although Philaster acts on the King in the way Dion describes, the scene as a whole does not suggest action and counteraction as often found between a pair of mutually antagonistic characters. Instead, it presents two reactions, and neither character responds to the other so much as to the impingement of the situation developing and changing before his eyes.

This presentation of immediate and absolute response to events and circumstances, developed by means of insidious shifts into a series of reactions, is the pattern of the Fletcherian play. But another characteristic appears, a corollary of the first. When Philaster and the King move apart, Fletcher introduces a covering speech in which Dion blames Philaster's insanity on the madness of the times. He observes with easy comprehensiveness:

> Every man in this age, has not a soule of Christall, for all men to reade their actions through: mens hearts and faces are so farre asunder, that they hold no intelligence. (249-252)

The speech presents a theoretical basis for the unpredictable reactions of characters throughout the play. Philaster and the King's pantomimic duologue commands our attention, and we may see in it a certain special significance, for it shows the essential unit whose proliferation comprises the form of the play as a whole. While one character speaks, the other listens as if entrapped; as the first uses carefully wrought language to explain his momentary stance, the other is unable to interrupt and so reacts pantomimically in a characteristically impassioned way.[14] In this manner what is heard and seen elicits complex response. But these diverse qualities not only maintain but actually increase the audience's interest. Exploiting the natural tension between the heard and the seen, the playwrights contrive to draw the spectators into the emotional center of the sequence, building it to its highest point for the sake of extreme effect and at the same time using it as a kind of net to trap their delighted audience and so carry them along in easy bondage from scene to scene.

[14] Thomas Rymer disapproved of this technique but did not fail to see its prominence, as in *The Maid's Tragedy*: "Certainly no spectacle can be more displeasing, than to see a man ty'd to a post, and another buffeting him with an immoderate tongue"—*The Tragedies of the Last Age,* in *The Critical Works of Thomas Rymer,* ed. Curt A. Zimansky (New Haven, 1956), p. 69.

Dion's speech also suggests the concept of dramatic character that gives rise to new and unpredictable situations. This concept becomes more clear in the "Scene of love" later in Act I. Arathusa begins by taking what seems an attitude best calculated to affront Philaster: she announces to him her determination to possess the two kingdoms for which he contends. Employing a rhetorical device typical of Fletcherian techniques, she withholds the one point that underlies and explains her position: she is in love with Philaster. She wants the two kingdoms *and* him, together, through marriage. Our first response to this ploy is perhaps as to a neat but not psychologically convincing trick. The joke is on Philaster, and we appreciate the joke; yet it seems implausible that Arathusa should deliberately jeopardize her hoped-for relationship by willfully making him think she opposes his claim. But in attacking supposed psychological inconsistency we miss the point. This apparent lack is based after all on a consistent premise, already voiced by Dion: human beings are unpredictable and inscrutable. The responses that "characterize" them are responses to situations that constantly change and so require protean adaptability. We cannot see into the soul of the character and so must judge, if at all, by appearance only. What we see and hear is subsumed in the *image of a person speaking*. Only on this may we depend. In withholding for a crucial moment the fact that she is in love with Philaster and desires his favorable response, Arathusa uses a rhetorical device that in effect protects her from having to declare her love until she can first discover Philaster's disposition. The recurrence of the word *danger* in the first act helps to suggest that these characters consistently use rhetorical ploys as means of self-defense against uncertainty. Having elicited the other's statement in strong and unequivocal terms, it is now safe for defenses to be let down and the "true" position of the character to emerge.

The first act of *Philaster,* then, establishes three important qualities of the Fletcherian dramatic character: his passionate responsiveness within the carefully prescribed limits of a scene or sequence; his perversion from some posited norm of reasoned conduct under pressure of extreme circumstances; and his apparent psychological inconsistency. What probably disturbs us most about this last quality is the evident *posturing* of the Fletcherian character. Constantly we notice that, in the act of taking an attitude and of using language to shape it into an absolute position, the character maintains a mental reservation that allows him to abandon this position a moment later. He seizes upon some one emotion and, with the suave playfulness of an accomplished rhetorician, rides upon its crest simply to see how far it will carry. When his tour de force is complete, he coolly abandons it with no sense of having compromised himself in any way. We may alternatively see, however, that a certain consistency lies in the character's constant attempts to protect himself with language. He uses rhetoric, not as a sword, but as a shield. Plunged into circumstances he could not have foreseen, he is forced to establish a figure of himself to which those around him can respond; simultaneously he examines this figure himself to determine its adequacy (and often to admire its bold lines). As circumstances change and new events intrude, he is forced into a series of redefinitions of himself, each a response to a unique situation. No doubt, an actor, once he has grasped this concept, could play Philaster with great conviction and liveliness. We must only remember that the norm of rational behavior from which the character finds himself perverted is not adequately defined, as it often is in Shakespeare—for example, in *Othello*. We see only the perversion, and Fletcher's technique implies that it is not relevant to infer the norm from which his character departs. The technique is wholly theatrical, oriented toward the involvement and pleasure of the audience.[15]

This concept of a "core-less" dramatic character in turn dictates the unpredictable outcome of the Fletcherian play. The structure of Fletcherian drama rests on the same withholding of

[15] Arthur Kirsch cites the scene with the country fellow in Act IV of *Philaster* as "a paradigm of Fletcherian dramaturgy" and explains that his uncouthness in challenging Philaster is so incongruous a joke that it "paradoxically insulates the boundaries of Beaumont and Fletcher's world of gay sights and protects its private sports and recreations; and his appearance compels us to take conscious delight in the artifice of the entire scene"—"*Cymbeline* and Coterie Dramaturgy," pp. 288-289. To see at once the difference between the "Fletcherian" and the "Shakespearean" techniques, one may compare the scene with a similar one in *King Lear* (IV.vi.225ff). In *Philaster* the country bumpkin who comes to the defense of "Bellario" is beaten off and swears never to go near that strange country again; whether intentionally or not, this exactly reverses the scene in *Lear*, on the heath, where the disguised Edgar assumes a country dialect but triumphs over the courtly Oswald, reinforcing through sympathy the thematic idea of human fidelity in a world of naked and terrifying reality.

essential information that characterizes the individual character's defensive rhetorical stance. For example, Fletcher uses the first two acts partly to set up the confrontation of Philaster and Bellario, Philaster's page, that follows in Act III. The entire scene burgeons with alternative possibilities engendered by what may be a mistaken or true assumption. Ambiguity is carefully prepared in Acts I and II, so that a certain credibility will inhere in this scene and in the course of subsequent events no matter how strange and unpredictable they appear in themselves. At the end of the play the audience may look back in satisfaction and reflect that the train of events has proceeded along a darkly circuitous but nevertheless "natural" path. Meanwhile, as foreshadowings gradually appear, the audience can enjoy situations whose variety is based on equivocation. The use of this technique lends itself to such interest in *the scene* that this, after all, may well seem its sole purpose. Two sets of possible outcomes have been prepared; each potentially cancels out the other but, because the characters' positions are presented as only momentary arguments, the two possibilities hang unresolved (or are restated in different terms) as the succession of scenes unfolds. There is no predicting what turn will come next, and so each seems to bear only the most tenuous relationship with its predecessor.

This linear development of the action provides what Shirley aptly describes. The audience becomes emotionally involved and at the same time has leisure to reflect on the subtle steps of its involvement. Moreover, the basic dramatic conflict in the play is not a personal one between two characters but a formal one between the temporality of the action and the spatiality of the characters' relation to it. The action develops straightforwardly, often at dazzling speed, within a certain span of time. But, at each turn, as new and unexpected developments ensue, the characters find it necessary to readjust their positions. Attempting to make sense out of what strikes them, if not wholly us, as a mystifyingly chaotic world, they erect "permanent" vantage points from which the bewildering complexity of events and circumstances around them can be viewed with a sense of comparative security. In their speeches they betray this motive to us (although almost never to each other). We see driving them a deep, instinctive desire to impose permanence on chaos by reining back, as it were, using emotion and will—sometimes intellect, always language—to bring all movement to a stop. Only by adopting this *attitude,* they seem to say, can they resist the attraction of the maze. And so they stand, in absolute and extreme positions, living emblems of resistance to change.

In some instances the habitual concern to oppose movement with stasis emerges with special emphasis through the presentation of emblematic word-pictures. *Philaster* contains its share of these, but *The Maid's Tragedy* provides the best-known example of the vivid set-piece which momentarily arrests all action. Fletcher blithely introduces it with Aspatia's call to her handmaidens: "Come, let's be sad, my girls." She begins by describing an emblem of grief in the story of the Queen of Carthage, "when, from a cold sea-rock,/Full with her sorrow, she tied fast her eyes/ To the fair Trojan ships. . . ."[16] If that wench were like Aspatia, she continues, she would stand "till some more pitying god Turn'd her to marble" (38-39). The emotion of self-pity is heightened by an alternative representation of permanence, a piece of needlework depicting Ariadne. Change only the detail of the "wild island," Aspatia says to her lady-in-waiting, and you will see the very image of me:

> Suppose I stand upon the sea-beach now,
> Mine arms thus, and mine hair blown with the wind,
> Wild as that desart; and let all about me
> Tell that I am forsaken. Do my face
> (If thou hadst ever feeling of a sorrow)
> Thus, thus, Antiphila: strive to make me look
> Like Sorrow's monument; and the trees about me,
> Let them be dry and leafless; let the rocks
> Groan with continual surges; and behind me,
> Make all a desolation. See, see, wenches,
> A miserable life of this poor picture! (68-78)

In relation to the surrounding action and the emotions of grief it elicits, the speech falls nicely into the pattern of tension between a linear movement in time and a graphic arrest of that movement in space. Moreover, Aspatia's glossing of the scenic details in the picture emphasizes its subjective orientation. The lifeless trees, the rocks battered by the ceaseless surge of waves, significantly

[16] *The Works of Francis Beaumont and John Fletcher,* Variorum Edition, ed. A. H. Bullen, 4 vols. (London, 1908), Vol. I, II.ii.27, 33-35.

anticipate the *paysage interieur* which, in Romantic art, leads the beholder from the contemplation of external surroundings into the mental state of the figure in the landscape.[17] Although the structure of the Fletcherian play presents a maze of intrigue, the rapid development of action is regularly impeded by pictorial tendencies—well illustrated in the subtitle of *Philaster* itself: *Love Lies A Bleeding.*

Finally, in the last scene of Act V, the issues are resolved and the structure of the play as a whole falls into place. Or perhaps *collapses* is the more accurate description. As Philaster points out to Euphrasia, who has finally relinquished her page's disguise,

> All these Jealousies
> Had flowne to nothing, if thou hadst discovered,
> What now we know. (V.v.149-151)

Here, in effect, is the paradigm for the typical Gothic or Romantic tragedy of suppressed information or missed opportunity. Many of these later plays (Cumberland's *The Carmelite* is a good example) have resolutions which at the last minute avoid the deaths that had seemed inevitable. In common with *Philaster* they are "near-tragedies" that depend on ignorance of the true state of external affairs, rather than Shakespearean tragedies depending on the inner illumination of character as well as on missed opportunity. Fletcher's characters, however great their faults, possess no tragic inevitability. The denouement can go either way, resolved "happily" or "tragically" with no real distortion of what has been built to lead up to it. The archetypal Fletcherian character is neutral, so to speak, with respect to the action. There is nothing in him that needs to be mirrored in the exterior world, except the uncertainty of his own nature. The fall, or even the stumbling, of princes is not so much the Fletcherian subject as the revelation of their grotesque, unbalanced posturing.

In Fletcherian drama begins the tendency to move away from the objective presentation of actions on the stage toward a more subjective presentation of their antecedents. The character does

[17] Maynard Mack has pointed out that the emotional landscape is a notable tendency in romance. Even in *King Lear*'s anti-pastoral heath, "Nature proves to be indifferent or hostile, not friendly—yet curiously expressive, as in romance, of the protagonist's mental and emotional states"—*King Lear In Our Time* (Berkeley and Los Angeles, 1965), p. 66.

not reveal himself in action so much as in reaction. Later in the course of English drama, such responses become the full explications of impassioned states of mind. A homogeneous dramatic tradition extends from the plays of Beaumont and Fletcher to those of Romantic writers like Joanna Baillie, "Monk" Lewis, Charles Maturin, Richard Sheil, and many others. This tradition may be aptly termed "the affective drama of situation." Plays of this sort have a structure based on a series of circumstances and events unconnected by a strict logic of causality (or Aristotelian "action"); their situations are deliberately brought out of the blue for the purpose of displaying human reactions to extreme and unexpected occurrences. In these plays the intelligible unit is not the thematic part, placed within a coherent series of other parts, but, as in Fletcherian drama, the scene, which exists in effect for its own sake.

CHAPTER II

The Persistence of the Fletcherian Mode

> A good play especially for ye passages and Plot. . . . Amidea a good part for a chast lady. act:3. about ye middle shee prevents ye Duke from ravishing her a scene well pennd
>
> —Abraham Wright, MS. comment on *The Traitor*

i. Shirley's *The Traitor*

CITING performance records of *The Traitor* that span a period of several centuries, a recent editor of the play singles out Sheil's adaptation, *Evadne,* for special interest "because it shows the nineteenth-century mind at work on the Jacobean material."[1] The continuity established by these records provides an important example of the influence of the Fletcherian pattern; at both their beginning and culmination the link with the Jacobean playwright is clear. A "true son of Fletcher," as Alfred Harbage has described him,[2] Shirley extensively exhibited his debt to the elder writer in *The Traitor* (licensed 1631). Again, when Richard Lalor Sheil re-dramatized the play for performance at Covent Garden in 1818-19, he found it convenient to incorporate the basic situation from *The Maid's Tragedy.* Between these two dates a theatrical history developed which, although broken for quite some years, illustrates the strength of Fletcherian influence on later generations of writers.

First published in 1635, *The Traitor* appears as one of a list of titles of the stock plays of Killigrew's company furnished to the Master of the Revels, Sir Henry Herbert, probably shortly after the Restoration.[3] Thus making its way into the new era, Shirley's tragedy established itself both early and late on the stage of this

[1] John Stewart Carter, ed., *The Traitor* (London, 1965), Intro., p. xii. All quotations are from this edition.

[2] *Cavalier Drama* (New York and London, 1936), p. 41.

[3] For the facts presented here see G. E. Bentley, *The Jacobean and Caroline Stage,* v (Oxford, 1956), 1150-53, and *London Stage,* Pt. I, p. 406 and *passim,* and Pt. II, *passim.*

period. As early as November of 1660 the play was performed by the King's Company. Pepys saw the production on four occasions between 1660 and 1667, and it was performed again in 1674-75. In 1691-92 a shortened version appeared at Drury Lane, a commentator in the April *Gentleman's Journal* observing that "it hath always been esteemed a very good Play, by the best Judges of Dramatick Writing." The remark extends the reputation Shirley's play achieved a few decades earlier. In 1671 Edward Howard cited it as among "the highest of our English Tragedies" along with such works as *Cataline* and *The Maid's Tragedy,* and G. E. Bentley concludes that "there seems to have been some disposition in the seventies to think of *The Traitor* as one of the great English tragedies of the past." In the somewhat truncated version of 1691-92 the play appeared again in 1699-1700, and, under the title *The Traytor; or, The Tragedy of Amidea,* it was performed in 1703-04 and again in 1704-05. In October 1718 a new production was mounted at Lincoln's Inn Fields, the text revised by Christopher Bullock. It ran for six performances during the 1718-19 season, again for two performances in 1719-20, and for a single performance in 1720-21.

At this point *The Traitor* disappeared from the stage, to reappear a hundred years later in the form of Sheil's *Evadne.* The century-long hiatus may seem to indicate that the eighteenth-century theater was abandoning the sort of play represented by Shirley's piece, just as it seemed to have abandoned Fletcher himself. But Sheil's play affords evidence that the Fletcherian mode, as practiced by both Fletcher and disciples like Shirley, was still a viable technique for producing successful performed drama. A comparison of Shirley's tragedy with Sheil's will make the latter's dependence clear.

The basic resemblance of *The Traitor* to the Fletcherian dramaturgical mode lies in the structure of its situations and the relationship of dramatic character to them. The setting of the play is Florence in the days of the Medici, a time and place that to English dramatists perennially suggest intrigue, bloodshed, political chaos, and treason. Shirley's plot develops the attempt of Lorenzo to wrest political power away from the present Duke by suborning trusted courtiers and pitting them one against another, meanwhile maintaining an image of himself as faithful to the credulous ruler. Two threads of action are established and then interwoven. One of these is a love plot involving two couples: Pisano, the friend of Cosmo, is in love with Amidea, while Cosmo himself woos Oriana. At the beginning of the play, however, we see this amicable double relationship already disrupted through the insinuations of the henchman Petruchio, acting on orders from Lorenzo. When Cosmo discovers that Pisano has shifted his affections to Oriana, Cosmo summarily relinquishes his beloved, a change of allegiance that serves to leave Amidea without a lover and in turn to incite her hot-headed brother Sciarrha to plan vengeance on Pisano. Related to Amidea's forlorn situation is the Duke's presence in the play, dictated only partly by his existence as the object of Lorenzo's treason. His primary motivation is not political but personal: he lusts after Amidea and so draws the enmity of her brother Sciarrha. In this way Sciarrha plays into the hands of Lorenzo, who hopes to make him the agent of the Duke's murder. So, either through Pisano or the Duke, Lorenzo hopes to distract attention from his own clandestine purpose of overthrowing the government and establishing himself as its new chief. The love plot, then, complex in itself, functions as an aspect of the central plot of treachery, behind which moves Lorenzo.

A summary of plot, however, tends to obscure the primary purpose and effect of the action. It is important to observe that Sciarrha has at least as many lines as Lorenzo, and important also to see that Lorenzo's relationship to Sciarrha is not one-sided but reciprocal. *The Revenger's Tragedy* offers a helpful contrast. Its main character, Vindice, is the indisputable center of interest, and his ingenious machinations provide the impetus for virtually every event. Constantly in control, Vindice responds to the unexpected by unerringly turning it to his purpose of vengeance on behalf of his sister against the Duke. In *The Traitor*—a play whose situations of vengeance often parallel Tourneur's—no similarly central figure appears. Sciarrha's singleminded defense of his sister's honor is every bit as strong as Vindice's, but he does not manage the action throughout; more regularly he responds to it, sometimes simply with monomaniac diatribes against the Duke's corruption. Nor is Lorenzo the deft, enterprising manipulator of other men's lives and passions that Vindice proves himself. Although Lorenzo's purpose of usurping Florentine power sets the action in motion, we see him principally in grave difficulties, thwarted by Sciarrha's quasi-independent responses to extreme situations and escaping undetected only through his talent at playing the hypocrite. On two separate occasions, in Acts I and III, Lorenzo comes within a hair's breadth of exposure by Sciarrha to the Duke, from which he saves himself by a complete hypocritical reversal. Again, in Act IV, Lorenzo manages to avert Sciarrha's accusation of hypocrisy only by pretending penitence.

What keeps the action of *The Traitor* in motion, then, is not the shrewdness of a single villain or avenger but the interaction of two such characters, neither self-sufficient. Their mutual lack of control over one another and over the unpredictable flow of events creates a greater sense of uncertainty than one derives from *The Revenger's Tragedy*. The "moral center" of *The Traitor* is no more than the familiar conventional ideal of womanly honor to which Sciarrha pays extensive service through word and deed. The true center of the play exists neither in an underlying concept of moral order nor in a self-embodied ideal of human behavior, but in a highly theatrical presentation of shocking and pathetic events and equally unprepared reversals of character.

Where, as Arthur Kirsch has suggested, the Cavalier playwright drove to extremes Fletcherian tendencies toward pattern and spatial design,[4] Shirley, as the heir of Fletcher, combines these tendencies with an emphasis on that dramatist's disjunction of character from event. The sense of dramaturgical pattern in *The Traitor*, although not as neatly geometric as in other contemporary (and early Restoration) playwrights, is nevertheless strong. In Shirley's hands, patterning is a formulaic device for heightening interest in a series of scenes, and the format is clearly that of *the trial*. Situations are created for the purpose of subjecting both the evil and the innocent to tests in which they prove themselves not wanting, incomprehensibly changed, or both simultaneously. This formulaic repetition intensifies the audience's enjoyment of intrigue, but still another and more pervasive pattern emerges. Within a given situation, whether governed or not by the idea of a trial, a pattern of character reversal predominates. The opening scene establishes this pattern by showing Pisano, the supposed lover of Amidea, as already having forsaken

[4] *Dryden's Heroic Drama* (Princeton, 1965), p. 70.

her for Oriana. Though his change of affections is completely conventional, Amidea's younger brother Florio subsequently comments, justifiably, "The alteration was strange and sudden" (II.i.319). After Lorenzo's suave self-transformation in the accusation scene ending Act I, Act II provides Pisano's farewell to Amidea in which he tells her his "heart's revolted" (i.295). "Some strange distemper," she laments, has "Invaded him" (i.314-315). This scene is followed by Cosmo's interview with Oriana in which, with selfless devotion to his ideal of friendship, he attempts to sway her affections from himself to Pisano. Oriana gives in, in mere baffled passivity.

This pair of scenes in Act II is patently the offspring of the Caroline playwright's genius for juxtaposition. But this patterned repetition is also more indigenously Fletcherian, for each scene presents a pair of characters, one of whom exploits the disadvantage of the other and so scores a temporary victory through persuasive rhetoric by reversing the attitude that the other character expects him to take. As this pattern proliferates through scene after scene, the "theme" of the play becomes clear: under the stress of extreme circumstances, human personality undergoes inexplicable change. It is a theme illustrated not by the meaningful coherence of a chain of events but by the severance of events from one another and from the characters who try to control them. Each scene carries its own rationale, and its hidden *donnée* serves to create suspense and at the same time to elicit sympathy for the vanquished character, who cannot penetrate the mask of the victor and so is prevented from grasping the "reality" of the situation.

The several scenes between Sciarrha and Amidea embody this disjunctive technique with increasing ingenuity on the playwright's part. In the most effective instance, in Act V, Sciarrha again attempts as in Act II to prompt Amidea to the Duke's bed. Having murdered Pisano for daring to forsake her, Sciarrha himself now faces death unless Amidea will use her charms to buy the Duke's pardon for him. Strongly reminiscent of the interview between the condemned Claudio and his chaste sister Isabella in *Measure for Measure,* the scene builds up a series of desperate resolves in which un-Shakespearean reversals accumulate with lightning speed. In the most pathetic tones he can muster, Sciarrha pleads with Amidea to save his life:

Then [i.e. in their first interview] I but tried thy virtue.
Now my condition calls for mercy to thee,
Though to thyself thou appear cruel for't.
Come, we may live both if you please. (V.i.98-101)

When she still refuses, Sciarrha suddenly offers to kill her if she will not relent. Amidea kneels, and the scene rushes to its climax:

Amidea [*aside*]. Forgive me, heaven, and witness
I have still
My virgin thoughts. 'Tis not to save my life,
But his eternal one.— *Rises.*
Sciarrha, give me leave to veil my face.
I dare not look upon you and pronounce.
I am too much a sister. Live. Hereafter
I know you will condemn my frailty for it.
I will obey the duke.
Sciarrha. Dar'st thou consent? *Wounds her.*
Amidea. Oh let me see the wound. *She unveils.*
'Tis well, if any other hand had done it.
Some angel tell my brother now I did
But seem consenting.
Sciarrha. Ha! But seem?
Amidea. You may believe my last breath.
Sciarrha. Why didst say so?
Amidea. To gain some time in hope you might call in
Your bloody purpose, and prevent the guilt
Of being my murderer. But Heaven forgive thee.
(V.i.126-141)

This brief passage contains three distinct reversals. Kneeling as if to prepare herself for death, Amidea prays instead for forgiveness for the sin to which she now acquiesces. As she rises, Sciarrha, who has urged her with supposedly full sincerity, abruptly stabs her when she appears to give in to his plea. And then Amidea reverses herself again by informing him that she only *seemed* to consent to his demands; she was bargaining for time. Amidea's kneeling and rising emphasize in a graphic way the reversal and counter-reversal characteristic of the structure of scenes throughout the play and summarized here, in effect, through condensed, rapid repetition. It serves also to emphasize the disjunctive spatial relationship of Fletcherian character to the linear movement of the play. As the scene mounts to its conclusion, no inevitability attaches to the characters' futile attempts to grasp the true "reality" of the climactic situation. Nor is this "reality" the primary object of the audience's interest. What draws their attention is not so much the culmination of a line of plot as the visual brilliance of the characters' kaleidoscopic enactment of it. The characters are a function of the scene and at the same time cut off from the totality of the "truth" toward which it moves. After Amidea is wounded and dying, Sciarrha reveals to her the hidden motive he brought to their last interview:

> Lorenzo . . . has
> My oath to send thee to his bed; for otherwise,
> In my denial, hell and they decree,
> When I am dead, to ravish thee. Mark that,
> To ravish thee. And I confess in tears
> As full of sorrow as thy soul of innocence,
> In my religious care to have thee spotless,
> I did resolve, when I had found thee ripe
> And nearest heaven, with all thy best desires
> To send thee to thy peace. (V.i.149-158)

The paradoxical fact remains, however, that Sciarrha did not stab her under these conditions but in response to her apparent abandonment of her chaste ideal. These climactic movements present no insight into the tragic nature of myopic human vision illustrated by King Lear's final posture, as we may infer it, bent low over the body of Cordelia. Their purpose is not thematic, not experientially philosophic, but theatrical. The failure of Amidea and Sciarrha to touch the hidden truth of their plight is not a function of their "human" fallibility but of the pleasurable pathos and surprised delight of their audience.

ii. Sheil's *Evadne* and Other Derivatives

The century-long gap that separates the early eighteenth-century production history of Shirley's *The Traitor* from Sheil's *Evadne; or, The Statue*[5] is not enough to obscure the close relationship of the two plays as examples of Fletcherian dramaturgy. Despite the wide and pervasive differences which distinguish the

[5] Covent Garden, 10 February 1819.

art and culture of the early nineteenth century from the Jacobean and Restoration ages, Sheil's "Romantic" tragedy exhibits the unmistakable traits of a method of writing plays first proved viable on the stages of aristocratic seventeenth-century playhouses.

In his excellent study of late Restoration tragedy, Eric Rothstein explains that the plays of such writers as Lee, Otway, and Rowe depart from the aesthetic duality of pathos and delight found in early Restoration drama, substituting a single emphasis on pathos alone.[6] Although generalization is hazardous, it seems clear that this departure was a response to audiences whose theatrical values were undergoing change. It is an easy step, but a false one, from this idea to the assumption that this "new" audience was losing its ability to respond to formal characteristics for their own sake. Pathos is the obvious stipend of serious drama in the ages of Otway and Sheil alike, but it must not be supposed that playgoers throughout this long period entered wholeheartedly into the illusion of reality on the stage with single-minded naïveté. Delight in the sort of planned artifice described and cultivated by Shirley did not survive intact, yet Romantic audiences remained very much aware of the formality of the dramas that evoked their tearful sympathies. Based on the pictorial symmetry of wing-and-backdrop scenery that endured from the seventeenth through the nineteenth centuries, this sense of formality took on several aspects, each relevant to the Fletcherian qualities of Sheil's play. One of these was the spectators' sense of acting style and its close association with particular star actors. Audiences were quite capable of responding to the emotional magnetism of a scene and at the same time applauding an actor for the vocal and physical skills that elicited their response. In addition, they had become increasingly aware of the dramatic conventions governing character types, which appeared in highly predictable and therefore aesthetically enjoyable combinations with one another through a succession of scenes. Romantic tragedy is an unusually derivative genre. The playwright treated these conventions overtly, drawing on scores of plays much the same as his. Formal homogeneity was so great that many of the serious plays of the early nineteenth century may be viewed as comprising a whole

[6] *Restoration Tragedy* (Madison and Milwaukee, 1967), Chaps. 5 and 6, esp. pp. 77-79.

series of "obligatory" scenes, villain, henchman, and dupe pitted against hero, heroine, father, and faithful servant in sequences whose formal characteristics were intimately known to an audience of constant theatergoers.

A comment on Sheil's *Evadne* by a viewer "who witnessed one of its earliest representations" illustrates how deeply ingrained was the sense of convention and formality. A reader unfamiliar with Sheil's play is for the moment at an advantage, since the comment deals with the plot as form rather than as narrative:

> The events on which the chief interest of the piece depends, are brought about with great skill. They are every one made "probable to thinking." It is impossible for *Vicentio* to resist the evidence which *Ludovico* offers him of *Evadne's* falsehood, when coupled with the changing of the pictures—it [is] impossible for *Colonna* to refuse the office which *Ludovico* forces upon him, of killing the *King*—and it is impossible for the *King* himself—young and not wholly depraved as he is—to withstand the appeal which *Evadne* makes to him, in the shadowy presence of her great and glorious ancestors. The minor incidents, too—the treachery of *Olivia*, the combat between *Colonna* and *Vicentio*—the intended sacrifice of his hand, which *Vicentio* makes to *Olivia*, &c., are all absolutely essential to the progress of the plot, and yet none have the appearance of being forced, or out of place.[7]

This eyewitness account presents a curious combination of interests. The writer has set out to demonstrate the probability, or naturalness, inherent in the events that comprise the plot. But the events he describes hold in common a quality that identifies them as discrete Fletcherian units: the irresistible attraction and response of a character to extreme and unexpected circumstances. The commentator sees a high degree of coherence in the play, observing that "the guilty ambition of *Ludovico* is the spring which sets every part in motion" and that "every incident flows naturally and intelligibly from its immediate and assigned cause. . . ." He considers this "quite enough of unity for all the purposes of the drama" (p. vi). But those purposes clearly point toward

[7] Quoted in Epes Sargent, ed., *Evadne: or, The Statue*, "Modern Standard Drama" (New York, 1847), Intro., pp. v-vii.

what the writer himself calls "the chief interest of the piece"—the "events," whose plausibility lies in the characters' absolute inability to resist their attraction.[8]

In adapting Shirley's tragedy to the Romantic stage, Sheil made certain changes to accord with the need for a shortened text and a reduced number of characters.[9] Its "fable," as a writer in the Oxberry edition found, is "more compact."[10] Substituting new names for the characters, the playwright retained the essential outline in which Lorenzo (now Ludovico) conspires with his henchman Petruchio (now Spalatro) to murder the Duke (now elevated to the monarchy of Naples) and so become chief of state. As in the earlier play, Sciarrha (now Colonna) becomes the villain's dupe, suborned into vengeance against the King through the latter's attempt on the honor of Evadne (formerly Amidea). Similarly, Sheil retains but simplifies the double love plot of *The Traitor*; Cosmo, the suitor of Oriana, is eliminated, resulting in a triangle in which Vicentio (formerly Pisano) transfers his affection for Evadne to her lady-in-waiting Olivia. Sheil's own contributions to this plot are to give the villain Ludovico a lustful interest in Evadne, to put the corruptible Olivia in his power, and to adapt the sensational situation from *The Maid's Tragedy* in which an unsuspecting young man discovers that his bride is the king's mistress.

These would be commonplace alterations were it not that each serves the purpose of heightening Evadne's plight and so provides increased scope for pathetic scenes. After an absence, Vicentio arrives home in expectation of marrying Evadne, only to be told by the scheming Ludovico that she has become the monarch's paramour. Given the character of Evadne as "a woman

[8] A nearly contemporary comment on *The Traitor* reveals this same notion of the "plot" as a device for providing highly theatrical scenes. At about mid-century Abraham Wright found it "A good play especially for ye passages and Plot. Lorenzo a good part for a cuning court flatterer, and a rogue. ye last scene of ye first act where hee quitts himselfe of treason very cunningly before ye Duke. Sciarra a good part for a brave spirit and ffawning baseness. ye 2. act: sc:1 Sciarrha is conferring with Lorenzo and Amidea about a revenge upon ye Duke for desining his sisters honour. . . . Amadea a good part for a chast lady. act:3. about ye middle shee prevents ye Duke from ravishing her a scene well pennd"—"Excerpta quaedam per A. W. Adolescentum" (ca. 1650-55), British Museum Add. MS. 22,608, fol. 74.

[9] All references are to *Evadne; or, The Statue: A Tragedy in Five Acts* (1819).

[10] (1821), Intro., p. iii.

in the truest and strictest, yet most delightful sense of the term,"[11] the supposition is incredible. Perversely, because it is just that, it works on Vicentio's credulous sense of the fortuitous and so establishes a dramatic foundation for his interview with Evadne. The Fletcherian principle of creating a hidden *donnée* underlies this scene, so that Evadne's expectation of a joyful reunion with her lover is ironically thwarted by his unexplained treatment of her as a base and perfidious strumpet. The difference between Fletcher's and Sheil's employment of the technique is simply that Sheil allows his audience prior knowledge. Consequently, since the motive for Vicentio's extreme behavior is known, the audience does not divide its interest equally between the two characters but concentrates more intensely on Evadne. This is a mutation of the familiar Fletcherian relationship of character, but its effect is nevertheless that Evadne's lover appears to her inexplicably changed. Put at great disadvantage by Vicentio's extended tirade, whose cause she cannot even guess at, Evadne is cut off from the supposed reality of the situation and so can only respond in hurt disbelief, an object of exquisite pathos.

Protracting the situation for three full pages of dialogue, Sheil at length allows Vicentio to accuse Evadne in precise words of infidelity and sin. The playwright exploits her horrified reaction by introducing now a series of quick reversals calculated to plunge his heroine into even deeper dismay. Vicentio, reacting to Evadne's shock by considering for a moment that she may indeed be innocent, asks to see the miniature of himself which he had hung around the neck of his beloved before departing. Evadne, unaware that the faithless Olivia has only moments before substituted a picture of the King, produces it for Vicentio's inspection. Again, the audience has been privy to Olivia's substitution and so is ready both for Vicentio's leap at this "final proof" and Evadne's gasp of fatalistic despair:

> Sure, some dark spell,
> Some fearful witchery. . . .
> I am confounded, maddened, lost, Vicentio!
> Some daemon paints it on the coloured air—
> 'Tis not reality that stares upon me!
>
> (II.ii, pp. 30-31)

[11] Quoted in Sargent, ed., p. vi.

This moment of irrational response serves, as in Fletcher, to halt the action in order to present a graphic image of intense reaction, summarizing Evadne's total severance from the reality of the situation.

John Genest, always ready to elucidate a playwright's blunders, found the exchange of pictures a "bungling incident" and observed that, instead of using common sense and perceiving Olivia had tricked her, Evadne, "like a true Tragedy Heroine, disclaims reason and talks nonsense. . . ."[12] Of course it goes without saying that the scene will not stand a test of this sort. It nevertheless remains true that this, Sheil's most successful play, appeared some thirty times on the Covent Garden stage during the 1818-19 season before audiences who evidently cared not at all for its failure to meet Genest's standard.[13] Although the argument for probability, quoted above, of the writer who witnessed an early performance may seem specious, particularly in light of Genest's denigrating comment, the reaction to Evadne as a "true Tragedy Heroine" remains the basis of her own credibility as a character and suggests as well the kind evident throughout the play. The conventional expectation for such a heroine is that she will have responses and lapses of exactly this sort. The fatalism of Fletcher's Arathusa—"Be mercifull ye gods, and strike me dead: What way have I deserv'd this?" (III.ii.129-130)—differs from Evadne's only in the specifics of language, not in conventionality. Sophisticated criticism may well assert that all the events of the play proceed from one efficient cause, Ludovico's ambition; but this is merely the "spring" that nourishes the gilded flower of pathos. The play gives the impression of a well-built, carefully sustained action, but its structure is nevertheless openly emotional. Like her original, Amidea in *The Traitor,* Evadne exists for the sake of eliciting pleasurable sympathy from her audience. Her characteristics are referable not primarily to life but to its simplification and, indeed, fragmentation on the stage. The métier for this "Simplicity of Passion"[14] is the highly charged, unprepared scene played by two characters, one of whom holds a heavy advantage

[12] *Some Account of the English Stage,* 10 vols. (Bath, 1832), VIII, 700-701.

[13] For the record of first-season performances see Genest, VIII, 699. Popular in both England and America, *Evadne* was acted as late as 1881—Carter, ed., p. xii.

[14] *St. James's Journal,* quoted above, p. 17.

over the other and uses it to vanquish or subdue. This is the formal unit whose proliferation through five acts makes up the substance of the play. More overtly conventionalized by Sheil's time, it remains essentially the same unit employed by Fletcher to produce interest and enthrallment in his audience.

Moreover, because the audience responds to the formal qualities of this paradigm of unhappy human relationships, the play like its Fletcherian predecessor can end either happily or tragically with no violation of "probability." It is significant that Sheil has effected a happy resolution without violating the terms of Shirley's bequest. The climactic moment in Act V of *The Traitor* is the stabbing and death of Amidea, followed in tested Renaissance fashion by other deaths to make "a heap of tragedies" (V.iii.155). The climactic scene in Act V of *Evadne,* borrowed from Act III of Shirley's play, combines the seduction scene, turned by Evadne to her own advantage and the King's repentance, with Colonna's exposure of Ludovico. The sequence begins with Evadne's reversal, modeled on Amidea's, in which she instructs her brother to let the King come to her. The scene—"*A vast Hall in Colonna's Palace, filled with Statues*" upon which "*the Moon streams in through the Gothic Windows*" (V.i, p. 67)—is appropriately foreboding, especially so because the audience is given no specific prior knowledge of Evadne's purpose. Sheil builds suspense by having Evadne give the King a guided tour of her silent marble ancestors. Elaborating this for almost four pages, the playwright allows the King to think that Evadne out of modesty is merely postponing going to his chamber with him, but the gambit is actually a device for awakening his conscience—a phenomenon that occurs when Evadne arrives at the statue of her father, who gave his life to save the King's. Unlike Shirley's, Sheil's heroine does not die in defense of her chaste principles but instead uses them to triumph over vicious adversity. This is enough to make the play no tragedy; yet Evadne comes near death (or to a fate worse than it), which is enough to make it no comedy. The spectators see before them a *heroine,* and so they know that Evadne prefers death to the loss of her honor. But as the scene builds they see that this heroine, helpless and pathetic through four acts, has unexpectedly found strength in her innocence, and their interest derives from watching Evadne use her feminine rhetorical wiles to elucidate the virtues of her forefathers and so bring her monarch to realize his guilt.

That Sheil calls his play "*A Tragedy, In Five Acts*" and yet uses the fifth act to accomplish the salvation of his heroine and the punishment of his villain involves no contradiction. *Evadne; or, The Statue* is neither comedy nor "Shakespearean" tragedy but Fletcherian tragicomedy, based on the disjunction, not the meaningful connection, of character and event. Where a character maintains neither a consistent control of events nor even a rudimentary grasp of his relationship to exterior reality, his actions become largely responses to the unexpected situations invented and exploited by the playwright to produce shock and pathos in his audience. Of Sheil's drama one can scarcely say what Swinburne said of *The Traitor*: "We are reminded of Fletcher at his best."[15] But the remembrance is strong all the same. Not at all an anomaly, *Evadne* is one of a host of plays performed in England in the early nineteenth century whose nature derives from the perpetuation, through the long history of the repertory theater, of dramaturgical ideas and techniques first developed on the indoor stages of the early seventeenth century.

A representative selection of works in this period which derive from specific plays in the Beaumont and Fletcher canon may partially indicate the extent of their latter-day influence.[16] Stephen Clarke's *The Kiss* (Lyceum, 1811-12) is an alteration of the comic plot of *The Spanish Curate,* previously mounted with alterations at Covent Garden in 1782-83. *The Noble Outlaw,* of unknown authorship (Covent Garden, 1814-15), is a comic opera founded on *The Pilgrim.* These are interesting simple instances, but a more extensive one appears in the history of *The Beggars' Bush.* First printed separately in 1661, the play was performed throughout the Restoration and, as *The Royal Merchant*: *or, Beggar's Bush,* became a popular favorite in the eighteenth century from as early as 1704-05.[17] Theatrical editions of the text slightly altered from

15 Algernon Charles Swinburne, "James Shirley," *Fortnightly Review,* n.s. CCLXXX (1890), p. 468.

16 The following examples of Fletcherian influence are derived partly from Genest, Vols. VII-IX; Allardyce Nicoll, *A History of English Drama,* III (Cambridge, Eng., 1955), 112-113; Donald J. Rulfs, "Beaumont and Fletcher on the London Stage, 1776-1833," *PMLA,* LXIII (1948), 1245-64; and partly from my own investigations.

17 See A. C. Sprague's comments on the problems of the theatrical text—

Cavalier development of Fletcherian drama, *Venice Preserv'd* is, as a *Times* reviewer said of a revival in 1904, "essentially a theatre-play, a thing of 'scenes,' of action and passions."[21]

Still other plays illustrate the specific Fletcherian effects derived from adaptation. The climax of Sophia Lee's *Almeyda: Queen of Granada* (Drury Lane, 1795-96) is borrowed directly from Shirley's *The Cardinal.* John Tobin's popular drama *The Curfew* (Drury Lane, 1806-07), which went through seven editions in the year of its first performance, is "a very happy imitation of the old dramatic writers," Genest finds, noting that it also perpetuates their faults, "particularly in the improbability of some parts of the plot" (VIII, 37). The "old dramatic writer" whose influence is most evident in the play is not Shakespeare or another Elizabethan but the Cavalier dramatist and later governor of Virginia, Sir William Berkeley, whose *The Lost Lady* (performed about 1638) was reprinted by Dodsley in 1744 and so lay waiting for Tobin. Finally, Lewis Theobald's *Double Falsehood* (Drury Lane, 1727-28), based on a manuscript the author claimed to be Shakespeare's lost play *Cardenio,* exhibits traits notably un-Shakespearean and, as John Crow has observed, "strikingly Fletcherian."[22] Richard Farmer was undoubtedly on the right track when he asserted that the play was by Shirley.[23] Its Fletcherian qualities are not surprising in view of its source in the Cardenio episode in *Don Quixote,* one of numerous Spanish romances whose characters and conventions were apparently ideal for adaptation by Fletcher (who, it seems, had a hand in the lost play) and fellow dramatists eager to produce fare attractive to aristocratic audiences. Suitably, *Double Falsehood* is reflected in Colman the Younger's *The Mountaineers* (Haymarket, 1793), also based on the story of the unfortunate Cardenio.

Examples multiply. As the contemporary Henry Weber ob-

[21] 14 June 1904, quoted by Taylor, p. 242. See also Rothstein's illuminating analysis of the play in *Restoration Tragedy,* pp. 103-109.

[22] Conversation with the present author. For discussions of the problem, see Walter Graham, ed., *Double Falsehood* (Cleveland, 1920), pp. 4ff, and John Freehafer, "*Cardenio,* by Shakespeare and Fletcher," *PMLA,* LXXXIV (1969), 501-513.

[23] ". . . from every mark of Style and Manner, I make no doubt of ascribing it to *Shirley*"—*An Essay on the Learning of Shakespeare,* 2nd edn. (Cambridge, Eng., 1767), p. 29.

served in his edition of Beaumont and Fletcher, "To trace all their lawful property in the more modern plays would be an endless and very thankless task."[24] It is perhaps now clear that the Fletcherian dramaturgical form produced, at first or second hand, a widespread effect on the drama of the late eighteenth and early nineteenth centuries. The foregoing discussion will not, I hope, imply a view that the only influence on the drama of this latter age was exerted by two playwrights whose innovations eclipsed the efforts of all others. I have attempted to show rather that their influence is, first, of a special and important kind and, second, that an understanding of it helps to explain the characteristics of plays all too often explained away as "bad Shakespeare" (or shelved as sub-literary to await the attention of sociologists). Further, I have tried to indicate that these plays must be studied in the surroundings in which they were performed, specifically by keeping in mind the long temporal context that identifies the English repertory theater as one of the most conservative of human institutions. The next chapter will continue to deal with the persistence of the Fletcherian mode by considering more directly the continuity of its development and by examining certain cultural phenomena whose reflections in the theater were full and lucid.

[24] *The Works of Beaumont and Fletcher*, 14 vols. (Edinburgh, 1812), I, Intro., cii.

CHAPTER III

Affective Drama and the Moment of Response

> In short, our Souls are at present delightfully lost and bewildered in a pleasing Delusion, and we walk about like the Enchanted Hero of a Romance, who sees beautiful Castles, Woods and Meadows; and at the same time hears the warbling of Birds, and the purling of Streams; but upon the finishing of some secret Spell, the fantastick Scene breaks up, and the disconsolate Knight finds himself on a barren Heath, or in a solitary Desart.
>
> —Addison, *Spectator* No. 413

i. The Fletcherian Mode in Transition

BY NATURE an openly conservative form of art, the drama consistently dresses itself out in the next-to-new of old fashion. Addison's *Cato*, for example, is in many ways a regressive work, its emotional structure and heroic character and blank verse oratory a clear résumé of Fletcher, Chapman and Dryden, Otway and Lee. Its justifiable impression of originality on Augustan audiences derived not from innovationary dramaturgy but from Addison's sense of how the past may serve the present. Although a special instance because of the heated political issue it framed, *Cato* illustrates the general truth that the seemingly new may preserve and reinvigorate tradition as well as undermine it. By exception, *Cato* also illustrates the rule that singularity in the drama is a rarity. By and large, the plays of the eighteenth and early nineteenth centuries manifest both conservative and radical tendencies moving slowly in uneasy coalition. Seen at short distance, they appear in rich heterogeneous detail. Viewed in longer perspective, they take on coherence of another sort. Fletcherian dramatic structure and character still provide the models on which many authors of this era patterned their serious dramatic works, while at the same time certain cultural developments of the post-Restoration period exerted influence in significant ways. New notions of human conduct in moral philosophy combined with new, subjective ideas of human psychology and changing concepts of the natural world to set an important "radical" precedent for playwrights. While apparently devoted to Fletcherian dramaturgical techniques as he understood them (without an inkling that they were Fletcherian), the tragic dramatist found available to him fresh ideas about human nature which he gradually incorporated within the traditional tragicomic structure of his play.

The psychology of perception initiated by John Locke and developed by later empirical philosophers and psychologists had profound effects over the course of the eighteenth century.[1] In the drama, this new view of man and his relationship to the world outside his mind established a theoretical basis for the presentation of human reactions unavailable to earlier playwrights. The quasi-autonomy of the scene remains a constant; but in Beaumont and Fletcher the character is shown from the outside, as it were, in action or reaction, whereas in later plays he is increasingly presented as revealed from within. Despite his presence in the scene, he is in an important way alienated from it because the playwright tends more to focus on the character's mental reactions while they are taking shape. Although the scenic fragment in the older drama is emblematic of extreme reaction, in later drama it becomes a kind of psychic spatial entity. Human response to the impinging external world is presented more explicitly as "dramatic sculpture" and so has essentially the same qualities and produces the same effects as, say, the "frozen moment" depicted in the Laocoön group, a favorite subject of late eighteenth-century theorists of the sublime and of the neo-Horatian dictum *ut pictura poesis.* In this sculpture the central figure is not shown at the point of full reaction but just before it. His mouth is half open; a scream of agony is about to burst forth but is only now at its threshold. We see, not culmination, but *process.*[2]

[1] Students of this subject must be indebted, as I am, to the studies of Marjorie Hope Nicolson; see *Newton Demands the Muse* (Princeton, 1946), *Mountain Gloom and Mountain Glory* (Ithaca, 1959), and *The Breaking of the Circle*, rev. edn. (New York, 1960). See also Ernest Tuveson, *The Imagination as a Means of Grace: Locke and the Aesthetics of Romanticism* (Berkeley and Los Angeles, 1960), and Kenneth MacLean, *John Locke and English Literature of the Eighteenth Century* (New Haven, 1936).

[2] Henry Fuseli translates Winkelmann's comment on the central figure in the Laocoön as follows: "Pangs piercing every muscle, every labouring nerve;

In his Introduction to *A Treatise of Human Nature* (1738) David Hume set down a premise derived from Locke but infused with the more overt scepticism that characterized Hume's investigations. "Tho' we must endeavour to render all our principles as universal as possible," he asserted, "by tracing up our experiments to the utmost, and explaining all effects from the simplest and fewest causes, 'tis still certain we cannot go beyond experience; and any hypothesis, that pretends to discover the ultimate original qualities of human nature, ought at first to be rejected as presumptuous and chimerical."[3] A germ of this scepticism can be found in Locke's notion of personal identity and its relationship to the existence of the soul. Locke considered it "probable" that one's consciousness of identity is "annexed to, and the affection of, one individual immaterial substance."[4] But, as one of his commentators has pointed out, Locke also maintained "our complete ignorance of the substance either of spirit or of body."[5] "Our faculties cannot arrive at demonstrative certainty about the immateriality of the soul," and so in this as in many things we

---

pangs which we almost feel ourselves, while we consider—not the face, nor the most expressive parts—only the belly contracted by excruciating pains: these however, I say, exert not themselves with violence, either in the face or gesture. He pierces not heaven, like the Laocoön of *Virgil*; his mouth is rather opened to discharge an anxious overloaded groan . . . ; the struggling body and the supporting mind exert themselves with equal strength, nay balance all the frame"—*Reflections on the Painting and Sculpture of the Greeks* (1765), pp. 30-31. For a convenient summary of the importance of the Laocoön for Renaissance and Neo-Classic aesthetic notions, see Margarete Bieber, *Laocoön: The Influence of the Group Since its Rediscovery*, rev. edn. (Detroit, 1967), esp. pp. 11-30. An example of the "Horatian" confluence of poetry and painting occurs in the Preface to the 1750 edition of Beaumont and Fletcher's plays. Thomas Seward quotes Aspatia's "Sorrow's monument" speech and then adduces Guido's painting of Bacchus and Ariadne as "the best *Comment* on these Lines. In both are the Arms extended, the Hair blown by the Wind, the barren Roughness of the Rocks, the broken Trunks of leafless Trees, and in both she looks like *Sorrow's Monument*. So that exactly *ut Pictura Poesis*; and hard it is to say, whether our *Authors* or *Guido painted best*"—*The Works of Mr. Francis Beaumont, and Mr. John Fletcher*, ed. Theobald, Seward, and Sympson, 10 vols. (1750), Pref., p. xxxi.

[3] Ed. L. A. Selby-Bigge (Oxford, 1888, repr. 1949), p. xxi.

[4] *An Essay Concerning Human Understanding*, ed. Alexander Campbell Fraser, 2 vols. (Oxford, 1894), II, xxvii, 25. Subsequent references are to this edition, cited as here by book, chapter, and section.

[5] A. S. Pringle-Pattison, ed., *An Essay Concerning Human Understanding* (Oxford, 1924), p. 269n. I am indebted to Pringle-Pattison for some of the ideas in this section.

must "content ourselves with faith and probability" (IV, iii, 6). Locke's concerted attempt to revise Cartesian doctrine suggests that if he had reformulated in a terse phrase his position with respect to Descarte's "Cogito" he would have written "Dubito ergo sum." For example, "It is past controversy," he explains, "that we have in us *something* that thinks; our very doubts about what it is, confirm the certainty of its being, though we must content ourselves in the ignorance of what *kind* of being it is: and it is in vain to go about to be sceptical in this, as it is unreasonable in most other cases to be positive against the being of anything, because we cannot comprehend its nature" (IV, iii, 6).

Locke's notion of the reality of the individual consciousness coupled with his admitted inability to demonstrate its nature with certainty supplies a psychological basis for the treatment of subjective and erratic states of mind increasingly evident in serious post-Restoration drama. The Scottish philosopher Thomas Reid was appalled by Hume's view of the relationship between man and the world outside his senses:

> If this is the philosophy of human nature, my soul enter thou not into her secrets. It is surely the forbidden tree of knowledge; I no sooner taste of it, than I perceive myself naked, and stript of all things, yea even of my very self. I see myself, and the whole frame of nature, shrink into fleeting ideas, which, like Epicurus's atoms, dance about in emptiness.[6]

Reid's language is extreme, but his dismay is nevertheless typical of the Romantic hero (or heroine). Faced with a world whose order and purpose seem to have become uncertain, even chaotic, he retreats to the only sure ground he can discover, his consciousness of himself. Here he is even more disconcerted to find that the benevolent design which seemed missing in the universe is equally elusive in the mind. Both Locke and Bishop Berkeley maintained a theistic assumption about the design of the universe. As Locke put it, "The coherence and continuity of the parts of matter; the production of sensation in us of colours and sounds, &c., by impulse and motion; wherein we can discover no natural connexion with any ideas we have, we cannot but ascribe them to the arbitrary will and good pleasure of the Wise Archi-

[6] *An Inquiry into the Human Mind, On the Principles of Common Sense*, 3rd edn. (1769), p. 22.

3. Garrick and Mrs. Cibber as Jaffier and Belvidera in *Venice Preserv'd*

4. Mr. and Mrs. Barry as Jaffier and Belvidera in *Venice Preserv'd*

5. Mrs. Siddons as Belvidera

tect" (IV, iii, 29). Hume relinquishes this assumption and restates the contrast between reason and experience: "One event follows another; but we never can observe any tie between them. They seem *conjoined*, but never *connected*."[7]

These new ideas of human perception and self-consciousness offered a theoretical groundwork for concepts of dramatic character notably anticipated in Fletcherian drama. Dion's speech in *Philaster* about the impenetrability of the human heart and mind becomes the unwitting cue for later writers to invert his point of reference. If, in communicating with others, a character must depend wholly on what appears, it is possible to describe the inner state of that character as fundamentally disconnected from what lies outside him. The course of serious English drama from the Restoration on reveals the playwright's mounting interest in investigating his characters' inability to make sense out of their environment. Events rush on with seeming purposelessness, and in the face of them the character resists their magnetic attraction by delving into his own mind in search of stability. But he is drawn on nevertheless, a victim of time, circumstance, and his own uncertain nature.

The dilemma of the dramatic character reflects a similar problem encountered by the dramatist himself. The moral philosophy synthesized by Shaftesbury presupposed the innate goodness and dignity of individual man and of the human species as a whole. Man is fallible but not fundamentally wicked. Although events may lead him astray, his instinctive response to the plight of those less fortunate than himself will extricate him—and, happily, his fellows as well—from whatever threatens the harmony and progress of society. The course of eighteenth-century comedy after Steele is to an important extent a series of dramatic demonstrations of this general idea.[8] But the writing of tragedy based on this premise poses a formidable question. Eighteenth-century au-

[7] *Enquiry Concerning the Human Understanding*, in L. A. Selby-Bigge, ed., *Enquiries Concerning the Human Understanding and Concerning the Principles of Morals by David Hume*, 2nd edn. (Oxford, 1902), Sec. VII, Pt. ii, ¶58 (p. 74). Hume goes on to point out that the idea of cause and effect is the product of seeing the same events habitually conjoined; one's idea of "*connexion*," then, comes from the fact that "he now *feels* these events to be *connected* in his imagination . . ." (VII, ii, 59).

[8] See the more detailed discussion of these notions in Chap. V and the scholarship cited there in note 3.

thors of serious drama faced the problem of reconciling a notion of inherent human goodness, supported by a benevolent Providence, with the presentation of death on the stage. Usually playwrights took one or the other of two avenues out of this difficulty. Some solved the problem by calling their plays tragedies but averting the final catastrophe by introducing some timely event or revelation. Such a play is Arthur Murphy's *The Grecian Daughter* (Drury Lane, 1771-72) or Charles Lamb's *John Woodvil* (1802). Other writers avoided the use of the sentimental *deus ex machina* (in effect, a *deus ex corde humano*) by exploiting more fully the capacities for human error implicit in the sentimental view of human nature. Their reasoning (if it may be called that) was based on the idea that virtue depends upon responsiveness. The benevolent man, by nature alive to the suffering of his fellow creatures, reacts to it with great immediacy and forcefulness. Sensibility to outward impressions, then, is the true mark of the noble mind. But the practice of this virtue entails an instinctive reaction, not a coolly reasoned one. In the heat of response the sensitive man may well fail to see that his reaction precipitates his own destruction.

In the late eighteenth century, play after play demonstrates the straddling of the moral issue implicit in this fallible logic. On the one hand, the man of essential virtue believes that in responding as he does he follows a course prompted by Divine Providence. On the other, if his response eventuates in grave misfortune or even death for him or for others, then his error simply becomes an occasion for pity over unmerited misfortune. As the course of English tragedy up to this time demonstrates, the Fletcherian structure is adaptable to alternatively "happy" or "unhappy" endings. The disjunction of character and event already evident in the Fletcherian play becomes, in the hands of playwrights influenced even at third or fourth hand by the spreading ideas of Locke and Shaftesbury, a much-used device for eliciting pity. If a man cannot really be blamed for displaying those qualities which make him human, and if audiences are shown his psychological propensities as inevitable processes leading up to reaction, they are convinced that so noble a mind could not have willed the evil that results from the function of untutored natural response. Where, then, lies the cause of misfortune? Of necessity it must lie in the operation of chance in the exterior world.

To this operation playwrights habitually assigned the ambiguous term *fate*. Audiences in this age, at least nominally Christian, gave lip service if not always real assent to the belief in a God whose hand shapes the course of history and men's lives. Yet they continued to applaud theatrical performances that offered an ill-defined sense of the inscrutable destiny attendant on human actions. Some two dozen or more plays produced in the eighteenth and early nineteenth centuries have the word *fatal* as part of their titles. The earliest instance after the Restoration is H. N. Payne's *Fatal Jealousie* (Dorset Garden, 1671-72), which combined with Massinger and Field's *Fatal Dowry*, Southerne's *Fatal Marriage* (Drury Lane, 1693-94), and a few others to form a precedent for numerous followers.[9] Playwrights, whether or not they employed the word, found the unpredictability of the Fletcherian structure a means of portraying an innocent character whose propensities for good are thwarted by the emergence of ungovernable events. Correlatively, employing the Fletcherian concept of character, they presented their own as perverted from a virtuous norm by the irresistible force of circumstance. Unduly tried by extreme situations with which nothing in their experience enables them to cope, they react in blind and impassioned responses which ironically bring about their destruction.

It is characteristic of George Lillo that he saw the pervertedness of the sentimental hero as a sort of moral depravity. Best known as the author of *The London Merchant: or, The History of George Barnwell* (Drury Lane, 1730-31), Lillo imbued the play that followed this with a set of qualities that make it almost a perfect transition piece. First presented by Henry Fielding at the Haymarket in 1736 under the full title *Guilt Its Own Punishment: or, Fatal Curiosity*, this domestic tragedy shows an unusual attention to character that enhances its importance in the history of the drama.[10] The reader who is fresh from *George Barnwell* and braced to endure a barrage of didactic assaults may well be surprised by the psychological development that precedes Lillo's explicit pointing of his moral towards the end of the last act. The

[9] For other titles see Allardyce Nicoll's alphabetical catalogue, *A History of English Drama 1660-1900*, VI (Cambridge, Eng., 1959), 155-156.

[10] Professor Nicoll calls attention to the superiority of *Fatal Curiosity* over *George Barnwell* and to its importance as a precursor of the German *Schicksalstragödie* and the serious domestic realism of later English plays—*History*, 3rd edn., III (Cambridge, Eng., 1955), 121-124.

three chief characters of *Fatal Curiosity* (the poverty-stricken merchant Old Wilmot, his despairing wife Agnes, and their son Young Wilmot) each demonstrate the mental aberration of excessive curiosity whose results are suggested in the title. Lillo goes to great lengths to demonstrate the psychological *process* of developing mental imbalance that eventuates in catastrophe for all three. Old Wilmot's fatal mistake, an excessive, Faust-like fascination with knowledge beyond the healthy use of man, leaves him free only to enjoy his "sad prerogative . . . To think, and to be wretched."[11] His thoughts, revealed in the soliloquy that opens the play, have led him to "that wisdom Whose perfection ends in knowing we know nothing." Although the sun continues its predictable orderly course, human life is composed of "Mere contradictions all! A tragic farce,/ Tedious though short, and without art elab'rate,/ Ridiculously sad" (I.i.14-18). Old Wilmot's disposition to inquire too minutely is complemented by a simpler kind of inquisitiveness on the part of his wife. Her desire to know the contents of the sumptuous cask left in her keeping by her disguised son brings about the climax of the play.

The most extensively detailed curiosity belongs to the son, Young Wilmot, a capable and adventurous fellow who has won great riches in trade and has now returned home to marry his patient, beloved Charlot, and to relieve his parents' misery and want. The plot shows many signs of the middle-class sentimental comedy which proliferates over the course of the century; but there are no feast and wedding at the end. The dramatist mounts an attack against the sentimental hero now fully evident in English drama. Young Wilmot returns with "wealth Enough to glut ev'n Avarice itself!" (II.i.137-138), is reunited with Charlot, and sets about relieving his parents' distress. In the "wanton" ease of his mind, he decides to make their happiness and his own more exquisite. "Why may I not Indulge my curiosity," he thinks, and meet them first as a stranger, so "to improve Their pleasure by surprise?" (II.ii.50-54). Entering his parents' home as a weary stranger seeking rest, he is astonished to see the depths of poverty to which they have fallen. In an aside, Lillo shows what pleasure his character takes in this pain:

> The joy to see them, and the bitter pain
> It is to see them thus, touches my soul

[11] *Fatal Curiosity*, ed. William H. McBurney (Lincoln, 1967), I.i.12-13.

With tenderness and grief that will o'erflow.
My bosom heaves and swells as it would burst,
My bowels move, and my heart melts within me.[12]

Resisting the impulse to reveal himself to his parents at once, Young Wilmot rationalizes delay by observing that a sudden revelation would kill them. They must instead be elevated into joy "By circumstances, then, and slow degrees . . ." (102). In these closing moments of Act II, it is clear that the young man has appropriated to himself the power of arranging Providence. "The darkest hours precede the rising sun," he arrogantly observes to his mother, "And mercy may appear when least expected" (75-76). Having placed his money-laden casket in her hands for safe-keeping, he retires to bed, asking Heaven to grant them patience for a few hours more.

In developing the murder sequence that forms the bulk of the third and last act, Lillo draws heavily on the analogous scene in *Macbeth*, but manages as well to conflate other important scenes in Shakespeare's tragedy so that its thematic development is condensed within one brief act. It is a credit to Lillo's craftsmanship that this heavily derivative scene carries its own weight dramatically and theatrically, for the playwright in preparation has spent two acts carefully building up the psychological perversion of these otherwise ordinary middle-class persons. Telescoping Shakespeare's sequence of character development, Lillo almost immediately follows the murder with Old Wilmot's cynical despair: "Sleep those who may. I know my lot is endless perturbation" (230-231). But in place of Lady Macbeth's sleep-walking scene Lillo assigns a brief dream-vision of the "dumb phantoms of despair and horror" (221) to Charlot, letting Agnes and Old Wilmot together discover the identity of the corpse. So, through their speeches and subsequent deaths, they serve as explicit *raisonneurs* of the terrible lesson evident in this bloody sequence of events. Old Wilmot's summary is the more inclusive:

Our guilt and desolation must be told
From age to age to teach desponding mortals
How far beyond the reach of human thought
Heaven, when incensed, can punish. (241-244)

[12] II.iii.45-49. McBurney explains the reference to bowels as in the Biblical sense of "tender feelings or pity" (p. 37n).

The moral issues in the play, however, are not really so easily resolved. Lillo apparently intends to demonstrate a correlation between the moral failings of those who abandon Providence and the punishment that attends on their apostasy. The recurrent image of the shining sun reinforces this idea and suggests ironically that human beings may forsake their faith in the benevolent design of the universe and so plunge into the darkness of sin and guilt. "The sun will shine, and all things have their course," Old Wilmot observes (III.i.238). Yet, while Lillo has carefully explicated the mental distress that leads to perversity of action, his control over the structure of the play has not been so sure. His concern to follow unity of time by restricting the action to the late afternoon and evening of one day results in a sequence of events that works against his moral purpose. For only a few hours will make the difference between a dreadful murder and the joyful reunion of parents and son.

A strong connection thus emerges between the rejection of Providence in the speeches of several characters and the implied rejection of it in this Fletcherian structure of withheld information and missed opportunity. In the introduction to his edition of *The London Merchant* and *Fatal Curiosity*, A. W. Ward stated that in the latter Lillo "exhibited destiny as operating to all intents and purposes independently of character" and that "the effect of this tragedy is therefore as hollow as it is horrible."[13] Such a conclusion is possible if we ignore Lillo's pointed emphasis, in the original title and throughout the work itself, on how much the characters deserve what they get. Yet, even when his skill in delineating psychological guilt is acknowledged, the contrary moral possibilities of the play still hang in uneasy suspension. In adapting the amoral Fletcherian structure to an Elizabethan tale of merited misfortune, Lillo unwittingly compromised himself. The compromise is perfectly evident in Old Wilmot's closing lines:

Yet let me say
You'll do but justice to inform the world
This horrid deed that punishes itself
Was not intended as he was our son;

[13] *The London Merchant . . . and Fatal Curiosity,* ed. Adolphus William Ward (Boston and London, 1906), Intro., p. liii.

For that we knew not, till it was too late.
(III.i.293-297)

Although not an adequate response to the moral complexity of *Fatal Curiosity,* Ward's judgment nevertheless serves to relate Lillo's psychological morality play to the radical disjunction of character and action in much English drama whose precedent lies in Fletcherian rhetorical structure. If his comment is not quite fair to Lillo, it is more just when aimed at the serious English drama that followed Lillo's transitional work.

ii. Character and Landscape in Home's *Douglas*

One of the many titles reflecting the fatalism evident on eighteenth-century stages occurs with John Home's *The Fatal Discovery* (Drury Lane, 1768-69). The title would have done almost as well for his earlier and best-known play, *Douglas* (Canongate, Edinburgh, 1756-57). Despite the accolades enthusiastic theatergoers showered on Home for having matched the genius of the great Elizabethan—"Whaur's yer Wully Shakspere noo!" one of them is said to have exclaimed[14]—an examination of the text leaves no doubt that the play employs the well-tested Fletcherian convention in order to unfold the psychological destruction of an innocent woman by mere chance. Although the title suggests that the central figure is the long-lost son of Lady Randolph, Home's focus almost never wavers from the noble wife and mother upon whose plight he constructs his "she-tragedy." Some measure of the play's phenomenal immediate popularity in Edinburgh must be accorded to Home's careful exploitation of his first audience's patriotic fervor and sense of place; but an attempt to explain its continued success elsewhere will more wisely pursue an idea of the relationships of character, language, and atmospheric detail.

Eighteenth-century aestheticians avidly debated the fine points of distinction between the sublime and the picturesque.[15] Yet, no

[14] James C. Dibdin, *Annals of the Edinburgh Stage* (Edinburgh, 1888), p. 87; see MacDonald Emslie, "Home's *Douglas* and Wully Shakspeare," *Studies in Scottish Literature,* II (1964), 128-129.

[15] Like all students of the subject, I have benefited from two basic books, Samuel Holt Monk's *The Sublime: A Study of Critical Theories in XVIII-Century England* (New York, 1935), and Walter John Hipple Jr.'s *The Beautiful, The Sublime, and The Picturesque In Eighteenth-Century British Aesthetic Theory* (Carbondale, Ill., 1957). The extensive and well-known

matter what their views, they stood agreed that the significance of these supposed qualities of the exterior world lay in their effects on the perceiving human mind. The nineteenth-century notion of the *paysage intérieur,* or mental landscape, grew out of the increasing sense in the eighteenth century that the human mind in a state of emotional excitement tends to adjust impressions from the outside world to accord with this inner condition. It became possible for poets and playwrights, as well as painters, to begin to depict landscape as in effect *expressive* of the mind in a state of imbalance or turmoil. The innumerable eighteenth-century discussions of the greater or lesser appropriateness of craggy rocks or smooth rocks, serpentine streams or swift-running brooks, of irregularity or sameness in general, suggest that landscape may be transformed in order to express in a more unified way some dominant emotion characteristic of human response to the external world. Yet the result of actual reformation, often careful and extensive, was that the "unity" of the new landscape had all the appearance of rude, unregimented, natural wildness—when viewed from the right point of vantage. Bishop Berkeley's diagrams of a lens and its field of vision present a theoretical analogue to the growing eighteenth-century emphasis on orienting landscape toward the eye of the subjective beholder who, as Wordsworth could later explain, both perceives and creates.[16] Conditioned by the Fletcherian disjunction between objective action and the subjective response of character, Home and the dramatists who followed him came increasingly to dwell on the "fatal" results of subjective vision. The emotional responses of characters to the impingement of the world outside themselves created chaos in a universe where order had once reigned.

Home begins by placing his central figure off by herself and supplying a soliloquy that sets both the mood and theme of the play. Matilda, Lady Randolph, first appears isolated in "*The court of a castle surrounded with woods,*"[17] but no immediate

scholarship that has grown since the publication of Monk's book needs no citation here.

[16] George Berkeley, *An Essay Towards a New Theory of Vision* (Dublin, 1709), in *Works,* ed. A. A. Luce and T. E. Jessop, 9 vols. (London, 1948-57), I; see esp. secs. 32ff, 88ff, and 109ff. For Wordsworth's view of the sympathetic human mind, see especially *The Prelude* (1850), Bk. II, ll. 232-260.

[17] *Douglas: A Tragedy. As it is Acted at the Theatre-Royal in Covent-Garden* (Edinburgh, 1757), Act I, p. 7. Since the scene remains unchanged

dramatic motive has forced her there. She is present, and alone, because it suits the playwright's convenience so to establish the relationship between Lady Randolph and her environment. Her speech reveals the extent to which past experience and her resultant emotional state condition her view of the surroundings:

> Ye woods and wilds, whose melancholy gloom
> Accords with my soul's sadness, and draws forth
> The voice of sorrow from my bursting heart,
> Farewel a while: I will not leave you long;
> For in your shades I deem some spirit dwells,
> Who from the chiding stream, or groaning oak,
> Still hears, and answers to *Matilda*'s moan.
> O, *Douglas! Douglas!* (I, p. 7)

In the following exposition the audience discovers that, almost a generation before, Matilda secretly married the warrior Douglas and bore him a child. At a fateful time shortly after, both her husband and brother were killed in battle and her young son, the namesake of his father, was lost and presumed dead. From that day, fidelity to their memory has been the principal activity of her life, even after her father coerced her into marriage with Lord Randolph some seven years before the action of the play begins. Melancholy having thus taken possession of her mind, her costume reflects the morbidity of the changeless affection that, she says, lies buried in Douglas' bloody grave. "These black weeds," remarks her impatient husband, who has come upon her alone in the courtyard, "Express the wonted colour of thy mind, For ever dark and dismal" (I, p. 8). As the exposition develops, Home introduces a scene in which Matilda reveals to Anna, her gentlewoman and confidante, the secret of her youthful marriage. Painting a vivid picture of the loss of her husband, she exclaims, like Fletcher's Arathusa before her, "Mighty God! What had I done to merit such affliction?" Continuing, she relates how her infant son was lost, a son whom she would have acknowledged, defying the rage and grief of her father, and would have led wandering "thro' the scorning world" (I, p. 13).

Obviously, Home is writing in the pathetic vein of Otway and

for each act, subsequent references are to Act and page only. I have used the first Edinburgh edition, a fuller text, in preference to the first London edition, which is a cut version of the former.

Rowe, establishing the plight of his innocent heroine in an unfeeling, antagonistic world. Around this center he builds a tale of woe and sorrow designed, as the London prologue unequivocally states, to elicit for "your suppliant all she begs, a tear" (p. iii). More explicitly, and with more sureness of hand than Lillo, Home provides a structure that nicely balances Providential order against the chaos of mere chance to precipitate Lady Randolph's doom. In working out the double recognition plot in which Lady Randolph reveals to young Norval that he is the son of Douglas and in which Norval recognizes Lady Randolph as his mother, Home emphasizes the idea that this reunion shows the workings of divine intelligence. "Eternal Providence!" exclaims Lady Randolph when, in Act III, she discovers that Norval is her son (p. 29). But "fatal love" (IV, p. 41), whose offspring now stands before her, is about to culminate in the evil destiny toward which it has always moved. "O Nature, Nature!" cries Lady Randolph, "what can check thy force?" Norval, trained by a soldier-hermit to become a peerless warrior, must go to defend his mother against the machinations of the villainous Glenalvon. With ironic force, Lady Randolph reassures him in parting that "as high heav'n hath will'd it all must be" (V, p. 55). Providence and fatalism, so conjoined, permanently sever when young Douglas, mortally wounded, re-enters.

The death scene that follows suggests that the battle of Providence and chaos, implicitly waged in the structure of the play and echoed in the atmospheric language, has no philosophic significance in itself. Its theatrical importance, however, is beyond doubt. The scene bears all the marks of a hand thoroughly adept at manipulating the emotions of an audience:

Douglas. Do not despair: I feel a little faintness;
I hope it will not last. [*Leans upon his sword*]
Lady Randolph. There is no hope!
And we must part! the hand of death is on thee!
O my beloved child! O *Douglas, Douglas!*
Douglas. Too soon we part; I have not long been *Douglas.*
O destiny! hardly thou deal'st with me:
Clouded and hid, a stranger to myself,
In low and poor obscurity I lived.

Lady Randolph. Has heav'n preserv'd thee for
an end like this?
Douglas. O had I fallen as my brave fathers fell,
Turning with great effort the tide of battle!
Like them I should have smil'd and welcom'd death.
But thus to perish by a villain's hand!
Cut off from nature's and from glory's course,
Which never mortal was so fond to run.
Lady Randolph. Hear justice! hear! stretch
thy avenging arm.
[*Douglas falls*]
Douglas. Unknown I die; no tongue shall speak
of me.—
Some noble spirits, judging by themselves,
May yet conjecture what I might have prov'd,
And think life only wanting to my fame:
But who shall comfort thee?
Lady Randolph. Despair! despair!
Douglas. O, had it pleas'd high heaven to let
me live
A little while!—My eyes that gaze on thee
Grow dim apace! my mother!—O, my mother!
[*Dies*]
(V, pp. 56-57)

Conveying a sense that blood ties are strongest, the double recognition plot now inverts into a double catastrophe with the death of Lady Randolph. Momentarily, Home protracts her agonies. Recovering from a fainting spell she finds herself "still in this wretched world!" and, in full despair, cries out against the fate that has chosen her as the object "On which Omnipotence displays itself,/ Making a spectacle, a tale of me,/ To awe its vassal, man" (V, p. 58). Almost mindless with her sense of injury, she rushes out. Anna, who has followed her, returns in sorrow to report her death. The description of Lady Randolph's suicide reflects the Fletcherian emblem of emotional stance, but it is here an emblem significantly infused with the sense of vastness and terror attached to contemporary notions of the sublime:

She ran, she flew like light'ning up the hill,
Nor halted till the precipice she gain'd,

Beneath whose low'ring top the river falls
Ingulph'd in rifted rocks: thither she came,
As fearless as the eagle lights upon it,

. . . .

O had you seen her last despairing look!
Upon the brink she stood, and cast her eyes
Down on the deep: then lifting up her head
And her white hands to heaven, seeming to say,
Why am I forc'd to this? she plung'd herself
Into the empty air. (V, pp. 59-60)

Anna's depiction of Lady Randolph's moment of hesitation is patently an icon of human bewilderment at the inscrutable forces which, upon mere whim, cast the pall of destiny upon idyllic young love. The figure of a human being poised upon a precipice and gazing down into the depths of an abyss had become, even in Home's time, a conventional figure for pathetic disaster. In Act II of Edward Moore's tragedy *The Gamester* (Drury Lane, 1752-53) Beverley's friend Jarvis reports that the world thinks of him "as of a good Man dead. Of one, who walking in a Dream, fell down a Precipice. The World is sorry for you."[18] Thomas Gray's bard is probably the best-known instance. Published in the same year as Home's play, Gray's poem describes the bard's sublime stance upon a promontory, prophesying doom for Edward I and his train who are passing far below.[19] Painted by Blake, Fuseli [see Plate 7], and others during the remainder of the century and after,[20] this moment stood as a symbol of what was inevitably to follow. Having completed his prophecy, "Headlong from the mountain's height Deep in the roaring tide he plung'd to endless night."[21]

[18] *The Gamester. A Tragedy* (1753), p. 19.

[19] "The Bard. A Pindaric Ode," *The Complete Poems of Thomas Gray*, ed. H. W. Starr and J. R. Hendrickson (Oxford, 1966), p. 19.

[20] For brief discussions of some of these renderings of Gray's bard and for a reproduction of Blake's, see *Romantic Art in Britain: Paintings and Drawings 1760-1860*, Catalogue of the Exhibition at Detroit and Philadelphia, 1968, ed. Frederick Cummings and Allen Staley (Philadelphia, 1968), pp. 160-161.

[21] Page 24. Gray himself was "greatly struck" by Home's play: "The Author seems to me to have retrieved the true language of the Stage, wch had been lost for these hundred years . . ."—*Correspondence of Thomas Gray*, ed. Paget Toynbee and Leonard Whibley, 3 vols. (Oxford, 1935), II, 515. *Biographia Dramatica*'s significant conjecture on Gray's source reinforces Home's notion of his heroine's essential innocence: "Dr. Johnson blames Mr. Gray

Again, only two years after *Douglas* was published, Adam Smith described in his *Theory of Moral Sentiments* the danger the sympathetic mind courts in following the natural dictates of passion. "Wearied and distracted with . . . continual irresolutions," he explains, such a person "at length, from a sort of despair, makes the last fatal and irrecoverable step; but with that terror and amazement with which one flying from an enemy throws himself over a precipice, where he is sure of meeting with more certain destruction than from any thing that pursues him from behind."[22] By 1820 the convention had become so deeply ingrained that Henry Fuseli, himself one of the most individualistic painters of "the sublime," could describe its operation as a fundamental artistic principle. Pointing out the best method of creating a background scene for *Macbeth*, he explained:

> Whatever connects the individual with the elements, whether by abrupt or imperceptible means, is an instrument of sublimity, as, whatever connects it in the same manner with, or tears it from the species, may become an organ of pathos: in this discrimination lies the rule by which our art, to astonish or move, ought to choose the scenery of its subjects. It is not by the accumulation of infernal or magic machinery, distinctly seen, by the introduction of Hecate and a chorus of female daemons and witches, by surrounding him with successive apparitions at once, and a range of shadows moving above or before him, that Macbeth can be made an object of terrour,—to render him so you must place him on a ridge, his down-dashed eye absorbed by the murky abyss; surround the horrid vision with darkness, exclude its limits, and shear its light to glimpses.[23]

---

for concluding his celebrated ode with suicide; a circumstance borrowed perhaps from *Douglas*, in which Lady Randolph, otherwise a blameless character, precipitates herself, like the Bard, from a cliff, into eternity"—*Biographia Dramatica; or, A Companion to the Playhouse*, ed. David Erskine Baker, Isaac Reed, and Stephen Jones, 3 vols. (1812), II, 175.

[22] *The Theory of Moral Sentiments; or, An Essay Toward an Analysis of the Principles by which Men naturally judge concerning the Conduct and Character, first of their Neighbors, and afterwards of themselves*, 9th edn., 2 vols. (1801), I, 331.

[23] *Lectures on Painting, Delivered at the Royal Academy* (1820), pp. 186-187.

Fuseli's advice shows with full adequacy how Home (and many dramatists who followed him) used the double principle of sublimity and pathos to elicit what aestheticians of the period still insisted on calling Aristotelian terror and pity. Home connects Lady Randolph "with the elements" by establishing her subjective association with the dark, foreboding gloom of the woods surrounding the castle. And he effectively severs her "from the species" by establishing the deep tie with her secret past which draws her away from human society to seek company in wild surroundings that mirror the deadly melancholy gripping her mind. Home's own sense of the emotional peaks reached by the end of the play was apparently so strong that he broke with tradition in writing his epilogue. Refusing to gratify the taste of the town for an after-speech of lighthearted wit as an antidote to tragic catastrophe, he has the actress who speaks his epilogue report the author as one who says, sadly,

> *that pity is the best,*
> *The noblest passion of the human breast:*
> *For when its sacred streams the heart o'erflow,*
> *In gushes pleasure with the tide of woe;*
> *And when its waves retire like those of Nile,*
> *They leave behind them such a golden soil,*
> *That there the virtues without culture grow,*
> *There the sweet blossoms of affection blow.*
> *These were his words:—void of delusive art*
> *I felt them; for he spoke them from his heart.*
>
> (p. 61)

So Home provides a pseudo-Aristotelian rationale for the sensational *coup de théâtre* just effected. Although a classic regularity appears in the action—Italianate, at least, in its emphasis on the autonomy of each of five acts—the action as a whole is neither Aristotelian nor Shakespearean, but Fletcherian. The circumstances that so rudely force the death of young Douglas, still dew-fresh from the Grampian hills, bear no relationship to the chain of cause and effect that endows the equally untimely death of Shakespeare's Cordelia with thematic resonance. Home's contrived circumstances are instead a function of the scene itself, conceived theatrically as Fletcher did his scenes for the emotional effect of the moment. The ignoble death of Douglas at the hands of a base villain and the consequent suicide of Lady Randolph could easily have been replaced by a scene in which Douglas encounters Glenalvon but triumphs over him, and is then joined by Lady Randolph who exults in his victory and proclaims his heroism (and paternity) to the assembled company. If such a resolution appears absurd, it nevertheless occurs in play after play where the impingement of Gothic atmosphere and shapes out of the past is equally weighty. The resulting emotional intensity is in either case the same, as Fuseli explained. This description of an alternative ending seems unfair to Home only because his skill in amassing the paraphernalia of Gothic fatefulness gives the illusion of a coherent, "Shakespearean" action. Attention to Home's epilogue helps to avoid the erroneous impression that *Douglas* is a latter-day Shakespearean tragedy. The meaning of the play exists only insofar as it relates to the emotions elicited from the audience, and these emotions are frankly sentimental.[24] Douglas and Lady Randolph do not die primarily because some deep failure of insight has blinded them to a knowledge of themselves and their place in the world they inhabit. They die because the audience's pleasure requires it. The egotistical satisfaction of the sentimental hero in doing good or, more commonly, in enjoying the prospect of doing good is closely analogous to the response Home looks for in his audience. Often disguised under the mask of selflessness adopted by the sentimental hero to achieve his ends, such satisfaction lurks uncommonly close to the surface in Home's epilogue. Plainly, the uses of tragic catastrophe are not confined to the fostering of sympathy for others. The "tide of woe" rushes in—but bearing "pleasure" on its crest.

The increasingly derivative nature of serious drama after Home shows, among other things, how fully *Douglas* had synthesized dominant trends in earlier drama and had at the same time endowed them with the peculiarly "romantic" qualities of the

[24] John Jackson defends Home's ending by explaining its affective rationale: "Had *Douglas,* with his youthful agility and fire, been permitted to have escaped the assassin's stab, and the play had finished with the exaltation of *Douglas,* and the happiness of *Lady Randolph,* . . . it would . . . have deprived the audience of those sympathising sensations of sorrow attendant upon distress, and the author, of presenting the world with one of the best short epilogues we ever remember to have heard"—*The History of the Scottish Stage* (Edinburgh, 1792), p. 329.

landscape of emotion. The orientation of landscape toward the sympathetic beholder produced in late eighteenth-century drama an increasing correlation between pictorialism in surroundings and the mental processes which lead to the moment of response. In exploiting this trend, dramatists found a considerable resource in the greater pictorial effects now possible on the stages of English theaters. In earlier days intimate playhouses with relatively small and only dimly lighted stages, their phenomenal enlargement in the late eighteenth and early nineteenth centuries allowed not only more spectators but a larger playing area and a consequent opportunity for more extensive spectacle. The innovation of side-lighting brought back by Garrick from France in the 1760's was followed in 1785 by the introduction of "patent lamps" on the Drury Lane stage whose "powerful effect," observed a reviewer in the *Public Advertiser,* "cannot be better seen than by a comparison of these new lights with the unusual dimness of the wax-candles in the vicinity of the Stage."[25] Brighter lights suggest the possibility of eliciting from spectators greater attention to what appears on the stage as a whole—not just on the forestage, the predominant acting area in Garrick's time. As lighting improved, later revolutionized by the introduction of gas light in the early nineteenth century, the action could retreat upstage and still be clearly visible.[26] Instead of playing in front of the scenery, actors could now move within it and so achieve a greater impression of reality. As the demand grew for more complicated machinery to represent the thrilling "horrors" of burning castles, crumbling bridges, and inundating floods, a greater opportunity

[25] 12 February 1785. See the discussion of Kemble's stagecraft in Pt. III, Chap. X below, pp. 248-249 and note 12. The exact nature of these lights remains uncertain; the lengthy, authoritative account of the subject in the *Oxford Companion to the Theatre* makes no mention of lighting innovations in 1785, although it details those introduced by Garrick some twenty years before—s.v. "Lighting, Stage, I. History. (a) From the beginning to the introduction of gas." Independent testimony from two contemporary newspapers (cited above and in Chap. X) nevertheless seems sufficient proof that a change indeed took place at this time; but my primary purpose is not to document precisely but to illustrate a notable and important trend.

[26] Robert Jephson's *The Count of Narbonne* (Covent Garden, 1781-82, adapted from Walpole's novel *The Castle of Otranto*) exemplifies the increasing use of the upstage area for spectacular or atmospheric effect: in the first edition (1781) the setting for the first scene is simply "*A Hall*"; in the second edition (1787) it is "*A Hall with Gothick ornaments; a full length picture of* Alphonso *in armour, in the center of the back scene.*"

also appeared for drawing the audience more deeply into the human action on stage. The dramatic "moment" could now take place in a theater more extensively equipped for visual effects. The psychological processes that eventuated in these "moments" could now be more fully suggested by the enhanced visibility of the Gothic landscape. In surrounding the distressed heroine or chained hero or agonizing villain on three sides, what had once been an atmospheric background now became more convincingly an environment. [see Plates 8 and 9]

Although in many cases this greater pictorialism in scenery and scenic effects contributed mainly to shock and sensation, a greater unity of production remained at least theoretically possible. In an important description of the aesthetic nature of a ruin, Sir John Summerson discusses the increased unity of subject and surroundings in architecture which also became evident on Romantic stages:

> The building has become comprehensible as a single whole—no longer an *exterior* plus one or more *interiors* but a single combination of planes in recession, full of mystery and surprise, movement behind movement; and since it retains all the while the character of architecture—a structure designed for use—it suggests its own participation in life: a fantastic participation. The doors and windows in a ruined building accent the drama of human movement, of through-going, out-looking and raise it to a transcendental plane.[27]

This assessment offers by inference a theatrical basis for the Romantic critical notion of the "theater of the imagination" conceived by Hazlitt and Coleridge.[28] The idea of artistic unity of effect conspicuous in the writings of Romantic critics derives in no small measure from the idea of the Gothic that seized hold of English culture during the course of the eighteenth century. This sense of unity found expression as early as 1762 in Richard Hurd's comparison of Gothic design in poetry and gardening. Describing "a wood or grove cut out into many separate avenues or glades," he explains that, while these walks had each their own destination, "the whole was brought together and considered

[27] *Heavenly Mansions and Other Essays on Architecture* (London, 1949), p. 236.

[28] See Chaps. XI and XII below.

under one view by the relation which these various openings had, not to each other, but to their common and concurrent center."[29] Translated into the aesthetics of theatrical performance, Hurd's description of unity implicit in the heterogeneousness of a maze suggests that the "center" which unites the proliferation of walks is the subjective consciousness of the central character and the pathos that his misfortunes evoke from the spectators. The Gothic sensibility has revivified the Restoration idea, inherited from the geometricians of Cavalier drama, that the intrigue plot of a play bears a visual analogy to the patterned confusion of a seventeenth-century garden.[30] "An actor, in a large theatre, is like a picture hung at a distance," remarked William Jackson in 1783.[31] If we combine this sense of the visual effect created by an actor on a stage, surrounded by an illusionistic environment, with the ever-present notion of the dramatic character as an innocent sufferer, we shall have in essence the nature of Romantic drama. "The death of the wicked cannot occasion pity," asserted one of the many contemporary theorists of tragedy, "and if innocence and virtue are not to fall beneath the stroke of oppression and injustice, where is the pathos, where is the tender sympathy?" The answer does not lie in the resolution of the play but in the maze of complications that precede it—"in the unmerited misfortunes, in the agonizing distress of the innocent; in seeing the virtuous involuntarily led to the perpetration of some horrid crime, or in

[29] *Letters on Chivalry and Romance* (1762), ed. Hoyt Trowbridge, Augustan Reprint Society Nos. 101-102 (Los Angeles, 1963), Letter VIII, p. 67.

[30] "Love! of thy laberinth of Art, what path Left I untroden?" exclaims a character in Sir William Habington's *The Queene of Arragon. A Tragi-Comedie* (1640), sig. [B4]. In a spirited defense of tragicomedy, Edward Howard explains that the inventive fictions of the dramatic poet lead "unto those pleasant retirements of the Muses, where as from various and beautiful platforms of Gardens, is beheld the particular designments of shades, walks, and flowers"—*The Womens Conquest: A Tragi-Comedy* (1671), Pref., sig. [a3^{v}]. A century later, the landscaped maze has become the subjective Gothic labyrinth, as in the old King Evander's prison in Arthur Murphy's *The Grecian Daughter*:

> On the sharp summit of the pointed rock,
> Which overhangs the deep, a dungeon drear:
> Cell within cell, a labyrinth of horror,
> Deep cavern'd in the cliff . . .
> —*The Grecian Daughter: A Tragedy* (1772), p. 4.

[31] *Thirty Letters on Various Subjects*, 2 vols. (1783), I, 101.

the dread apprehension of having already committed it, or tottering on the very brink of perdition."[32]

The interest, the pathos of Romantic drama, as of its Fletcherian predecessor, lies in the danger not the death.[33] The resolution of the play may indeed leave corpses strewn upon the stage, but such an outcome is no more a violation of its structural implications than is the prevention of catastrophe by some happy accident. The comments gathered here on the nature of the drama and allied arts in the late eighteenth and early nineteenth centuries reflect the aesthetic norms of the age. An account of some representative plays produced in this period will further illustrate how the Fletcherian form persists, following established norms and at the same time adapting itself to important theatrical changes. During this time the two essential qualities of Romantic drama emerge: the triumph of pictorialism, and the development of spiritual sickness in the dramatic hero.

[32] [Edward Taylor], *Cursory Remarks on Tragedy* (1774), p. 47.

[33] See Philip Edwards' discussion of this phrase in "The Danger not the Death: The Art of John Fletcher," *Jacobean Theatre*, Stratford-Upon-Avon Studies, I (London, 1960), 159-177.

CHAPTER IV

Romantic Heroism and Its Milieu

> The spirit, the soul, the every thought and sensation of the first character in this piece, De Monfort, is clearly discerned by the reader, and he can account for all the events to which they progressively lead: but the most attentive auditor, whilst he plainly beholds effects, asks after causes; and not perceiving those diminutive seeds of hatred, here described, till, swollen, they extend to murder, he conceives the hero of the tragedy to be more a pitiable maniac, than a man acting under the dominion of natural propensity.
>
> —Elizabeth Inchbald, "Remarks" on *De Monfort*

i. The Fletcherian Pattern in Late Eighteenth-Century Drama

ALTHOUGH little known, and deservedly so, William Hodson's *Zoraida: A Tragedy* (Drury Lane, 1779-80) was produced late enough to reflect in an important way the development of pictorialism in late eighteenth-century drama and yet early enough so that the new lighting effects possible by 1785 were not present to draw from Hodson too complex a response. Those who believe that heroic drama died a century before Hodson may find confirmation in a reading of his play. Bearing many characteristics of the earlier form, *Zoraida* seems in fact to have been written after a fresh review of *The Conquest of Granada.*[1] In both plays the exterior situation is a struggle between two countries whose principal differentiation is religious, and both present an idealized heroine and incessant talk of love and honor. These facts by themselves set Hodson's work in the tradition of eighteenth-century high tragedy which, following Dryden, made a fetish of oriental or otherwise exotic subject matter. But *Zoraida*'s repetition of certain names suggests an open derivativeness that in turn shows how far Hodson departed from his text. Zulema, the old Zegry in Dryden's play, undergoes a change of sex

[1] References are to *Zoraida: A Tragedy . . . To which is added a Postscript, containing Observations on Tragedy* (1780).

and becomes Zoraida's waiting woman. Ozmyn becomes Osman and is robbed of his own love interest in Benzayda to emerge as a stock Gothic figure, the loyal assistant forced to masquerade as a tool of the chief villain and doubling conveniently as an expository character. Almanzor becomes Almaimon, and with emasculation of name loses his power as a warrior. A monomaniacal lover who risks all, even death, for the life and reputation of his mistress, Almaimon is nevertheless consistently bettered by the villain, Selim, through capture—or by the playwright himself through the imposition of adverse fate. Hodson has adapted the heroic play to now-familiar Gothic conventions, one of which requires that the heroine be allotted sufficient time to agonize over the worsening situation before the long-absent hero delivers her some seconds before the curtain descends. When Zoraida's deliverance comes, it is in the form of the venerable revelation of obscure birth, but with a twist: it is the heroine's obscure birth, not the hero's, that comes to light. Almaimon's pedigree is clear enough; he emerges the quintessential man of feeling, the pathos of whose situation derives in part from his total ineptness on stage despite his reported prowess when out of sight. He, and Zoraida too, would have been lost through his luckless attempt at her rescue in Act V, were it not for the guilt feelings of Zirvad, the dervise, who announces the secret of Zoraida's relationship with Selim just in time to avert Almaimon's death and an incestuous marriage between Selim and his now-discovered sister.

If such materials do not seem conducive to significant drama, Hodson's development of character and plot nonetheless bears a filial resemblance to the Fletcherian pattern of intrigue followed by a revelation that clarifies blood relationships (or dissipates their threat of incest, as in *A King and No King*) and so neatly dodges impending disaster. For the student of dramatic convention, Hodson's play exemplifies both the persistence of several closely related traditions and the unhappy fact that a playwright may create a perfectly lifeless work by employing them, not as a staff, but as a crutch.

In a wider perspective of ideas and cultural trends, *Zoraida* affords additional interest. Following a penchant for theorizing observable in many writers of his age, Hodson appended to the first edition a short treatise entitled "Observations on Tragedy." The pictorialism evident in his play is given a theoretical framework in his discussion of the function of action. To an educated eighteenth-century man, the word *action* in this context would immediately suggest Aristotle, a figure whose eminence continued to cast long shadows in this day.[2] But an examination of Hodson's theory reveals only that he sensed the direction in which the drama, quite independent of Aristotelian unity, was moving. "Both on the antient and modern theatre," Hodson observes, "the action, as being in nature the primary object, must be the prominent feature of Tragedy, where it answers to the principal figure in a picture, while Character, and Manners, may be aptly compared to the attendant groups. If these are heterogeneous to the main design, or if just and pertinent, are brought too forward, and set in too strong a light, by eclipsing the principal figure, they at least diminish, if they do not destroy, the effect of the whole" (p. 83). Hodson of course echoes Aristotle's idea that character must be subordinate to action, which itself must have a beginning, middle, and end. But if the reader is surprised to find an emphasis on action, in this period, at the expense of an emphasis on character, he may reassure himself by reflecting on Hodson's metaphor. "The main design," in Hodson's words, is another phrase for the maze-like intrigue of his play. Its twists and turns are the primary object, not the development of character. But Hodson's sense that this object corresponds to the grouping of human elements in a historical painting undermines the force of his argument. Although the development of an intrigue is by nature linear, or temporal, rather than spatial, Hodson uses a spatial metaphor to suggest that the play as a whole must be considered *pictorially*. No hint of logic appears in the sequence of events as Hodson conceives of them. Instead, the events considered together correspond to the central human figure in a painting, whose relationship to surrounding objects and groups is determined by the focus that a carefully laid out perspective effects.

This conflation of character and action, evident throughout the play itself, combines with great pictorial qualities in the climactic

[2] See Clarence C. Green, *The Neo-Classic Theory of Tragedy in England During the Eighteenth Century* (Cambridge, Mass., 1934); René Wellek, *A History of Modern Criticism: 1750-1950*, Vol. I: *The Later Eighteenth Century* (New Haven, 1955); John W. Draper, "Aristotelian 'Mimesis' in Eighteenth Century England," *PMLA*, XXXVI (1921), 372-400; and Earl R. Wasserman, "The Pleasures of Tragedy," *ELH*, XIV (1947), 283-307.

scene where Zoraida, in despair, attempts suicide. This, the last scene of Act V, presents a grand procession gathered in honor of the forced marriage of Zoraida to the villain Selim. An epithalamium is sung and the ceremony is about to proceed when Zoraida produces a dagger and raises it over her breast in sight of the assembled guests. Surely no dramatic reason exists for Zoraida's attempted self-destruction here, for she could with much greater ease and possibility of success have dispatched herself in the privacy of her tent. Obviously, the scene is at once an opportunity for spectacular visual effects and a chance for the playwright to avert catastrophe by having his hero Almaimon burst from concealment and stay her "frantic hand." At this point, as Zoraida and Almaimon stand unmoving, paralyzed by the surprise and emotional intensity of the sudden revelation that he is still alive, the old dervise Zirvad appears and announces the second revelation, of Zoraida's true identity as the sister of Selim.

This revelation of a blood tie between heroine and villain serves, as Bertrand Evans has shown, to further his developing redemption, a process that takes place with remarkable swiftness in plays produced at the beginning of the nineteenth century.[3] But in the two decades that separate Hodson's "heroic tragedy" from that time, the more immediately important phenomenon is the development of the perverse or at least unorthodox unity that underlies the combination of striking visual effects with moments of equally stirring psychological stress or astonishment.

As Shakespeare well knew, a shipwreck offers an excellent chance to bring distress to a crisis and at the same time provides dramatic momentum for reuniting long-lost persons. Yet Richard Cumberland's *The Carmelite* (Drury Lane, 1784-85) depends much less on the thematic intricacy of a comedy like *Twelfth Night* than on relatively simple formulaic qualities commonly found in Fletcherian drama. Patterned repetition, an important aspect of Shirley's *The Traitor,* is the central device of Fletcher's *The Knight of Malta,* whose structure derives from the requirement for becoming a knight in that revered company: a period of testing during which the postulant proves himself

[3] *Gothic Drama from Walpole to Shelley* (Berkeley and Los Angeles, 1947), pp. 86-89. Evans' is the only existing study that comes to grips with the complex nature of dramatic convention in the serious plays of this age. It will be evident from the ensuing discussion that I have drawn extensively on his findings.

worthy of admittance. By the time the crisis occurs in Act IV, at least seven instances of testing have occurred, almost all based on departures from, or even perversions of, the ideal of true knighthood. Fletcher's *The Loyal Subject* provides an even better precedent. In this play one character, the old general Archas, undergoes a whole series of trials himself. On the idea of the attempted degradation of a true hero, Fletcher builds a tragicomedy composed of over a half-dozen critical scenes each of which tests Archas' honor by submitting him to rejection and scorn for his principles. Steadfast to the end, he becomes "honour's martyr"[4] and at the last moment reaps the rewards of patience and fortitude. Cumberland follows a formulaic pattern much like this, but his subject is double, not single. His device is to set forth a series of revelations of identity which culminate in the reunion of husband, wife, and son; but before this happy event takes place the playwright subjects two persons to a series of inordinate trials based on the suppression of truth. *The Carmelite* thus combines the technique of formulaic repetition with the equally familiar accumulation of pathetic and shocking scenes.[5]

It becomes evident early in the first act that the monk who, along with his companion Hildebrand, has been rescued from the sea is really the husband of Matilda, the unhappy mistress of the nearby castle. The monk plans to make clear his identity, but the situation holds an impediment. It appears that Hildebrand believes he murdered the noble crusader Saint Valori, husband of Matilda. Saint Valori, disguised as the monk, plans to take Hildebrand before the king's court and vengefully expose him but is distracted by his belief that the young Montgomeri is his wife's lover. This impediment, involving the "fatal" mistakes of both Saint Valori and Hildebrand, is basis enough for Cumberland to spin out a cleverly managed intrigue, punctuated by revelations, through four and three-quarters acts. What has kept Matilda alive for the twenty years since Saint Valori departed for the Crusades has been the secret knowledge that Montgomeri is her son and the hope that her husband will some day return. What has kept Hildebrand alive for the same period is the extreme activity of his conscience; he cannot die without forgiveness. Upon

[4] *Works of Beaumont and Fletcher*, Variorum edn. (London, 1908), III, 332.

[5] References are to *The Carmelite: A Tragedy* (1784).

this duplex cornerstone Cumberland constructs his edifice of impassioned scenes leading to the well-paced crisis in Act IV, where first Hildebrand reveals to Matilda his identity as the supposed slayer of Saint Valori, and then Saint Valori reveals himself to Hildebrand. Meanwhile, the continuity of the play depends on the passivity of Hildebrand and Matilda. Possessed by a deadly malady of spirit, from the beginning he appears a doomed man—self-doomed, in fact, by an act of violence for which his conscience in retribution is gnawing away at his soul. Matilda performs the same passive dramatic function with her grieving. At several times we see the lady in her habitual attitude, on her knees before the altar in the private chapel, lamenting a husband's loss. [see Plate 10] These two emblematic figures of guilt and grief establish an impression of stasis, against which, as in the Fletcherian pattern, works the impending force of fate, invoked through the mounting revelations that eventuate in Act IV with the death of Hildebrand after Saint Valori has shown himself to the stricken man and showered him with forgiveness. Act V carries out the last set of double clarifications in Saint Valori's revelation of his identity to Matilda and the mutual discovery of Saint Valori and Montgomeri that they are father and son.

Although the plot of Cumberland's tragicomedy is easy to follow in reading, no special dramatic exigency dictates the appearance and order of scenes. Matilda's revelation of her maternity to Montgomeri, for example, has been postponed twenty years only so that it may contribute to the theatrical effectiveness of Act II. The same holds to a great extent of Saint Valori's revelation of himself to Hildebrand in Act IV. While the knight's postponement for the sake of vengeance remains plausible, the plain fact is that an earlier discovery would have spoiled the play, since, as in *Philaster,* the fabric hangs on the point of suppressed identity. Meanwhile the play maintains theatrical effectiveness partly because, in keeping his identity secret, Saint Valori exacts from Hildebrand the most exquisite atonement a human being may make. Cumberland deftly avoids any suggestion of cruelty on Saint Valori's part, but to the disinterested reader (undoubtedly not to the theater audience) cruelty abounds. Cumberland skillfully alternates scenes in which Hildebrand writhes under the "agenbite of inwit" (as it was anciently called) and scenes in which Matilda is made to suffer excessively for her supposed fall from virtue.

Saint Valori's use of the monkish disguise in accomplishing his ends suggests that, if any play of Shakespeare's exerts some influence on Gothic drama, it is *Measure for Measure.* Though the pattern of the Gothic genre remains essentially Fletcherian, Shakespeare's dark comedy contains many elements later exploited by dramatists of Cumberland's day. The ineffectual Gothic hero, often in prison or otherwise in bonds through much of the action, bears a resemblance to Shakespeare's unfortunate Claudio. Its heroine is as devoted to virtue and under as much of an attack on her chastity as Isabella, although the Gothic heroine often proves more resourceful in keeping her antagonist at bay. The friar, whose saffron garb sometimes cloaks a truer identity, may manipulate the action as assiduously as Shakespeare's Duke and Cumberland's Saint Valori.[6] In addition these plays hold in common an atmosphere of impending doom deliberately heightened by the playwright to achieve maximum suspense and intensity, as in the frequent appearance of prison scenes with their aura of gloomy dankness. Finally, the Gothic happy ending brought out of the blue bears at least a distant kinship to Shakespeare's scheme of multiple marriages, with the major difference, however, that Shakespeare's analogous tests of individual characters carry out a thematic concern, while the Gothic playwright's series of unpredictable and theatrically effective crises conventionally leads to a fortunate resolution bestowed as a free gift.[7]

In still another way the Gothic dramatist subordinates whatever Shakespearean influence may exist in order to exploit an important technique of Fletcherian dramaturgy. Full of Shakespearean echoes, Cumberland's language nevertheless presents arresting graphic images of human distress. Cumberland (at least in the period represented by this play) exercises more restraint than other writers, who seldom fail to include a procession, a conflagration, or some such spectacular effect. Yet he presents emblems of human misery whose qualities reflect the Fletcherian monument of sorrow. In Act I Matilda grants refuge to the two victims of shipwreck with these words:

[6] An unusually lucid later example of the manipulating friar is the character of Coelestino in M. G. Lewis's *Venoni, or, The Novice of St. Mark's* (Drury Lane, 1808-09).

[7] See Evans, *Gothic Drama*, pp. 78 and *passim.*

Oh, approach and enter.
If you can weep, we will converse whole days,
And speak no other language; we will sit,
Like fountain statues, face to face oppos'd,
And each to other tell our griefs in tears,
Yet neither utter word. (p. 12)

Even where Cumberland's debt to Shakespeare is most explicit, it emerges in forms associated with that playwright's evocative language, not with his structural or characterizing techniques. In an important instance, in Act III, Hildebrand recounts a fearful dream to his father-confessor, the disguised Saint Valori. Obviously modeled on Clarence's nightmare in Act I of Shakespeare's *Richard III* (a sequence Colley Cibber excised from his swiftly paced redaction of that play[8]), the speech demonstrates how Cumberland follows the tendency in his age to combine the description of a fantastic, terrifying environment with a delineation of the inner sufferings of character:

Methought but now by shipwreck I was plung'd
Into the foaming ocean; on the shore
Your figure stood with beck'ning hand outstretch'd
To snatch me from the waves; chear'd with the sight,
Thro' the white surf I struggled; with strong arm
You rais'd me from the gulph; joyful I ran
T'embrace my kind preserver—when at once
Off fell your habit, bright in arms you stood,
And with a voice of thunder cried aloud,
"Villain, avaunt! I am Saint Valori!"—
Then push'd me from the cliff: down, down I fell,
Fathoms on fathoms deep, and sunk for ever! (p. 31)

The imagery, as in Clarence's nightmare, is of drowning, and, like Clarence's, Hildebrand's dream holds a prediction of truth. But Cumberland's enhancement of the fall by calling up a cliff from the vasty deep elicits from his audience the sublime emotion that images of deathly falls from precipices invariably drew forth. Such emotion may be labeled Aristotelian "terror" but is in

[8] See the discussion of Cibber's *Richard III* in Pt. III, Chap. IX below, pp. 224-229.

fact a sympathetic reaction to the highly subjective fears of the character himself.

A decade and a half after *The Carmelite,* there appeared on the enlarged stage of the Drury Lane (rebuilt in 1794) a play that fully synthesizes Cumberland's exploitation of mental distress with the pictorial atmospherics evident since *Douglas.* But the synthetic qualities of Joanna Baillie's *De Monfort,* important though they are, are secondary to its innovations. The issues raised by this uncommonly ambitious tragedy reflect at once the imminently crucial dilemma of the patent houses[9] and the complex problems of dramaturgy implicit in the rise of the Romantic hero. "The scenery was magnificent," observed the theatrical composer Michael Kelly of the production at Drury Lane in April of 1800, and "the cathedral scene, painted by Capon, was a *chef d'oeuvre. . . .*"[10] Despite such magnificence, Kelly recalled, the play "would not suit the public taste" and was withdrawn, a demonstrable failure, after eight poorly attended performances.[11] It is possible to speculate why, and in doing so to explore some of the characteristics that even then were "stigmatizing" the legitimate drama, from which, as if to spite itself, the closet drama was splitting off and beginning its own anemic growth. Without taking a vindictive attitude toward playwrights who write from theory instead of from first-hand experience, one may see in *De Monfort* the inordinate influence of psychology on a playwright concerned perhaps as much as any other living writer with the forces that drive men to act.

Man has a natural desire to see his fellow human beings tested for "the fortitude of the soul," Joanna Baillie asserted in her lengthy "Introductory Discourse" in the first volume of her *Plays on the Passions,* as they are familiarly called.[12] The idea is based on a predilection that informs all of her writing. It is not so much

[9] See the discussion beginning Sec. ii, and note 15, below.

[10] *Reminiscences of Michael Kelly,* 2 vols. (1826), II, 177.

[11] Of the last few performances Thomas Dutton wryly observed, "The crowded houses, and unbounded applause, with which *De Montfort* [sic] continues to be received, are unhappily confined to the *Play-bills*"—*The Dramatic Censor; or, Weekly Theatrical Report,* II (1800), 134.

[12] *A Series of Plays: In Which it is Attempted to Delineate the Stronger Passions of the Mind. Each Passion Being the Subject of A Tragedy And A Comedy,* p. 7. Published in London in 1798, it was augmented by a second and yet a third series over succeeding years; for full citations see Allardyce Nicoll's handlist in his *History,* 2nd edn., IV (Cambridge, Eng., 1960), 257-258.

with culmination that Joanna Baillie is concerned, but with process. The trouble with the common tragic hero of the day, she claims, is that he is introduced at the very apex of his fury; similarly, the fault of contemporary theatrical production is that it concentrates too much on events (pp. 38-39). In effect, she points out, these qualities are gross distortions of the true purpose of tragedy, which is "to unveil to us the human mind under the dominion of those strong and fixed passions, which, seemingly unprovoked by outward circumstances, will from small beginnings brood within the breast, till all the better dispositions, all the fair gifts of nature are borne down before them . . ." (pp. 30-31).

From dissatisfaction with the superficial display of current drama, both serious and comic, grew Joanna Baillie's plan for reform. In a series of plays she would "delineate the progress of the higher passions in the human breast," each passion forming the subject of a tragedy and a companion comedy (pp. 41, 56). Certainly few more ambitious projects had fired the lofty minds of her age. The "scientific" comprehensiveness of the idea rivals Sir Joshua Reynolds' design to set forth the history of western art in a series of carefully inclusive lectures. Yet, while it vividly reflects contemporary intellectual and cultural tendencies, just as Reynolds' *Discourses* do, the fruits of her plan bear only minimally on the practice of playwrights who succeeded in mounting their products on early nineteenth-century stages. Minimally, that is, except in one major area where the resemblance is crucial: in the concept of dramatic character.

The relationship of her concept to that evident on the boards of London theaters and in contemporary criticism appears both in *De Monfort* itself and in the brief description of the tragedy included in the "Introductory Discourse." Expectedly, she defines the passion that forms the subject of the play. Hate, she affirms, is "that rooted and settled aversion, which from opposition of character, aided by circumstances of little importance, grows at last into such antipathy and personal disgust as makes him who entertains it, feel, in the presence of him who is the object of it, a degree of torment and restlessness which is insufferable" (p. 64). The play will be devoted to depicting this insupportable agony, and the character who manifests the passion in all its subtlety will be one with whom we wholly sympathize. Hate itself is vicious, without question. But, under Joanna Baillie's direction, "it is the passion and not the man which is held up to our execration" (p. 65). This statement of a fundamental divorce of character from the emotion that consumes him places her theory and the play which endeavors to support it in the mainstream of developing notions apparent in the drama, acting, and criticism of this new age. The date of the production of *De Monfort* at Drury Lane just at the turn of the century conveniently sets it at a point of transition from influential eighteenth-century tradition to the innovations that swiftly followed.

The first three acts, comprising some eight scenes dominated almost completely by the chief character, establish the inveterate hatred for Rezenfelt which De Monfort has for many years harbored in his heart. Not until the second scene of Act III do we discover, from Rezenfelt himself, that from their youth De Monfort had allowed this fixed hatred for him to feed almost unaccountably on boyish rivalries. Rezenfelt's unsympathetic description of De Monfort's proud youthful vying for "pre-eminence" (p. 362) can do little at this late point to displace the sympathy for him already established over the space of two and one half acts. This "retrospective" structure (p. 64) allows room both for the attention the playwright gives to the present circumstances of her troubled hero and for her unorthodox way of relating him to other characters. From his first entrance in Act I, De Monfort appears possessed by a melancholy which, try though he may, he cannot shake. Having returned to the house of his former landlord, he must greet the local gentry and so confronts his dread enemy, now a wealthy landowner and suitor for the hand of his sister Jane. In the first two acts the dramatist openly departs from several well-established Gothic patterns. The mutual discovery and reunion of brother and sister take place, not in Act V, but in Act II. More important, the conventional evil genius who predictably torments hero and heroine for almost the whole play has here been transformed into the discreetly polite and friendly Rezenfelt. De Monfort considers him a consummate hypocrite, but Rezenfelt's behavior contradicts this judgment. The most he can be accused of is an understandable impatience with De Monfort's monomania.

The meaning of these dramaturgical innovations, slight as they may seem, is of great importance for understanding the concept of dramatic character developed in this tragedy. Heavily indebted to notions of man's essential goodness, late eighteenth-century drama and criticism had contrived to remove the source of evil from man himself and place it outside him in the form of gratuitous chance, usually labeled *fate* or *destiny*. Joanna Baillie has gone one step further: she returns the source of evil to the breast of man; but in doing so she does not compromise the sentimental premise under whose weight her pen moves. The relegation of evil to this interior position creates a character who manifests a fundamental division between virtuous nature and vicious passion. The Fletcherian disjunction of character and event has been redefined as an ethical disjunction of human virtue from human acts. Gothic drama, beginning with Home's *Douglas*, placed special emphasis on an event that took place years before and continues to exert its effects thereafter. *De Monfort* internalizes this convention by redefining it as a psychological process in which an evil passion inexplicably takes root in the fallow soul of man and slowly chokes away his life force. Since the operation of fate has now been relegated to the human soul, the dramatist has no reason to base her play on a series of impassioned encounters with forces in the outside world, least of all anything so pettily obvious as the machinations of a villain or the fifth-act discovery of a sister. She has informed the reader in her introductory treatise that she eschews the sensationalism of performed drama. What she does not say is that she has single-handedly (and perhaps unwittingly as well) effected on the stage a transformation in the nature of dramatic character whose repetition in the closet drama of subsequent years appears unmistakably evident.[13] The reader's comparison of *De Monfort* with *Manfred* will go far toward illuminating the unexplained sickness of soul which drives Byron's melancholy hero to attempt suicide by hurling himself from a precipice in the Alps.

A reason may now be suggested for the failure of *De Monfort* on the stage. To call the play undramatic is to cloud the issue. Its failure more probably lies in the simple fact that it was too revolutionary in concept for an audience so accustomed to convention. Strictures may justly be applied to many dramas of this period for merely exploiting sensationalism. But the author who wrote such dramas to order was nevertheless able to catch up his audience in an intriguing series of predictably "unpredictable"

[13] See Pt. II, Chap. VII below.

events to which characters respond with passion and often with utter bewilderment. Reactions of this kind may bear only superficial fidelity to the psychological processes explored by Locke, Hume, and others; they nevertheless demonstrate a *theatrical* correlation of events and mental responses missing from *De Monfort* and from the closet drama that enshrines the tendencies it manifests. "Some sprite accurst within thy bosom mates To work thy ruin," Jane De Monfort laments to her brother early in the play (II.ii, p. 339). This force, and not that of exterior happenings, brings about his unspeakable death, by a kind of spiritual internal bleeding. The events especially of the fourth and fifth acts serve only as inconsistent and distorted reflections of what is essentially interior and formless.

To be sure, the play has a share of qualities eminently realizable on the Drury Lane stage. The wood in which De Monfort murders Rezenfelt in Act IV is genuine horrific Gothic, a perfect environment for a man wandering the trackless forest of his own mind where, De Monfort mutters to himself,

> As in the wild confusion of a dream,
> Things horrid, bloody, terrible, do pass,
> As tho' they pass'd not; nor impress the mind
> With the fix'd clearness of reality. (IV.i, p. 377)

Similarly, the pencil of William Capon, a master of atmospheric and antique scenery, contributed great effectiveness to the closing scenes, including the celebrated "cathedral" scene, laid in the halls and chambers of a convent isolated in the wood.[14] But no amount of scenery and lighting, even when complemented by the musical *savoir faire* of Kelly and the acting virtuosity of Kemble as De Monfort and Mrs. Siddons as the noble Jane, could apparently compensate for the lack of theatricality implicit in the fact that the essential conflict of the play is severed from objective reality and entombed within the mind and heart of its chief character.

In Romantic drama the Fletcherian structure of character and event has taken on fresh shape. Disjunctiveness is still present in affective scenes, but, as in De Monfort's speech in the dark wood,

[14] See Sybil Rosenfeld and Edward Croft-Murray, "A Checklist of Scene Painters Working in Great Britain and Ireland in the 18th Century," *TN*, XIX (1964), 13-15; and Rosenfeld, "Scene Designs of William Capon," *TN*, X (1956), 118-122 and plates.

6. Miss O'Neill as Belvidera

7. Henry Fuseli, "The Bard," an illustration accompanying Gray's poem

8. Thomas Greenwood the Elder, scene design, Gothic landscape

9. Thomas Greenwood the Elder, scene design, Gothic prison

10. Mrs. Siddons as Matilda in Cumberland's *The Carmelite*

11. "Carlo, the Roscius of Drury-Lane Theatre"

The LAST NIGHT but ONE of performing till the HOLIDAYS.
The FIRST NIGHT of the NEW PANTOMIME. 52.

THEATRE ROYAL, DRURY-LANE.

This present MONDAY, December 22nd, 1800.

Their Majesties Servants will act a Tragedy called The

STRANGER.

The Stranger, Mr. KEMBLE,
Count Wintersen, Mr. HOLLAND, Baron Steinfort, Mr. BARRYMORE,
Mr. Solomon, Mr. WEWITZER, Peter, Mr. SUETT,
Francis, Mr. PALMER, Tobias, Mr. DOWTON.
Mrs. Haller, Mrs. SIDDONS,
Countess Wintersen, Miss HEARD, Charlotte, Mrs. SCOTT.
The Vocal Parts by Miss STEPHENS, Miss B. MENAGE.
Principal Dancer, Signora BOSSI DEL CARO.
After the Play a new Pantomime, (never performed,) called

HARLEQUIN-AMULET;

or,

THE MAGICK OF MONA.

With New SCENERY, MACHINERY, DRESSES and DECORATIONS,
To conclude with

A MOVING PANORAMA.

The New Overture, Songs, and Chorusses, by Mr. SHAW,
with Selections from the late Mr. STORACE, and Mr. KELLY.
The Pantomime Tunes Selected from the Welch Bards by Mr. BYRNE.
Accompanied on the HARP by Mr. WIEPART.
Harlequin, Mr. BYRNE,
Pantaloon, Mr. GOODMAN The Bard, Mr. COOKE,
Morcar, (the Magician Mr. DE CAMP,
Pero, Mr. CHIPPENDALE, Scaramouch, Mr. MORTRAM,
Clown, Mr. GRIMALDI.
Columbine, Miss B. MENAGE,
Joan, Mr. BAYZAND.
With a variety of Pantomimick Characters by
Messrs. Fisher, Evans, Sparks, Rhodes, Webb, &c.
Masters Chatterley, W. Chatterley, Walter, Ellis, Wells, Johnson,
Tokeley, Weal, Smith, Beton, &c.
Mesds. Chippendale, Coates, Maddocks, Cuyler, Haskey, &c.
THE PRINCIPAL VOCAL PARTS BY
Mr. DIGNUM, Mr. TRUEMAN,
Mrs. MOUNTAIN, Miss STEPHENS, and Miss DE CAMP.
CHORUS OF WARRIORS.
Messrs. Cooke, Tett, Caulfield, Jun. Sawyer, Dibble, Aylmer, Gallot, Jones, Elliot & Rhodes, &c.
CHORUS OF BARDS,
Messrs. Cook, Bardoleau, Willoughby, Clark, Dabby, Danby, Jun. Maddocks, Evans, &c.
CHORUS OF GIPSIES AND PEASANTS
Mesds. Arne, Menage, Bristow, Coates, Wentworth, Maddocks, Jacobs, Williams, &c.
The DANCES composed by and under the Direction of Mr. BYRNE.
The SCENES designed by Mr. GREENWOOD,
and painted by him, Mr. BANKS, and Assistants.
The MACHINERY, DRESSES and DECORATIONS, designed by
Mr. JOHNSTON,
and executed by him, and under his Direction,
by Mr. UNDERWOOD, Mr. GAY, and Assistants.
The Female Dresses by Miss REIN.
BOOKS of the SONGS, &c. to be had in the Theatre.
Boxes 6s. Pit 3s. 6d. Gallery 2s. Upper Gallery 1s. NO MONEY TO BE RETURNED.
Nothing under FULL PRICE will be taken.
Printed by C. Lowndes, next the Stage-Door. *Vivant Rex et Regina.*

To-morrow, the Tragedy of MARY QUEEN OF SCOTS.
Being the Last Time of Performing till the Holidays.

Theatre Royal, Drury Lane. 61

This present SATURDAY, January 24, 1801,
Their Majesties Servants will act (5th time) a revived Tragedy in Five Acts called

KING LEAR.

King Lear, Mr. KEMBLE, Duke of Burgundy Mr. DIGNUM,
D. of Cornwall, Mr. RAYMOND, D. of Albany, Mr. HOLLAND,
E. of Kent, Mr. WROUGHTON, E. of Glocester, Mr. PACKER,
Edgar, Mr. BARRYMORE, Edmund, Mr. C. KEMBLE
1. Knight, Mr. Caulfield, 2. Knight, Mr. Rhodes, 3. Knight, Mr. Wells,
Physician, Mr. Maddocks, Captain of the Guard, Mr. Trueman,
Officer, Mr. COOKE, Oswald, Mr. PALMER,
Herald, Mr. Chippendale, Esquire, Mr. Fisher, Old Man, Mr. Waldron,
Edward, Mr. De Camp, Pages, Master Chatterley, Master Tokely,
Ruffians, Mr. Webb, Mr. Evans.
Goneril, Mrs. HUMPHRIES, Regan, Mrs. POWELL,
Cordelia, Mrs. SIDDONS,
Aranthe, Miss TIDSWELL.
After the Play, (TWENTY-FOURTH TIME,) a new Pantomime called

HARLEQUIN-AMULET;

OR, THE MAGICK OF MONA.

The New Overture, Songs, and Chorusses, by Mr. SHAW.
The Pantomime Tunes Selected from the Welch Bards by Mr. BYRNE.
Harlequin, Mr. BYRNE,
Pantaloon, Mr GOODMAN, The Bard, Mr. COOKE,
Morcar, (the Magician,) Mr. DE CAMP,
Pero, Mr. CHIPPENDALE, Scaramouch, Mr. MORTRAM,
Clown, Mr. GRIMALDI.
Columbine, Miss B. MENAGE,
Joan, Mr. BAYZAND.
THE PRINCIPAL VOCAL PARTS BY
Mr. DIGNUM, Mr. TRUEMAN,
Miss STEPHENS, and Miss ARNE.
The SCENES designed by Mr. GREENWOOD,
and painted by him, Mr. BANKS, and Assistants.
The MACHINERY, DRESSES and DECORATIONS, designed by
Mr. JOHNSTON, and executed by him, and under his Direction,
by Mr. UNDERWOOD, Mr. GAY, and Assistants.
The Female Dresses by Miss REIN.

The Doors to be opened at a Quarter past FIVE, and to begin at a Quarter past SIX.
Places for the Boxes to be taken of Mr. FOSBROOK, at the Box-Office, in Little Russell-Street.
Boxes 6s. Second Price 3s. Pit 3s. 6. Second Price 2s. Gallery 2s. Second Price 1s.
Upper Gallery 1s. Second Price 6d. NO MONEY TO BE RETURNED.
Printed by C. Lowndes, next the Stage-Door. *Vivant Rex et Regina.*

HARLEQUIN-AMULET; or, THE MAGICK OF MONA,
will be performed on Tuesday and Wednesday next week.
The Tragedy of PIZARRO
continuing to be received with the greatest approbation by brilliant and crowded
Audiences, will be repeated, (for the 13th time this Season, on Monday next,
With the Musical Entertainment called OF AGE TO-MORROW.
On Tuesday (2nd time.) the revived Comedy of The DOUBLE GALLANT.
On Wednesday, the Comedy of SHE STOOPS TO CONQUER.
On Thursday will be revived the Tragedy of
The DISTRESSED MOTHER.
After which (for the first time) a New Comick Opera, in two Acts, called
The VETERAN TAR.
The Overture and Musick, entirely new, composed by Dr. ARNOLD.

Theatre Royal, Drury Lane. 72

This present THURSDAY, January 29, 1801,
Their Majesties Servants will act a Tragedy called

JANE SHORE.

Duke of Glocester, Mr. RAYMOND,
The Lord Chancellor, Mr. MADDOCKS,
Lord Stanley, Mr. WEBB,
Lord Hastings, Mr. KEMBLE,
Sir Richard Ratcliffe, Mr. TRUEMAN,
Sir William Catesby, Mr. CAULFIELD,
Dumont, Mr. WROUGHTON,
Belmour, Mr. HOLLAND,
Servants, Mr. EVANS, Mr. FISHER.
Alicia, Mrs. POWELL,
Jane Shore, Mrs. SIDDONS.
After which, a New Comick Opera, in Two Acts, (never performed,) called

The VETERAN TAR.

The Overture and Musick, entirely new, composed by Dr. ARNOLD.
The Characters by
Mr. BANNISTER, Jun.
Mr. DE CAMP,
Mr. WEWITZER,
Mr. SUETT,
Mr. TRUEMAN,
Mr. CHIPPENDALE, Mr. WEBB,
Mrs. SPARKS,
Miss STEPHENS,
Mrs. MOUNTIAN.
CHORUS of SAILORS and VILLAGERS.
Messrs. Cooke, Danby, Danby, Jun. Evans, Fisher, Maddocks Rhodes, Cook,
Clarke, Dibble, Aylmer, Sylvester, Jones, Sawyer, Willoughby, Tett, Bardoleau,
Elliot, Caulfield, Jun. &c.
Mesds. Arne, Bristow, Coates, B. Menage, Wentworth, Menage, Kelly, Maddocks,
Saunders, Chippendale, Butler, Jacobs, Williames, &c. &c.
BOOKS of the SONGS, &c. to be had in the Theatre.

☞ On account of the Indisposition of Mr. BARRYMORE, the Tragedy of
The DISTRESSED MOTHER is deferred.

The Doors to be opened at a Quarter past FIVE, and to begin at a Quarter past SIX.
Places for the Boxes to be taken of Mr. FOSBROOK, at the Box-Office, in Little Russell-Street
Boxes 6s. Second Price 3s. Pit 3s. 6. Second Price 2s. Gallery 2s. Second Price 1s.
Upper Gallery 1s. Second Price 6d. NO MONEY TO BE RETURNED.
Printed by C. Lowndes, next the Stage-Door. *Vivant Rex et Regina.*

Those Ladies and Gentlemen who have been disappointed of Places for the Revived
Tragedy of KING LEAR, are respectfully informed, that it will be acted
(for the 6th Time) on Saturday next.

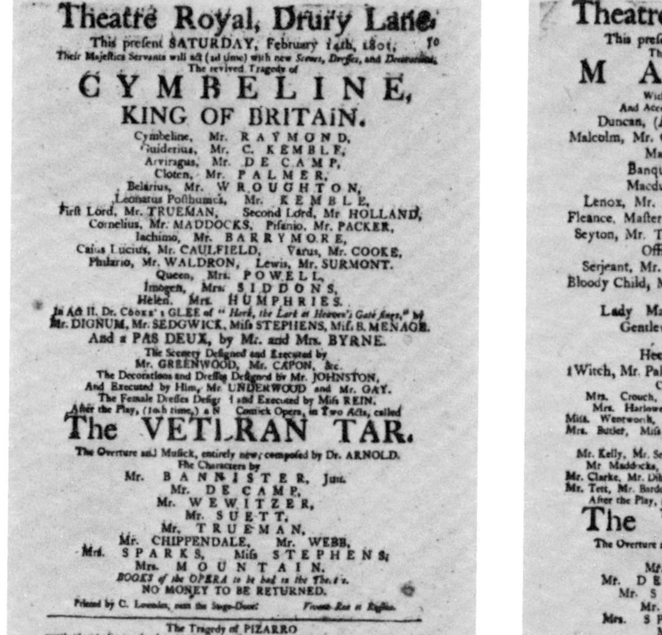

Theatre Royal, Drury Lane.
This present SATURDAY, February 14th, 1801,
Their Majesties Servants will act (1st time) with new Scenes, Dresses, and Decorations,
The revived Tragedy of
CYMBELINE,
KING OF BRITAIN.
Cymbeline, Mr. RAYMOND,
Guiderius, Mr. C. KEMBLE,
Arviragus, Mr. DE CAMP,
Cloten, Mr. PALMER,
Belarius, Mr. WROUGHTON,
Leonatus Posthumus, Mr. KEMBLE,
First Lord, Mr. TRUEMAN, Second Lord, Mr HOLLAND,
Cornelius, Mr. MADDOCKS, Pisanio, Mr. PACKER,
Iachimo, Mr. BARRYMORE,
Caius Lucius, Mr. CAULFIELD, Varus, Mr. COOKE,
Philario, Mr. WALDRON, Lewis, Mr. SURMONT.
Queen, Mrs. POWELL,
Imogen, Mrs. SIDDONS,
Helen, Mrs. HUMPHRIES.
In Act II. Dr. Cooke's GLEE of "Hark, the Lark at Heaven's Gate sings," by
Mr. DIGNUM, Mr. SEDGWICK, Miss STEPHENS, Miss B. MENAGE.
And a PAS DEUX, by Mr. and Mrs. BYRNE.
The Scenery Designed and Executed by
Mr. GREENWOOD, Mr. CAPON, &c.
The Decorations and Dresses Designed by Mr. JOHNSTON,
And Executed by Him, Mr. UNDERWOOD and Mr. GAY.
The Female Dresses Designed and Executed by Miss REIN.
After the Play, (10th time,) a New Comick Opera, in Two Acts, called
The VETERAN TAR.
The Overture and Musick, entirely new, composed by Dr. ARNOLD.
The Characters by
Mr. BANNISTER, Jun.
Mr. DE CAMP,
Mr. WEWITZER,
Mr. SUETT,
Mr. TRUEMAN,
Mr. CHIPPENDALE, Mr. WEBB,
Mrs. SPARKS, Miss STEPHENS,
Mrs. MOUNTAIN.
BOOKS of the OPERA to be had in the Theatre.
NO MONEY TO BE RETURNED.
Printed by C. Lowndes, next the Stage-Door. Vivant Rex et Regina.

The Tragedy of PIZARRO
continuing to be received with the greatest approbation by brilliant and crowded
Audiences, will be repeated, (for the 16th time this Season,) on Monday next.
The third and fourth nights of the revived Tragedy of
CYMBELINE,
will be on Tuesday and Thursday next.
The New Comick Opera of The VETERAN TAR will be repeated every
evening next week.
A New Historical Drama, called
DEAF AND DUMB;
or,
THE ORPHAN PROTECTED,
is in Rehearsal, and will be produced as soon as possible.
There is a New Edition of CYMBELINE, as it is acted by Their
Majesties Servants, (printed faithfully from the Prompter's Copy by C. Lowndes,
with permission of the Proprietors) to be had at the Theatre Royal, Drury Lane.

Theatre Royal, Drury Lane.
This present SATURDAY, February 21st, 1801,
Their Majesties Servants will revive Shakespeare's
MACBETH.
With the Original Musick of Matthew LOCKE,
And Accompaniments by Dr. ARNE, and Mr. LINLEY.
Duncan, (King of Scotland) Mr. PACKER,
Malcolm, Mr. C. KEMBLE, Donalbain, Mr. DE CAMP,
Macbeth, Mr. KEMBLE,
Banquo, Mr. WROUGHTON,
Macduff, Mr. BARRYMORE,
Lenox, Mr. SURMONT, Rosse, Mr. HOLLAND,
Fleance, Master CHATTERLEY, Siward, Mr. SPARKS,
Seyton, Mr. TRUEMAN, Physician, Mr. MADDOCKS,
Officers, Mr. EVANS, Mr. WEBB,
Serjeant, Mr. Caulfield, Armed Head, Mr. Chippendale,
Bloody Child, Miss Kelly, Crown'd Child, Master Tokeley,
Apparitions of Eight Kings.
Lady Macbeth, Mrs. SIDDONS,
Gentlewoman, Miss TIDSWELL,
Lords, Ladies, Attendants and Soldiers.
Hecate, Mr. SEDGWICK,
1 Witch, Mr. Palmer, 2 Witch, Mr. Wewitzer, 3 Witch, Mr. Suett,
CHORUS of WITCHES and SPIRITS.
Mrs. Crouch, Miss De Camp, Miss Stephens, Mrs. Mountain,
Mrs. Harlowe, Miss B. Menage, Miss Arne, Mrs. Coates,
Miss Wentworth, Mrs. Maddocks, Miss Menage, Mrs. Chippendale,
Mrs. Butler, Miss Williams, Miss Bristow, Miss Jacobs, Miss Kelly,
Miss Saunders, &c. &c.
Mr. Kelly, Mr. Sedgwick, Mr. Dignum, Mr. Cooke, Mr. Evans, Mr. Fisher,
Mr. Maddocks, Mr. Rhodes, Mr. Cook, Mr. Danby, Mr. Danby, Jun.
Mr. Clarke, Mr. Dibble, Mr. Aylmer, Mr. Sylvester, Mr. Jones, Mr. Willoughby,
Mr. Tett, Mr. Bardoleau, Mr. Elliot, Mr. Caulfield, Jun. Mr. Sawyer, &c &c.
After the Play, (14th time,) a New Comick Opera, in Two Acts, called
The VETERAN TAR.
The Overture and Musick, entirely new, composed by Dr. ARNOLD.
The Characters by
Mr. BANNISTER, Jun.
Mr. DE CAMP, Mr. WEWITZER,
Mr. SUETT, Mr. TRUEMAN,
Mr. CHIPPENDALE, Mr. WEBB,
Mrs. SPARKS, Miss STEPHENS,
Mrs. MOUNTAIN.
BOOKS of the OPERA to be had in the Theatre.
NO MONEY TO BE RETURNED.
Printed by C. Lowndes, next the Stage-Door. Vivant Rex et Regina.

The Tragedy of CYMBELINE cannot be repeated for some time, on account
of the Preparations for the production of the New Historical Drama.—But those
Ladies and Gentlemen who were on Thursday night disappointed of places, may
rely on having due notice of its next Representation.
The Tragedy of PIZARRO
continuing to be received with the greatest approbation by brilliant and crowded

Theatre Royal, Drury Lane.
This present MONDAY, April 6th, 1801,
Their Majesties Servants will act a Tragedy in Five acts called
PIZARRO.
The SCENERY, DRESSES, and DECORATIONS, entirely New.
The Musick, Airs, Choruses, and Marches, incidental to the Piece,
Composed by Mr. KELLY.
PERUVIANS.
Ataliba, Mr. POWELL
Rolla, Mr. KEMBLE,
Orozembo, Mr. DOWTON,
Topac, Master CHATTERLEY, Orano, Mr. TRUEMAN,
Hunalo, Mr. FISHER, Harin, Mr. EVANS, Capal, Mr. WEBB,
Huasca, Mr. SPARKS, Hualpa, Mr. CORY,
Cora, Miss BIGGS;
Fernando, Miss SMALLEY.
SPANIARDS.
Pizarro, Mr. BARRYMORE,
Alonzo, Mr. C. KEMBLE, Almagro, Mr. CAULFIELD,
Gonzalo, Mr. COOKE, Davila, Mr. DE CAMP,
Las Casas, Mr. PACKER,
Valverde, Mr. PALMER, Centinel, Mr. HOLLAND,
Pedro, Mr. MADDOCKS, Sancho, Mr. CHIPPENDALE,
Elvira, Mrs. POWELL,
The Vocal Parts by
Mr. SEDGWICK, Mr. DIGNUM,
Mrs. CROUCH, Miss DE CAMP,
Mrs. MOUNTAIN, Miss STEPHENS,
After the Play, (THIRTY SECOND TIME,) a new Pantomime, called
HARLEQUIN-AMULET;
OR, THE MAGICK OF MONA.
The New Overture Songs, and Chorusses, by Mr. SHAW,
The Pantomime Tunes Selected from the Welch Bards by Mr. BYRNE.
Harlequin, Mr. BYRNE,
Pantaloon, Mr. GOODMAN, The Bard, Mr. COOKE,
Morcar (the Magician,) Mr. DE CAMP, Pero, Mr. CHIPPENDALE,
Clown, Mr. BAYZAND,
Columbine, Miss B. MENAGE,
Joan, Mr. MORTRAM,
THE PRINCIPAL VOCAL PARTS BY
Mr. DIGNUM, Mr. TRUEMAN, Miss STEPHENS and Miss ARNE.
Places for the Boxes to be taken of Mr. FOSBROOK, at the Box Office, in Little R. Russell-street.
Boxes 6s. Second Price 3s. Pit 3s. 6d. Second Price 2s. Gallery 2s. Second Price 1s.
Upper Gallery 1s. Second Price 6d. NO MONEY TO BE RETURNED.
Printed by C. Lowndes, next the Stage-Door. Vivant Rex et Regina.

DEAF and DUMB, Or, The ORPHAN PROTECTED,
continuing to be received with the highest applause by brilliant and overflowing
Audiences, will be repeated for the Sixteenth Time, To-morrow.
With (for the last Time this Season) BLUE-BEARD; Or Female Curiosity.
On Wednesday, The Comedy of The COUNTRY GIRL.
with HARLEQUIN AMULET, or, The MAGICK of MONA.
On Thursday, (the 17th Night of) DEAF and DUMB.

12. Six playbills for the Drury Lane season 1800-01

13. Edmund Kean as Bertram in Maturin's tragedy

14. Kean as Bertram

15. Mrs. Jordan

16. William Barrymore

17. Robert Palmer

18. Charles Kemble as Hamlet

environment has become a function of the character's mind. Both character and landscape are now seen, together, as cut off from the normal course of human events and the normal surroundings in which they take place. Tragedy in this age possesses strong qualities of fantasy. The heavy reliance of writers since Shakespeare and Fletcher on romance materials as sources for their plays developed a notion of serious drama as imaginatively distinct from life. The affective structure of late seventeenth-century pathetic tragedy encouraged the audience's warm response to these materials despite (or perhaps because of) their separateness from real experience. What happens as the eighteenth century moves to its close is that the spectators now find themselves able to penetrate the mind of the character who undergoes experience in his isolated world, where "Simplicity of Passion" makes their emotional leap just that much easier. The tragic figure, based in earlier years on a decorous sense of Aristotelian separateness from the multitude, has now come to embody the deeply irrational fears and longings of an audience deeply committed to extreme emotional response. The reader of serious plays of the late eighteenth and early nineteenth centuries may well find himself stifled by the evident baldness of "Simplicity" in its various forms: in the rigid decorum of character, in the repetition of predictable situations, in the thermostatic white heat of language. He must not let these qualities blind him to the fact that they are now indicative of the disturbed, hypersensitive, and ever-responding mind of a universalized type of human nature whose idealized aspirations and failures mirror in graphic epitome those of his audience.

ii. Issues in the Early Nineteenth Century

Almost two centuries before Joanna Baillie wrote, the fundamental change in the theaters of Shakespeare's day took place, some of whose results have been examined in the course of discussion. The breaking up of a homogeneous popular theater into two groups, one for the masses of playgoers, the other for the aristocratic and well-to-do, produced in the private theaters a type of play whose influence, as we have seen, extends into the early nineteenth century. But ironically, even while this tradition continued to exert its strength, an analogous transformation was occurring. It is perhaps characteristic of the complexity of late eighteenth- and early nineteenth-century English culture that this fragmentation came not just in two but in three parts. The legitimate theaters of London, although beset with increasing financial difficulties, continued to present as main pieces Gothic drama, spectacular or "Gothicized" Shakespeare, and historical plays of pseudo-antiquity, all of which had become over the course of years the stock resources for serious theatrical performance. At the same time, certain authors who disdained the spectacular and the sensational, or who simply and totally disregarded performed drama and its theatrical demands, were writing works designed for the privacy and leisure of the closet. Finally a new kind of drama was breaking ground, suitable for audiences who either lacked interest in the "higher" products of the patent houses or could not afford their prices. Offered a variety of inexpensive entertainment, many Londoners turned either to the circus or to other theaters where plays could be seen whose characters and subjects more closely approximated people and situations in ordinary life. Melodramas like T. J. Dibdin's *The Murdered Guest* (Royal Coburg, 1818-19)—an adaptation of Lillo's *Fatal Curiosity* —and nautical plays beginning as early as J. C. Cross's *The Purse*: *or, Benevolent Tar* (Haymarket, 1794) were attractions to which Drury Lane and Covent Garden responded mainly by offering increasingly spectacular pantomimes or equestrian, canine [see Plate 11], or asinine extravaganzas, often billed with a *King John* or *King Lear* mounted with all the scenic resources at their command.[15]

[15] A series of playbills for the 1800-1801 season at Drury Lane illustrates the incipient theatrical situation. [see Plate 12] Shakespeare's plays form an important part of the repertory offerings, but they seem almost a sop to culture in comparison with what is evidently the real attraction: the spectacular afterpiece. Cordal Powell's *Harlequin-Amulet,* introduced on 22 December 1800, has played almost nightly through 24 January 1801, when *King Lear* appears; it is replaced on 29 January by S. J. Arnold's new nautical comic opera *The Veteran Tar.* (Notably, each new afterpiece is billed under an established favorite: Kotzebue's *The Stranger* or Rowe's *Jane Shore,* both enhanced by the acting of Sarah Siddons and John Kemble.) By 14 February, when the new production of *Cymbeline* makes its second appearance, *The Veteran Tar* becomes a veteran of ten performances. A week later, on 21 February, *Cymbeline* is withdrawn in order to devote all energies to "the New Historical Drama"; *The Veteran Tar* continues to add audiences for Shakespeare, this time *Macbeth.* The new play, Thomas Holcroft's *Deaf and Dumb*; *or, The Orphan Protected,* runs some twenty-four nights; but the novelty dwindles, and in early April Drury Lane resorts again to the tried-

The decline of the drama thus seemed universally in evidence. It is often suggested, not wholly in sport, that the descent from Parnassus began with the appearance of the most significant tragedy of the eighteenth-century English theater: the Stage Licensing Act of 1737. Undeniably, the literary qualities of serious drama declined in the eighteenth century and reached a notorious nadir in the early nineteenth. For this reason little scholarly attention has been paid in the past to a number of works that subsist on vital qualities unconnected with literary excellence. Recent studies of melodrama have begun to assess this vitality by placing these plays in their immediate contexts of theater and audience.[16] But scant interest has been shown in those vestigial works of early nineteenth-century "tragedy" whose liveliness, such as it is, is of another sort. The development of new dramatic forms in melodrama coincides with a desperate (and self-defeating) effort

---

and-true spectacular: Sheridan's *Pizarro* and *Harlequin-Amulet*—"THIRTY SECOND TIME."

The most accurate and illuminating account of the dilemma of the patent theaters at this time is provided in Gary James Scrimgeour's Ph.D. dissertation, "Drama and the Theatre in the Early Nineteenth Century" (Princeton, 1968), Chap. IV, "The Fall of the Majors." For a convenient outline sketch of the difficulties see Nicoll, *History*, IV, 223-224. In 1832 a Parliamentary committee appointed to inquire into the causes of the decline of the drama offered the following summary of several hundred pages of testimony:

> Your Committee find that a considerable decline, both in the Literature of the Stage, and the taste of the Public for Theatrical Performances, is generally conceded. Among the causes of this decline, in addition to those which have been alleged, and which are out of the province of the Legislature to control, such as the prevailing fashion of late dinner hours, the absence of Royal encouragement, and the supposed indisposition of some Religious Sects to countenance Theatrical Exhibitions, Your Committee are of opinion, that the uncertain administration of the Laws, the slender encouragement afforded to Literary Talent to devote its labours towards the Stage, and the want of a better legal regulation as regards the number and distribution of Theatres, are to be mainly considered.

Report from the Select Committee on Dramatic Literature: With the Minutes of Evidence. Ordered, by The House of Commons, to be Printed, 2 August 1832, p. 3.

[16] In addition to the Scrimgeour dissertation cited in note 15 above, see Eric Bentley's discussion of melodrama in *The Life of the Drama* (New York, 1964); Michael R. Booth, *English Melodrama* (London, 1965); Robert W. Corrigan, "Melodrama and the Popular Tradition in the Nineteenth-Century British Theatre," *Laurel British Drama: The Nineteenth Century* (New York, 1967); and Frank Rahill, *The World of Melodrama* (University Park, Pa., 1967).

on the part of legitimate theaters to rescue a dying tradition. It is with this conservative effort that the present investigation is concerned. The influence of melodrama is vividly apparent on the stages of the Drury Lane and Covent Garden theaters; nevertheless, the tragedies performed there exhibit certain traits identifiable only by viewing them in the long temporal perspective of the English repertory theater. Elsewhere in this book, studies of some of these plays appear: Sheridan's *Pizarro,* Coleridge's *Remorse,* Milman's *Fazio,* Sheil's *Evadne,* Shelley's *The Cenci.* An account here of plays contemporary to these by "Monk" Lewis and Charles Maturin will briefly illustrate and summarize the circumstances dominating performed tragedy in the first two decades of the nineteenth century.

Adelgitha; or, The Fruits of A Single Error burst forth on the Drury Lane stage early in 1807, only after three editions of the play had appeared the year before to titillate the sensibilities of the reading public.[17] The play is perfect evidence of "Monk" Lewis's accomplishments as a purveyor of Gothic high voltage. It is great fun to read even today. Nor was Lewis himself lacking in a sense of humor, as his postscript to the printed text confirms. Having just disposed of the unfortunate seduced maid and mother Adelgitha through her suicide at the end of the play, Lewis proceeds to inform the reader of his primary intention. It was, he confides,

> to illustrate a particular fact; viz. "the difficulty of avoiding the evil consequences of a first false step."—It appeared to

[17] References are to the first edition, *Adelgitha; or, The Fruits of a Single Error. A Tragedy* (1806). After some hesitation I have concluded that discussion here should focus on this play rather than on Lewis's much superior *Alfonso, King of Castile* (Covent Garden, 1801-02). In addition to the important presence in it of a culpable yet "innocent" heroine, *Adelgitha* is more representative of the type of super-spectacular drama most familiar in Lewis's earlier *The Castle Spectre* (Drury Lane, 1797-98). Although my discussion emphasizes the playwright's pragmatic response to the demands of a mass audience, I must in fairness refer the reader to *Alfonso,* a work of high competence and no inconsiderable power of language whose Fletcherian characteristics are notably similar to those of Fletcher's own *The Knight of Malta*; see especially Lewis's scene in the Gothic chapel (IV.ii), in which a sudden revelation elicits a swift, unprepared reaction and is in turn followed by a second revelation that builds ingeniously, almost like a structural reflex, on the first. For a discussion of *Alfonso* in relation to closet drama, see Pt. II, Chap. VII below, pp. 158-159.

> me, that the more venial the offence, and the more amiable the character of the offender, the more strongly would the above position be proved; and the very nature of my object made it necessary, that Adelgitha should be the constant victim of her single transgression in *this* life, and only receive the reward of her many virtues in the life to come.—But above all I must request, that no one will mistake Adelgitha for a *heroine*—I meant to represent in her—"A woman, with all her sex's weakness,"—whose natural inclinations were virtuous and benevolent; but who was totally unprovided with that firmness of mind, which might have enabled her to resist the force of imperious circumstances.—Accordingly she gives way to them one after another, and is led on gradually and involuntarily from crime to crime, till she finds herself involved in guilt beyond the possibility of escaping.

"Such was my plan," Lewis concludes, "though perhaps the defects of its execution may have prevented the reader from discovering it till now" (p. 127). Of course, no such defects are perceivable in the play, whose expert emotional structure reveals at every seam the burnished joints of a master craftsman. Around the central character described in his confessional note, Lewis builds a plot whose sensationalism and intricacy defy summary. Page after page of perfervid dialogue blazes the trail of errors that ensue from Adelgitha's fatal unmaidenly step. The play presents the Fletcherian situation and concept of character pressed to extremes almost beyond belief. With unflagging invention Lewis plunges his essentially innocent "non-heroine" and her inept, witless son (first of the many fruits of her single youthful error) into situations where the only consistency is the sure elicitation of terror and pathos. Villains, heroes, maidens upright and fallen, henchmen and servants alike respond unfalteringly and with rhetorical superlatives to the demands of a scene, then blithely reverse themselves a moment later without discoverable loss. In its exploitation of backstage ingenuity and its concern with the horrified responses of an innocent and unprepared human being to events that form an exit-less maze around her, *Adelgitha* reads like a parody of everything serious in the drama for fifty years past. Nor does the play lose an ounce of its effect if this possibility be granted. It is not so incredible that parody too was what Lewis had in mind when he explained, "Such was my plan."

A rereading of *De Monfort* after experiencing *Adelgitha* might well suggest that, despite her shortcomings, Joanna Baillie had gifts which might have revivified the English stage. Examining the dramas of an age when one sometimes finds himself thankful for small favors, one cannot help being impressed, to a degree, with the energy that Charles Maturin infused into the character whose name gives title to his tragedy *Bertram*.[18] Despite the wild implausibilities of the plot, as Coleridge observed in withering detail in *Biographia Literaria*,[19] Maturin presents in his central character a distillation of the half-explained sickness of soul and the complementary sense of melancholy grandeur that began to characterize the English villain-hero in Joanna Baillie's De Monfort. A clergyman by profession and perhaps more familiar as the author of the novel *Melmoth the Wanderer*, Maturin produced only three plays, of which *Bertram* was the first and by all odds the most popular. Brought to the Drury Lane stage in 1815-16 with Edmund Kean in the title role, the play, as an unidentified hand comments on the flyleaf of the British Museum copy, "was received with great favour and acted many times. . . ."[20] The seven editions published within the year attest to the reception of a work that, perhaps more than any other performed drama of its day, sums up the nature of the Romantic hero more familiar to general readers in the plays of Lord Byron.

Bertrand Evans has pointed out the essential lines of this figure's development in observing that, as time moved on, playwrights devoted increasing attention to presenting the activity of the villain's conscience in revolt against his criminal deeds. The predisposition of the age was such that, as the agonies of the villain became more obvious and more detailed, greater sympathy was elicited for him. So by degrees the villain turned a hero who,

[18] *Bertram; or, The Castle of St. Aldobrand; A Tragedy* (1816).

[19] Reference is to the edition by J. Shawcross, 2 vols. (Oxford, 1907), Chap. XXIII, cited below as *BL*. Coleridge's critique of *Bertram* originally appeared as five letters published in *The Courier*, 29 August and 7, 9, 10, and 11 September 1816.

[20] Genest records a first-season total of twenty-two performances—*Some Account of the English Stage*, 10 vols. (Bath, 1832), VIII, 532. For a competent account of Maturin as a playwright, see Willem Scholten, *Charles Robert Maturin: The Terror-Novelist* (Amsterdam, 1933), Chap. III.

through circumstances beyond his control, had become possessed by some evil force which drew him on to sin and despair, a force against which his conscience struggled valiantly but ineffectually.[21] The early nineteenth-century hero represents a further development of this phenomenon. Heavily dependent on the eighteenth-century tradition, it is a development difficult to define, but the character of Bertram offers a precise illustration.

The playwright draws a character stricken with a deep spiritual malaise, in whom despair is so firmly rooted that conscience seems to have been stifled altogether. Bertram indeed has a heart of adamant. It requires the influence of events spread out well into the last act to bring him to his knees; even then he is clearly a man more sinned against than sinning. Meanwhile, throughout previous scenes, the great energy and intensity of his vengeful purpose carry him along in a manner calculated to impress an audience with a sense of grandeur and high wonder. The loftiness of his aspiring mind maintains itself in the face of the vulgar accidents and petty situations that contrive to bring about his ruin. The less than fully explained motives behind Bertram's hatred for Saint Aldobrand, who has forced marriage on Bertram's beloved Imogine during his long absence, somehow associate with his great sensibility, his feeling soul, so that his desire for vengeance can neither be fully condemned nor condoned. The audience cannot plumb the depths of that soul, but they recognize all the outward signs of the fortitude, coupled with the deadly illness, which reigns there. Thus sympathy is heightened into wonder by the spiritual strength of this man, full of hate and vengeance as he is. The force that drives him is closely akin to the power George Frederick Cooke infused into his Richard III, acted in London at the beginning of the century just at the time when Joanna Baillie's innovationary *De Monfort* appeared. Although Maturin does not provide such a line for him, Bertram has full cause, like Richard, to exclaim, "I am—myself alone!"[22]

Conventional as Bertram is, Maturin somehow manages to endow him with an ostensible uniqueness whose complexity makes

[21] Evans, *Gothic Drama*, pp. 86-89.

[22] Cooke's Richard is discussed in Pt. III, Chap. X below, pp. 271-276. For illustrations suggestive of Bertram's paradoxical weakness and grandeur see Plates 13 and 14, where the character's ambiguous combination of passivity and idealized power is especially evident.

him a subject too difficult for simple moral judgment. Coleridge grasped Maturin's intention when, in his analysis, he set the play in its proper light. Clearly, as Coleridge observes, Bertram is the legitimate heir of the outlaw character that first appeared in Schiller's *Die Räuber* and speedily cut a wide swath through the English drama of the late 1790's and early 1800's, including Wordsworth's regrettable *The Borderers.* But behind these immediate circumstances lies a long tradition, Coleridge perceives, beginning with the Don Juan character in an old Spanish play, *Atheista Fulminato.* Briefly tracing its extensive popularity, Coleridge shows that the perennial appeal of this figure stems from the fact that it seizes upon a duality inherent in human nature. Coleridge puts himself in the place of a member of the audience to show in detail how this double response works itself out:

> There is no danger (thinks the spectator or reader) of *my* becoming such a monster of iniquity as *Don Juan*! *I* never shall be an atheist! *I* shall never disallow all distinction between right and wrong! *I* have not the least inclination to be so outrageous a drawcansir in my love affairs! But to possess such a power of captivating and enchanting the affections of the other sex!—to be capable of inspiring in a charming and even a virtuous woman, a love so deep, and so entirely personal to *me*!—that even my worst vices (if I *were* vicious), even my cruelty and perfidy (if I *were* cruel and perfidious), could not eradicate the passion! to be so loved for my *own self,* that even with a distinct knowledge of my character, she yet died to save me! this, sir, takes hold of two sides of our nature, the better and the worse. For the heroic disinterestedness, to which love can transport a woman, can not be contemplated without an honourable emotion of reverence towards womanhood: and, on the other hand, it is among the miseries, and abides in the dark ground-work of our nature, to crave an outward confirmation of that *something* within us, which is our *very self,* that something, not *made up* of our qualities and relations, but itself the supporter and substantial basis of all these. Love *me,* and not my qualities, may be a vicious and insane wish, but it is not a wish wholly without a meaning. (*BL,* II, 188)

Obviously, as Coleridge indicates, an analysis of the conventions of dramatic character is incomplete without assessment of their effect on an audience. Evidence of "restless and anatomizing casuistry"—Shelley's phrase in his Preface to *The Cenci*—lies in the dual response of readers and theatergoers explained by Coleridge and already seen implicit in the structure of Fletcherian drama. Looking back at the plays of Beaumont and Fletcher, George Darley observed that "the works of these poetic creators are like worlds produced by a sort of Manichean power, a double principle of Good and Evil, wherein the latter much predominates as to *quantum,* but the former is pre-eminent as to *qualitas,* and each counteracts the other without pause."[23] The ending of Maturin's tragedy epitomizes this felt complexity. The love of Bertram for Imogine has been thwarted, before the action of the play commences, by Bertram's luckless persecution at the hands of Saint Aldobrand, by his subsequent flight, and by Imogine's apparently forced marriage to Saint Aldobrand. In the climax of the play Bertram, coerced by circumstances into becoming a murderer driven by insane thoughts of revenge, melts only at the last moment when he sees the effects of his vengeance in the terrifying madness and death of his beloved. Bertram's own brief death speech sums up the essential conflict of the Romantic stage hero—only secondarily with external forces or with other men whose vile machinations seek his ruin:

> Bertram hath but one fatal foe on earth—
> And *he is here—(stabs himself.)* (p. 80)

Only a faint possibility remains of moral condemnation from an audience which, having progressed through five acts of terrible crises and bewildering turns of events experienced by a man and woman who are no match for them, now sees their lifeless forms stretched out upon the stage. Pity for Imogine, pity for Bertram. And wonder, also, that two human beings so ideal and at the same time so "unique" could be brought to death in so dreadfully undeserving a way.

A reader moving directly from *Philaster* or *The Maid's Tragedy* to *De Monfort* or *Bertram* might find it difficult to see in

[23] *The Works of Beaumont and Fletcher,* 2 vols. (1840), Intro., I, xxxvi-xxxvii.

these plays the ties that bind them. But the ties nevertheless are there, evident enough when serious Romantic plays are viewed in the perspective of the seventeenth-century drama and theater from which they ultimately derive. The process of this derivation may well be described as decadence. But there is as much innovation in the Romantic concept and presentation of dramatic character as there is slavish imitation of what has come before. No modern scholar can pretend to have discovered the influence of Fletcherian drama on the plays of the English Romantic age. I have simply attempted to add substance to the conviction of other readers that the plays of Beaumont and Fletcher have exerted considerable effect on subsequent English drama. If anyone can be credited with this discovery, it is surely Coleridge. Describing the inordinate influence of the German drama on the English around the end of the eighteenth century, Coleridge states his belief that the so-called "German" school is really native English in origin. Similarly, he disposes of the crediting of Shakespeare "for the most anti-Shakespearean drama" of this age. If we wish to search for models, Coleridge concludes, we need only look to those "two poets who wrote as one, near the age of Shakespeare, to whom, (as the worst characteristic of their writings) the Coryphaeus of the present drama may challenge the honor of being a poor relation, or impoverished descendant. For if we would charitably consent to forget the comic humor, the wit, the felicities of style, in other words, *all* the poetry, and nine-tenths of all the genius of Beaumont and Fletcher, that which would remain becomes a Kotzebue" (*BL*, II, 184).

The comment is a sobering one but nevertheless impossible to dismiss. Coleridge's devastating treatment of *Bertram* ranks as one of a host of reminders that the drama of the Romantic age sadly went begging for the qualities we admire in the plays of Shakespeare's and Fletcher's day. But this drama is still worth study, in company with the acting and criticism to which it gave rise, for the view it presents of dramatic character and its relationship to human nature. Not only does this notion go far toward illuminating the cultural qualities of the age of Keats and Hazlitt; it is in fact still very much with us, informing many of our cherished assumptions about the unique response of the individual human mind to those forces, within and without, which move it to perceive and to act.

PART II

Tradition and Innovation in Characters and Plays

CHAPTER V

The West Indian: Cumberland, Goldsmith, and the Uses of Comedy

> As to the Character of Sir *John Falstaff*, it is chiefly extracted from *Shakespear*, in his 1st Part of King *Henry* the *IVth*; But so far as *Sir John* in *Shakespear's* Description, sinks into a *Cheat* or a *Scoundrel*, upon any Occasion, he is different from that *Falstaff*, who is designed in the following *Essay*, and is entirely an amiable Character.
>
> —Corbyn Morris, *On Wit and Humour* (1744)

i. Cumberland and the Characters of English Life

PREVIOUS discussion has traced the growth, persistence, and mutation of Fletcherian dramatic character and form in the serious English drama written over a span of two centuries. In the three chapters that follow, length of historical perspective is reduced, with a consequent enlargement of scale; concentration on the individual work remains unchanged. The reader will observe that the plays examined cluster around three points: the early 1770's, the end of the century, and the period of about 1820. This is an intentional arrangement, but its purpose is not simply historical. The present essay seeks to illustrate the nature of the sentimental man by examining him in his clearest guise, as the hero of sentimental comedy. The chapter on Sheridan's *Pizarro* builds on this illustration by investigating the more complex (or, at any rate, involuted) characteristics of that figure in early Romantic tragedy. Finally, Shelley's *The Cenci* is set in the theatrical, philosophical, and imaginative traditions available to the Romantic poet, who at once explored them and attempted to reject them. Together, these discussions offer detailed evidence of a shift toward subjectivity in the drama of the late eighteenth and early nineteenth centuries and, along with this, evidence of a developing concept of innocence as the distinguishing characteristic of ideal human nature.

Among the papers Oliver Goldsmith left at his death in 1774 were some unfinished verses published that same year as *Retaliation: A Poem . . . Including Epitaphs on the most Distinguished Wits of this Metropolis.* Among the writers memorialized in Goldsmith's series of mock epitaphs was Richard Cumberland—civil servant, playwright, and self-appointed physician to the moral ills of English life. Suitably, the author of *Retaliation* directed his barbs at the penetrable target of Cumberland's almost messianic purpose:

> Here Cumberland lies having acted his parts,
> The Terence of England, the mender of hearts;
> A flattering painter, who made it his care
> To draw men as they ought to be, not as they are.
> His gallants are all faultless, his women divine,
> And comedy wonders at being so fine;
> Like a tragedy queen he has dizen'd her out,
> Or rather like tragedy giving a rout.
> His fools have their follies so lost in a croud
> Of virtues and feelings, that folly grows proud,
> And coxcombs alike in their failings alone,
> Adopting his portraits are pleas'd with their own.
> Say, where has our poet this malady caught,
> Or wherefore his characters thus without fault?
> Say was it that vainly directing his view,
> To find out mens virtues and finding them few,
> Quite sick of pursuing each troublesome elf,
> He grew lazy at last and drew from himself?[1]

Goldsmith's lines read like the perfect rejoinder to a vain, myopic, self-approving man. Yet Cumberland managed to take them as a perfectly sincere tribute to his genius and even went so far as to offer Goldsmith his "gratitude for the epitaph he bestowed on me. . . ."[2] In fact, Cumberland's response is exactly the behavior that characterizes the man of sentiment whose portrait he himself so often limned. In much the same way that Steele's Bevil Junior in *The Conscious Lovers* rearranges reality to conform with his idealized image of himself, Cumberland reinter-

[1] *Retaliation,* pp. 10-11.

[2] *Memoirs of Richard Cumberland,* 2 vols. (1807), I, 369. Subsequent references are cited by volume and page.

prets Goldsmith's retaliatory motive in order to make it redound to his own credit.[3] The argument supporting this reinterpretation is not difficult to infer. Although the general race of men are pathetic in their faults, their excesses may be idealized as amiable qualities which maintain the health of society by cementing the bonds of friendship among its members. Where the greatest crime is anti-social behavior, the greatest virtue is the subordination of self-interest to the good of the whole. When Cumberland thanked Goldsmith for his magnanimous tribute, it was (one must suspect) with the fullness of heart that only the truly benevolent man can bear toward the failings of his unlucky fellow.[4]

As much as any playwright of his day, Cumberland felt that the end of dramatic comedy was not only to entertain and instruct, but actually to reform the hearts of one's countrymen as only a privileged man of unusual perspective and lofty purpose could hope to do. This, it would seem, was a particularly appropriate goal, for the function of the comic dramatist since Roman times had been to show how disruptive forces in society may be redirected for the benefit of all its members. Few writers of his age were as conscious as Cumberland of the dramatic tradition to which they were heirs; certainly none was more energetic in exploring ways to adapt it to present needs. Sheridan's mockery of

[3] For this analysis of Steele and for other ideas about sentimentality in this chapter, I am particularly indebted to the following works: Ronald S. Crane, "Suggestions Towards a Genealogy of the 'Man of Feeling,'" *ELH*, I (1934), 205-230; Ernest Tuveson, "The Importance of Shaftesbury," *ELH*, XX (1953), 267-299; Arthur Sherbo, *English Sentimental Drama* (East Lansing, Mich., 1957); Tuveson, *The Imagination as a Means of Grace: Locke and the Aesthetics of Romanticism* (Berkeley and Los Angeles, 1960); and Paul E. Parnell, "The Sentimental Mask," *PMLA*, LXXVIII (1963), 529-535. Sherbo's bibliography (*Sentimental Drama*, pp. 173-175) brings together many useful works on the subject.

[4] Cumberland's patronizing attitude toward Goldsmith is evident in the anecdote he relates of their first meeting: "It was now, whilst his labours [on *She Stoops to Conquer*] were in projection, that I first met him at the British Coffee-house. . . . When I perceived an embarrassment in his manner towards me, which I could readily account for, I lost no time to put him at his ease, and I flatter myself I was successful. As my heart was ever warm towards my contemporaries, I did not counterfeit, but really felt a cordial interest in his behalf, and I had soon the pleasure to perceive that he credited me for my sincerity—'You and I,' said he, 'have very different motives for resorting to the stage. I write for money, and care little about fame—' I was touched by this melancholy confession, and from that moment busied myself assiduously amongst all my connexions in his cause"—I, 365-366.

him as Sir Fretful Plagiary in *The Critic*[5] was the unhappy but probably inevitable result of the reputation Cumberland had earned—not only as a mender of hearts but as a mender of plays. On the appearance of his *The Choleric Man* in 1774-75 critics attacked him for having plundered wholesale from Shadwell's *The Squire of Alsatia* as well as for having presumed to adapt Terence's *Adelphoi,* as Cumberland himself had acknowledged.[6] They might as well have attacked him on much the same grounds for such earlier plays as *The West Indian* (Drury Lane, 1770-71) and *The Fashionable Lover* (Drury Lane, 1771-72), since these too depended heavily on a traditional structure whose roots extend far back beyond Fletcher and Shakespeare to the comedies of Plautus and Terence and to the Greek playwrights of the New Comedy from which they drew. Cumberland's debt is more obvious in *The Choleric Man*; nevertheless, this play as well as its predecessors is innovative in a way much like Shakespeare's *Comedy of Errors,* obviously a variation on a theme by Plautus.

Cumberland sketched out his innovations in a general way in his *Memoirs.* It is after all no wonder that he was pleased by Goldsmith's supposed tribute, since Goldsmith had summarized in it what Cumberland himself felt to be his unique and wholly laudable purpose:

> As the writer for the stage is a writer to the passions, I hold it matter of conscience and duty in the dramatic poet to reserve his brightest colouring for the best characters, to give no false attractions to vice and immorality, but to endeavour, as far as is consistent with that contrast, which is the very essence of his art, to turn the fairer side of human nature to the

[5] See Stanley T. Williams, *Richard Cumberland: His Life and Dramatic Works* (New Haven, 1917), pp. 145-147.

[6] Cumberland published *The Choleric Man* early in 1775 with a dedication "To Detraction," an ill-tempered rejoinder to his critics in which he attempted to illuminate their dark minds on the nature of literary and dramatic tradition. Unfortunately, in this instance his learning as a scholar is much superior to his skill as a playwright; the faults of *The Choleric Man* are all the more noticeable for its being deliberately set against the *Adelphoe.* Ironically, Cumberland says in his *Memoirs* that his chief detractor was a certain author whose "tract" *An Essay on the Theatre* "professes to draw *a comparison between laughing and sentimental Comedy,* and under the latter description particularly points his observations at *The Fashionable Lover*"—I, 379-380. It is of course possible that Cumberland really did not know that Goldsmith was the author of the essay.

public, and, as much as in him lies, to contrive so as to put men in good humour with one another. (I, 272)

Amiability is the primary mark of the healthy society, Cumberland would seem to say. Consequently we must see immorality for what it really is and, in contrast, see the fair ideal to which human nature may aspire and indeed attain. Presumably the triumph of the idealized man of virtue, whose "fouler side," so to speak, has been carefully expunged from the portrait, will have the salutary social effect of putting the audience into a spirit of convivial harmony. "Men as they ought to be, not as they are" is Cumberland's self-acknowledged purpose. Hardly a more explicit statement of intent could have come from a writer who by common consent was the foremost sentimental dramatist of his day.[7]

Yet Cumberland saw a problem peculiarly his because of the age in which he lived. It was not enough to realize the fruitful possibilities that lay in traditional comedy simply by following its plots and adapting the manners and "sentiments" of Terence's or Shadwell's characters to those of his own time; to do only this would be to produce a pervasive flatness, even insipidity. If he could not "put life and spirit into his man or woman of virtue, and render them entertaining as well as good," then he had better abandon the stage altogether (I, 272). Vitality is elusive nowadays, he explained in the Advertisement to *The Fashionable Lover*, for "the level manners of a polish'd country, like this, do not supply much matter for the comic muse, which delights in variety and extravagance. . . ." Consequently Cumberland found it necessary in both *The West Indian* and *The Fashionable Lover* "either to dive into the lower class of men, or betake myself to the out-skirts of the empire; the center is too equal and refined for such purposes."[8]

As anyone knows who has studied the antipathy Goldsmith encountered to the presentation of "low" characters on the stage[9] (an aversion he brilliantly satirized in the tavern scene in *She Stoops to Conquer*), Cumberland's latter possibility was a much

[7] See Williams' account of the growth of Cumberland's reputation in *Cumberland*, esp. Chap. IX.

[8] *The Fashionable Lover; A Comedy: As it is acted at the Theatre-Royal in Drury-Lane* (1772), p. vi.

[9] Typical of adverse reactions to the "low" characters in *The Good Natur'd Man* is John Hoadly's comment in a letter to Garrick quoted below, p. 119.

more viable alternative. To the outskirts of the British empire he accordingly made his way, he explains in his *Memoirs,* his imagination armed with a new purpose which might enlarge the sympathies of those for whom he wrote:

> I fancied there was an opening for some originality, and an opportunity for shewing at least my good will to mankind, if I introduced the characters of persons, who had been usually exhibited on the stage, as the butts for ridicule and abuse, and endeavoured to present them in such lights, as might tend to reconcile the world to them, and them to the world. I thereupon looked into society for the purpose of discovering such as were the victims of its national, professional or religious prejudices; in short for those suffering characters, which stood in need of an advocate, and out of these I meditated to select and form heroes for my future dramas, of which I would study to make such favourable and reconciliatory delineations, as might incline the spectators to look upon them with pity, and receive them into their good opinion and esteem. (I, 274)

With one produced comedy—*The Brothers* (Covent Garden, 1769-70)—and several comic operas already to his credit, he now began *The West Indian* with the idea of pairing two characters, each the victim of contemporary prejudice, each implicitly requesting the redemption that was his due. The conventional stage Irishman, farcically inept and humorously extravagant in behavior and language, reemerged in all the freshness Cumberland's sympathetic attitude could endow him with in Major O'Flaherty. In this character, the playwright explained, may be seen the courageous and gallant man, loyal to monarch and country, whose religion has disqualified him for service in the king's army and so has forced him to hire out as a mercenary. "I gave him courage," he recalls, "for it belongs to his nation; I endowed him with honour, for it belongs to his profession, and I made him proud, jealous, susceptible, for such the exiled veteran will be, who lives by the earnings of his sword, and is not allowed to draw it in the service of that country, which gave him birth, and which of course he was born to defend . . ." (I, 275). Cumberland's innovation, then, was to combine the external characteristics of the stage Irishman, which excite laughter and ridicule, with those of the stalwart professional defender of the nation's liberty, which could give rise only to admiration. In no way did he depart from the essential hilarity of the conventional figure. This, the second "hero" of the comedy, he observed in the prologue, is "A brave, unthinking, animated rogue, With here and there a touch upon the brogue."[10] So far the familiar object of an Englishman's scorn. There is nevertheless a redeeming difference: "Laugh, but despise him not, for on his lip His errors lie; his heart can never trip."

The first "hero," Belcour, makes an even more extensive claim on audience sympathy, as his name itself reveals. It is deceptively easy now to take him as simply another erring, sentimental hero, although drawn with uncommon boldness of line. For Cumberland's audience, however, the boldness extended to a virtually complete departure from customary attitudes toward the "creole," as the West Indian was commonly called. The measure of Cumberland's daring is clear from the fact that, at the first performance, a large group of West Indians presented themselves in the audience, ready to disrupt the proceedings and denounce the playwright, should their national character be maligned.[11] To understand the height of this minority feeling it is helpful to review, as Wylie Sypher has, the popular attitude toward this figure in the eighteenth century. The creole in actual history was the probably inevitable result of the British exploitation of the West Indies, where inbreeding among colonists and natives produced children of often uncertain ancestry. Typical of these was the offspring of a white planter and his native mistress, who might well become heir to the plantation and in turn take both a white wife and one or more native mistresses. Far from considering themselves inferior, this ethnic group (if it can be called that) developed a certain characteristic pride. Creole children of white plantation owners were sent back to England for education, where their affluence enabled them to attend the best schools and generally to lord it over their contemporaries. The great increase in the price of sugar in the middle years of the century gave returning planters and their families the wherewithal to congregate at resorts and to crowd fashionable London streets with their car-

[10] *The West Indian: A Comedy. As it is Performed at the Theatre Royal in Drury-Lane* (1771).

[11] See Williams, *Cumberland*, pp. 70-71.

riages. Undeniably, the West Indian was upsetting English social order and was duly resented as a proud and extravagant interloper.[12]

Against this considerable prejudice Cumberland directed his energies in creating the character of Belcour. His ability to portray the type exactly is reflected in the authoritative description of the West Indian in Edward Long's *History of Jamaica*. Published in 1774, only three years after Cumberland's comedy appeared at Drury Lane, Long's *History* offers a verbal picture of the creole that might have been drawn from Cumberland's character, so close did he come to the mark.[13] Belcour is replete with benevolent virtues and predominantly amiable faults. The playwright himself summed up his creation as an ideal mixture of virtue and sociability:

> To the West Indian I devoted a generous spirit, and a vivacious giddy dissipation; I resolved he should love pleasure much, but honour more; but as I could not keep consistency of character without a mixture of failings, when I gave him charity, I gave him that, which can cover a multitude, and thus protected, thus recommended, I thought I might send him out into the world to shift for himself. (I, 274-275)

Such was the character which, like some new and exotic object of the hunter's aim, was "started full in view" of the first night's audience, as Cumberland described in the first lines of his prologue. The West Indians among the assembly were ready to riot at the use of such a metaphor, but Cumberland's verses calculatedly promised that his character sketch was not only faithful to life but complimentary as well. When "critics" run this creature to earth, he assured them, they will discover "Some emanations of a noble mind;/ Some little touches, which, tho' void of art,/ May find perhaps their way into the heart."

Minority feelings thus assuaged, the audience as a whole settled down to enjoy the first of twenty-eight Drury Lane performances that season, a highly successful record.[14] The play of

[12] Sypher, "The West-Indian as a 'Character' in the Eighteenth Century," *SP*, XXXVI (1939), 504.

[13] Long, *History of Jamaica* (1774), II, 261-284, quoted by Sypher in "The West-Indian," p. 506.

[14] My count of performances listed in *The London Stage 1660-1800*, ed. George Winchester Stone, Jr., Pt. 4, Vol. III (Carbondale, Ill., 1962).

course did not single-handedly destroy anti-West Indian prejudice, but when this appeared, as in at least one review, it served to make Cumberland's innovation even clearer. Never departing from the figure easily recognized by contemporary Londoners, Cumberland applied the catalyst of sentiment to produce pure gold from the base metal of the original. No playwright before him had so studiously labored on behalf of victims of social prejudice. It is undeniable that the flighty Belcour and the irrepressible Major O'Flaherty are significant characterizations when seen in the context of the dramatic tradition and social conditions from which they spring.

ii. Morality and Mirth: The Terentian Theme Recast

Yet it must not be supposed that Cumberland's efforts to enlarge his audience's hearts were, however noticeable at the time, unique. Cumberland was fully capable of feeling that he waged a one-man battle against those who would denigrate the purity and loftiness of his intentions. But in fact his efforts to elicit admiration for characters supposedly outside the pale of human sympathy were only part of a large and important shift in sensibilities taking place at this time. Important instances of this change occur in the transformation of villain into hero begun by Garrick's subjective interpretation of Richard III and, at the same time, Charles Macklin's revolutionary portrayal of Shylock as a serious figure of tragic proportions instead of a red-headed comic buffoon.[15] By the time Cumberland's *The Jew* (Drury Lane, 1793-94) presented audiences with the first sympathetic treatment of this figure in a contemporary play, the revivified and now "understandable" Shylock was a commonplace on eighteenth-century stages.[16]

[15] Francis Gentleman's description of Macklin in the role is representative: ". . . there is no doubt but Mr. MACKLIN looks the part as much better than any other person as he plays it; in the level scenes his voice is most happily suited to that sententious gloominess of expression the author intended; which, with a sullen solemnity of deportment, marks the character strongly; in his malevolence, there is a forcible and terrifying ferocity . . ."—*The Dramatic Censor; or, Critical Companion* (1770), I, 292.

[16] Hazlitt's analysis of the character in 1817 indicates the extent of the shift: "The desire of revenge is almost inseparable from the sense of wrong; and we can hardly help sympathising with the proud spirit, hid beneath his 'Jewish gaberdine,' stung to madness by repeated undeserved provocations, . . . till the ferociousness of the means by which he is to execute his purpose,

Still another Shakespearean character underwent essentially the same transformation. In describing its immediate origin in Corbyn Morris's essay of 1744 on wit and humor, Stuart M. Tave has summarized the change in Sir John Falstaff as one from "a fat parcel of gross humors—a cowardly, lying, gluttonous buffoon" to "an entirely lovable old rogue—a courageous, honest, trim-figured philosopher."[17] Shaftesbury's notion of human nature, itself a synthesis of dominant tendencies in the Latitudinarian religion and Lockean psychology of the late seventeenth century, undoubtedly contributed to the change that overtook the character.[18] Examination of the writings of Shaftesbury and Steele suggests that they helped to foster the sense of the inherent dignity and honor of human nature that underlies the attempts of Corbyn Morris and, after him, Maurice Morgann to rescue Falstaff from charges that discredit the species.[19] Like Morgann, Morris presupposes an integral humanity in the character, which Shakespeare himself violated after first introducing him. Falstaff's appearance in *The Merry Wives of Windsor* Morris finds "greatly below his true Character," and his imprisonment and death in the second part of *Henry IV* seem to Morris a base attempt to avoid the imputation of encouraging "*Idleness* and mirthful *Riot*. . . ."[20] The Falstaff of the first part of *Henry IV* is, then, the quintessential character. There, for Morris, no alloy intrudes to render its abundant good nature impure. Morris outdoes himself in cataloguing the virtues of this engaging figure: "Generosity, Chearfulness, Alacrity, Invention, Frolic and Fancy superior to all other Men . . ." (p. 28). From Shakespeare's unparalleled success Mor-

---

and the pertinacity with which he adheres to it, turn us against him; but even at last, . . . we pity him, and think him hardly dealt with by his judges"—*The Characters of Shakespear's Plays*, in *Complete Works*, ed. P. P. Howe (1930-34), IV, 320.

[17] "Corbyn Morris: Falstaff, Humor, and Comic Theory in the Eighteenth Century," *MP*, L (1952), 102. See also Tave, *The Amiable Humorist: A Study in the Comic Theory and Criticism of the Eighteenth and Early Nineteenth Centuries* (Chicago, 1960), pp. 106-139.

[18] See Ernest Tuveson's excellent studies of this subject cited in note 3 above.

[19] See the discussion of Morgann's study of Falstaff below, Pt. III, Chap. VIII, pp. 205-206.

[20] [Morris], *An Essay Towards Fixing the True Standards of Wit, Humour, Raillery, Satire, and Ridicule. To which is Added, an Analysis of the Characters of An Humourist, Sir John Falstaff, Sir Roger De Coverly, and Don Quixote* (1744), Intro., p. xxviii.

ris thus infers the crucial principle for creating such a character; it is, simply, *"in drawing the Persons exhibited, with such chearful and amiable* Oddities *and* Foibles, *as you would chuse in your own* Companions *in* real life . . ." (p. 30). For it is obvious, says Morris, that whoever cannot be endured as a friend *"will never become, for the very same Reasons, a* favorite comic Character *in the Theatre"* (p. 31). The essence of a humorous character lies in his amiable nature. Sociability is the tie that unites men in society, minimizing their faults and lapses and molding them into a healthful company. Following the lead of ideas like this, Cumberland had simply taken the additional step of solidifying a general attitude into an overt comic principle. Just as Morris openly asserts his intention to present an "entirely . . . amiable Character" (p. xxviii), so Cumberland proposed "to turn the fairer side of human nature to the public, and . . . to contrive so as to put men in good humour with one another" (I, 272).

Cumberland's method of reforming the hearts of his countrymen emerged naturally from his knowledge of dramatic comic tradition and his sense of the amiable eccentricity of character that native English genius could produce. He was consequently in a position to take maximum advantage, consistent with his own presuppositions, of comic form and structure as old as the Roman. Roman comic playwrights left two closely related legacies to their British and continental followers. The first of these, and undoubtedly the more important, was a strong sense of community. Despite their differences, Plautus and Terence shared a view of Roman society as an integrated and largely harmonious mixture of diverse but not intractable elements. Their plays depended on the existence of a society in which the various roles of its members were defined clearly enough to become stage conventions upon which playwrights might rely. The basic plot of Roman comedy—so basic that we tend to ignore the different Aristophanic type and take it as the plot of comedy in general—is the temporary disruption of a highly structured society, followed by its eventual restoration.[21] This disruption is due almost inevitably to friction between the older and younger generations (the two main classes of characters presented on the Roman

[21] I am of course employing here the ideas of Northrop Frye; see the sections on comedy in *Anatomy of Criticism* (Princeton, 1957), and see also George E. Duckworth, *The Nature of Roman Comedy* (Princeton, 1952), Chaps. VI-XI, *passim.*

stage); and implicit in this friction is an idea about human society that has persisted from that time to our own. The basic realities of growth and change imply that the younger generation must inevitably supplant the older, in wealth, status, and success. Friction is caused by what appears to the older generation as the importunate attempt of the younger to usurp authority and freedom before having gained the wisdom necessary to exercise them with temperance. The formal qualities of Roman comedy derive from this basic conflict of interests and values. Because comedy, essentially optimistic in its view of life, finds a satisfactory resolution implicit in temporary disorder, the play conventionally ends with a feast or a wedding, or both. The too rigid older generation has been made to bend, and the younger generation has effected a meaningful assimilation of itself into society—cause enough for celebration.

The second legacy to which Cumberland and his forbears fell heir came as a codicil to the first. Statistically a minor fortune, it derives not from Roman comedy in general but from one play by Terence, the *Adelphoi*. Terence's play does not differ fundamentally from the others in its genre, but it holds in addition to the familiar conflict of generations a more explicit thematic idea. With unconventional philosophic interest Terence explores the implications of the familiar comic line of action in which tempestuous youth seeks a responsible and satisfying place in the adult world. As Cumberland himself acknowledged, a dramatist employs the basic device of contrast to make his meaning clear. Terence sets up two pairs of brothers, drawing a contrast between those of the younger and older generations. But within each generation the playwright also illustrates two opposing philosophies of education, one based on strict watchfulness and Spartan restraint, the other on virtually unlimited freedom. The question implicit in this double conflict is: Which system will produce the better citizen? The answer, worked out in the scheme of events leading to the happy resolution, is that youth must be allowed some freedom to err in order to discover for itself the necessity for responsible conduct. At the same time, Terence emphasizes the fact that each philosophical position contains elements of extremeness that war against peaceful transition. Moderation consistent with the opportunity for reasoned choice appears, after all, the soundest method.

"I rejoice that you wept at ye West-Indian," Garrick wrote to his clergyman friend John Hoadly toward the end of the first season of its performances.[22] The remark came in answer to Hoadly's letter of high praise for the play, tempered with helpful criticism of the plot, in which he declared: "You prophesied that the 'West Indian' would make my *mouth water* to read. I suppose you meant after your character of it: you might have added, that it would make *my eyes water,* which it did twenty times in the reading."[23] A similar but more comprehensive response appeared less than a month after the play opened at Drury Lane on 19 January 1771. A writer who signed himself "Veritas Theatrica" unburdened himself of his feelings in a letter to the *Whitehall Evening Post.* "My breast," he confided, "is not superior to terror,—my heart is, I hope, open to sensibility,—my eye no stranger to compassion,—but at a comedy I expect and love to laugh; and I took up the pen to make my acknowledgments to an author who has gratified his inclination,—who has introduced laughter without dismissing sentiment,—and who has showed morality and mirth to be far from incompatible!"[24]

For this writer at least, Cumberland's educational purpose had become a felt reality. Reassessment of the familiar Terentian theme had evidently led Cumberland to see in it the possibility of producing a strong vindication of the sentimental premise basic to his thought and writings. Morality and mirth might be rendered compatible by demonstrating that laughter at the excesses of an untutored young man denies him neither dignity nor a place in society. Instead, it conveys a tacit acknowledgment of sympathy for those natural responses that prompt him to extravagant behavior. Although his impulsive reactions may throw society into temporary chaos, the events precipitated by the fluctuations of his own behavior finally produce a reordered and once more flourishing community. So Cumberland adapted the Roman comic premise, combining it with the more explicit Terentian notion of meaningful experience as a prerequisite for entrance into society. The only departure from his models that Cumberland allowed himself was the one on which his fame (or, perhaps, noto-

[22] Letter dated 9 May 1771 in *The Letters of David Garrick,* ed. David M. Little and George M. Kahrl, 3 vols. (Cambridge, Mass., 1963), II, 739.

[23] Letter dated 28 April 1771 in *The Private Correspondence of David Garrick,* [ed. James Boaden], 2 vols. (1831-32), I, 420.

[24] 9 February 1771, quoted in Williams, *Cumberland,* pp. 76-77.

riety) rests. The Roman playwright dramatizes extravagance but in the end mediates it with some notion of temperate behavior. Cumberland, in contrast, shows that extravagance contains the seeds of its own vindication. The tempering of society as a whole is not achieved by the imposition of reasoned restraint but by allowing excess its rightful way. Accordingly, *The West Indian* presents, in the most vital dramatic form with which Cumberland could endow it, the just triumph of natural response.

The structure of *The West Indian* is plainly designed to suit this purpose. The basic device Cumberland uses to effect the victory of his noble protagonist and of his noble theme is one long familiar to theater audiences. One of the most frequent of all dramatic situations is the trial, which tests the chief character's ability to respond successfully and so prove his worth in the eyes of others. There are, it need hardly be said, many possible variations. Cumberland's approach is to inform the audience at the very beginning that Belcour stands to gain—or lose—great moral approbation, according to what his conduct shall merit. In the opening exposition, a conversation of the wealthy merchant Stockwell with his clerk Stukely, Cumberland arranges to let the audience in on the essential fact of Belcour's identity: Stockwell, who has agreed to introduce Belcour to English life and to manage his affairs for him, is in reality his own father. But Belcour will not yet be allowed knowledge of his paternity. "Before I publickly reveal myself," Stockwell explains to his clerk, "I could wish to make some experiment of my son's disposition; this can be only done by letting his spirit take its course without restraint; by these means, I think I shall discover much more of his real character under the title of his merchant, than I should under that of his father" (p. 4).

In allowing his audience a share in the secret of Belcour's birth, Cumberland in effect enables them to concentrate on the period of trial with the foreknowledge that Belcour will emerge not unscathed but nevertheless victorious. They are now aware that the obligatory scene in Act V will be that in which Stockwell informs the young man of his heritage and consequently claims him as a rightful member of the society in which, for the space of over four acts, he has appeared as an interloper. As a reward for good behavior, Belcour will win the knowledge of his identity, which has already supported the audience's sympathetic interest in him from even before his first entrance on stage.

So employing a notion of paternity as a means of grace, Cumberland produces an unusual tightness of structure that gives direction to the period of trial. From his first appearance it is clear that Belcour, the most exuberant and agreeable of young men, is capable of earning his place in society. His primary difficulty is not so much his inherent extravagance as his supposed origin, for a West Indian after all is essentially an outsider importunately demanding accord and respect. This is the primary conflict out of which Cumberland's redemptive process grows. The audience begins by being willing to allow Belcour almost every sort of excess, since it is his nature to possess a mercurial temperament. But they would customarily grant this to all West Indians while still retaining their prejudice against the group. Cumberland exploits this prejudice by having Belcour fulfill the expectations of his audience but at the same time establishing that his hero is of pure English stock. Belcour is the product of a secret marriage between Stockwell and the legitimate daughter of a West Indian planter, now dead. Forced by circumstances to introduce their child into the family as a foundling, Stockwell and his now-deceased wife found their hopes justified when the planter benevolently adopted the young man as his own son and made him heir to his vast Jamaican holdings. Having come into his property, Belcour has set sail for England to try out the civilization of his foster father while still believing himself a creole. Cumberland thus arranges for Belcour to flaunt all the characteristics of a native of that sultry climate but at the same time provides a loophole through which the young man can crawl to respectability. The audience must perforce accept him as one of their number because of his birth. But they may still reject him because of his acquired traits. Yet, if they accept him, they do so not as an outlander but as a native English son. Carefully establishing these conditions at the outset, the playwright proceeds to make his audience reconsider the attributes desirable in a young man, regardless of his origin. His play, then, is designed for a kind of double redemption: events will serve to deliver Belcour from the onus placed upon him by prejudice while leaving him essentially unchanged, and the audience will be forced to acknowledge that, in excluding the West Indian from society, they have proscribed an essential element of its cohesiveness.

Cumberland's strategy in effecting all this is to allow his hero to fall into error only through acts of great benevolence or mere youthful misjudgment. In so doing he is obviously laying claim to the actions of the archetypal *adulescens* of Roman and British comedy, but at the same time he carefully changes the value judgments that would conventionally apply. Traditionally, youthful excess draws the protagonist into difficulty, while experience and temperate judgment exist, at least by implication, as standards for behavior. On the surface *The West Indian* follows this paradigm. For example, when in the first act Belcour announces to Stockwell (who already knows) that he is rich and has come to England to spend his money, the merchant paternally cautions him to treat wealth "not as a vassal, over whom you have a wanton and despotic power, but as a subject, which you are bound to govern with a temperate and restrained authority" (p. 8). And further on, when Belcour has managed to elicit a challenge to duel from young Dudley, whose sister Louisa Belcour has mistakenly approached as a vivacious woman of the town, Stockwell stands in as his second and offers a timely explanation to prevent bloodshed. But despite this ostensible fidelity to the familiar pattern, Cumberland does not in fact make it the basis for any supposedly necessary reformation of his extravagant hero. Instead, he uses this very extravagance as the means to contrive his resolution.

Belcour's first action after leaving Stockwell is to see Louisa Dudley and, breathless with anticipation, to pursue her to her lodgings. But no sooner does he arrive in futile hopes of discovering her than he is made aware of the financial needs of the elderly Captain Dudley. Without so much as a wasted gesture he accommodates himself to the new situation:

> I've lost the girl it seems; that's clear: she was the first object of my pursuit; but the case of this poor officer touches me; and, after all, there may be as much true delight in rescuing a fellow creature from distress, as there would be in plunging one into it. . . . (p. 27)

It is Belcour's promptness to follow his own inclinations and so serve his own pleasure which leads him to place in Captain Dudley's hands an envelope containing two hundred pounds. This same charity, as Cumberland designed, covers Belcour's subsequent multitudinous sins. Through sheer inexperience he is led by the conniving landlady Mrs. Fulmer to believe that Louisa Dudley only passes as the sister of young Charles Dudley and is actually his kept mistress. Considering her a legitimate object of conquest, Belcour gives Charlotte Rusport's jewels, entrusted to him by Stockwell, to Mrs. Fulmer to purchase Louisa's affections, and so elicits the challenge from her brother Charles. Meanwhile he offers Charlotte jewels of superior value that he just happens to have in his pocket. Egregious as these errors are, Belcour's naïveté in committing them seems designed to ingratiate him not only with the audience but even with those other characters supposedly most likely to take offense at them. When Stockwell hears of Belcour's gift to Captain Dudley he exclaims, "I must disclose myself to Belcour; this noble instance of his generosity . . . allies me to him at once; concealment becomes too painful; I shall be proud to own him for my son . . ." (p. 78). When it appears that Mrs. Fulmer has trapped Belcour into parting with the diamonds, Stockwell tells him that his ingenuousness is "no match for the cunning and contrivances of this intriguing town" (p. 82). And finally, when Stockwell has averted the catastrophic consequences of the duel and brought Louisa Dudley and Belcour together, he intercedes for him in a speech addressed as much to the audience as to the young girl:

> You will not be over strict, Madam, in weighing Mr. Belcour's conduct to the minutest scruple; his manners, passions and opinions are not as yet assimilated to this climate; he comes amongst you a new character, an inhabitant of a new world and both hospitality as well as pity recommend him to our indulgence. (p. 90)

The proviso scene that now ensues attempts in dramatic summary the same rationalization of Belcour's considerable faults. Apparently like the traditional rake, lewd for above four acts, Belcour begs Louisa to "cease . . . to reflect upon the libertine addresses I have paid you, and look upon me as your reform'd, your rational admirer" (p. 92). But Louisa has already told him that no reparation is necessary for his conduct except his "more favourable opinion for the future . . ." (p. 91). And indeed no atonement is due, since Cumberland has Belcour explain that his first glimpse of Louisa fired an essentially noble passion. "There's a healing virtue in your eyes," he observes; ". . . I cannot be a villain in your arms" (p. 92). Since there is really nothing to forgive, momentary error may be easily forgot. The natural human instinct that has prompted Belcour's actions from the start is now fully justified. Out of the jungle of egotism, natural responsiveness emerges victorious, for it is this primal force that brings together in marriage two virtuous young persons and so renews society. As if to suggest that a still younger generation is now pressingly imminent, Belcour claims Louisa's hand in a surging speech that upholds impassioned response as the greatest good pursued by man:

> By Heav'n my soul is conquer'd with your virtues more than my eyes are ravish'd with your beauty: Oh, may this soft, this sensitive alarm be happy, be auspicious! Doubt not, deliberate not, delay not: If happiness be the end of life, why do we slip a moment? (p. 93)

Thus self-certified, Belcour presents himself to Stockwell, who now reveals the identity of the "father, who observes, who knows, who loves you" (p. 101). Official approbation is now awarded for those qualities Belcour himself has warranted as free from all impurity. "I have watched you," Stockwell confesses as he gives his blessing, "with a patient, but enquiring eye, and I have discover'd thro' the veil of some irregularities, a heart beaming with benevolence, an animated nature, fallible indeed, but not incorrigible; and your election of this excellent young lady makes me glory in acknowledging you to be my son" (pp. 101-102).

If the resolution of *The West Indian* reads like a pamphlet on "The Proceedings of Providence Vindicated, Written by a Society for Mutual Esteem," it is because Cumberland's method contains intrinsic proof of its "validity." His acknowledged purpose was to mend the hearts of his audience by delivering them from the vanity and snobbery that impoverished their lives. But his way of accomplishing this purpose was to *reinterpret* motives supposedly egotistical and therefore anti-social in order to show that the private responses of the individual are precisely those which restore health and integrity to the world of men. The audience is now able to feel benevolence for the social outcast without having really compromised its own social position. Egotism has been given a seal of approval by deftly disguising its viciousness as "pardonable irregularity." If the author were taken to task for having deliberately and hypocritically sought to falsify human nature, his defense would be simply that he purposed to show men, not as they are, but as they ought to be. When the playwright shoulders the heavy burden of teaching men their faults, he must not compromise his integrity by displaying on the stage one whose virtues and vices stand in equal balance. Moral purpose requires selectivity. Only the "fairer side of human nature" bears showing to those from whom dramatic art elicits sympathetic response. True comedy not only mirrors life as we know it but exhorts its viewers to give back the image they see.

iii. Goldsmith and the Context of Retaliation

And so "coxcombs," said Goldsmith, who was not in the vein, "Adopting his portraits are pleas'd with their own." Goldsmith's consciously assumed role as antagonist of sentimental comedy is so well known that it may seem pointless to raise the subject once again. But criticism has not made sufficiently clear the extent to which the dramaturgical methods employed by Goldsmith conditioned the form and meaning of his attack. A close reading of *She Stoops to Conquer* (Covent Garden, 1772-73) suggests that Goldsmith, as much as Cumberland, was aware of formal and thematic trends in contemporary drama and that he was able to see these in the perspective of dramatic tradition extending back to the Romans. The issues raised by his play are essentially those elucidated only a few months earlier in his "Essay." This critical assault on sentimentalism and the dramatic assault that followed are usually taken as classic examples of their kind. While they no doubt deserve such a place in the history of the drama and of dramatic criticism, their significance becomes clearer when they are placed in the context of certain developments that occurred some five years before. Within the space of a week in 1768, there appeared two plays, each of which attempted in different ways to grapple with the question of sentimental behavior.

Hugh Kelly's *False Delicacy* (Drury Lane, 23 January 1768) and Goldsmith's *The Good Natur'd Man* (Covent Garden, 29 January 1768) are commonly viewed as representing the two opposing camps of sentimental and of anti-sentimental or "laughing" comedy. Allardyce Nicoll's assessment, a case in point, takes *False Delicacy* as "a highly moral work written in rivalry" to Goldsmith's play; he employs Goldsmith's preface to it to show that the author of *The Good Natur'd Man* was attacking "genteel" plays which lack both character and "humour."[25] Richard Garnett sums up the relationship by citing *False Delicacy* as "a vapid sentimental comedy of the kind that Goldsmith most disliked. . . ."[26] Ricardo Quintana has achieved a more judicious view. Rightly emphasizing the fact that many of the comedies produced in the late eighteenth century were not strictly speaking sentimental or were simply comedies of manners based on an assumption of general good nature, Quintana finds considerable variety of treatment even in plays whose sentimentality is supposedly clear. "One of the most curious variants," he observes, is *False Delicacy*, "glorifying sentimentalism and laughing at it in alternate scenes."[27] Quintana's idea of a fundamental divisiveness in the play provides a more adequate measure of its complexity. But the critical practice of polarizing what seem to be discordant qualities in an individual play or in two different plays is a simplification that leads to misunderstanding. A fresh look at this, Kelly's first comedy, is in order.

The basic problem and consequently the basic cause for the misinterpretation of *False Delicacy* is that the fifth act does not fulfill the promise of the first four. Kelly's play is a competent and entertaining comedy of manners that sets out to cast ridicule on false delicacy—an excessive sensitivity to standards of supposedly ideal social conduct. The chief practitioners of this extremely nice behavior are Sidney, engaged to Colonel Rivers' daughter; Lady Betty Lambton, a young widow who has already rejected the suit of Lord Winworth (whom she would very much like to have) on the principle that "a woman of real delicacy shou'd never admit a second impression on her heart";[28] and Miss Marchmont, Lady Betty's orphan ward, who also dismisses Lord Winworth out of

[25] Nicoll, *A History of English Drama 1660-1900*, III (Cambridge, Eng., 1955), 130, 158.

[26] Garnett, ed., *Goldsmith: Selected Works*, "The Reynard Library" (London, 1950), p. 666.

[27] Quintana, "Goldsmith's Achievement as a Dramatist," *UTQ*, XXXIV (1965), 165.

[28] *False Delicacy: A Comedy; as it is performed at the Theatre-Royal in Drury-Lane* (1768), Act II, p. 17.

regard for the feelings of her benefactor (and, besides, she prefers Sidney). In addition to these three appears Colonel Rivers, a retired army man who spouts sentiments about the prostitution of young women through marriages for money but who is perversely willing to allow his daughter to elope with Sir Harry Newburg, a rich young pleasure-hunter, so that she will have the satisfaction of putting her father in an early grave. In opposition to this group of solemn mannerists, Kelly introduces the elderly family friend Cecil and the effervescent Mrs. Harley—surely one of the most well-executed comic characterizations of the century—as agents for the chastisement of extravagant behavior. Through their mutual efforts Cecil and Mrs. Harley contrive to bring these self-destructive *delicatistes* to an understanding of their errant behavior, Mrs. Harley exclaiming in the last scene, "Why now all is as it shou'd be,—all is as it shou'd be—this is the triumph of good sense over delicacy" (p. 87).

Yet the triumph is less than complete, owing to Kelly's difficulty in arriving at a final synthesis of the value judgments implicit in the action as he has arranged it. What Kelly has failed to clarify is the function of self-interest in human society. It is not a matter of condemning it outright or of extolling it as a virtue before which all others pale. It is a matter of establishing an intelligent and explicit distinction between actions that satisfy human desires while promoting the general welfare and actions that set private gratification at odds with community benefit. Kelly conducts the first four acts of *False Delicacy* with what seems a well-planned effort to expose various individuals who affect a kind of martyr complex: they would not be so base as to gratify their private instincts when it is plain that society demands the utmost in selflessness. Chiefly through the agency of Mrs. Harley, the playwright points out that these persons are actually the grossest of egotists. Their pretensions to selfless behavior mask their real intent to be thought of as ladies and gentlemen of superior virtue. Mrs. Harley, especially effective in dealing with the affectations of her friend Lady Betty, arranges for her to see that rejecting Lord Winworth serves no purpose except to make both of them miserable. Having worked his way through four acts of witty and entertaining chastisement of this sort, Kelly arrives at Act V—and somehow manages to lose his sense of direction.

The scene presents a confrontation of Colonel Rivers and his prospective son-in-law, Sidney, a young man whom Mrs. Harley characterized when, at the beginning of the play, she described "those half-soul'd fellows, who are as mechanically regular as so many pieces of clock-work, and never strike above once an hour upon a new observation—who are so sentimental, and so dull—so wise and so drowsy" (I, p. 4). The target clear, Kelley takes careful aim, but his comic purpose misfires. Sidney wants to break off his engagement with Miss Rivers because, as he says, her inclinations lie elsewhere and he has too much "sensibility" to do them "the smallest violence" (V, pp. 72-73). Colonel Rivers, an egregious sentimentalist where only he himself is concerned, recognizes and states the egotism behind Sidney's politeness: Sidney simply wants to be free to marry Miss Marchmont and so has contrived an elaborately "honorable" exit from his obligation. At such a moment of exposure, a Sheridan might have allowed this Joseph Surface an exclamation of "Confusion!" and sent him scurrying unredeemed to the wings. But the present playwright, who apparently cannot bring himself to such harshness, proceeds to blunt the pointedness of his theme by reinforcing the outlines of Sidney's mask of sentiment. Adopting a tone of distinct moral superiority, the young man charitably condescends not to take offense:

> Miss Marchmont, Colonel, is greatly above this illiberal reflexion; as for myself, I shall be always ready to justify an action which I know to be right, though I should be sorry ever to meet you but in the character of a friend.
>
> [*Exit.*] (V, pp. 74-75)

As Colonel Rivers charges off, bellowing in impotent rage, Mrs. Harley and Cecil are with weak contrivance brought on to arrange the denouement. It is evident now that Kelly has mistaken the true object of his attack, for instead of keeping his sights trained on sentimentality itself he has granted one of its exemplars a permanent victory over another. Mrs. Harley and Cecil, commenting on what they have seen, are made to say that this all fits in with their plan. But its purpose is now other than certain. Cecil immediately observes that Sidney is "a noble young fellow" who richly deserves the hand of Miss Marchmont (V, p. 75). Accordingly, three marriages are swiftly arranged: Miss Rivers' with the would-be eloper Sir Harry, now in good graces with the

Colonel; the lachrymose Miss Marchmont's with the righteous Sidney; and the chastened and grateful Lady Betty's with the long-suffering Lord Winworth. Kelly has rescued all except one of his principal objects of ridicule without more than scratching their self-esteem. Having paid with spurious coin his immense debtorship for the thing done (as George Meredith later described the consequences of human action),[29] the playwright finishes his comedy by blithely restating the motives that have prompted Cecil and Mrs. Harley to their good works. Drafted by the author into pseudo-Jonsonian service through four acts, they now relinquish their scourges, turn benefactors, and join the ranks of the mutual admirers. Cecil generously matches Winworth guinea for guinea in funds awarded to Sidney and Miss Marchmont, then congratulates himself for having "a little common understanding" of the needs of others. "This," says Mrs. Harley, with a force of which Kelly was evidently unaware, "is the triumph of good sense over delicacy." Presumably in this society no delicacy is "false" enough to cavil at accepting a windfall fortune. And so it appears that the "plan" hinted at by Mrs. Harley and Cecil was not really to restore a sense of balance to society but simply to add to its numbers. In case anyone has been unintentionally hurt in the match-making process, Kelly has Winworth reassure the audience that "the noblest of all lessons is the forgiveness of injuries." Yet, lest it appear that all are now on an equal footing, Colonel Rivers reminds us that a certain class of mortals stands out above the rest:

> . . . The principal moral to be drawn from the transactions of to-day is, that those who generously labor for the happiness of others, will, sooner or later, arrive at happiness themselves. (V, p. 87)

And so the play ends, the sentimental premise stated and vindicated. Implicit in this vindication is the ambiguous value attached to the morality of human conduct. According to the meaning imposed by the structure of the play, false delicacy is condemned because it prevents society from replenishing itself. But, according to the sentiments evinced at last by the characters themselves, it is condemned because it interferes with the grati-

[29] In *The Egoist*; a definition given popular currency by Stephen Daedalus in *A Portrait of the Artist as a Young Man.*

fication of one's own desires. Mrs. Harley and Cecil have known this all along but have conveniently kept it a secret from the others until such time as they could reveal it in triumph. And yet in the very act of revealing egotism as the effective basis of human action, they perversely glory in the merit stored up for them through selfless acts. The only thing better than gratuitous forgiveness is generosity—which repays the donor a hundredfold.

It is no wonder, then, that *False Delicacy* has been often interpreted as a straightforwardly sentimental play and that Kelly's name has been coupled with Cumberland's as a distinguished purveyor of such merchandise. To be sure, Kelly wrote his own ticket of admission into the august company of the "Terence of England, the mender of hearts" when he severed his fifth act from the comic purpose that had governed the first four. But it is a mistake to imagine that Kelly was alone in his infirmity of purpose. The play that appeared at the rival theater six nights after *False Delicacy* opened at Drury Lane manifests a similar unsureness. Allardyce Nicoll found it necessary to apologize for placing his account of *The Good Natur'd Man* in his section on "Comedies of Manners" rather than in "Sentimental Comedy." Despite Goldsmith's declared purpose, Professor Nicoll observes, "elements of sentimentalism mar its general tone, so that the conclusion is forced and vapid."[30] Ricardo Quintana accounts for the extreme statement of reformation uttered by young Honeywood at the end of the play by explaining that Goldsmith's true purpose was to burlesque sentimental comedy by carrying its idiom to ridiculous extremes. A reading of the play supports Quintana's view, but he himself is careful to point out that Goldsmith's method is over-subtle. The serious deficiency of the play, he finds, is that it fails "to point up the true norm which lies behind its comic action. . . ."[31] It might be added that it is asking a great deal of even the seasoned parodist to exceed the blatant thematic summary of Kelly's Colonel Rivers. However much Goldsmith may have wished, as he declares in his preface to the first edition, to eschew "genteel" comedy and to emulate the "nature," "humour," and "character" of the comedies of the last age,[32] the lack

[30] Nicoll, *History of English Drama*, III, 158.

[31] Quintana, "Goldsmith's Achievement," p. 170. See also Quintana, *Oliver Goldsmith: A Georgian Study* (New York and London, 1967), pp. 147-151.

[32] *The Good Natur'd Man: A Comedy. As Performed at the Theatre-Royal in Covent Garden* (1768), p. v.

of dramatic clarity in *The Good Natur'd Man* is well demonstrated by John Hoadly's description of the audience's response to Goldsmith's mock-sentimental hero. The scene with the bailiffs and its attendant "low humour," Hoadly wrote to Garrick in 1773, degraded his hero, whom the audience were taught to pity and respect, into "a low buffoon, and what is worse, into a falsifier, a character unbecoming a gentleman."[33] The degradation of the man of fine feeling was, of course, exactly the point. Hoadly unwittingly parried the satirist's blow by appealing to decorum, an elevated principle that Goldsmith seems to have felt had its basis only in the fantasies of playwrights, not in life.

So did Goldsmith learn the need for a comic structure sufficiently bold in outline. Although there is no evidence that he had considered the rehearsal form, it is certain that in writing *The Good Natur'd Man* he had attempted to contrive the kind of mock-serious structure characteristic of the spirit of Buckingham's original burlesque. His problem, then, was to take advantage of possibilities for satirizing sentimental drama and at the same time to create dramatic characters and a dramatic form that would expose sentimentality in actual life. For this complex purpose the rehearsal form was perhaps too limited. At any rate, Goldsmith turned elsewhere, in fact to his own imagination, in quest of an adequate form.

In conducting his search, Goldsmith could hardly have forgotten the principal critical objection to *The Good Natur'd Man.* Kelly had successfully compromised the comic tendencies of the first four acts of *False Delicacy* by contorting his play into a vindication of sentiment effected by unexceptionably genteel characters. Goldsmith, on the other hand, had found himself misun-

[33] Letter dated 1773 by Boaden in *Private Correspondence of Garrick,* I, 506. Goldsmith's view of lowness was clearly at odds with Hoadly's: ". . . by the power of one single monosyllable, our critics have almost got the victory over humour amongst us. Does the poet paint the absurdities of the vulgar; then he is *low*: does he exaggerate the features of folly, to render it more thoroughly ridiculous, he is then very *low.* In short, they have proscribed the comic or satyrical muse from every walk but high life. . . . The truth is, the critic generally mistakes humour for wit, which is a very different excellence. Wit raises human nature above its level; humour acts a contrary part, and equally depresses it"—*An Enquiry into the Present State of Polite Learning,* Chap. XI, quoted by Arthur Friedman, ed., *Collected Works of Oliver Goldsmith,* 5 vols. (Oxford, 1966), v, 13n. All quotations from Goldsmith have been checked against Friedman's excellent text.

derstood and castigated for presenting *lowness* on the stage and so compromising the integrity of his chief character. Consequently his retaliatory method was to seize on this very objection and exploit it for all its worth. Gathering his resources for an assault on determinedly genteel audiences, he prepared the way with a brief salvo published in the *Westminster Magazine* in January 1773, less than three months before *She Stoops to Conquer* appeared on the boards of the Drury Lane on 15 March. "An Essay on the Theatre; Or, A Comparison between Laughing and Sentimental Comedy"[34] attempts to establish the true subject matter of comedy by an appeal to tradition. There has always been a distinction between comedy and tragedy, Goldsmith observes, yet modern playwrights have mistakenly attempted to conflate the two. For a right understanding of their essential difference Goldsmith turns to Aristotle, who, he says, defines comedy as "a picture of the Frailties of the lower part of Mankind" and so distinguishes it from tragedy, "which is an exhibition of the Misfortunes of the Great." In this manner (not original, but serviceable) Goldsmith elucidates the precedent on which depends the argument of his essay and of his imminent comedy as well. The two qualities most offensive in the modern, or sentimental, comedy are that it introduces "the Distresses, rather than the Faults of Mankind" and that it disdains everything *low*. Terence, he protests, always stopped short before coming to "the downright pathetic," and Vanbrugh and Cibber, following in his wake, delighted in presenting "Low Comedy." Modern writers, traitors to this tradition, offer characters who are almost always "good" and "exceedingly generous":

> If they happen to have Faults or Foibles, the Spectator is taught not only to pardon, but to applaud them, in consideration of the goodness of their hearts: so that Folly, instead of being ridiculed, is commended, and the Comedy aims at touching our Passions without the power of being truly pathetic. . . . (pp. 4-5)

Having established the governing malady, Goldsmith concludes with a suggestion for its remedy. Sentimental comedy, he says, is "a kind of *mulish* production, with all the defects of its opposite parents, and marked with sterility." The best way to get rid of it

[34] *Westminster Magazine,* I (1773), 4-6.

is simply to administer a dose of its own medicine: "If we are permitted to make Comedy weep, we have an equal right to make Tragedy laugh, and to set down in Blank Verse the Jests and Repartees of all the Attendants in a Funeral Procession" (p. 6).

Goldsmith's dramatic purpose and method in *She Stoops to Conquer* may easily be inferred from the points raised in his "Essay." The general form of the play will derive from the dramatic contrast of lowness and genteelness, encompassing the traits customarily associated with these two opposite modes of behavior. Closely connected with this contrast will be the deliberate use of language wholly unsuited to the social position and "identity" of the character who speaks it. Finally, beneath all this, Goldsmith will have built the solid foundation upon which good comedy must rest: an adequate sense of its relationship to life. Jests at a funeral violate decorum, but mournfulness in life is everywhere accompanied by mirth.

Yet all of this, opportune as it appears, might have failed to carry Goldsmith's purpose to fruition, had it not been for the brilliant structural idea enabling him to wed the thematic contrast between the low and the acceptable to successful creation of comic character. Kelly, Ben Jonson, and other playwrights had divided their characters into two groups, the satirized and the agents of satire. Goldsmith followed their example in the latter case by providing Tony Lumpkin and Kate Hardcastle. But he also went a crucial step further and arranged that *each* of his characters would assume at least two distinct and mutually contradictory identities. The primary target of this device was of course young Marlow, who, as his friend Hastings says, is "impudent enough" with females not blessed by rank but who considers "a modest woman, drest out in all her finery" as "the most tremendous object of the whole creation."[35] Goldsmith's comic strategy places Marlow in situations where he must alternately address the one and then the other, and his genius lay in making both of these persons in reality the same woman. Very much the heir of Shakespeare's comic heroines, Kate is fully aware of her own fundamental identity and also of the pretensions of others deficient in self-knowledge. She consequently can assume and then doff her disguises of the lady of feeling and of barmaid at an

[35] *She Stoops to Conquer: or, The Mistakes of a Night. A Comedy. As it is acted at the Theatre-Royal in Covent-Garden* (1773), Act II, pp. 20-21.

inn without damage to her integrity or to her down-to-earth sense of life. Tony Lumpkin is similarly endowed with the gift of being himself. He plays the ardent lover of Miss Neville for the edification of his society-conscious mother, but there is no doubt that he cares for nothing save sport of all kinds. The rest of the characters (except for Sir Charles Marlow, who appears only at the end) betray affected attempts to be other, and better, than they are, and thus become the established victims of Goldsmith's scheme. In arranging their exposure, Goldsmith devises a double presentation of "the low": Tony Lumpkin low by status and inclination, Kate Hardcastle low by design. The result is that the decorum of character gravely maintained by sentimental playwrights comes in for a thorough reduction to absurdity. Goldsmith pokes holes in the supposed integrity of Marlow, playboy and man of sentiment, by revealing the fundamental egotism that prompts him to idealize himself as his needs require. But the playwright brilliantly proliferates this man-and-mask idea, giving it not only to false pretenders to respectability but also to completely unsentimental or low characters who use it to conquer just as all the others do.

In this way the whole structure of the sentimental play collapses, and the audience is forced to regard points about human individuality conventionally obscured by the single-minded artificiality of "weeping" comedy and, for that matter, of much eighteenth-century high tragedy as well. The enforced re-evaluation of the relationship between art and life carries through the play from the prologue itself. Garrick, its author, evidently caught up in the spirit of Goldsmith's enterprise, sent his actor on tearfully mourning the imminent death of the comic muse. He tries his best to mouth the sententious phrases of the man of sentiment—"All is not gold that glitters, Pleasure seems sweet, but proves a glass of bitters"—but he cannot bring it off. "*To make you laugh,*" he concludes, as Goldsmith himself had in his essay, "*I must play tragedy.*" Similarly, under Goldsmith's direction, the hypocritical Marlow finds himself in a sentimental interview with a most sentimental young lady. "I love to converse," he observes, "only with the more grave and sensible part of the sex." "There is nothing I like so much," she returns, "as grave conversation myself; I could hear it for ever. Indeed I have often been surprized how a man of *sentiment* could ever admire those light airy pleasures, where nothing reaches the heart" (II, pp. 35-36). Yet not much later Kate, impersonating the barmaid of this house that, as Mrs. Hardcastle observes, "looks for all the world like an inn" (I, p. 2), finds Marlow accosting her, vowing she is "vastly handsome," requesting a taste of the "nectar" of her lips, and offering to accompany her to her chamber to judge her embroidery (III, pp. 59-62).

For these sins Marlow must dearly pay. Accordingly Goldsmith sets up a proviso scene combined with a discovery scene which sums up the point of the play by taking the corresponding scene from sentimental comedy and turning it upon its head.

BELCOUR.

> . . . Since the first moment that I saw you, every instant has improv'd you in my eyes, . . . by principle as well as passion I am unalterably yours, in short there are ten thousand causes for my love to you, would to Heaven I could plant one in your soft bosom that might move you to return it!
>
> (V.v, p. 92)

Goldsmith gets the tone of this kind of language just right and at the same time uses it to emphasize the reversal of high and low:

MARLOW.

> Your beauty at first caught my eye; for who could see that without emotion. But every moment that I converse with you, steals in some new grace, heightens the picture, and gives it stronger expression. What at first seem'd rustic plainness, now appears refin'd simplicity. What seem'd forward assurance, now strikes me as the result of courageous innocence, and conscious virtue. (V, p. 101)

Hardcastle and Sir Charles promptly emerge from behind the screen where they have been observing these unaccountable proceedings and take the offender mercilessly to task. All his offenses are thrown open to scrutiny—his "indifference," his "uninteresting conversation," his "cold contempt," his "formal interview." By all standards of sane conduct, Marlow deserves unceremonious rejection. But now Goldsmith, playing his concealed ace, blithely invokes forgiveness. Hardcastle, restraining Marlow from making a hurried exit, offers warm comfort and reassurance:

> I know she'll forgive you. Won't you forgive him, Kate. We'll all forgive you. Take courage, man. (V, p. 103)

Universal forgiveness runs rampant now as the thwarted elopers, Hastings and Miss Neville, are brought within the boundaries of compassion. "Pshaw, pshaw," says Mrs. Hardcastle, driving home the point, "this is all but the whining end of a modern novel" (V, p. 105).

Goldsmith's burlesque of the happy ending constitutes one of the most successful moments of his comedy. Yet there is a sense in which it justifies itself as a dramatic conclusion independent of the satirical purpose that has generally guided the structuring of the play. Because Marlow at last openly repudiates the sentimental basis for his actions—"O, curse on my noisy head," he says; "I never attempted to be impudent yet, that I was not taken down" (V, p. 103)—he has achieved the kind of sanity and self-recognition that make him a satisfactory match for Kate. While fulfilling his desire to lampoon the high astounding seriousness of sentimental behavior on the stage, Goldsmith has not lost sight of his more fundamental purpose to restore a sense of natural character to a society where artificiality (what Cumberland saw as "the level manners of a polish'd country") has become increasingly the mode of life. *She Stoops to Conquer* is both a criticism of the theater and a criticism of life. It would not have been consistent with Goldsmith's comic plan to have sent Marlow off unredeemed. He, as much as Terence, Farquhar, and the other playwrights whose works he invoked as precedents, believed in the soundness of the comic view. It was its perversion, not its essential aim, to which he objected. There are no villains in Goldsmith's play, not only because there are none in the sentimental comedies he set out to expose, but because in his view man is capable of redemption if only he will see himself as he is. A society based on self-knowledge as well as on mutual esteem was, for him, the salutary combination upon which it might subsist and grow. Hardcastle's concluding speech to Marlow so neatly summarizes this idea that it passes itself off as the most natural of hopes:

> So boy take her; and as you have been mistaken in the mistress, my wish is, that you may never be mistaken in the wife. (V, p. 106)

CHAPTER VI

Sheridan's *Pizarro*: Natural Religion and the Artificial Hero

> Such then is MAN, thus venerable in his frame, thus godlike in his nature! How glorious would have been his history; how exalted his attainments; how exquisite and permanent would have been the felicity of this lower world, had man been duly conscious of himself! But alas! whilst other creatures around us remain inviolably true to the original order of their being, it is MAN, and MAN alone, revolts!
>
> —Charles Bulkley, *Apology for Human Nature* (1797)

i. Sheridan and Kotzebue

IF THE NAME of Richard Brinsley Sheridan were not attached to it, *Pizarro* (Drury Lane, 1798-99) might now lie buried in obscurity even deeper than it has found. Modern readers who open a complete edition of his plays continue to discover in astonishment that it was indeed Sheridan, author of *The School for Scandal* and *The Rivals,* who proudly put his name to a work translated from the German of Kotzebue. Even in his own time, Sheridan was regarded by some as a traducer of those high principles of dramatic art illustrated in the composition of his earlier plays and reasserted through irony in *The Critic. Pizarro* seems the work of a playwright perversely adopting the requirements of his own character Puff, who cries out, "Now then for my magnificence!—my battle!—my noise!—and my procession!"—judiciously combining them with those suggested by Don Whiskerandos' love scene: "SITUATION and STAGE EFFECT, by which the greatest applause may be obtained, without the assistance of language, sentiment or character. . . ."[1] Reading Sheridan's grand operatic tragedy today, the student of English drama is apt to shrug his shoulders in tacit acknowledgment that the play, de-

[1] *The Critic,* in *The Plays of Richard Brinsley Sheridan,* ed. R. Crompton Rhodes, 3 vols. (Oxford, 1928), II, 239, 235. Except as noted, subsequent references to Sheridan's plays are to this edition, cited by volume and page.

spite the name of its author, is only too much like the many other dramas of the time that subsist on pathos and parade.

And yet Sheridan's last full-scale theatrical effort produced, in its own day, a response almost totally different from that of uninvolved modern readers. If the play does nothing for Sheridan's reputation as a dramatist, it nevertheless indisputably proves his sure sense as a manager of what Drury Lane audiences would most willingly pay to see. Because his theater was in deep financial difficulty, Sheridan seems to have felt bound to retrieve it from the debts into which his own extravagant management and the ever-increasing costs of scenes and machines had driven it. Surviving records demonstrate that, once he had discovered the possibilities of Kotzebue's *Die Spanier in Peru oder Rollas Tod,* he decided to stake his own reputation and the fortunes of his invalid theater on this one, superb theatrical vehicle. In doing so he brought to bear not only the full acting and designing talent of his company but his own sense, as an author and manager well acquainted with his public, of what would most likely mirror its tastes and interests.

A proved commercial success in its own time, *Pizarro* achieved a popularity comparable in the eighteenth century only to that of *The Beggar's Opera* and so elicits from theater historians the interest aroused by any phenomenally successful play. But behind this unprecedented popularity lie qualities which, for the student of English drama, establish *Pizarro* as perhaps the most representative play of its era. Its political—and politic—concern with the issues of human liberty, then under threat from Napoleonic France, were enough in themselves to rouse the patriotic fervor of British hearts and so insure the success of the play. But with these topical qualities Sheridan combined others of a more "lasting" sort: an appeal to an audience's great attraction to spectacle and general interest in novelty; a lavish outpouring of competent operatic music, processional hymns, and lyrical songs; and an extensive cultivation of the insatiable appetite for pathetic situations. Added to all this was the magnetic force exerted by Drury Lane's stellar company, John Philip Kemble and Sarah Siddons in the ascendant and trailed by the delightful Mrs. Jordan, by the blunt-featured Barrymore and the suave, competent veteran Palmer, and by the highly promising actor of juvenile roles, Charles Kemble, the younger brother of Drury Lane's chief tragedian. [see Plates 15, 16, 17, and 18] Although the playbill according to custom did not mention the name of the author, no reader of London newspapers could have escaped knowing that all this was to issue fully formed from the head of Sheridan, who gathered the entire range of his company's talents to surround the ideally heroic central figure of Rolla, the Peruvian warrior. *Pizarro* merits study, then, by all whose interests lie in the serious contexts—theatrical, political, social, cultural—of a commercial stage success. Sheridan and Kemble worked closely together in creating a hero who somehow draws all these interests together, an archetypal Romantic hero whose responses characterize his life, and death.

The critic for the *Times* summed up the universal response to the first performance on 24 May 1799, pointing out how well Sheridan had judged both his audience and his material:

> The *Death of Rolla*, by KOTZEBUE, and the universal applause with which it was received on the German Stage, induced our English TERENCE to emulate his foreign cotemporary in a similar exhibition. He has closely adhered to the outlines, and has in most instances preserved the sentiments of the original piece, but the language is entirely re-written from the translation with which he was furnished. Mr. SHERIDAN has, after successful exertions in the various lines of Comedy, Opera, and Farce, attempted a production with the boldness and extent of which he does not appear to have been sufficiently impressed. To gratify the present taste in favour of the German drama, and to strengthen a performance constructed after that manner, with the additional attractions of striking machinery, scenic grandeur, and the fascinations of appropriate music, were objects that seemed calculated to combine the different suffrages of the votaries of extreme sensibility and the admirers of romance and spectacle. With these views he has taken up the bow of KOTZEBUE, and supplied it from his own quiver with arrows with which he often dexterously hits the mark, though he frequently scatters them at random. (25 May 1799)

Random shafts were inevitable in a hastily mounted play that, on the first night, occupied close to five hours in representation. The inordinate length of the performance was almost the sole objection registered by the critics; clearly, the play had to be cut. First to go was a grotesque comic sequence in the first act involving a starved underling of Pizarro's.[2] By lopping and cropping individual speeches and portions of scenes throughout the play and at the same time smoothing out the operation of machinery and scene changes, Sheridan quickly brought his piece within acceptable limits. On the second night it was a mere hour and a half too long, the third performance ended shortly after ten o'clock, and after the fourth the critics announced that the play "increases in its effect on every succeeding representation" and that "the Scenes having been considerably shortened, go off with a promptitude and facility that no longer protracts the original interest of the story. . . ."[3] All that was lacking to Sheridan's complete success was remedied when the royal family, having neglected to grace Drury Lane with their presence for some four years, attended the tenth performance on 5 June.

Pathos, spectacle, song, and the peculiar attractiveness of the Germanic—these, unanimously agreed the reviewers, were the ingredients combined so successfully in Sheridan's perfectly balanced recipe. Although Sheridan may easily be convicted of lapses of taste, there is no reason to doubt the sincerity of his dedication of the play to his wife, "whose approbation of this

[2] For an account of this sequence, see the detailed plot summary in the *Oracle, and The Daily Advertiser* review of the first performance (25 May 1799).

[3] For estimates of decreasing performance length see reviews in the *Oracle, and The Daily Advertiser,* 27 May; *Morning Chronicle,* 28 May; and *Morning Herald,* 29 May 1799. According to Crompton Rhodes, the only copy of the play abridged as acted at Drury Lane is in the Garrick Club—*Harlequin Sheridan: The Man and the Legends* (Oxford, 1933), p. 182 and n. This copy, which I have examined, is a first edition, interleaved. Numerous speeches (especially in Act III) have been cut in whole or in part, and many verbal changes introduced into the text, mostly for the sake of decorum or elegance; the entire volume is extensively and meticulously marked for production. Although it is difficult to be certain, the hand is in all likelihood Kemble's. Since the first edition itself must be the product of the cuts and alterations referred to in the paragraph above, the Garrick Club volume must then represent a further stage of revision; one might speculate that it represents Kemble's fresh production of the play after his move to Covent Garden several years later. A timetable written in the margin of the last page indicates a total playing time of two hours fifty-eight minutes (exclusive of intervals between acts). A generation earlier, the average playing time was not much over two hours, and the longest—for *Oedipus*—was two hours forty-eight minutes—J. Brownsmith, *The Dramatic Time-Piece: or Perpetual Monitor* (1767).

Drama," he wrote in the first edition, "and whose peculiar delight in the applause it has received from the Public, have been to *me* the highest gratification its success has produced. . . ." Despite his self-confessed reputation for indolence and procrastination, Sheridan clearly spent considerable effort in making Kotzebue's "Spanish" play suitable for English audiences.

Kotzebue's drama of the Spaniards in Peru was not based on historical accounts such as William Robertson's but on Jean François Marmontel's "roman poétique" *Les Incas* (Paris, 1777).[4] Kotzebue's chief characters are Pizarro, the basely-born Spaniard who rose to become a conqueror of the New World; his paramour Elvira, whom he seduced when she was still a novice in a convent; Alonzo, a young Spanish warrior who discovered Pizarro's cruelty for what it was, defected to the Peruvians, and "married" the lovely young Cora; and Rolla, the chieftain of the Inca's troops, whose early virtuous love for Cora has been sublimated but has not decreased after her marriage to Alonzo. The action of the play occurs in and around the Inca's fortress, the series of battles waged by Spanish and Peruvian troops precipitating the main events. When Alonzo is captured by the Spanish forces, Rolla, knowing full well what may happen to him, disguises himself as a monk and insinuates his way into the dungeon where Alonzo has been thrown preparatory to his execution the following day. Having exchanged clothing with Alonzo and seen him on his way

[4] The Scottish historian Robertson's *The History of America*, 2 vols. (1777), was translated into German in 1777 and into French in 1778. It is clear, as the contemporary antiquary John Britton asserted, that Marmontel is Kotzebue's source—*Sheridan and Kotzebue* (1799), p. 69. Although exotic settings had long been attractive to English readers and playgoers, Dryden and Howard's *The Indian Queen* (Bridges Street, 1663-64) and Dryden's sequel, *The Indian Emperor* (Bridges Street, 1664-65), form a specific elder precedent for English plays about the New World. Within Sheridan's lifetime, as in Dryden's, French romances exerted a strong influence on the subject matter of English drama, Marmontel's *contes* being important exemplars. As early as 1785-86, *The Peruvian . . . By a Lady* (Covent Garden), a comic opera, acknowledged its source as Marmontel's *Coralie, ou L'Amitié à l'Épreuve*—a romance that also provided the plot for Hugh Kelly's *The Romance of an Hour* (Covent Garden, 1774-75); see Allardyce Nicoll, *A History of English Drama 1660-1900*, 2nd edn., III (Cambridge, Eng., 1955), 120-121 and 206 for these and other instances of Marmontel's influence. The subject of New World drama on the English stage has been studied in Benjamin Bissell, *The American Indian in English Literature of the Eighteenth Century* (New Haven, 1925), and Lois Whitney, *Primitivism and the Idea of Progress in English Popular Literature of the Eighteenth Century* (Baltimore, 1934).

to escape, Rolla is discovered by Elvira, who, now disenchanted with Pizarro, plots his murder. Pretending to agree to it, Rolla goes to the tent of Pizarro, who starts up from his sleep but then accepts Rolla's challenge to his magnanimity by setting him free. Alonzo meanwhile returns safely to his beloved Cora, but Rolla is again captured and sentenced to death. When he sees that two Spanish soldiers have kidnapped the infant son of Alonzo and Cora, he swiftly takes the child from their hands and escapes by traversing a bridge over a mountain stream. A bullet from a Spanish weapon mortally wounds him, and he returns dying to the Peruvian stronghold. There, tenderly placing the child in the arms of its grateful mother, he expires.

Sheridan was faithful to this outline, but his task nevertheless loomed large. Examination of his translated text apparently convinced him of its great possibilities for heroic dialogue, particularly in the expression of patriotic sentiment, which he proceeded to "graft" onto the existing text. At the same time he attempted to soften the coarseness of Elvira, little more than a soldier's trull in the original, so that she began to take on some of the characteristics of a high-minded, however low-fallen, heroine. Sheridan began by cutting out as much as he could of the tedium of the first scene, condensing many brief interchanges into slightly longer single speeches and omitting much splenetic dialogue. Evidently concerned to motivate more clearly Elvira's subsequent repudiation of the tyrannical Pizarro, Sheridan has her emerge as a woman with no illusions, taking her passion for Pizarro for what it is but at the same time maintaining her view of the ideal hero and conqueror that Pizarro still has it in him to be. This heightening of Elvira forms part of Sheridan's general concern to elevate his prose to a dignity befitting the lofty aspirations of his characters. Throughout the play a careful reader (and there were not a few such perspicuous readers in Sheridan's own day) can mentally transform his prose into almost perfect iambics. Elvira's impassioned speech to Pizarro after he first enters is typical:

> O, men! men! ungrateful and perverse! O, woman! still affectionate though wrong'd! The Beings to whose eyes you turn for animation, hope, and rapture, through the days of mirth and revelry; and on whose bosoms in the hour of sore calam-

19. A "Peruvian's Vengeance": Barrymore as Pizarro, Kemble as Rolla in Sheridan's *Pizarro*

20. Kemble as Rolla

21. Scene from a command performance of *Pizarro,* Covent Garden, 1804

22. [?Ansell], "PIZZARO [sic] a NEW Play or the DRURY-LANE MASQUERADE" (11 June 1799)

23. Robert Dighton, Kemble as Rolla: "We serve a KING whom we LOVE = a GOD whom we ADORE" (June 1799)

24. Guido Reni (attrib.), Beatrice Cenci

25. Miss O'Neill as Juliet

ity you seek for rest and consolation; THEM, when the pompous follies of your mean ambition are the question, you treat as playthings or as slaves! (III, 25)

Almost everywhere Sheridan attempts this kind of tone, sometimes cutting or transposing speeches not only for the sake of added clarity but with an ear for the full and balanced flow of rhetoric. Although himself not an actor, Sheridan had like his father before him a high interest in declamation and musical intonation.[5] James Boaden's friend Stuart confided to Boaden that he went up into Sheridan's private box about the third night and there observed how the playwright's attention was fixed on the business of the scene. "He repeated every syllable after each performer," Stuart reported, "counting poetically the measure upon his fingers, and sounding with his voice like a music-master, with a degree of earnestness beyond my power to describe."[6]

In Act II Sheridan continued in this vein, combining the enhancement, almost the deification, of Rolla with a variety of dramatic and startling effects. Where Kotzebue depended on narration of off-stage event, Sheridan has the Peruvian ruler Ataliba captured on stage by Spanish soldiers. Not content with this, he transforms Kotzebue's narrated account of how Rolla called back his fleeing forces into a striking presentation of the hero himself, announced by blaring trumpets and stalking on in high indignation, rallying his fear-stricken men under the banner of the Incas and so turning defeat into victory. At this late point Sheridan inserts Kotzebue's earlier scene of an old blind man and a young boy who climbs a tree to report the bloody events, so compressing a haphazard sequence of brief scenes into a splendid moment of triumph as Rolla rescues his captured monarch.

Sheridan then reverts to the German playwright's version, continuing the idealization of his central figure while carefully excising the overt sexuality of Kotzebue's play. Evident throughout is Rolla's superbly simple nobility coupled with an aristocratic flair for polite behavior. Sheridan's cuts manage to eliminate almost all traces of the cool desperation, a product of Rolla's unrequited love for Cora, which motivates him in the original play. The motives of Sheridan's Rolla are more easily assigned: he combines

[5] See Esther K. Sheldon, *Thomas Sheridan of Smock-Alley* (Princeton, 1967).

[6] Boaden, *The Life of Mrs. Jordan* (1831), II, 16-17.

a strong instinct for friendship with a pained sense of unfruitful, virtuous love. Nor does Sheridan spend as much time as Kotzebue in developing motivation; except for his early attention to Elvira, he consistently gives it brief and explosive dramatic statement, as in the scene where Rolla discovers Pizarro asleep in his tent. Here, Rolla sends Elvira away and then in a brief monologue delivered over the motionless body of the tyrant points out the results of criminal ambition. Sheridan goes on to make two basic changes in this scene, both indicative of a purposive shift in the presentation of his dramatic hero. Where in Kotzebue the tyrant starts out of his sleep on his own accord to see Rolla raising a dagger over his breast, Sheridan's Rolla deliberately awakens Pizarro and proclaims his refusal to act in the manner of a base assassin. Consistent with Rolla's high-minded ideals, Sheridan has him execute instead a "Peruvian's vengeance" by throwing the dagger at Pizarro's feet. [see Plate 19] As the conqueror "*walks aside confounded,*" Rolla states the moral lesson implicit in his act: "Can Pizarro be surprised at this! I thought Forgiveness of Injuries had been the Christians' precept—Thou seest, at least, it is the Peruvian's practice" (III, 68).

The last page of the scene is a brief but fiery debate over the qualities of the truly noble man. When Pizarro ruefully admits that "I can face all enemies that dare confront me—I cannot war against my nature," Rolla responds with a definition of the ideal to which he might aspire:

> Then, Pizarro, ask not to be deem'd a hero—To triumph o'er ourselves, is the only conquest, where fortune makes no claim. In battle, chance may snatch the laurel from thee, or chance may place it on thy brow—but in a contest with yourself, be resolute, and the virtuous impulse must be the victor. (III, 71)

It is little wonder that, after such an eloquent assault, Pizarro is stunned into letting Rolla go. When he has left, Pizarro remains alone, a composite of Richard III in the tent scene and Macbeth after his many murders:

> Ambition! tell me what is the phantom I have follow'd, where is the one delight which it has made my own? My fame is the mark of envy—my love the dupe of treachery—my glory

eclips'd by the boy [Alonzo] I taught—my revenge defeated and rebuked by the rude honour of a savage foe—before whose native dignity of soul I have sunk confounded and subdued! I would I cou'd retrace my steps—I cannot—Would I could evade my own reflections!—no living!—thought and memory are my Hell.[7]

Rolla's character is now complete; all that remains is his equally heroic death. To accomplish this, Sheridan made perhaps the most important single change in the play, inventing a brilliant *coup de théâtre* whose scenic sublimity caps Sheridan's inveterate concern to achieve the utmost in visual splendor, magnificence, and picturesque detail. Following the same tendency evident in Kemble's opulent production of *Macbeth* five years before,[8] Sheridan translates imaginative suggestiveness into a completely realized scene of spectacular sights and sounds. Where Kotzebue had provided a soldier to relate how Rolla escaped from the Spaniards and at the same time rescued Cora's child, Sheridan substitutes a new scene laid in "*The Out-Post of the Spanish Camp.—The back ground wild and rocky, with a Torrent falling down the Precipice, over which a Bridge is formed,*" to which for good measure is added "*A fell'd Tree*" (III, 76). So employing the elaborate talents of his painters and machinists, Sheridan begins the scene downstage with Pizarro and a group of his soldiers sadistically confronting Rolla with their possession of the infant. In a desperate feat, Rolla snatches the child from the soldiers' grasp, runs off, and a moment later appears well up-stage, near the back scene, crossing the wooden bridge high over the cataract and pursued by soldiers who at Pizarro's command fire at him. Mortally wounded, Rolla staggers to the other side of the bridge where he "*tears from the rock the tree which supports the bridge*" (III, 78), sends it plummeting down, and then disappears. The crucial moment of rescue, just as the hero has retrieved the infant from the Spanish soldiers, finds Kemble holding the child high in one hand, an attitude made famous by Sir Thomas Lawrence's painting of him and reflected also in an engraving of a

[7] III, 71. The above reference to Richard III and Macbeth may convey a sense of the importance of Shakespearean analogy in the contemporary drama of the late eighteenth century. For discussions of the critical and theatrical response to these two figures in this period see Part III.

[8] See Pt. III, Chap. X, pp. 261-264.

command performance of *Pizarro* at Covent Garden in 1804. [see Plates 20 and 21] These depictions of one of Kemble's most memorable "points" show him evidently just as he utters his heroically defiant threat, "Who moves one step to follow me, dies upon the spot" (III, 78). Together they fully illustrate Sheridan's combination of lavish scenic display with the heroic sentiment—and imminent pathetic destruction—of his central figure.[9]

The next scene, as in Kotzebue, presents Rolla returning to Peruvian ground. Sheridan, pruning away all hints of the superfluous, writes a scene composed of five brief speeches in which Rolla restores the child to its mother, apologizes for bloodying its gown, and falls lifeless. The obvious effect is of a single moment, a graphic emblem of self-sacrificing human virtue. To maintain its visual impact Sheridan ignores Kotzebue's ending of the play at this point and adds his own concluding sequence. A flagrant violation of the facts of history, Sheridan's ending by no means violates any of the principles that have guided him in the adaptation of his German source. The playwright arranges to have Rolla die in the midst of the Spaniards' last attempt to capture the Inca fortress. Multitudes of Peruvian warriors rush onto the stage followed by multitudes of the enemy. But, in true Homeric style, the promised carnage is averted by Pizarro and Alonzo's decision to determine the fate of nations by single combat. As Pizarro is about to slay Alonzo, the penitent Elvira suddenly appears, dressed in the costume of her novitiate in which Pizarro first saw and desired her. Her unexpected presence distracts the Spaniard long enough for Alonzo to rally himself and dispatch the hated tyrant with his sword.

Nor is this conclusion enough for Sheridan. Neither Rolla nor Drury Lane's capabilities for spectacle must be forgotten. Marshalling almost his entire cast of principals, subordinates, supernumeraries, and chorus onto the boards, Sheridan stages a grand procession in which the body of Rolla is carried to the center of the scene on a bier "*surrounded by Military Trophies.*" As priests and priestesses chant a dirge,[10] Alonzo and Cora "*kneel on either*

[9] See the discussions of these graphic works and of a recently discovered painting of the scene in Anthony Oliver and John Saunders, "De Loutherbourg and Pizarro, 1799," *TN*, XX (1965), 30-32 and Plate I; and Raymond Mander and Joe Mitchenson, "De Loutherbourg and Pizarro, 1799," *TN*, XX (1966), 160 and Plate II.

[10] The dirge, as well as the rest of the vocal music of the play—all by

side of it, and kiss ROLLA'*s hands in silent agony. . . .*" The last great pictorial—and thematic—effect arranged by the playwright is evident from his concluding stage direction: "*In the looks of the King, and of all present, the Triumph of the Day is lost, in mourning for their Hero*" (III, 81).

However much some critics objected to Sheridan's engrafted conclusion, the majority reaction fully justified his efforts. The reviewer for the *Morning Chronicle* pointed out that, in effect, Sheridan knew very well what he was doing and that he should be praised for his accomplishment. "It has been so constantly the practice to waste enormous expence in the decoration, machinery, dresses, and processions of pieces which had no other merit than their shew," he said, "that it is a new thing to the Theatre to have the utmost possible magnificence combined with a drama, which arouses all the best emotions of the soul, and is animated in parts by the most glowing eloquence." The scenery, dresses, and music, he went on, are "grand and magical." But "when to these are added the skilful development of the most vehement passions, by language at once simple and nervous, in which, without being overloaded by ornament, there are images at once beautiful and new, with periods of the most exquisite tenderness, it must be the general sentiment that the performance is a great acquisition to the stock of theatrical amusement" (25 May 1799). An early nineteenth-century critic suggests the comprehensiveness of the *Chronicle*'s estimate in calling the play "one of the most beautiful specimens of the *romantic drama* that exists." Some of the scenes, he observes, are "most strikingly thrown together," while others "(to use common language) *run away with the heart*."[11] Sheridan's expert combination of elegant spectacle and touching pathos produced the results he anticipated. But it must not be forgotten that the success of the play was due in great part not only to its essential dramatic and theatrical qualities but to the additional fact that it appeared at a particularly critical moment in the history of the British nation. Many of the sentiments expressed were, as Sheridan must have shrewdly calculated, designed to appeal to

Michael Kelly—is preserved in *The Music of Pizarro* (1799); a copy exists in the British Museum. For Kelly's entertaining account of his involvement in the production, see his *Reminiscences* (1826), II, 160-163.

[11] Henry Mercer Graves, *An Essay on the Genius of Shakespeare, with Critical Remarks on the Characters of Romeo, Hamlet, Juliet, and Ophelia* . . . (1826), p. 65.

the Briton's high sense of patriotism and so, in a special sense, to "run away with his heart."

ii. England Under the Incas

The visit of George III and his royal family to the theater in Drury Lane created a stir of excitement seldom equalled. Not only was the theater itself crowded to capacity but adjacent streets and alleys were congested with those unable to force their way inside. Many who did manage that feat paid the higher price for a box seat and then clambered over the box into the pit, where they might see as well as be seen. The royal box, the object of Sheridan's special attention, had been lavishly decorated with spring flowers and shrubs. Sheridan was exploiting the singular occasion for all its worth. Along with the other two proprietors, Richardson and Grubb, he met the royal party at the door of the theater and escorted them to their places, each of the three walking before and lighting the way with a pair of candles.[12] "On the entrance of the Royal Party," reported the *London Packet,* "the roar of acclamation from all parts of the Theatre was prolonged for nearly ten minutes" (5-7 June 1799). When the King and his entourage were settled in their places, the Drury Lane chorus and soloists came onto the stage, accompanied by the Duke of York's band, and sang *God Save the King.* So great was patriotic fervor that the hymn was promptly encored.

A few days later the political caricaturist Ansell brought out a satirical print that captures much of the situation's flavor. Seizing on the fact of Sheridan's long membership in the opposition in Parliament, he depicted the playwright holding a flaming candle aloft to lead George III and his party to their seats. As Sheridan calls out for *God Save the King* to be played "Louder," the King on entering his box observes, "No! no! no Jacobins here, all Loyal, all Loyal. Charming Man the Author eh charming Man, never saw him in such a good light before."[13] [see Plate 22] It was indeed obvious that Sheridan's own politics were involved in the situation, and political commentators and caricaturists took the occasion as an opportunity to brand him a turn-coat or, at

[12] *Morning Chronicle,* 6 June 1799.

[13] "PIZZARRO a NEW Play or the DRURY-LANE MASQUERADE," Print Room, British Museum, No. 9397 in B.M. *Catalogue of Personal and Political Satires,* ed. Mary Dorothy George, VII (1942).

least, a hypocrite. The *Anti-Jacobin Review* published a print depicting a conniving Sheridan and captioned, "In Pizzarro's [sic] plans observe the Statesman's wisdom guides the *poormans Heart*."[14] Others strongly hinted that Sheridan was no more than an opportunist, making both political and financial capital out of an improbable piece of fustian rhetoric. One of the most sharply barbed of such attacks, captioned "PIZARRO returning from the Gold Mines of Peru!" shows the author reeling across the stage under the weight of an immense bag thrown over his shoulder and leaving behind a trail of coins which have fallen through a hole in the bottom. As he labors along, Sheridan is made to say: "I must hurry home or I shall be waylaid by the Jacobin Banditti! My heart sinks and my sack seems lighter every step I go. Pizarro, Pizarro, what a fortunate General thou has been, with the aid of a single Officer, the great Rolla, to have work'd such wonders!!"[15]

Although Sheridan made vast amounts of money from his scheme, the royal visit to his theater was of course not to be interpreted as a personal favor to him. What undoubtedly drew the King was his curiosity to see a play that had become overnight a famous piece of loyalist propaganda. Reviews as early as the first performance had praised the play for arousing patriotic feeling at a time when the safety of the British nation was severely jeopardized by the activities of the French. One critic observed that Rolla's harangue to the Peruvian army before the battle contained "some very happy allusions to the contest in which we are at present engaged with the inveterate enemies of social order and happiness. . . ."[16] Sheridan's inserted speech bears the imprint of a seasoned parliamentary orator able to judge in advance the exact effect his carefully chosen words will produce:

> My brave associates—partners of my toil, my feelings and my fame!—can Rolla's words add vigour to the virtuous energies which inspire your hearts?———NO—YOU have judged as I have, the foulness of the crafty plea by which these bold invaders would delude you—Your generous spirit has compared as mine has, the motives, which, in a war like this, can animate *their* minds, and OURS. THEY, by a

[14] IV (1799), p. 318.
[15] Print Room, British Museum, No. 9397.
[16] *Evening Mail*, 24-27 May 1799.

> strange frenzy driven, fight for power, for plunder, and extended rule—WE, for our country, our altars, and our homes. —THEY follow an Adventurer whom they fear—and obey a power which they hate—WE serve a Monarch whom we love—a God whom we adore. . . . [see Plate 23] The throne WE honour is the PEOPLE'S CHOICE—the laws we reverence are our brave Fathers' legacy—the faith we follow teaches us to live in bonds of charity with all mankind, and die with hope of bliss beyond the grave. Tell your invaders this, and tell them too, we seek no change; and, least of all, such change as they would bring us. (III, 37)

The *Times* reported that His Majesty was "peculiarly gratified" with Rolla's address (6 June 1799). The moment was, to use the fashionable word for such things, "electric." Rolla's speech drew a burst of applause that lasted, according to one estimate, for a full five minutes.[17] The reviewer for the *Morning Post,* little short of ecstatic, found it "hardly possible to describe the rapturous bursts of loyalty and patriotism that arose . . ." (6 June 1799). Even those who saw a purpose less lofty behind Sheridan's interpolated speech could not help being impressed with "the dexterity with which he has engrafted his loyal *clap traps.*"[18]

Although many critical notices, both at the opening and on the occasion of the King's visit, confined themselves to such obvious reflections, others viewed the play within a wider and more significant context. The central contrast of the production, said one of these writers, derives from the opposition of the characters of Pizarro and Rolla. While the first is completely callous, a low and unprincipled scoundrel, the latter is the chief spokesman for the high morality of the play, a hero who "sacrifices his happiness and his life to the impulse of the noblest feelings." Thematically the point of this contrast is that it juxtaposes "European" cruelty, which we justly abhor, with the happy characteristics of "a peaceable and virtuous people." The representation of this noble race on the stage, the reviewer explained, "excites the pity and interest of humanity" in their favor.[19] Similarly, the critic for the *Morning Chronicle* cited what he thought were the distinctive qualities of the play: its piety, spirit of independence, love of jus-

[17] *London Packet,* 5-7 June 1799.
[18] *Monthly Magazine,* VIII (1799), 1056.
[19] *Evening Mail,* 24-27 May 1799.

tice and humanity, and exhortation to benevolent concern. This last characteristic, he found, was perhaps the most necessary, since its effect is "to rouse us from that ignominious apathy to the fate of our fellow creatures, which is too truly imputable at this moment to the English people" (27 May 1799). Still another writer pointed out the fundamental connection between benevolent interest in others and the quality of one's own life which gives rise to it. Because the play inspires a sense of "genuine religion," he said, it will prove to be a school for the nation's youth, serving to revive in them a "glorious feeling of generosity."[20]

It is impossible not to infer from these comments that Sheridan built his sturdy political edifice upon the familiar foundation of English sentimentalism. The playwright spent considerable effort in shaping the rhetoric of his literal translation and in enhancing its possibilities for elaborate spectacle, but he undoubtedly took interest also in working out the implications of the political issues involved. In a sense, the drama is a *pièce à clef*. Sheridan must have known that Rolla's perfervid oratory on the subject of God, King, and Country would immediately suggest to his audience that the Peruvians under threat of subjugation by foreign imperialists were emblematic of the peaceable and orderly English menaced by the Napoleonic *conquistadores* just across the channel. There are, however, no explicitly parallel characters, with the possible exception of Pizarro as a figure for Napoleon himself. Certainly, not even those critics most ready to see the play as a kind of political allegory made connections between Pizarro and the French general, between the Inca king Ataliba and George III, or between Rolla and any corresponding leader of English forces like Nelson. Sheridan seems to have avoided any hint of precise correlation and to have sought instead a general parallel between the piety and natural goodness of the Peruvian primitive and those same qualities that Englishmen saw, through glistening eyes, in themselves. Perhaps he felt that anything closer to home would have given his play some of the qualities of political satire observable in *The Beggar's Opera*, a work that deliberately sets out "to asperse *somebody* in Authority."[21] Obvi-

[20] *General Evening Post*, 23-25 May 1799.

[21] "A Compleat Key to the Beggar's Opera, by Peter Padwell of Paddington, Esq." (1728), quoted by William Eben Schultz, *Gay's Beggar's Opera: Its Content, History, & Influence* (New Haven, 1923), p. 181.

ously, as a vehement member of the opposition Sheridan could hardly afford to jeopardize the financial success of *Pizarro* by laying open old wounds and so exposing his play to the charge of arousing political controversy. If a precedent exists, it is not Gay's ballad opera but Addison's *Cato,* a solemn high Augustan tragedy whose central figure almost magically united the warring factions of Whig and Tory in the cause of selfless devotion to home and country.[22] Sheridan carefully raised his audience's sense of patriotism above the level of mere partisan conflicts, exploiting its more general and subtle implications until the spirit of the true patriot became indistinguishable from the spirit of the truly benevolent man.

Undoubtedly, a great measure of Sheridan's success derived from his ability to suppress anything specific enough to appeal to one faction at the cost of alienating another. Whig and Tory prejudice are skillfully avoided, but Sheridan went even further than this. Apparently because religious denominational bias could ruin the play just as quickly as political bias, he allowed nothing in the dialogue or situations to point either at the established church or any recusant congregation. His safety lay in the distance of geography and history that separated late Georgian England from the Spanish conquest of South America. Primitives like the Peruvian Indians could hardly be expected to know of the Christian deity. Before Pizarro and his hordes descended upon them they simply followed the dictates of their consciences in paying obeisance to the sun-god, whose unfailing warmth brought life, health, and sustenance to his people and inspired in them the natural virtues that kept them at peace with one another. When the Spanish did come, it was clear that their version of religion, although professedly Christian, served merely as a pretext for slaughter and rapine. Sheridan's treatment of Rolla and his compatriots thus

[22] In John Oldmixon's account, Addison's *Cato* was produced "at the latter End of Queen *Ann*'s Reign, when the old *English* Spirit of Liberty was as likely to be lost as it had ever been since the Conquest"; Addison's motive, Oldmixon said, was "to support the old *Roman* and *English* Public Spirit, which was then so near being suppressed by Faction and Bigotry"—*An Essay on Criticism* (1728), p. 6. M. M. Kelsall, who adduces Oldmixon's view, calls attention to the fact that the historical Cato was a brilliant choice of Addison's, since Cato combined the exemplary philosophical virtue of a Socrates with distinct qualities of political heroism, so uniting two themes in one—"The Meaning of Addison's *Cato,*" *RES,* XVII (1966), 149-162.

makes the most of a doctrine dear to the English benevolist's heart, the notion of the noble savage.

English fascination with primitive societies was never higher than in the late eighteenth century. As students of the history of ideas have shown, one of the fundamental tenets of sentimental moral philosophy was that man, being essentially good, could trust that his first responses were inherently virtuous.[23] Even the primitive man, isolated from his supposedly enlightened Christian fellows and living in the bleak discomfort of an arctic clime or amidst the luxuriant vegetation of a tropical isle, displayed a belief in an all-powerful, all-loving deity. Unerringly following their own natural impulse to be guided by providential order, such men achieved lives of virtue unaided by sober reflection or conversion to Christianity. Bishop Butler's *Analogy* was only one of many theological treatises written in the age of Johnson and afterwards which attempted to show that man is by nature a religious creature.[24] In an age when belief in God was being put

[23] The summary here and in subsequent paragraphs of ideas about primitivism and of sentimental moral philosophy depends partly on scholarship cited in Chap. V, note 3, and partly on the following representative works: C. B. Tinker, *Nature's Simple Plan* (Princeton, 1922); A. O. Lovejoy, "The Supposed Primitivism of Rousseau's Discourse On Inequality," *MP*, XXI (1923), 165-186; Hoxie Neale Fairchild, *The Noble Savage: A Study in Romantic Naturalism* (New York, 1928); Lovejoy, "Monboddo and Rousseau," *MP*, XXX (1933), 275-296; Lovejoy and George Boas, *Primitivism and Related Ideas in Antiquity* (Baltimore, 1935); Edith Amelie Runge, *Primitivism and Related Ideas in Sturm und Drang Literature* (Baltimore, 1946); and Whitney, *Primitivism and the Idea of Progress.*

[24] Joseph Butler, *The Analogy of Religion, Natural and Revealed, to the Constitution and Course of Nature* (1736). Among earlier works, Samuel Clarke's Boyle Lectures of 1705, printed as *A Discourse Concerning the Unchangeable Obligations of Natural Religion, and the Truth and Certainty of the Christian Revelation* (1706), evinced a notable attempt to prove that man's basic religious impulses stem from his moral sense, of which revealed religion acts as a preserver or restorative. By mid-century the notion had developed sufficiently to allow Lord Kames to identify man's moral sense with the selfless principle of benevolence, which at once checks the appetites and passions and prompts him to seek the happiness of all his fellow men—*Essays on the Principles of Morality and Natural Religion* (Edinburgh, 1751). The supposed universality of man's natural religious sense is summed up most familiarly by Pope in his *Essay on Man*:

> For Modes of Faith, let graceless zealots fight;
> His can't be wrong whose life is in the right:
> In Faith and Hope the world will disagree,

seriously to the test by the writings of Hobbes, Gibbon, Hume, and other materialistic, mechanistic, or otherwise unorthodox thinkers, sincere believers were forced to re-examine the foundations of their religion. One of the most often-employed strategies for proving the existence of God thus became the attempt to draw an analogy, as did Bishop Butler, between revealed religion and its "natural" counterpart. Proponents of natural religion, as it was called, held that all men, irrespective of the influence of conventional, institutionalized religion, are naturally inclined toward moral behavior, thus demonstrating the presence of the deity that created them and teaches them how to live by operating on their instincts. The radical nature of this argument can hardly be ignored. Whereas traditional proofs for the existence of God were founded on reason and dealt with a first cause and with the observed order of the universe, the proof through natural religion came to be based instead primarily on instinct, or what amounted to such. Lord Kames's statement of the idea in his *Essays on the Principles of Morality and Natural Religion* is representative:

> . . . to found our knowledge of the Deity solely upon reasoning, is not agreeable to the analogy of nature. We are not left to gather our duty by abstract reasoning, nor indeed by any reasoning. It is engraved upon the table of our hearts. We adapt our actions to the course of nature, by mere instinct, without reasoning, or even experience. Therefore, if we can trust to analogy, we ought to expect, that God will discover himself to us, in some such manner, as may take in all mankind, the vulgar and illiterate, as well as the deep thinking philosopher. (p. 316)

Man's untutored natural responses, then, are enough to establish the fact that God lives and acts for good in the hearts of men.

Sheridan's play clearly reflects this argument. In addition to providing in the character of Rolla the epitome of the noble savage, Sheridan also takes care to make Kotzebue's youthful warrior Alonzo a spokesman for the idea. His choice of Alonzo is an

---

> But all Mankind's concern is Charity:
> All must be false that thwart this One great End,
> And all of God, that bless Mankind or mend.
> (III, 305-310)

obvious and felicitous one, since the German playwright had presented him as a member of Pizarro's band of cutthroats who had undergone a kind of conversion and defected to the Peruvian side. Alonzo's experience provides exactly the perspective required. In the second act, after being captured by the Spaniards, he is brought in chains to the tent of Pizarro. The Spanish general upbraids him mercilessly for deserting, but Alonzo's response reveals the purity of his motive. "When those legions," he retorts, "lured by the abhorred lust of gold, and by thy foul ambition urged, forgot the honour of Castilians, and forsook the duties of humanity, THEY deserted ME" (III, 53). Alonzo goes on to explain the good that has come of his defection. When he first saw the fields of Quito they were barren, but his industry has brought about the "sweet bashful pledges of delicious harvest, wafting their incense to the ripening sun. . . ." Where before had existed injurious customs and "superstitions strange and sullen" which had worked for evil on the believing minds of those innocents, he can now point with justifiable pride to the villages where "they live like brethren, social and confiding, while through the burning day Content sits basking on the cheek of Toil. . . ." Finally, and most impressively, Alonzo boasts that pure religion lives uppermost in the hearts of these men. He fondly describes them "at that still pause between exertion and repose, belonging not to pastime, labour, or to rest, but unto Him who sanctions and ordains them all. . . ." At this point in their daily lives, Alonzo observes, one may find "many an eye, and many a hand, by gentleness from error won, raised in pure devotion to the true and only God!"[25] Evidently Sheridan is not at all bothered by petty inconsistencies. On the one hand, the Incan civilization, historically a

[25] III, 54. Alonzo's description of the ideal society of the Peruvians bears a striking resemblance to Bishop Butler's description of a society founded on natural virtue: "But let us return to the Earth, our Habitation; and we shall see this happy Tendency of Virtue, by imagining . . . a Kingdom or Society of Men upon it, perfectly virtuous, for a Succession of many ages; to which, if you please, may be given a Situation advantageous for universal Monarchy. In such a State, there would be no such thing as Faction: but Men of the greatest Capacity would of Course, all along, have the chief Direction of Affairs willingly yielded to them; and they would share it among themselves without Envy. Each of these would have the Part assigned him, to which his Genius was peculiarly adapted; and others, who had not any distinguished Genius, would be safe, and think themselves very happy, by being under the Protection and Guidance of those who had"—*Analogy*, p. 63.

highly developed and complex one, is presented in the play as a nation of simple primitives living in a ripe Golden Age. On the other, Alonzo's Spanish "know-how" has transformed barrenness into fertility through the benevolent imposition of Westernizing "civilization."

Sheridan is clearly having it both ways at once. If Alonzo's description sounds like the satisfied report of a zealous Christian missionary, the suggestion that the Peruvians have converted to Christianity is effectively neutralized by consistent references in the play to a god at once the Christian deity introduced by Alonzo and the time-honored sun. At the most important of these points Alonzo, imprisoned and, as he thinks, about to die, pronounces a soliloquy in which he addresses the presiding power. "For the last time, O sun!" he laments, "I shall behold thy rising. . . ." As the sun comes up on cue Alonzo resolves not to watch, but simply to offer his "last prayer to thee, Power Supreme" for his wife and child (III, 60-61). Enough ambiguity appears in this soliloquy to suggest that Alonzo in effect identifies belief in the God of the Christians with belief in the Sun of the Incas. It is evident that the light of the world is the power worshipped by Peruvians and Christians alike. The forms of religion may vary widely, but when discovered in its irreducible essence religion is no less than that force which brings all men to acknowledge and love the one omnipotent, benevolent god. This same power moves men to act with truly selfless and noble purpose. "I thought Forgiveness of Injuries had been the Christians' precept," Rolla says as he throws his dagger at Pizarro's feet; "Thou seest, at least, it is the Peruvian's practice" (III, 68).

In this way Sheridan has the best of both worlds. By introducing Alonzo's Christian charity and energy, partly the product of his Castilian upbringing, he could avoid giving the impression of exalting Peruvian religious life at the expense of the Christian way known to all Englishmen. At the same time, by making Pizarro the scapegoat for all that was decadent in conventional religion, he increased by contrast his audience's sense of the natural virtue demonstrated in the heroic acts and even the daily lives of South American "savages." Sheridan thus succeeded in skirting issues that might divide his audience and, worse still, drive them out of the theater. And so his play realized, at least as far as Drury Lane audiences were concerned, the aspirations that he held perhaps from the moment that his anonymous translator put into his hands the Englished text of Kotzebue's melodramatic Spanish tale.

Yet the very fact that Sheridan had avoided giving offense to so many became, perversely, the cause of offense to others. Reviewers during the initial run of the play unanimously acclaimed the high sentiment, lofty expression, patriotic fervor, and engaging spectacle of *Pizarro*, but the criticism that grew up over succeeding months took a less simple view. Often spurred by a reading of the printed text as well as, or instead of, experiencing the play in the theater, certain writers began to attack it for its moral duplicity.

An essay in the *Lounger* in 1785 anticipated the main points of this critical attack in discussing the relationship between character and the moral effect of dramatic representations. Modern audiences, the writer of the essay suggested, are no longer willing to accept characters whose actions are easily discernible as completely good or vicious. Refined theatergoers now require "shades of character more delicate. . . ." The consequence is that "the bounds of right and wrong are often so uncertainly marked" that poetic power and eloquent sentiment may be used on behalf of either, with an evident, debilitating effect on the minds of the youthful and inexperienced.[26] In the next number the writer went on to explain that "the dignity of the scene" may well hide the very real evils inherent in the subject matter. By thus falsifying or ignoring the true moral nature of circumstances, the play allows us to indulge ourselves in "the fantastic and imaginary distresses" which it presents.[27] He describes the character of Macbeth, whom he acknowledges a tyrant and murderer, as one we are nevertheless disposed to pity rather than to hate. That the offender is finally punished is not enough to disengage the play from its morally hurtful tendencies, since the "striking incidents" and "sentiments running through the tenor of a piece" may well leave a more telling impression than the last-minute punishment with which it ends (p. 111). In fact the very virtues of such "mixed" characters as Macbeth are often dangerous bases on which to form principles, because instead of leading to moral actions in real life they may remain merely "shining and showy

[26] *Lounger,* No. 27 (6 August 1785), p. 108.
[27] No. 28 (13 August 1785), p. 110.

qualities" that arouse vanity and trap applause. Perhaps the most distressing quality of performed tragedy, the writer concludes, is that it seems impossible to separate an act virtuous in itself from the vicious effects it may produce: "The extreme, the enthusiasm even of a laudable propensity, takes from its usefulness to others, and degenerates into a blind and headlong indulgence in the possessor" (p. 112).

Palliation of guilt, then, according to this observer, is the primary characteristic of "modern" tragedy and modern audiences as well. Yet he offers no real solution to the difficulty, and indeed the only one available seemed to be to avoid plays altogether. For the eminent moral philosopher William Richardson, as for this lesser writer and many others of his day, there appeared to be no moral consistency in the fact that man's ability to respond sympathetically often led him unwittingly to immorality and even self-destruction. One was the result of the other, yet both somehow remained subsumed within the supposedly innate goodness of man. Richardson's way out of the difficulty was the unsatisfactory one of saying that we should observe in others the tendency to let one passion dominate the mind and heart, and by seeing the dire effects of it to avoid it ourselves.[28] For the many critics who found *Pizarro* inconsistent in this way, however, it was apparently enough simply to vilify the playwright for moral laxity or at least to demonstrate in a general way that the subjective approach to character held implicit in it the destruction of all traditional, objective codes of behavior.

"Kotzebue is fond of singularity," observed a reviewer of Sheridan's published text. Far from following established models for the creation of character, he instead delights in giving common events an unexpected turn or in focusing on a passion found more frequently in books than in real life.[29] Another writer (perhaps the only theater critic who broached the subject) asserted that Kotzebue deals with the "bold delineation of dangerous Passions," and he is even bolder in asserting their claims in the face of condemnation by civil and religious institutions. Because of this daring venture into forbidden areas, the popularity of Kotzebue's plays throughout Europe is extraordinarily high. Readers

[28] *Essays on Shakespeare's Dramatic Characters,* 6th edn. (1812), p. 196. For a discussion of Richardson's idea see Pt. III, Chap. IX below, pp. 201-205.
[29] *Critical Review,* XXVI (1799), 308.

approach his works not only with "anxious avidity" but with "curiosity and alarm."[30] Because of the unusual attractiveness of Kotzebue's characters and their unbridled passions, many critics felt bound to attack *Pizarro*. Some were highly indignant that the celebrated Sheridan could stoop so low as to foist on the English public "the filthy effusions of this German Dunce!"[31] Others proceeded with only a little more restraint to examine "the most subtle and dangerous poison" they thought lurked beneath the characters of Elvira and Rolla and behind the "veil of sentiments of the most noble nature" in the play as a whole.[32]

Typical of these attacks is the analysis of Elvira offered to the readers of the *Anti-Jacobin Review*:

> Elvira is one of the most reprehensible characters that was ever suffered to disgrace the stage, and yet she goes off unpunished. We see here a fresh attempt, perfectly reconcileable, however, to the new system of philosophy—we behold the principles of a prostitute held up in an enviable light, and, as the author tells us, endeavouring to draw down our pity and our admiration—vice, of a nature the most threatening to the well-being of society, is rendered amiable by the poet's aid—there is not a girl of any elevation of spirit and ignorance of the world, who will not, on witnessing the effusion of this unusual personage in the drama, cry out, "How admirable Elvira's sentiments and conduct are!"[33]

It is not surprising, after this, to find the writer's political bias brought into play. "I maintain," he almost shouted, "that Elvira is nothing less than a complete Godwinite heroine, stark staring *Mary* all over!" (p. 209). This condemnation—a case of guilt by association with Mary Wollstonecraft—illustrates the perennial connection in the popular mind between unorthodox political belief and immoral conduct, in this instance between British radicalism and German "immorality." Such a complete and indignant rejection of Sheridan's play might be dismissed as no more than an attack on the playwright's own politics, were it not that other writers of no discoverable political bias said much the same thing, if in less strident tones. The pseudonymous author of

[30] *St. James's Chronicle*, 25-28 May 1799.
[31] *Anti-Jacobin Review*, III (1799), 210.
[32] Philipus Philaretes, *Adultery Analyzed* (1810), p. 122.
[33] III (1799), p. 208.

Adultery Analyzed neatly and coolly summarized Sheridan's purpose "to elevate Elvira to the rank of an heroine in the estimation of the audience. . . ." The sentiments of courage and precepts of goodness that she utters in the course of the play, he explained, betray the playwright's open attempt to controvert the "first grand principle of morals, that those may be truly great who are not truly good" (p. 130).

This sense of the heroic serves to establish the most important aspect of Elvira's "alternately amiable and profligate" character.[34] In Kotzebue's play the character is interesting for her impassioned criticism of Pizarro, but plainly she remains hardly more than a camp-follower. Sheridan was faced with the task of "improving" the character sufficiently to make it palatable to decorous English audiences. That he succeeded, at least to some degree, is evident in the reviews of the first performances. But later critics with more leisure to reflect upon the niceties of consistent characterization conveniently forgot that Nicholas Rowe had performed the same task in rendering pathetic the mistress of Edward IV. Although Sheridan obviously had the precedent of *Jane Shore,* still frequently performed, on which to base his portrait of Elvira, these critics insisted that the playwright's penitent heroine did no more than display the "latitude of modern principles" according to which a degraded female character is elevated "into the first rank of heroines, by the splendour of her conduct at the conclusion. . . ."[35]

Elvira's pretensions as a heroine were thus suspect to many, and it is easy to understand that, in a period of English life when women were often ceremoniously idealized, not a few writers could view any hint of inconsistency in the dramatic portrait as a slander upon the sex. Less easy to understand, at least initially, are the objections raised to the character of Rolla. These are admittedly minor when placed beside the predominant view of him as the epitome of nobility and virtue. Yet, because they relate so closely to the central philosophical and moral issues of the play, these objections must be considered in attempting to provide a balanced view of Romantic attitudes toward the dramatic hero.

The *Anti-Jacobin Review,* ever vigilant in the cause of the English constitution and English morality, provided a typical depre-

[34] *British Critic,* XIV (1799), 64.

[35] *Gentleman's Magazine,* LXIX (1799), 691.

ciatory analysis of *Pizarro*'s central character. In a review of Anne Plumptre's *The Virgin of the Sun* (Kotzebue's earlier play, *Die Sonnenjungfrau*, to which *Rollas Tod* forms the sequel) the *Anti-Jacobin* explained the principle underlying the sense of virtue exhibited in the play. This principle, said the writer, is simply "that which permits the full gratification of passion, without any regard to existing institutions. . . ."[36] Consequently the character of Rolla, although masquerading as the pattern of masculine excellence, is actually an instance of "the flimsy and false morality which makes virtue consist in acting agreeable to the impulse of passion, instead of fixed principles" (p. 443). A writer in the *Gentleman's Magazine*, concentrating on this same notion, perceived a close connection between the tendency of *Pizarro* to exalt "Deism," or "natural religion," and its concept of dramatic character. The notion of instinctive response consequently explains not only the religion of the Peruvians but their every action as well:

> Human feeling seems to be the grand principle of action. Rolla acts from feeling; Ataliba acts from feeling; Elvira is made up of these feelings, and in such a manner, that a show of what are called good [sic] may cover most portentous sins, and hold up her character to admiration. By this conduct it is that Kotzebue endeavours to gain his hearers and readers. By flattering the passions, he attempts powerfully to interest the heart; and, when that is gained, insidiously instils his venomous principles.[37]

Moral ambiguity lurks at the very center of the play, according to these writers. Almost to a man, they blamed the collapse of British morals, as James Boaden later did, on vicious Germanic forces that had infiltrated and undermined the purity of the English drama.[38] It was, they contended, the phenomenal attractive-

[36] III (1799), p. 441.

[37] LXIX (1799), 833-834. One may see the result of what this writer views as a pernicious process in John Britton's response to Sheridan's revisions: "Pizarro in the original is left unpunished, unreclaimed, contrary to the general practice of dramatic exhibitions. Elvira's fate is unknown. But Mr. Sheridan, however it may offend the *prudish critic*, has produced a contrition in this magnanimous female, which cannot fail of pleasing the *candid Christian*"—*Sheridan and Kotzebue* (1799), p. 124.

[38] See Boaden's comment on the German drama quoted below, Pt. III, Chap. X, p. 278.

ness of Kotzebue and German sensationalism which had taken by storm the supposedly impregnable fortress of British correctness and forthright morality and sent it thundering down. Blind to the fact that the compromise of objective moral values had lain implicit in the English drama through the long years in which subjective character had developed on English stages, these critics insisted that nothing in their own tradition could have given rise to such double-dealing. Only tendencies from without could have caused the loss of firm moral principle. The English drama itself was blameless.

The psychology of this reaction is interesting to contemplate. For it bears a striking analogy to the sentimental concept of human nature prevalent in British moral philosophy in the eighteenth century and in the philosophical criticism of Lord Kames, William Richardson, Maurice Morgann, and their many fellows of similar cast of mind. Kames assumed that it had to be an exterior force which led unfortunate human beings to catastrophe, since man himself possessed instincts only for good.[39] The critical and theatrical treatment of Shakespeare's characters had become increasingly dependent on this idea—so much so, in fact, that the tyrannical murderer Macbeth had by this time become a figure for all virtuous men seduced and irredeemably betrayed by outside influences and, paradoxically, by their own innate sensibilities. The sign of the truly noble man is his instinctive responsiveness, agreed many writers of Sheridan's generation. That way heroism lies. Almost as if to present a definitive demonstration of this notion, Sheridan seized on the morally ambiguous character of Rolla in Kotzebue's play (without, one strongly suspects, recognizing its ambiguity) and enhanced it by infusing notions of the hero which came down to him from preceding generations. In so doing he participated in the transformation of the traditional English hero of Marlowe, Chapman, and Dryden into an epitome of the Romantic man of feeling, a man whose heroism consists in the greatness and nobility of his beating heart's responses.

iii. Rolla's Lineage and the Form of Romantic Tragedy

The artificiality of Sheridan's Rolla is the most notable characteristic of a play that seems to depend almost exclusively on the

[39] This is the premise on which Kames's analyses of human nature in his *Elements of Criticism* (Edinburgh, 1762) are based. See the discussion of Kames below, Pt. III, Chap. VIII, pp. 193-195.

artificial. Readers of English drama often dismiss the Romantic hero, of whom Rolla is the abstract and sad chronicle, for his contrived sentiment, hollow rhetoric, and shop-worn melancholy. Nevertheless, because of the importance of defining the concept of dramatic character that distinguishes this age, it is necessary to come to grips with this invariably embarrassing figure. To insist that Rolla does not possess the vitality of the highest order of dramatic characterization is to labor the obvious. Although a leader of armies, he is no Agamemnon. Nor is he a Falstaff. Yet he shares with his knighted predecessor a quality that few dramatic characters possess, a synthetic quality of unusual richness. Seen within the contexts available to the theatrical and dramatic historian, to the student of cultural and political history, in fact to all those interested in the popular manifestation of enduring yet changing ideas and conventions, Rolla appears to us in the fresh light cast on him by passing time. The purpose, here pursued, of establishing these contexts now leads to the task of relating his character to the form and conventions of the drama in which he emerges.

The closest analogue to Rolla is the hero of sentimental comedy. The play resolves happily because of the essential goodness of that hero's uninstructed natural responses. But in comedy, as in Steele's *The Conscious Lovers* or Cumberland's *The West Indian,* the sentimental hero is a character of ordinary reality, presented as one might encounter him in a city square or fashionable drawing room. Similarly, the "world" of sentimental comedy represents a close approximation of the everyday reality familiar to audiences. The artificial hero of sentimental tragedy, however, is artificial in the first place because of his obviously extreme separateness from ordinary life. No one expects to meet a Rolla in Fleet Street, haranguing passing barristers and merchants, any more than he thinks of finding a Belcour in gleaming armor atop a mountain peak in Peru. Yet this artificial hero, for all his distinctness, carries a certain indefinable conviction for the audience. They do, of course, recognize that the precedent for such a character is to be found in literature, not life, but this admitted distinction does not prevent them from taking Rolla as seriously as he is intended. The critic for the *Times* found that, by the fourth performance, enough excrescence had been cut away so that "the mind is led, with almost uninterrupted interest, to contemplate the heroic fate of *Rolla.*" The highly stylized acting of

Kemble was ideally suited to the role, the critic went on; his excellent manner "graces the virtuous and dignified character of *Rolla* with every noble display of the mimic art. . . ."[40]

It is the whole-heartedness of Rolla (however over-simplified we may find it) that proved his greatest attraction for Romantic audiences, and behind his single-minded commitment to a noble cause lie the two characteristics of which he is composed. He is ideally good, because of both his physical courage and moral virtue. But he is also ideally human, for he finds within himself a conflict between his private good responses (his love for Alonzo's faithful Cora) and his public good responses (his loyalty to king, country, and fellow man). This ideal conflict precipitates the tragic outcome of the play. Rolla's way out of his difficulty is the predictable one of self-immolation. When Cora unjustly accuses him of having contrived Alonzo's capture and certain death so that he himself may marry her, Rolla's instinctive response is to defend and prove the purity of his motives. Consistent with the extremeness that characterizes his every thought, word, and deed, he substitutes himself for the captured Alonzo, knowing full well that his action is suicidal. Objectively considered, this is a completely private and egotistical way of showing how wronged he is—as if to say, "You'll be sorry when I'm dead." But this is not the view imposed in the play. Instead, Rolla's gesture is made to appear purely noble, a supreme act of selfless benevolence: no greater love hath a man. . . . This act, than which no act public or private can be greater, ultimately reconciles Rolla's personal conflict by making the distinction between public and private good irrelevant. The reaction elicited from the audience, as the reviews consistently show, is simply a great sense of loss. It does not even begin to partake of an awareness that the egotisti-

[40] 29 May 1799. Summarizing the characteristics of "the grand style" as set down by Sir Joshua Reynolds and others, Edgar Wind presents an idea helpful in explaining the aesthetic distance of dramatic heroes such as Rolla. Late eighteenth-century academicians, he observes, "declared that the grand style and the faithful portrait manner are incompatible with one another, and that artists ambitious to paint heroes should take care not to make them look too much like themselves or their neighbours, or like the soldiers they saw walking about in the streets. If it is true that familiarity breeds contempt, the advice was sound that the hero should not be represented as a familiar figure"—"The Revolution of History Painting," *JWCI*, II (1938), 116. See my discussion of this point in "John Hamilton Mortimer and Shakespearean Characterization," *Princeton University Library Chronicle*, XXIX (1968), 193-207.

cal premise of sentimental behavior, as in the cases of Steele's Bevil Junior and Cumberland's Belcour, is fully in operation here. Conveniently closing their eyes to the fact that emotional indulgence lies at the source of Rolla's singular attitude, the audience refuse, just as Rolla himself refuses, to acknowledge duplicity either in his acts of heroism or in the concept of virtuous behavior that underlies the play as a whole. By substituting himself for Alonzo, Rolla makes a complete offering of himself; presumably he understands that he is to lose his life as a result. But the sentimental code does not approve of death in this manner. Rolla deserves to be let off the hook at the last minute, since the forces of evil embodied in Pizarro and his cruel Spanish cohorts cannot be allowed to prevail. And so evil is in fact momentarily controverted by the same benevolent impulse when Pizarro sets Rolla free. But the essential irony of the play (as indeed of Romantic drama in general) is that, although overt evil cannot triumph over noble human impulses, mere chance unfortunately can. Accordingly, it is an uncontrollable, fortuitous event that takes Rolla's life: one bullet out of hundreds finds its way to his breast. This unforeseen happening creates immeasurable pathos in his death and at the same time reduces evil from the level of premeditated act to the level of inexplicable external event. There is no good reason for Rolla's death. That, paradoxically, is why he must die.

The death of an undeserving innocent through the agency of chance seems on the surface to have little connection with the activities of the heroic hero familiar in English drama from the time of Marlowe. But it is nevertheless true that the genealogy of the artificial hero descends in a straight line from Tamburlaine through Dryden's Almanzor and Aureng-Zebe and Addison's Cato to Rolla. Perhaps the most obvious mark of this figure is not so much his action as his speech. The heroic vaunts of Tamburlaine, derived in their turn from the blustering Herod of the medieval mystery play, set the standard for this figure for centuries to come:

> I hold the Fates bound fast in iron chains,
> And with my hand turn Fortune's wheel about,
> And sooner shall the sun fall from his sphere
> Than Tamburlaine be slain or overcome.[41]

[41] *Tamburlaine the Great*, ed. John D. Jump (Lincoln, 1967), Pt. I, I.ii.174-177.

So Tamburlaine boasts, in resounding terms that became the mark of the heroic hero even as he spoke. But splendid rhetoric was not enough by itself to form the truly noble man, as Chapman's profound raisonneur of heroism, Bussy D'Ambois, explained:

> So when we wander furthest through the waves
> Of glassy Glory and the gulfs of State,
> Topp'd with all titles, spreading all our reaches,
> As if each private arm would sphere the world;
> We must to Virtue for her guide resort,
> Or we shall shipwrack in our safest Port.[42]

Not only heroic acts, but virtuous motives to support them, are the twin requirements for the man of true valor. Already, in the little time that separates Marlowe's play from Chapman's, a change in the concept of this hero has occurred, one that becomes fully evident only later in the plays of Dryden. The tendency of Marlowe's Tamburlaine to focus on qualities of self-reliance gradually begins to separate the hero from the surrounding world through which he cuts a path to greatness. In depending as did Richard III on "himself alone," Bussy and Almanzor both suggest that the source for principles of virtuous behavior is not to be found in some external system of objective conduct but, instead, within themselves. No order is observable in the universe against which they pit their strength and wits. It is demonstrably a chaotic, purposeless world, providing only opportunities for the hero to prove his nobility and virtue by imposing control upon it according to his own lights. The recurrent metaphor for the heroic stance is that of a tall, stalwart tree, rooted so firmly that the winds of chance which buffet it long and hard cannot unseat it from its grip upon the earth. It is hardly surprising that, after so many repetitions, this image of self-reliance issues once again from the mouth of Rolla.[43]

The qualities of heroism that characterize Sheridan's noble savage are, then, those of his heroic forebears. But it is essential to see that the close similarity of these traditional figures is accom-

[42] *Bussy D'Ambois*, ed. Nicholas Brooke (London, 1964), I.i.28-33.

[43] ". . . I am as a blighted Plantain," Rolla says to Alonzo, whom he has come to rescue, "standing alone amid the sandy desart—Nothing seeks or lives beneath my shelter" (III, 63). The irony of the metaphor as Rolla uses it needs no comment.

panied by crucial changes that mark them off in vivid distinction from one another. Tamburlaine, as he himself acknowledges,[44] is the scourge of God, the agent whereby evil men meet a just doom—even though he himself is, if not evil, at least amoral. His triumph at the end of the first part of Marlowe's drama is the wondrous one of a man singularly able to escape the time-honored consequences reserved for those who mount upon Fortune's wheel. Almanzor, like Tamburlaine, is uniquely himself. He owes allegiance to no country and no king, only to the ideal of heroism that he quite consciously embodies in himself. But he is no scourge of God. The world inhabited by Tamburlaine, where objective values of good and evil are conventionally operative (although rendered practically inoperative by Tamburlaine's climb to success and fame), has disappeared. In its place exists a cosmos in which fortuitous events are contained by acts of sheer heroism. Glimmerings of a new order emerge in *Aureng-Zebe* and *Cato*, where domestic and philosophic forces have subdued the fiery spirits of their heroes. Finally, in Sheridan's Rolla appears the coalescence of them all, a pious hero over whom no antagonistic human power can stand victorious. But, significantly, fortuitous event no longer falls under the sway of this god-like man. Tamburlaine scorns it; Cato rises above it; Rolla succumbs to it.

The death Rolla suffers at the end of *Pizarro* is inexplicable as the operation of poetic justice. It is in fact an open violation of the aesthetic norm by which evil is punished and virtue rewarded. Thomas Rymer might well ask of this play, as of *Othello*, "If this be our end, what boots it to be Vertuous?"[45] For in this drama both evil, in the person of Pizarro, and virtue, embodied in Rolla, meet their irreversible demise. Sheridan sums up the enigma in describing the faces of those assembled around Rolla's bier: "*The Triumph of the Day is lost, in mourning for their Hero*" (III, 81).

But, if this is indeed a paradox, it is one built into the very form of the play as well as into the sentimental concept of the dramatic hero that buttresses Sheridan's efforts. The generic difference between romantic comedy and Romantic tragedy may now be adduced to resolve the mystery posed by the death of

[44] 2 *Tamburlaine* II.iv.80.

[45] *A Short View of Tragedy*, in *Critical Works*, ed. Curt A. Zimansky (New Haven, 1956), p. 161.

this blameless man. Frank Kermode has observed of Shakespeare's romances, particularly *The Tempest,* that this form shows the apparently universal operation of certain laws which we know in real life work only intermittently. Such laws include the notion that no evil can dwell in a beauteous form, or that the forces of good, specifically fertility, triumph in the end, usually in a feast or a wedding. In romance, Kermode observes, certain ideas develop "with ideal clarity, as if to show us that a formal and ordered paradigm of these forces is possible when life is purged of accident. . . ."[46] In Romantic tragedy we find the same idealized, "artificial" world. But tragedy, as Fletcher, Shakespeare, and playwrights in general assume, is closely bound up with the presentation of death on the stage. Romantic tragedy encompasses this presentation in the midst of an ideal world through the deliberate introduction of accident—with invariably "tragic" results. The idea that doom can be brought about by mere chance may seem quite at odds with classical ideas of inexorable fate or flaws in human nature. But the impression gained from genuine Romantic tragedy (although not from tragedy aborted into a happy ending, as in Charles Lamb's *John Woodvil*) is that the force of sheer chance has its own inexorable quality. Pathos is the inescapable effect of the death of a noble man of virtue. Discovering himself in a world he never made, he can do no more than respond to it with the passion that springs from his inherent sensibilities. But to do so is to fall prey to the operation of chance. His fatal extravagance, fatal curiosity, in fact his fatal good nature, are no match for the lawless movements of an inscrutable universe that ironically elicit his sympathetic response. Faced with the spectacle of a man whose life and environment are both so uncertain, we can always be sure that something completely unexpected will happen. And so we come always to expect it.

[46] *The Tempest,* 6th Arden edn. (Cambridge, Mass., 1958), Intro., pp. liv-lvi.

CHAPTER VII

The Cenci: The Drama of Radical Innocence

God,
Who sees the motive and the deed regards not,
Bade us go down and save her from the demons,
Who do not know the deed can never bind.
—Yeats, *The Countess Cathleen*

i. Variations on a Theme by Dryden

I DRAW a stroke over all those *Dalilahs* of the Theatre," Dryden said, repenting authorial excesses in his Epistle Dedicatory to *The Spanish Fryar,* "and am resolv'd I will settle my self no reputation by the applause of fools."[1] Not the first to consider what posterity would make of him, Dryden was nevertheless the self-conscious father of those writers who have sensed their allegiance divided between ideals of permanent truth and the demands of professional life. His distaste for the stage was that of a dramatist who had experienced both success and failure and knew the uncertainty of either as a sign of merit. Amazed by the "glaring Colours" of the star-like *Bussy D'Ambois* in the theater, he read it, found himself "cozen'd with a Jelly" (Sig. A2^{v}), and grew determined to avoid its example: ". . . as 'tis my Interest to please my Audience, so 'tis my Ambition to be read; that I am sure is the more lasting and the nobler Design" (Sig. A3^{v}).

It is easy enough to accuse Dryden of cynicism or inconsistency, or both, but impossible to ignore the precedent his divisive attitude set for subsequent poets and critics. A century and a half later, its contrary tendencies had become polarized but not essentially changed. In the preface to *Marino Faliero* (1821) Byron declared:

> I cannot conceive any man of irritable feeling putting himself at the mercies of an audience:—the sneering reader, and the loud critic, and the tart review, are scattered and distant

[1] *The Spanish Fryar, or, The Double Discovery* (1681), Sigs. A2^{v}-A3.

> calamities; but the trampling of an intelligent or of an ignorant audience on a production which, be it good or bad, has been a mental labour to the writer, is a palpable and immediate grievance, heightened by a man's doubt of their competency to judge, and his certainty of his own imprudence in electing them his judges. Were I capable of writing a play which could be deemed stage-worthy, success would give me no pleasure, and failure great pain.[2]

Irritable feeling had Dryden too, and scorn for those "half-witted Judges" in the theater who as often praised his plays as condemned them.[3] In view of Dryden's comments, it will hardly do to dismiss Byron's as those of a "spoilt child" who egotistically refused to submit his person to rigorous discipline and his writings to public judgment.[4] M. G. Lewis, in this respect one of the most accommodating dramatists of Byron's day, recognized too that an impasse had been reached. For *Alfonso, King of Castile*—indisputably Lewis's finest play and the only one that pleased the author himself throughout—he had but dim hopes of theatrical success. His chief reason for printing it before it appeared in production was, he explained in the preface to the first edition, his "very grave doubts, whether even an *excellent* Tragedy, if written in blank verse, would succeed on the Stage at present: of course I do not flatter myself that mine will; and, after the cold reception of *De Montfort* [sic], I am not vain enough to expect that *Alfonso* will meet with a kind one. I therefore rather wish this production to be considered as a dramatic poem. . . ."[5]

[2] *Marino Faliero, Doge of Venice. An Historical Tragedy, in Five Acts* (1821), Pref., p. xviii.

[3] *The Spanish Fryar*, Epistle Dedicatory, Sig. A3.

[4] Allardyce Nicoll, *A History of English Drama 1660-1900*, 2nd edn., IV (Cambridge, Eng., 1963), 63. For an intelligent discussion of Byron's complex relationship to the contemporary theater, see T. H. Vail Motter, "Byron's *Werner* Re-estimated," *Essays in Dramatic Literature: The Parrott Presentation Volume*, ed. Hardin Craig (Princeton, 1935), pp. 243-275.

[5] Pref. dated 12 December 1801, repr. in *Alfonso, King of Castile: A Tragedy, in Five Acts*, 2nd edn. (1802), p. vi. For other examples of the developing "split" between the stage and the study, see the following: Henry Fielding, *The Author's Farce and the Pleasures of the Town* (1730), I.vi; [George Colman the Elder], *Critical Reflections on the Old English Dramatick Writers* (1761); Horace Walpole, Postscript to *The Mysterious Mother* and "Thoughts on Tragedy," in *The Works of Horatio Walpole, Earl of Orford*, 5 vols. (1798), I, 125-129 and II, 305-314; Anon., "The British Theatre," *London Magazine*, XL (1771), 262-265, 311-313; William Cooke, *Elements of Dramatic*

Lewis's blank-verse tragedy achieved performance after all but, as the playwright himself anticipated, could not touch the popularity of *The Castle Spectre* or even *Adelgitha*, superior though it was to both.[6] The "stage" and the "closet" had become felt antinomies for the writers of this age. A sense of dichotomous aims comes across, perhaps more strongly than any other quality, to the modern student of early nineteenth-century drama. The clichés have been rehearsed again and again. Men of literature had forsaken the theater, and no wonder: audiences were lewd and riotous; plays could be only seen, not heard; managers were traitors to dramatic tradition; playwrights were prostitutes to the appetites of the masses. The alleged debasement of performed drama, the alleged lifelessness of the dramatic poem—each half of the double image of the drama of this period has, in our eyes, reinforced the outline of the other. The pressing need, it would seem, is not for yet another history of the period, but for a way of understanding the histories that already exist. Beginning either with disdain or with thinly veiled special pleading, modern historians have attempted to define Romantic poetic drama according to the dramatist's putative intention, declared or implied, not to write for the stage,[7] or according to its technical qualities ("Romantic drama is drama in blank verse"[8]). In this pantomime for

---

Criticism (1775), p. 204; Robert Dodsley, ed., *A Select Collection of Old Plays*, 12 vols. (1744), 2nd edn. [ed. Isaac Reed], 12 vols. (1780), Prefaces; [William Hodson], "Postscript, containing Observations on Tragedy," appended to *Zoraida. A Tragedy* (1780); J. Aikin, "On the Impression of Reality attending Dramatic Representations," *Memoirs of the Literary and Philosophical Society of Manchester*, IV (1793), pt. 1, 96-108; George Walker, "On Tragedy & the Interest in Tragical Representations," *Memoirs of the Literary and Philosophical Society of Manchester*, V (1802), pt. 2, 331; Richard Payne Knight, *An Analytical Inquiry into the Principles of Taste* (1805), pp. 344-345; Henry Siddons, *Practical Illustrations of Rhetorical Gesture and Action, Adapted to the English Drama* (1807), p. 331; [Frederick Howard, Earl of Carlisle], *Thoughts Upon The Present Condition of The Stage*, new edn. (1809); and Hannah More, *Tragedies* (1818), Preface.

6 Genest notes that the play was acted "about 10 times" and explains, as Lewis did, that the ending was altered in performance—*Some Account of the English Stage* (Bath, 1832), VII, 553.

7 See Nicoll, *History of English Drama*, 2nd edn. (Cambridge, Eng., 1955), III, 217ff; and IV, 155, where Professor Nicoll softens and readjusts his earlier pronouncements.

8 Richard M. Fletcher, *English Romantic Drama 1795-1843* (New York, 1966), p. 19. Like Fletcher, Bernice Slote appears to assume that first-rate poets do not allow themselves to be influenced except by other first-rate

scholars, Harlequin Showman duels endlessly with Fra Lippo Lippi, neither recognizing the other as his twin.[9]

This chapter will illustrate an alternative way of studying nineteenth-century poetic drama. My premise is that the antinomies sensed by contemporary writers and widely observed by subsequent readers should be apprehended as in felt tension with one another rather than simply as mutually exclusive. Both Dryden and Lewis could wish to appeal to *both* playgoer and reader; and each knew, or thought he knew, whose judgment would confer success and whose would better stand the test of time. Description of Romantic poetic drama should depend on the dramatist's awareness of these tensions and on the sense he conveys of two differing audiences, not merely on the formal qualities of his language or on a purpose to ignore, reform, or shame the stage. Similarly it is necessary to see this drama itself not in opposition but in relation to performance in the theater. Closet drama is stage drama *manqué*, drama aspiring to a state of performance either actual or imagined, but not produced, or producible, on the contemporary stage because of some special circumstance (for example: its language is insufficiently intelligible or unsuited to the spoken voice; the effects it calls for cannot be realized; the kind of stage it requires no longer exists; its subject matter is indecorous; the author fears it will be damned; or praised; and so on). I suggest that the term *closet drama* should be used to indicate a tendency, or set of tendencies, rather than a "pure" generic identity of the sort implied by such terms as *tragedy* or even *melodrama*. In most periods, but especially in this one, certain plays were written frankly for the stage but not produced (at least, not in their authors' lifetimes); witness Keats's *Otho the*

---

writers. Coleridge's *Remorse*, she says, was "the only successful so-called literary drama for Keats to follow" in writing *Otho the Great*, a play she views as handicapped by having been "written for a particular actor," Kean—*Keats and the Dramatic Principle* (Lincoln, 1958), pp. 99, 104. It may be added that *Doctor Faustus*, *Hamlet*, *Philaster*, and other plays suffer from a similar defect.

[9] This is not, of course, to say that no history of nineteenth-century drama commands attention. Although Professor Nicoll lacks powers as a critic, his extensive and painstaking scholarship has put all students of English drama in his debt. In addition to the volumes of his *History* and their valuable handlists of plays, cited above, see the good brief account by Harold Child, "Nineteenth-century Drama," *Cambridge History of English Literature*, ed. Sir A. W. Ward et al. (Cambridge, Eng., repr. 1961), XIII, 255-274.

Great. Others were avowedly not composed for the stage but produced anyway, like Byron's *Sardanapalus*. Rather than call any of these exceptional, it is better to distinguish between "closet" plays and "acting" plays by examining the playwright's preparation. If nurtured on Home, Cumberland, Jephson, Holcroft, and others, he may well have his play accepted and produced; if his debt is primarily to Marlowe, Shakespeare, Ford, Webster, and their like, his play will probably be published and read. But neither possibility excludes the other. With regard also to the presentation of character, the distinction between closet drama and the performed play is one of tendency or degree, not kind. Stage characters in this period reflect the disposition of roles in a repertory company and even the preferences and styles of particular leading actors (as, for instance, the steady melancholy of Penruddock in Cumberland's *The Wheel of Fortune* [Drury Lane, 1794-95] suggests John Philip Kemble's relentless, careful grace—as it should, since the play was written as a vehicle for him). Characters in unperformed drama not aimed at production may also reveal this assemblage of familiar types, a possibility that interferes not at all with the attempt, common to both "kinds" of drama but often considered indigenous to the closet play, to create deliberately universalized states of passion.[10]

The fact is that the so-called "closet drama" has strong tendencies to be "of the theater, theatrical" but at the same time to approach the extra-theatrical condition of one (or more) of the other arts—painting, poetry, music. It seems a reductive simplification to treat such works as generically pure creations. They are perhaps the least uncontaminated of any plays in a period especially significant for the breakdown of old genres, old ideas, and old values. A representative work which also happens to be (in my opinion) the best and richest example of poetic drama in the Romantic age is *The Cenci*. I shall examine it with two purposes in mind: to demonstrate the need of reading works of this sort in as wide a perspective of forms, ideas, and aims as the reader's experience can afford; and to elucidate one idea in particular, the Romantic notion of radical innocence. One of the most deeply derivative of ideas about human nature manifest in nineteenth-century imaginative writing, it is also, paradoxically, the most

[10] See Nicoll, *History*, III, 224-225 and IV, 156-157. For discussions of "universality" in performed drama, see the closing sections of Pt. I, Chap. IV and Pt. II, Chap. VI above.

original. A product of the long history of developing concepts of dramatic character explored in earlier chapters and also in Part III of this book, human innocence in Romantic drama combines the eighteenth-century idea of the blameless hero or heroine beset by calamity, or the villain by his own conscience, with a new, "poetic" notion of the relationship between art and life. As in the experiential duality of the urn in Keats's ode, the radically innocent character of Romantic drama lives in a guileless world out of time, and yet ironically must render up his innocence in a "dramatic" world where time and circumstance enchain a once free, joyous spirit.

This brief description is offered in advance of analysis in order to provide a sense of direction over difficult ground. The path is, I believe, much the same for each of the plays, notorious and usually avoided or carefully explained away, of the five major Romantic poets; the same also for forgotten or neglected works like Thomas Maurice's *Panthea, or The Captive Bride* (1789), Frederick Howard, Earl of Carlisle's *The Step-Mother* (1800), and Thomas Lovell Beddoes' *The Brides' Tragedy* (1822). *The Cenci,* however, embodies the issues in question in their clearest and most widely implicating form and so calls for, and bears, extensive examination.

ii. Sources and Issues

In approaching a poet whose intellectual range and consequent breadth of reading were as wide as Shelley's, it often seems that the greater part of Western literature and thought lies implicit in his works. So, in *The Cenci,* we may find a drama whose characters appear to derive from Sophoclean and Euripidean tragedy transformed by Elizabethan richness of imagery and extravagance of rhetoric; or we may discover a dramatic forcefulness that seems the product of Aristotelian notions of pity and terror curiously stratified within an Italianate five-act structure. *The Cenci* is, in addition, rich in ideas. The play reflects complex associations of Christian stoicism and Shelley's familiar idiosyncratic Platonism with the more obscure but equally relevant concepts of Zoroastrian religious thought. Yet, in exploring fruitful contexts like these as aids toward understanding Shelley's ambitious tragedy, we are prone to overlook influences close at hand whose sensuous immediacy may have fed the poet's imagination as much as the heady substance of his reading. Two such influences have remained largely unexamined, perhaps because they are obvious enough to be taken for granted. One of these is the now disputed portrait of *La Cenci* by Guido, described at length in Shelley's preface to the play; the other is the compelling theatrical style of Eliza O'Neill, the young Regency actress whose impression on the poet is recorded in Mary Shelley's notes. Studied together, these two influences cast fresh light on Shelley's play and on its central figure, Beatrice. Customarily readers concern themselves with the pathos of her dilemma and with the problems of moral choice and responsibility raised by the murder of her father and by her subsequent denial of guilt. But we should also take care to place the character and motivations of Beatrice within the context of Shelley's prevailing ideals. In doing so, we may employ Guido's portrait and Miss O'Neill's acting to elucidate both the structure of the play and the complex problem of sympathy raised by Shelley's unorthodox treatment of pathetic tragic character.

Saving his discussion of Guido's portrait for the end of his preface, Shelley begins by describing the character of Beatrice Cenci as he found it in his manuscript source: "The young maiden, who was urged to this tremendous deed by an impulse which overpowered its horror, was evidently a most gentle and amiable being, a creature formed to adorn and be admired, and thus violently thwarted from her nature by the necessity of circumstance and opinion."[11] The poet relates the tragic nature of his character to the crucial problem of moral responsibility, then proceeds to attack the corollary problem of an audience's sympathetic response. Although men generally see a kind of statutory guilt in her deed, Shelley finds, they sense at the same time great pathos in her situation. This moral paradox leads to the heart of the play as a dramatic structure:

> It is in the restless and anatomizing casuistry with which men seek the justification of Beatrice, yet feel that she has done what needs justification; it is in the superstitious horror with which they contemplate alike her wrongs and their re-

[11] *The Complete Poetical Works of Percy Bysshe Shelley*, ed. Thomas Hutchinson ("Oxford Standard Authors"; new edn., London, 1943), p. 275. Subsequent references to Shelley's works and to Mary Shelley's notes are to this edition.

> venge, that the *dramatic* character of what she did and suffered, consists. (pp. 276-277, emphasis added)

When placed beside Shelley's initial description of Beatrice, this passage reveals the peculiarly divided nature of his heroine. At first a young woman of eminent gentleness and elegance, she at length finds herself immured by horrible circumstances which cause her to be "violently thwarted from her nature." The extreme situation poses a problem so immense that nothing in Beatrice's original character equips her to deal with it. Abruptly she is forced to commit a heinous crime "by an impulse" which overcomes the revulsion she might originally have felt. Shelley thus presents two distinct Beatrices: one who exists in a hypothetical life outside the events of the story, and another, a "dramatic character" whose fundamental nature derives from the act she commits under extraordinary duress and from its effect on the minds of an audience which must somehow evaluate it. Shelley's deft manipulation of the "real" Beatrice and her dramatic counterpart determines the form of his play. A certain radical innocence in the character underlies the dramatic events, so that the crime she commits is somehow separable from the integral real person of Beatrice herself. The author of Count Cenci's murder is not this historically attractive person but the separate *dramatic character* that shadows the real, a character created by the unpredictably extreme force of circumstance and manifested through a purely momentary impulse.

Within this context, Guido's painting appears to have conveyed much more to Shelley than simply the graphic image of a pathetic young Renaissance woman. Describing the portrait at the end of his preface, Shelley reveals that he saw in it a precise relationship between pathos and the moral paradox he discovered in Beatrice's act. At the same time he underscores the artistic paradox of "real" and dramatic character that emerges from the preface as a whole. Contemplating the "fixed and pale composure" of Beatrice's countenance, radiant even in despair, Shelley observes that the lips reveal a "permanent meaning of imagination and sensibility" and that the eyes, although swollen from weeping, remain "beautifully tender and serene":

> In the whole mien there is a simplicity and dignity which, united with her exquisite loveliness and deep sorrow, are in-

> expressibly pathetic. Beatrice Cenci appears to have been one of those rare persons in whom energy and gentleness dwell together without destroying one another: her nature was simple and profound. The crimes and miseries in which she was an actor and a sufferer are as the mask and the mantle in which circumstances clothed her for her impersonation on the scene of the world. (p. 278) [see Plate 24]

Here again the suggestion appears that Shelley conceives of his character in the double sense I have explained. In Guido's portrait she retains those qualities that made her one to adorn and be admired, but the unspeakable events and circumstances which occur between the original state of the young maiden and Guido's pathetic spectacle have effected a kind of schizophrenic duality. We sense the presence of a dramatic persona, a tragic mask that for a brief but conclusive moment obscures the bright, serene reality within.

Shelley was unusually drawn to such elegant, dignified, radiantly pathetic figures. In a series of enthusiastic letters to Thomas Love Peacock, the poet records impressions of other Renaissance paintings seen during frequent visits to Italian museums. Again and again he betrays his fascination for portraits of young women whose expressions mirror pathetic situations. A Danae of Titian excites his admiration for "the softest & most voluptuous form with languid & uplifted eyes & warm yet passive limbs," and he responds again to "a Maddalena by Guido with dark brown hair & dark brown eyes and an earnest soft melancholy look."[12] Describing a crucifixion by Guido, he conveys his intense interest in the Magdalene "clinging to the cross with the look of passive & gentle despair beaming from under her bright flaxen hair. . . ."[13] Evidently, Shelley's habitual response to the graphic representation of women is to find the same pathos which, for him, characterized Guido's Beatrice.

The connection between Guido's portrait and the acting of Eliza O'Neill exists in the similarly pathetic features Shelley discovered in them, and it bears greatly on Shelley's conception of Beatrice and the paradoxical response of an audience to her situation. Fortunately, surviving records establish the nature of Miss

[12] Letter to T. L. Peacock, dated 25 February [1819], in *The Letters of Percy Bysshe Shelley*, ed. Frederick L. Jones (Oxford, 1964), II, 81.

[13] Letter dated 9 November 1818, in Jones, ed., *Letters*, II, 50.

O'Neill's acting and so make it possible to assess the influence she exerted on Shelley.

On 6 October 1814 this young Irish actress, flushed with success in Dublin, made her London debut as Juliet. Her triumph was instantaneous. Audiences rushed to acclaim the genius of the unknown provincial actress, some spectators even paying her the ultimate compliment of fainting under the spell of her power. Critics who habitually cast a knowing eye on playbills containing such phrases as "Juliet by Miss O'NEILL, (Of the *Theatre Royal, Dublin*) being her first appearance in London"[14] forgot their cynicism and petulance and began to hail the newcomer as the only heiress apparent to Mrs. Siddons' tragic throne. Eliza O'Neill so began a brilliant career that included many heroines of standard English repertory and a number of new characters as well, notably the central roles in Sheil's *Evadne* and Milman's *Fazio*. Her name might well be as familiar now as Helen Faucit's or Ellen Terry's, had she not chosen another more tranquil career while "in the zenith of her glory," as Mary Shelley remarks in her notes to *The Cenci* (p. 336), and left her profession for marriage in December 1819 after only five years on the London stage.

The qualities of Miss O'Neill's style became at once apparent. William Charles Macready, recalling her self-abandonment to character, described her as "an entirely modest woman; yet in acting with her I have been nearly smothered by her kisses." Elsewhere he praised his sometime leading lady for her "native elegance, . . . feminine sweetness, . . . unaffected earnestness and gushing passion."[15] Notices of her debut as Juliet reflect the comprehensiveness of Macready's remarks, Hazlitt's in the *Champion* emphasizing the general fascination with Miss O'Neill's expressive features. Her face, he asserted, "has that mixture of beauty and passion which we admire so much in some of the antique statues." Impressive yet simple in her actions, she blended voice and movement to achieve uncommon results. When she is told of Romeo's death, Hazlitt recalls, "in the silent expression of feeling, we have seldom witnessed any thing finer," and in lamenting

[14] Covent Garden bill for 6 October 1814, Folger Shakespeare Library.

[15] Lady Pollock, *Macready as I Knew Him* (London, 1885), p. 29, quoted by Alan S. Downer, *The Eminent Tragedian: William Charles Macready* (Cambridge, Mass., 1966), p. 78; *Macready's Reminiscences, and Selections from His Diaries and Letters*, ed. Sir Frederick Pollock (London, 1875), I, 86.

Romeo's banishment she "marked the fine play and undulation of natural sensibility, rising and falling with the gusts of passion, and at last worked up into an agony of despair, in which imagination approaches the brink of frenzy."[16] Here in essence are the features implicit in Guido's portrait as Shelley viewed it; the same qualities emerge in the dramatic character of Beatrice as she resolves on the murder of her father. [see Plate 25 and compare Plate 6 above]

Boundless suffering, powerful responsiveness, touching pathos —these traits of exquisite feminine misfortune were the making of Miss O'Neill's fame. Shortly after her retirement Hazlitt summarized her theatrical qualities by explaining how she drew from her audience an extraordinary sympathetic response. His analysis strikingly suggests the combination of "energy and gentleness" that Shelley saw in Guido's portrait. Miss O'Neill's acting, said Hazlitt, possessed both "the utmost force" and "the purity and simplicity" of tragedy, for she revealed all passions through her "simple and undefinable" responsiveness:

> She did not work herself up to the extremity of passion, by questioning with her own thoughts; or raise herself above circumstances, by ascending the platform of imagination; or arm herself against fate, by strengthening her will to meet it; no, she yielded to calamity, she gave herself up entire, and with entire devotion, to her unconquerable despair:—it was the tide of anguish swelling in her own breast, that overflowed to the breasts of the audience, and filled their eyes with tears. . . .[17]

Knowing Hazlitt's perennial dissatisfaction with any performer save the incomparable Siddons, one can scarcely help being impressed by his judgment of Eliza O'Neill. For Hazlitt the imaginative ideal was realized in Mrs. Siddons, who alone could summon up "that terrible reaction of mental power on the scene, which forms the perfection of tragedy."[18] Yet his admiration of Miss O'Neill's "simple and undefinable" reaction to extreme circumstances remains to engage attention. Together with natural

[16] 16 October 1814, repr. in *A View of the English Stage, Complete Works,* ed. P. P. Howe (London, 1930), v, 199.

[17] *Complete Works,* ed. Howe, xviii, 284-285.

[18] *Complete Works,* ed. Howe, xviii, 196.

elegance and "the spirit of perfect innocence and purity" that Macready to his delight discovered in her,[19] this responsiveness was in all likelihood the quality to which Shelley felt himself similarly and compulsively drawn.

Shelley's animosity toward the theater ran high throughout his life. The principal source for knowledge of Shelley's playgoing, Mary Shelley's journal, records only infrequent and apparently reluctant attendance. In the fall of 1814, a week after Miss O'Neill had made her debut, Shelley and Mary saw Hamlet performed by the actor who the previous January had taken London by storm, Edmund Kean. Mary's comment on the experience implies Shelley's fixed attitude:

> The extreme depravity and disgusting nature of the scene; the inefficacy of acting to encourage or maintain the delusion. The loathsome sight of men personating characters which do not and cannot belong to them. Shelley displeased with what he saw of Kean.[20]

Peacock recalls that the pains he took to rid Shelley of his prejudice against the stage met no success, even when he managed to confront the poet with the artistry and wit of *School for Scandal*.[21] Generalizing from records like these, Newman Ivey White declared that Shelley regarded the legitimate theater as a "corrupter of principles" whose loss could hardly compensate for an hour's entertainment.[22]

In the face of these records, however, stands another that flatly contradicts the rest. In her notes to *The Cenci* Mary explains that Shelley wrote in hopes of performance and points out that the memorable acting of Eliza O'Neill influenced his composition of the play. Before they departed for Italy, Shelley saw Miss O'Neill "several times" and was "deeply moved . . . by the graceful sweetness, the intense pathos, and sublime vehemence of passion she displayed." Not only did he wish her to take the part of Beatrice, Mary recalls; she was "often in his thoughts as he wrote . . ." (p. 336). Appropriately enough, a close similarity

[19] *Reminiscences*, ed. Pollock, I, 97.

[20] *Mary Shelley's Journal*, ed. Frederick L. Jones (Norman, Okla., 1947), entry for 13 October 1814, p. 20.

[21] *Peacock's Memoirs of Shelley with Shelley's Letters to Peacock*, ed. H. F. B. Brett-Smith (London, 1909), p. 39.

[22] *Shelley* (New York, 1940), I, 521.

lies in the attributes critics perceived in Miss O'Neill and those of the historical Beatrice Cenci as Shelley describes them in the preface to his play. The singular qualities of Eliza O'Neill apparently moved Shelley to disregard for once his inveterate distaste for the actors and productions of his day. Specifically, it was Miss O'Neill's style as Shelley sensed it in one particular role that made the crucial impression. Unfortunately Mary's journal seldom reveals whether Shelley accompanied her to the theater on every visit she records, but there are four productions we can be sure the poet saw: Kean's Hamlet in October 1814; *The Merchant of Venice,* 11 February 1817; *School for Scandal,* a production of uncertain date; and Henry Hart Milman's *Fazio,* a tragedy printed in 1815, acted at the Surrey in 1816-17 as *The Italian Wife,* and performed under its original title at Covent Garden on 5 February 1818.[23] On 16 February of that year Shelley, Mary, and Peacock went to see Milman's drama, already familiar to the poet and his wife from a previous reading, and Peacock was struck with Shelley's "absorbed attention to Miss O'Neill's performance of Bianca," its heroine.[24] During the summer of 1819 when at work on his own drama, the memory of this performance and of the play that made it possible led Shelley to keep the actress strongly in his thoughts. Mary's recollection that Shelley saw her perform "several times" may be correct, but for lack of other evidence I shall concentrate on Milman's play.

Fazio—a work Shelley later dismissed as "miserable trash"[25]—was written in the waning light of a venerable English tradition, the revenge tragedy. But while the characters and language betray some symptoms of the deadly disease of Elizabethanism, its fundamental qualities are the product of a later innovation, the Romantic tragedy of betrayal through circumstance, displaying characters in situations so extreme and unexpected that no previous experience of the world can aid them in emerging unscathed. So it is with Fazio and his unfortunate wife, Bianca. Living in pure domestic felicity while Fazio vainly explores the mysteries of alchemy, they find their lives suddenly disrupted by the prospect of real gold within their reach. Appropriating the riches of

[23] Nicoll, *History,* IV, 356.

[24] Jones, ed., *Mary Shelley's Journal,* pp. 64, 72, 92; *Peacock's Memoirs,* ed. Brett-Smith, p. 39.

[25] Letter to Lord Byron, dated 4 May 1821, in Jones, ed., *Letters,* II, 290.

his neighbor, the mysteriously murdered usurer Bartolo, Fazio sets up house in a palatial mansion; but he is almost immediately lured away by Aldabella, a coquette of the Florentine court from whom marriage to Bianca had temporarily rescued him. Driven insane by jealousy, Bianca pursues a fanatical revenge. She informs the Duke that the missing corpse of the old usurer lies buried in the garden of Fazio's former house. A warrant is immediately issued, Fazio is condemned to death, and Bianca, only now fully aware of the wrong she has done the husband she still loves, dies of a broken heart.[26]

The revenge play, then, has become the vehicle for a tale of innocence traduced through circumstance. Fazio succumbs when he sees the dead Bartolo's fortunes gleaming at his fingertips, and Bianca irretrievably falls from grace when driven mad by Fazio's momentary faithlessness. One might observe that Milman's notion of human personality suffers from acute "British-heroinism"; Bianca would need to be desperately beside herself not to see the consequences of denouncing her husband in open court. But consistency in character is not Milman's concern. The *Times* reviewer explained what obviously was the playwright's concern when he commented that the drama affords "singular opportunities for the display of histrionic talent."[27] Eliza O'Neill must have been thoroughly at home in the role of Bianca. Milman ignores plausibility for the more pressing need of providing a barrage of theatrical effects. Typical is the scene in which the distraught Bianca denounces her husband to the amazement of the Duke's entourage, or the scene in which the penitent heroine, taking her last leave of Fazio in the condemned prisoner's cell, is turned almost to stone by the bell which summons him to death. Using this effective combination of sudden occurrence and instantaneous response to engage his audience's sympathies, Milman works relentlessly toward his theme: we see two essentially innocent characters led by circumstances outside their control to destroy the blissful unity of their once guileless lives. Through the playwright's skillful arrangement of accidental events, two pathetic unfortunates immolate themselves on the altar of their own keen sensibilities.

Writing to Peacock in April 1818 about a proposed tragedy on

[26] *Fazio,* in *The Poetical Works of the Rev. H. H. Milman,* 3 vols. (1840), III, 115-206.

[27] 6 February 1818.

Tasso's madness, Shelley stated his hope that it would have "better morality than Fazio."[28] Yet the boldest fact emerging from a comparison of Shelley's and Milman's plays is their common casuistical treatment of a virtuous human being seduced into committing a vicious act. It is imperative to see that the problem of "morality" in *The Cenci* derives from the same concept of human nature implicit in Milman's drama. While violating the conventional ethical premise of human responsibility for action, the concept at the same time affords great scope for the development of pathos. Although Shelley's characterization and language undeniably overshadow Milman's, the peculiar moral problem in Shelley's play cannot be squarely faced except by setting his drama in the context provided by the radical practice of Romantic playwright's casuistical display of "innocence" wronged must to cast his own heroine in this particular mold. The Romantic actor's emphasis on moments of intense reaction and the Romantic playwright's casuistical display of "innocence" wronged must be seen in close relationship in order to grasp the complexity of Shelley's Beatrice. For Shelley too employs the typical structural methods of the Romantic playwright in concentrating on the theatrical moment of response.

That Shelley himself related the techniques of the Romantic actor and the Romantic playwright appears both in his own comments and in Mary Shelley's summary of his play. In a letter asking Peacock to arrange for a production at Covent Garden, Shelley explained that "the principal character Beatrice is precisely fitted for Miss O Neil [sic], & it might even seem to have been written for her—(God forbid that I shd. see her play it—it wd. tear my nerves to pieces). . . ."[29] Shelley's suggestion that Miss O'Neill would fully realize the extreme emotions of the character fits nicely with Mary's description of the play as a theatrical composition. Quoting Shelley's letter in her notes, she adds, "There is nothing that is not purely dramatic throughout; and the character of Beatrice, proceeding, from vehement struggle, to horror, to deadly resolution, and lastly to the elevated dignity of calm suffering, joined to passionate tenderness and pathos, is touched with hues so vivid and so beautiful that the poet seems to have

[28] Letter to T. L. Peacock, dated 20 April 1818, in Jones, ed., *Letters*, II, 8.

[29] Letter to T. L. Peacock, dated [ca. 20] July 1819, in Jones, ed., *Letters*, II, 102.

read intimately the secrets of the noble heart imaged in the lovely countenance of the unfortunate girl" depicted in Guido's painting (p. 337). Here, on a single page of commentary, are all the materials needed to connect Guido's portrait, the acting of Eliza O'Neill, Milman's Bianca, and Shelley's Beatrice. With this connection freshly in mind, we may examine Shelley's play.

iii. Casuistical Structure and Divided Audience

After an opening scene introducing Count Cenci and his consummate success in evil deeds, Shelley brings on his chief character and quickly relates her to surrounding figures and events. This second scene of the play provides a model for those to follow. At the outset Shelley carefully establishes his heroine's unblemished innocence and moral strength. "Pervert not truth, Orsino," she cautions the scheming priest. "You have a sly, equivocating vein That suits me not" (ll. 1-2, 28-29). The first purpose of the scene is to introduce these two contrasting characters, but its effect is to make perfectly clear Beatrice's pathetic situation. Already persecuted by the Count, she can turn to no one except Orsino, whose falseness she rightfully suspects. The scene falls naturally into two parts. Beatrice breaks off with Orsino, since he offers only an illicit relationship. This movement is swiftly reversed when Beatrice reaffirms her dependence on him—"Here I stand bickering with my only friend!" (l. 46). Between these two movements Beatrice appears already in desperation. "Ah, wretched that I am!" she exclaims, "Where shall I turn?" (ll. 29-30). Because her situation has even now no remedy, Shelley allows her to suggest what becomes increasingly apparent as the play progresses—that untoward circumstance is wrenching her out of her true nature. "Sorrow," says Beatrice, "makes me seem Sterner than else my nature might have been" (ll. 34-35).

Shelley employs the banquet scene that follows to develop the perversion of Beatrice from her original nature. Using a method much like Milman's treatment of Bianca in the Duke's court, he seizes every opportunity to draw forth impassioned reactions from Beatrice and to emphasize her helplessness before the relentless force of Cenci's evil purpose. As the Count hints at the cruel death of her two brothers, Beatrice exclaims, "Great God! How horrible!" and, again, "Ah! My blood runs cold" (ll. 34, 36). Shelley manages to make of this scene both a black mass (with

Cenci offering the blasphemous sacrifice) and a recasting of the banquet scene in *Macbeth*. As a kind of innocent Lady Macbeth, Beatrice begs the noble guests not to depart, pleading with them to rescue her and her foster mother Lucretia. Somehow Beatrice does not hear Cenci's threat to anyone who might lend assistance, and so her next speech has an even greater pathetic effect:

> Dare no one look on me?
> None answer? . . .
> . . . .
> O God! That I were buried with my brothers!
> And that the flowers of this departed spring
> Were fading on my grave! And that my father
> Were celebrating now one feast for all! (ll. 132-140)

In the first scene of Act II Shelley builds to an even higher pitch Beatrice's agony at the fate about to overwhelm her. The governing action of the scene is simple: Beatrice flees from the Count, who at any moment may overtake her. Shelley uses this line of action in the best Gothic tradition, combining the trick of building false suspense and the complementary trick of a totally unprepared entrance.[30] Beatrice first thinks that Cenci is about to enter, but only the servant appears (ll. 18ff). Then, when she has momentarily recovered, the Count bursts in and so impels Beatrice back into her former state of uncontrollable fear. "*She shrinks back, and covers her face*" (stage direction, l. 105), and in a moment we see her "*staggering towards the door*" (stage direction, l. 111). Cenci now sends Beatrice to her chamber, ominously hinting at his ultimate design.

So far Beatrice has passed through the first two steps—vehement struggle and horror—that Mary outlines in describing the progress of the character. Although Shelley's experience of Romantic plays in both the theater and the study seems to have been minimal, he has evidently grasped their basic method. For a writer with no practical experience in the theater, these first two acts display a remarkably sure hand. Everything contributes to place Beatrice in a series of gradually worsening situations, al-

[30] St. John Ervine was apparently the first to notice Shelley's use of this technique; see "Shelley as a Dramatist," *Essays by Divers Hands, Transactions of the Royal Society of Literature of the United Kingdom* (London, 1936), n.s., xv, 96-98, quoted in Kenneth M. Cameron and Horst Frenz, "The Stage History of Shelley's *The Cenci*," *PMLA*, LX (1945), 1088.

lowing her to react to them with impassioned frenzy and so building up a portrait of an undeniably pathetic young woman whose innocence and love of truth and virtue provide no defense against the assault of evil, personified in the strange, errant genius of her father.

The stage has now been skillfully set for the two crucial scenes in the play: Beatrice's oath of vengeance and her subsequent trial in court. Act III consists almost entirely of one long scene whose action leads directly to the murder of Count Cenci. A true measure of Shelley's poetic ability, the mad scene here recalls Bianca's madness in the presence of the Duke and is at the same time a much more successful piece of stage writing:

> There creeps
> A clinging, black, contaminating mist
> About me . . . 'tis substantial, heavy, thick,
> I cannot pluck it from me, for it glues
> My fingers and my limbs to one another,
> And eats into my sinews, and dissolves
> My flesh to a pollution, poisoning
> The subtle, pure, and inmost spirit of life!
> My God! I never knew what the mad felt
> Before; for I am mad beyond all doubt!
>
> (ll. 16-25)[31]

Bianca and Beatrice explicitly announce that they are mad, and their styles of expression are equally extravagant. More important, the same dramatic technique and purpose support the language in each case. In Milman's play, the servant's chance mention of the Duke's assembled court impels Bianca to reveal her husband's secret and ultimately drives her mad. Like Milman, Shelley seizes on a momentary impulse which overpowers the spiritual potency of his heroine's innocent nature and irrevocably

[31] Compare Bianca's lines:

> Oh, I am mad, wildly, intensely mad.
> 'Twas but last night the moon was at the full;
> And ye, and ye, the sovereign and the sage,
> The wisdom and the reverence of all Florence,
> E'en from a maniac's dim disjointed tale,
> Do calmly judge away the innocent life,
> The holy human life, the life God gave him.
>
> (III, 176)

moves her to revenge. Driven insane by Cenci's crime and caught up in the awareness of her own demented state, Beatrice resolves on

> something which shall make
> The thing that I have suffered but a shadow
> In the dread lightning which avenges it;
> Brief, rapid, irreversible, destroying
> The consequence of what it cannot cure.
> Some such thing is to be endured or done:
> When I know what, I shall be still and calm,
> And never anything will move me more.
> But now! . . . (ll. 87-95)

These two impassioned speeches clarify the dualistic concept of dramatic character that Shelley assumes in his preface. The first speech presents the essential dramatic moment of the play. In precipitating Beatrice's madness, Cenci's horrendous assault is the immediate impulse moving her to act; this "most gentle and amiable being" becomes "violently thwarted from her nature by the necessity of circumstance. . . ." The second speech underscores the importance of the first by emphasizing the brevity of the moment and by stating that the impulse will lead to an act of even greater passion and finality. And so we perceive a character momentarily and yet totally "transformed"—as Beatrice herself affirms (l. 109). Fully conscious now of the impetus driving her toward something "to be endured or done," Beatrice emerges as the dramatic character Shelley describes in his preface. In this moment of suffering and action, Beatrice puts on "the mask and the mantle in which circumstances clothed her for her impersonation on the scene of the world."

Immediately after the murder sequence, whose extensive echoes of *Macbeth*[32] reveal Shelley's attempt to create an atmosphere of horror, the Pope's legates arrive with a warrant for Count Cenci's arrest. Here Shelley borrows the Romantic playwright's widely employed technique of irony enlisted in the service of pathos. The tragedy of insufficient information or of missed opportunity, developed in the Fletcherian drama of the early seventeenth century, had been a characteristic of English Gothic

[32] See Ernest Sutherland Bates, *A Study of Shelley's Drama The Cenci* (New York, 1908), p. 54, and Daniel Lee Clark, "Shelley and Shakespeare," *PMLA*, LIV (1939), 278-286.

drama as early as Walpole's *The Mysterious Mother* (Strawberry Hill, 1768).[33] In this instance, Savella and Bernardo arrive in order to have Cenci answer "charges of the gravest import" (IV.iv.12). In the light of this unexpected event, the murder of the Count now appears to have been unnecessary, since the legates have a warrant for his "instant death" (l. 28). Consequently the position of Beatrice is even more pathetic now than at any previous point. Moreover, through Shelley's economical dramaturgy, the arrival of the legates serves an equally important thematic purpose of setting up the casuistical argument by which Beatrice at her trial will defend her innocence and justify the deed committed.

The basic difference between Milman's and Shelley's heroines is that Beatrice possesses a commanding intellect, whereas Bianca proceeds more by blind instinct and feminine intuition. Yet, in the trial scene, Beatrice employs essentially the same casuistical arguments that Milman puts into the mouth of Bianca. Both characters conduct their own defenses on the grounds that the innocent sufferer deserves to be vindicated. In a long and impressive speech, Beatrice asserts that the world has lost all discrimination between innocence and guilt when it condemns parricide and yet allows wrongs far greater than this to go unpunished and even unmentioned (V.ii.115-157). The bloodhounds of the law perversely insist on prosecuting the lesser crime. Marzio, the luckless agent of Cenci's death, reflects this idea when he cries out, in his parting speech, "She is most innocent! Bloodhounds, not men, glut yourselves well with me . . ." (ll. 165-166), an epithet directly echoing the Duke's condemnation of Bianca for setting "the bloodhounds of the law" on her husband's track (p. 171).

The two remaining scenes of the play take place in prison. E. S. Bates long ago pointed out their close similarity to the two prison scenes in *Fazio*.[34] Together, these final moments offer conclusive testimony to what has been apparent through the play. When Shelley saw Eliza O'Neill perform Bianca, a train of associations began which eventually led to a drama consciously

[33] See Bertrand Evans, *Gothic Drama From Walpole to Shelley* (Berkeley and Los Angeles, 1947), pp. 228-232 and *passim*. Although Evans does not discuss the important influence of *Fazio* on Shelley, I am nevertheless indebted to him for setting Shelley's play within the significant context of popular drama.

[34] *Shelley's Drama*, p. 55.

written to suit the emotive talents of an exceptionally compelling actress. Milman's dramatic use of a series of impassioned responses to extreme situations naturally complemented Shelley's vivid memory of Miss O'Neill's Bianca. Finally, Milman's concept of tragic dramatic character as that of innocence betrayed through the irresistible force of circumstances served Shelley in his own more complex creation of the genuine Beatrice hidden behind the dramatic mask of suffering. As far as he followed the paradigm conveniently set for him by Milman, Shelley succeeded in providing a vehicle for Miss O'Neill's eminently pathetic style of acting, a vehicle whose inherently sensational subject and intense dramatic interest far exceed its model.

Shelley also succeeded in writing a play whose qualities as dramatic literature transcend the influences of Eliza O'Neill's acting and Milman's play. Shelley's manipulation of sympathy for his heroine cannot be adequately summarized simply by pointing to his intention to have Miss O'Neill enact the role of Beatrice. There is at work in this play an additional complicating force. In attempting to create a character whose radiant innocence and purity and gentle dignity shine through the tragic events which close her life, Shelley neglected to take account of certain conditions necessary to hold unabated the sympathetic interest of his audience.

Production records of *The Cenci* indicate that sympathy for Beatrice is lost somewhere toward the end of the drama. Research has shown that the first performance, by the Shelley Society in 1886, drew great acclaim from the audience but that its critical reception was unfavorable. Disturbed by Beatrice's denial of her guilt in the trial scene, critics of this production asserted that she had alienated the sympathies of the audience. At the first professional production, in London in 1922, critics and audience unanimously acknowledged the emotional power of the play.[35] Yet, by this time, in the work of Bates, Newman White, and their followers, an independent critical attitude had arisen to complement the important nineteenth-century critical view of the problem of sympathetic response.[36] Although *The Cenci* does hold the

[35] Cameron and Frenz, "Stage History of *The Cenci*," pp. 1081-91.

[36] See especially Carlos Baker, *Shelley's Major Poetry: The Fabric of a Vision* (Princeton, 1948), pp. 138-153; Melvin R. Watson, "Shelley and Tragedy: The Case of Beatrice Cenci," *K-SJ*, VII (1958), 13-21; Robert F. Whitman, "Beatrice's 'Pernicious Mistake' in *The Cenci*," *PMLA*, LXXIV

stage, especially if judiciously cut to fall within conventional time limits,[37] modern readers continue to insist that, in the closing moments of the play, Beatrice becomes something other than a simple object of pathos. To set aside either the series of successful productions or the repeated adverse critical commentary is to ignore the real complexity of the problem.

A solution appears, however, if we adopt a perspective previously unsought. It is possible that Shelley had a purpose beyond the conventional tragic response of pity and terror assumed by most critics who discuss the play. In his extensive examination of the characters of *The Cenci,* Carlos Baker views the critical discomfort over Beatrice's behavior in the last act as a failure to appreciate Shelley's purpose. The poet's intention, he says, "is to display the perhaps inevitable corruption of human saintliness by the conspiracy of social circumstances and the continued operation of a vindictive tyranny."[38] After trying every conceivable method of converting her father to peace and love, Beatrice at length exchanges the armor of righteousness for the cloak of resolute vengeance. Explicitly rejecting the moral position that has guided her in the past, she adopts the implacable hardness necessary to accomplish the design necessity has imposed on her, and she maintains this new spirit of self-possession to the very end (pp. 148-150). A solution to the problem of sympathetic response may be found by setting Baker's analysis, particularly his notion of Beatrice's last unbending stance, within the context of Shelley's treatment of the theatrical audience for whom, out of necessity, he intended his tragedy to be performed.

In IV.iii the murder of Count Cenci is accomplished. Early in the following scene, Beatrice advises her foster mother Lucretia about their future conduct:

Be faithful to thyself,
And fear no other witness but thy fear.

(1959), 249-253; Paul Smith, "Restless Casuistry: Shelley's Composition of *The Cenci,*" *K-SJ,* XIII (1964), 77-85; and Charles L. Adams, "The Structure of *The Cenci,*" *Drama Survey,* IV (1965), 139-148.

[37] See Bert O. States, "Addendum: The Stage History of Shelley's *The Cenci,*" *PMLA,* LXXII (1957), 633-644, and Marcel Kessel and States, "*The Cenci* as a Stage Play," *PMLA,* LXXV (1960), 147-149.

[38] *Shelley's Major Poetry,* pp. 147-148.

For if, as cannot be, some circumstance
Should rise in accusation, we can blind
Suspicion with such cheap astonishment,
Or overbear it with such guiltless pride,
As murderers cannot feign. (IV.iv.40-46)

Beatrice here sets forth the moral position underlying all her arguments at the trial. She believes that it is morally right to pretend innocence because by eternal law the crime was justified. So, in the trial scene, she argues for what ordinary human reason would infer from the appearances surrounding the crime: if she had really been guilty of murder, she would have avoided the stupid mistakes which seem to implicate her (V.ii.93ff). It is easy enough to understand that, beginning late in Act IV, Shelley attempts to establish the inadequacy of human law in dealing with the special circumstances presented in Beatrice's case. His purpose is apparently to create sympathy for her position, not so much by pointing up its pathetic qualities as by emphasizing the divine rightfulness of her act. Presumably the audience should acquiesce *rationally* to her position, at odds with human law but justified through casuistical argument, and through this rational act achieve a profound sympathy for her plight.

But the methods of defense that Shelley allows his heroine fall into the same category with the "restless and anatomizing casuistry" which in his preface he imputes to those men who inconsistently seek justification for Beatrice's act while themselves believing it to have been just. When Shelley has Beatrice suggest to Lucretia that any means are justified to defend what is in itself a just act, he crosses the threshold of a problem that has no conventional solution. On the one hand, he is writing for an audience which would presumably respond with great sympathy to Beatrice's dilemma. On the other, he is at the same time introducing an attitude with which a conventionally minded audience could not be expected to agree: the condoning of deliberate falsification *in esse*. The result is a curious ambivalence pervading the closing sections of the play. Shelley means us to take seriously and straightforwardly Beatrice's contention that human justice is inadequate and even irrelevant to her own unique situation. Yet he has already introduced irony into Beatrice's conviction that retribution is in itself justified. He asserts in his preface:

> Revenge, retaliation, atonement, are pernicious mistakes. If Beatrice had thought in this manner she would have been wiser and better; but she would never have been a tragic character: the few whom such an exhibition would have interested, could never have been sufficiently interested for a dramatic purpose, from the want of finding sympathy in their interest among the mass who surround them. (p. 276)

In this passage Shelley confronts the unpleasant fact that his own personal ideals are uninteresting to the mass of mankind and that consequently dramatic interest can be found only in the un-ideal, the fallibly human. The poet betrays his fundamental distrust of the audience for which any acting drama must be written, preferring instead "the few" with special insight comparable to his own. "It is in the superstitious horror," he wrote at the conclusion of the paragraph, "with which [men] contemplate alike her wrongs and their revenge, that the dramatic character of what she did and suffered, consists" (pp. 276-277). Shelley implies that, in order to create a *dramatic* and therefore *un-ideal* character, the artist must capitulate to the superstitious false premises basic to the motives and interests of the masses. But Shelley cannot really capitulate; his preface tells us that he cannot.

So the play inadvertently sets up a moral paradox for its viewers. The audience is expected to accept Beatrice's (and Shelley's) idea of the inadequacy of human justice and to take straightforwardly Beatrice's conviction of her own righteousness. But at the same time the audience is to perceive the blind partiality of Beatrice's view; it is not really expected to agree that retribution is just. There is, then, a basic inconsistency in Shelley's presentation of the character of Beatrice which makes it impossible to maintain sympathy for her in the concluding minutes of the play. When, in the trial scene, we hear Beatrice emphatically deny her implication in the murder, we are aware that she feels justified in this outright lie because she has already abjured the responsibility to be bound by conventional human justice and morality. But our sympathies, already unbalanced, are permanently alienated when Beatrice appears willing to allow the hired murderers to bear full responsibility for the crime. Her contempt for human law now extends to human lives. So it appears that Shelley's own sympathy for the plight of his heroine conflicts with his own ideal of personal heroism and with his attitude toward the only audience he would expect to congregate in a theater. "There is nothing" in the play, Shelley observed in his letter to Peacock requesting a London performance, "beyond what the multitude are contented to believe that they can understand. . . ."

On the contrary, I think there is something in the play of which the poet himself was not fully aware. Through his great inventive and linguistic powers, Shelley created a theatrical character whose stature towers over that of any other in the period. But because of his individualistic approach to ethics and his fundamental distrust for the conventions, moral and social as well as legal, which governed his audience, he failed to create a unified tragic structure that would fix the minds and hearts of his audience on the catastrophe of his distressed heroine. A playwright can hardly present a successful tragedy to an audience for which he feels nothing other than contempt. Shelley is obviously on the side of the angels, but he obviously does not believe his "demon" audience (as Yeats thought of the uncomprehending populace) will be so too. Yet he insists on treating Beatrice as a "tragic" character, blinded by momentary impulse into an act of retribution—with which Shelley himself cannot sympathize. Too many variables therefore destroy the possibility of a unified tragic response. Beginning late in Act IV, the reader of *The Cenci* feels himself disengaged from his involvement in the play. He can do nothing except follow the events to their termination in a spirit of enforced detachment.

As I have suggested, however, this disengagement of sympathetic response may form part of some more profound plan than that Shelley chose to explain in his preface. The detachment effected by the closing action of the play parallels Beatrice's own detachment, born of despair, which just precedes her execution. A few moments before she is led off to her death, Shelley introduces a brief scene that contrasts the frenzy of Lucretia and Giacomo with Beatrice's own stony indifference. "Whatever comes my heart shall sink no more," Beatrice says,

> And yet, I know not why, your words strike chill:
> How tedious, false and cold seem all things. . . .
> . . . .
> You do well telling me to trust in God,

I hope I do trust in Him. In whom else
Can any trust? And yet my heart is cold. (V.iv.78-89)

Perhaps Shelley's ultimate goal in tracing the tragic end of his pathetic heroine is to remove her—and his audience as well—to a state beyond terror and pathos, a state described in his poem "On the Medusa of Leonardo da Vinci in the Florentine Gallery." Shelley finds that the power and agony of the painter's subject have an effect that moves through pathos to something beyond. "Its horror and its beauty are divine":

Yet it is less the horror than the grace
  Which turns the gazer's spirit into stone,
Whereon the lineaments of that dead face
  Are graven, till the characters be grown
Into itself, and thought no more can trace;
  'Tis the melodious hue of beauty thrown
Athwart the darkness and the glare of pain,
Which humanize and harmonize the strain. (p. 582)

The gazer's spirit turns to stone obviously not from indifference but from the artist's rendering of great, pathetic beauty "athwart the darkness and the glare of pain." Out of this meeting of extreme qualities emerges a larger, harmonizing wholeness. The aesthetic effect of the Medusa painting is the same as that of Guido's portrait of *La Cenci*. "There is a fixed and pale composure upon the features," Shelley observed. "She seems sad and stricken down in spirit, yet the despair thus expressed is lightened by the patience of gentleness"; her eyes "are swollen with weeping and lustreless, but beautifully tender and serene" (p. 278). In facing the spectacle of Beatrice's defeat at the end of Shelley's tragedy, the viewer may well be apprehending the same divine *stasis* that Shelley discovered in Guido's painting and described in his verses on the Medusa. "Here, Mother," Beatrice says at the very end,

tie
My girdle for me, and bind up this hair
In any simple knot; ay, that does well.
And yours I see is coming down. How often
Have we done this for one another; now

We shall not do it any more. My Lord,
We are quite ready. Well, 'tis very well.

In perceiving the humanizing conjunction of beauty and suffering, the onlooker becomes himself a kind of sculpted figure, arrested in an attitude of intense vision beyond terror, beyond pity. The moment of impassioned response, in which Beatrice is impelled like the typical Romantic heroine toward her irremediable act, finally becomes the purified emblem of both the heroine herself and those who contemplate the image of her suffering. The melodious continuity of life in the figure has been transfixed, frozen in space, while the viewer also stands unmoving, caught in a timeless moment as he beholds

A woman's countenance, with serpent-locks,
Gazing in death on Heaven from those wet rocks.

iv. Dramatic Character in the Romantic Age

"Suppose I stand upon the sea-beach now," Aspatia suggests in *The Maid's Tragedy*,

Mine arms thus, and mine hair blown with the wind,
Wild as that desart; and let all about me
Tell that I am forsaken. Do my face
(If thou hadst ever feeling of a sorrow)
Thus, thus, Antiphila: strive to make me look
Like Sorrow's monument. . . .

Aspatia, Ariadne, Beatrice, the Medusa—all are analogous monuments to human sorrow but monuments also to the continuity of English drama over the two hundred years from Fletcher to Shelley.[39] The timeless pathos of these graphic subjects does not, of course, adequately summarize either the aesthetic or experiential nature of that drama. And yet the contrarieties of time and eternity, distress and peace, captured in these painted and verbal descriptions come as close as any single moments can to the larger sense of life that lies implicit in them and in the drama they attempt to epitomize.

[39] For the comparison of Aspatia and Ariadne see Seward's comment on Guido's painting of Bacchus and Ariadne quoted in Pt. I, Chap. III above, note 2.

The dramatic artist of any age, writing for any stage and audience, must render "the moment" present, must forsake narrative for the artifice of actuality. But the plays that fall into the stream of continuity examined in the preceding pages make of these moments a special thing. The art of tragicomedy is, as I have tried to show, to seek meaning in the intermediate, the disjunctive; in the separable part, the coherent fragment. That art is closely allied to the art of Romantic tragedy and, it would seem, especially to the art of the Romantic play whose tendency draws it away from collective response in the theater toward the singular creativity of the individual imagination. For in these plays "the moment" not only seeks to embrace the totality of human essence and response but operates according to a new aesthetic of time itself. In this aesthetic the moment of response is presented as disjunct from the past. Our impression is of an unprepared, violent upheaval or reversal, and in this moment the character becomes perverted from the norm of innocence under the pressure of circumstance. Nevertheless, this moment is referable to time that has gone by. The past, in the guise of "fate," impinges on the present. What happened in some remote time is operative even now; perhaps especially now. These two notions of time past and time present together supply the single most extensively employed technique in Romantic drama, the development of pathetic irony of character. The analogue of human nature in the Romantic play is caught up in the flow of time, yet he appears disconnected from the events that impel him on. An "alter ego" exists by implication outside the play, a projection of the "ego" of the dramatic character. But the innocence of this alter ego requires us not to condemn the stage ego for any action, no matter how reprehensible or horrifying. Despite the behavior which a perverse or malignant destiny draws from him, the character's radically innocent "true self" remains an ideal state apart from the world in which, for better or worse, he must act. It is when the corrupting power of this world is imposed upon him that, ironically, he acts *for the moment* against his true nature and so elicits sympathy from all who observe his pathetic dilemma.

In this "Romantic" responsiveness the Fletcherian disjunction of character and event appears in its ultimate mutation: action is forced on a character by circumstance, but action neither defines personality nor conditions subsequent behavior; only *motive* defines the person and sustains it through subsequent time. And motive is, by its very nature, anterior to the act and private to the agent. Only the audience may share in its revelation. Here, in this dramaturgical situation, lies the quality that produces the "undramatic" tendency we sense in closet drama. Where motive and not action, soliloquy and not dialogue, define personality, the character tends to lose its primary reference to the other characters. Its reference instead is to an audience that has leisure to contemplate the minutiae of subtle mental revelation: a reader, an "audience of one." The basic characteristic of closet drama is its combination of the writer's special attitudes toward the character and toward the reader. As the character "turns away" from the other characters toward the audience, the visual movement from profile to full face suggests the unfolding of his true nature as a radically innocent "human being." Such a character, however attractive, is fundamentally exterior to the play. The auditor becomes the sympathetic silent reader, drawn into the imaginative reality of the character's mind, heedless that processes culminate in ends, that motives issue in action, that events, even on a stage, are no less "real" than the dramatic psyche that perceives (or distorts) them.

Lewis's *Alfonso*, when produced in the theater, was a poetic drama; when read in the privacy of the study, a dramatic poem—the same work, largely the same words, but rendered in two different modes before two differing audiences. This is the divisive tension that fragments numberless plays written in the early nineteenth century, robbing all too many of dramatic integrity, that is to say, of vitality. The crux of the situation, it may be suggested, is that the notion *ut pictura poesis*, while an important agent of imaginative creation in Romantic lyric and narrative verse, became an ultimately devitalizing one for Romantic drama. True, it could lead to the capturing of an impassioned moment, richly suggestive of unalloyed human responsiveness. But the "poeticizing" of this moment, drawn out until climax gave way to anticlimax and that to no climax at all, severed graphic epitome from the language that supported and refined its meaning. The moment "frozen" out of time and set down as a kind of speaking sculpture ultimately and inevitably succumbed to the influence of the "Laocoön" theory of passion imprisoned, with its stultifying implication of process uneventuating in action. The only usefulness that remained in the idea was to serve later poets like Tennyson and Arnold in describing the deep frustrations of an age that sought, largely in vain, for spiritual guidance from its visionary leaders. Before this larger cultural failure took place, the more private and personal dilemma of the Romantic artist was working itself out in the bifurcation of sensibilities and aims explored in this chapter. *Ut pictura mimesis,* so to speak, is the divisive concept at the root of the Romantic playwright's difficulty. Poetic dramas and dramatic poems continued, through the nineteenth century, to act as bastard half-brothers contending for a patrimony to which neither had a right. Simultaneously another natural son, melodrama, was already proving its claim to the disputed legacy of vitality.

An account of the gradual transformation of melodrama into the realistic play might properly begin with the impasse reached by the drama of the early nineteenth century. Not the best of times but the worst of times, so far as the quality of its plays gives evidence, the period of Siddons and Sheridan, Shelley and Kean nevertheless produced a concept of dramatic character that shapes and exemplifies the spirit of the age. From the incipient subjectivity of the arts in the eighteenth century the Romantic imagination drew a revolutionary idea of man's innocence of heart and ironic banishment to that vale where, as John Keats, the wisest innocent of all, realized, he must himself create his soul. It is typical of revolutionary ideas that this concept came trailing intimations of its own demise, but typical also that, while it flourished, it engaged the minds of men much like ourselves who, with alternate gratitude and disdain, receive and refashion the gifts tradition bears.

PART III
Shakespearean Character in the Romantic Age

CHAPTER VIII

Macbeth and Richard III: Dramatic Character and the Shakespearean Critical Tradition

> The painter, the poet, the actor, the orator, the moralist, and the statesman, attempt to operate upon the mind in different ways, and for different ends; and they succeed, according as they touch properly the strings of the human frame. Nor can their several arts ever stand on a solid foundation, or rise to the dignity of science, until they are built on the principles of the human constitution.
>
> —Thomas Reid, *An Inquiry into the Human Mind* (1763)

i. The Study of Shakespearean Character

ALONGSIDE the growing new drama in eighteenth-century England there developed an interest in Shakespearean plays and their chief characters which, by the end of the century, amounted to high devotion. Not only had Shakespeare usurped the place of Beaumont and Fletcher in the eyes of theatergoers; his works had claimed equal priority from their professionally critical contemporaries—many of whom apparently never entered a theater. The history of eighteenth-century literary criticism is to an important extent the history of Shakespearean criticism in this age. Because this is so, a study of the developing critical fascination with the Elizabethan playwright's great tragic figures provides an index to dominant contemporary intellectual interests. Between Johnson and Hazlitt, notions of dramatic character evolve alongside the theory of sympathetic imagination.[1] As the new drama also shows, developments in psychology parallel

[1] See T. M. Raysor, "The Study of Shakespeare's Characters in the Eighteenth Century," *MLN*, XLII (1927), 495-500, valuably supplemented by the introduction to his edition of *Coleridge's Shakespearean Criticism*, 2 vols. (London, 1930), I, xvii-lxi. See also D. Nichol Smith, ed., *Eighteenth Century Essays on Shakespeare*, 2nd edn. (Oxford, 1963), Introduction, *passim*; David Lovett, "Shakespeare as a Poet of Realism in the Eighteenth Century," *ELH*, II (1935), 267-289; and Walter Jackson Bate, "The Sympathetic Imagination in Eighteenth-Century English Criticism," *ELH*, XII (1945), 144-164.

the growth of interest in landscape as a meaningful stimulus to emotions.[2] These changing conceptions of man's nature and his place in the world about him are extensively reflected in contemporary study of two of Shakespeare's most popular characters. Although Hamlet, King Lear, and others draw consistent attention, eighteenth-century criticism of *Richard III* and *Macbeth* develops in richness and breadth of interest until, by 1785, the comparison of their central characters encompasses in a special way the most important critical concerns of the age. In fact, by the last quarter of the century, Macbeth and Richard III emerge as two opposite types of dramatic character and, at the same time, their "minds" become archetypes of the human mind in its varied reactions to the impinging outside world.

The orientation of this criticism, however, is not always easy to establish. When an aesthetician like Archibald Alison can offer an illuminating comment on Shakespearean performance, or a practicing playwright like William Hodson can write a treatise on the theory of tragic character, one must distinguish degrees of shading between theatrical and "closet" criticism without allowing a useful distinction to become blurred. Fortunately a substantial body of criticism exists which depends mainly on perceptive reading and ignores those problems treated by writers interested in theatrical performance. Concerned with plays largely as materials for the study of human psychology, such criticism provides a helpful contrast to the different complexity of dramatic character in the theater.

At the same time, an investigation of this body of writing establishes the necessary background for understanding the concept of dramatic character which finally emerged in the nineteenth century in the writings of Coleridge and Hazlitt, Leigh Hunt, Lamb, and others. This chapter will present a synthesis of significant ideas propounded by their eighteenth-century predecessors, and in doing so will establish a vantage point from which to view the treatment of Shakespeare on the late eighteenth-century stage. In order to maintain a depth otherwise impossible, the re-

[2] See Chap. III above. For the interrelation of these and other dominant intellectual and cultural trends, see Walter Jackson Bate, *From Classic to Romantic: Premises of Taste in Eighteenth Century England* (Cambridge, Mass., 1946), and M. H. Abrams, *The Mirror and the Lamp: Romantic Theory and the Critical Tradition* (Oxford, 1953).

maining pages of this book will focus on Richard III and Macbeth, two characters whose special significance will, it is hoped, become apparent as the discussion proceeds. These two Shakespearean characters elicited from eighteenth- and early nineteenth-century actors and critics a response that comes as close as any to epitomizing the attitudes of their age, not only toward Shakespeare and his plays, but toward the nature of man and of his reactions to the world outside himself.

ii. Shakespearean Character through Johnson and Mrs. Montagu

In the period up to 1765, interest in dramatic character becomes only gradually a major critical concern. Comments on the characters of Richard and of Macbeth and his wife are infrequent up to the publication of Johnson's *Shakespeare,* occurring only as occasional signs of the concentrated critical attention later to come. Although periodical essays in the early decades devote intermittent attention to these characters, interest in the theory of the Longinian sublime and in the aesthetics of dramatic "design" plainly outweighs interest in dramatic character.[3] Nevertheless, by the 1740's, character analysis sometimes competes with the traditional concern for structure. Following the precedent set by Samuel Johnson in his anonymous *Miscellaneous Observations on the Tragedy of Macbeth* (1745)—a work whose influence is discussed below—critics now begin to address themselves to the important and basic idea of Macbeth's self-deception. Only a year later, the remarks of John Upton in his *Critical Observations on Shakspeare* (1746) show that this notion has already begun to grow in complexity. Upton devotes primary attention to Macbeth's ruling passion and its destructive effects on his character. Although not lacking in conduct and courage, he explains, Macbeth mistakenly responds to the lures of his "master-passion," ambition, and his mind becomes "agitated and convulsed, now virtue, now vice prevailing." Not surprisingly, reason eventually gives way to inclination, and Macbeth's subsequent atrocities

[3] See, for example, *Tatler* No. 90 and *Spectator* No. 141, as well as modern discussions in Samuel Holt Monk, *The Sublime: A Study of Critical Theories in XVIII-Century England* (New York, 1935), pp. 10-28 and *passim,* and Walter John Hipple, Jr., *The Beautiful, The Sublime, and The Picturesque in Eighteenth-Century British Aesthetic Theory* (Carbondale, Ill., 1957), p. 23 and *passim.*

serve to point the great lesson of the play, that "wickedness draws on wickedness" (pp. 42-50). The moral orientation of Upton's criticism does not distract him from presenting a detailed account of Macbeth's struggle against evil impulse. His view of Macbeth as a virtuous man vacillating between good and evil establishes the most important single notion of his character for criticism up to Hazlitt. In addition, the attention Upton pays to the development of character overshadows his slight regard for structure. His work is an indication that interest in the interaction of supernatural and natural elements in *Macbeth*, manifest in Johnson's *Observations*, will disappear as later critics begin to concentrate on the struggle within Macbeth's mind. Supernatural elements will come more to be seen as reflections of psychological anguish. For Upton, the influence of Lady Macbeth on her husband is apparently more important than the witches' prophecy. She works herself up to such a high pitch of cruelty that Macbeth in his treasonous murder of the king becomes a mere agent of her own self-love (p. 45).

William Guthrie's *Essay upon English Tragedy* (1747) reworks Upton's notion of Lady Macbeth's relationship to her husband. Surprisingly, considering the date of his work, Guthrie's view of dramatic character is based explicitly on a naturalistic criterion. Recognizing that the "prepossession of a whole age" is against him, he nevertheless maintains that "there is not the least necessity for the chief personage in a play to have either courage, wisdom, virtue, passion, or any other quality, above what is to be found in his real history, or in common life" (p. 20). Translating a Latin source for the history of Macbeth, he points out how Shakespeare has improved on the original without violating the truth of history. Macbeth, the source reports, "of himself impatient, was spurred on by the almost daily reproaches of his wife, his bosom counsellor in all his designs." Guthrie admires the finish Shakespeare gives to these two wicked characters and points out "how artfully" the playwright has "conducted and described the human heart through every stage of guilt, rising and reluctant in the man, ready and remorseless in the woman" (p. 22). Guthrie views as immaterial the lack of intenseness he sees in the lesser characters of *Macbeth*, considering it sufficient if "one or two characters, at most, in a play, are thus worked up . . ." (p. 19).

Guthrie's criteria of natural truth in character and consistent focus suggest a shift in interest which later critics will substantiate. Concern with the central figure of a play is beginning to ıerge from the older notion, common since Dryden's essay "On Grounds of Criticism in Tragedy," of Shakespeare's ability to ke subtle discriminations between characters.[4] Guthrie reflects h of these interests, for in addition to his comment on *Mac- h* he sets down the first direct comparison of the characters of cbeth and Richard III. Praising Shakespeare for his variation uilty ambition in a number of characters, Guthrie observes:

> Ve see Hamlet's father-in-law, Macbeth, King John, and ing Richard, all rising to royalty by murdering their kinlred kings. Yet what a character has Shakespeare affixed to very instance of the same species. Observe the remorse of he Dane, how varied it is from the distraction of the Scot: nark the confusion of John, how different from both; while he close, the vigilant, the jealous guilt of Richard is peculiar o himself. (pp. 12-13)

thrie's perception of Macbeth's distraction and its difference n Richard's closely guarded guilt sets the pattern for compar- critical views of these two figures. Important for anticipat- est in the individuality of Shakespeare's major charac- cially those of similar circumstances and cast of mind, *Essay* is also notable for his insistence on naturalness er. As the sentimental movement grows in the latter he century, response to the Shakespearean character depend on the notion that he is a figure for all men influence of passion. The reader responds, Guthrie im- he suffering of a man entirely like himself, a man whose ank is no barrier to sympathy between like hearts and

years before the appearance of Johnson's edition and its preface, the Scottish philosopher Henry Home, Lord published his influential *Elements of Criticism.*[5] As in n, one of Kames's chief criteria for art is verisimilitude, an erest that moves him to criticize Shakespeare's portrayal of

[4] *Of Dramatic Poesy and other Critical Essays,* ed. George Watson (London, 1962), I, 252.

[5] 3 vols. (Edinburgh, 1762). As in citations in Pts. I and II, the place of publication of works issued before 1850 is London unless otherwise indicated.

certain characters. Kames's premise is simply that "in any severe passion which totally occupies the mind, metaphor is unnatural" (III, 132).[6] On this principle Queen Elizabeth's lamentation over the death of the princes in *Richard III* is in "bad taste," as is Macbeth's speech beginning "Methought I heard a voice cry, Sleep no more . . ." (II, 227; III, 132). Kames's treatment of Lady Macbeth is similar but involves a more subtle psychological point. Citing examples of "immoral sentiments exposed in their native colours, instead of being concealed or disguised," he finds Lady Macbeth's speech beginning "The raven himself . . ." unnatural for its failure to conform to psychological reality. Although his norm is arbitrary and although he may be convicted of misunderstanding Shakespeare's technique, his explanation is still noteworthy for its sentimental premise. Kames refuses to believe that even "the most hardened miscreant" ever murdered a trusting guest unless forced to do so. He cites Lady Macbeth's extreme agitation and her invocation of infernal spirits as factors that contribute to the stifling of remorse. However, he continues, in this mental state "it is a never-failing device of self-deceit, to draw the thickest veil over the wicked action, and to extenuate it by all circumstances that imagination can suggest. And if the crime cannot bear disguise, the next attempt is, to thrust it out of mind altogether, and to rush on to action without thought." Macbeth follows the latter course, Kames observes, but Lady Macbeth follows neither. Instead, she deliberately attempts to strengthen her heart to commit a horrible crime without even trying to conceal her motive. This, Kames thinks, is simply unnatural:

> I hope there is no such wretch to be found, as is here represented. (II, 189-191)

It is not difficult to imagine Kames shuddering as he writes the last sentence. His idea, predicated on a notion of essential human goodness, is that only the extreme influence of forces foreign to man's nature can seduce him to the commission of crime, for he has no criminal propensities of his own. Unfortunately Kames offers no discussion of the motives of Richard III, a character

[6] The idea closely echoes the principle of decorum based on verisimilitude found in Johnson's well-known comment on the invalidity of Milton's lament for Lycidas: "Where there is leisure for fiction there is little grief"—*Lives of the English Poets*, ed. George Birkbeck Hill (Oxford, 1905), I, 163.

whom subsequent criticism consistently views as his own tempter. As it stands, Kames's analysis prepares the way for more sympathetic treatment of villainy by removing the source of evil from the villain's heart and placing it in some exterior place of influence. By 1786, in the criticism of Richard Cumberland, this palliation of human guilt is overt enough to allow full and unabashed sympathy for the criminal despite even the most despicable crimes.

Three years after Kames's *Elements* appeared, Samuel Johnson brought out his edition of *The Plays of William Shakespeare*[7]—a landmark in the history of English criticism both as a summary of tradition and as a harbinger of what follows. As modern scholars have observed, the Preface reflects the tenets of neo-classic criticism and follows its well-established pattern, while the notes to the plays reveal Johnson's interest in the newer criticism of character.[8] The evolution of Johnson's critical thinking on *Macbeth* by itself sums up eighteenth-century trends. The changes he introduced by way of accretion and shift in emphasis emerge from a comparison of his 1765 notes with his preparatory efforts two decades earlier in the *Miscellaneous Observations*. There, as in the edition of 1765, a long note appears on Shakespeare and the history of witchcraft which relates character to structure. Shakespeare, Johnson says, made the entire action of the tragedy depend on enchantment and produced the main events with the help of supernatural agents; within this scheme, he suggests, the two central characters work out their destiny (p. 99). Johnson's view of dramatic character within the framework of supernatural elements is notable for its early appearance here. More remarkable, however, is another point that later becomes central to *Macbeth* criticism: the question of courage. "I dare do all that may become a man," Macbeth retorts to his wife's cruel jibes early in the play; "Who dares do more, is none." Finding these lines the most impressive and moving in the play, Johnson takes pains to set them in dramatic context. He perceives that Lady Macbeth

[7] 8 vols. (1765).

[8] *Samuel Johnson on Shakespeare*, ed. W. K. Wimsatt (New York, 1960), pp. 70-71; Wimsatt here cites D. Nichol Smith's earlier observation. Their appraisal should be qualified by the comment that Johnson's treatment of the unities does not look backward toward their traditional defense but forward to their demise, and that Johnson's rationalistic view of dramatic illusion is more peculiar to him than to any body of critical thought before or after.

appeals to her husband's soldierly instinct of courage, "a glittering Idea which has dazzled Mankind from Age to Age . . ." (p. 22). Although the lines are a perfect rejoinder to Lady Macbeth's imputation of cowardice, Macbeth is stung into acquiescing and, momentarily deluding his conscience, he follows out the oaths he has sworn to kill Duncan.

Johnson's conception of Macbeth is of a man goaded into a feat of courage that causes him to ignore the distinction he himself makes between true and false fortitude. He implies that Macbeth becomes less a man for wilfully ignoring his dependence on a divine creator whose laws govern all human conduct. Concern with the morality of human action is always near the surface in Johnson's criticism, but the specific connection he makes between required standards of conduct and Macbeth's self-delusion sets up a context for a long series of subsequent critical refinements. In its general concern with character and its specific delineation of Macbeth, Johnson's early criticism establishes both precedent and point of departure for his followers.

One of the most important later refinements was introduced by Johnson himself, whose edition of 1765 includes a brief but crucial general comment appended to the notes first written in 1745:

> This play is deservedly celebrated for the propriety of its fictions, and solemnity, grandeur, and variety of its action; but it has no nice discriminations of character, the events are too great to admit the influence of particular dispositions, and the course of the action necessarily determines the conduct of the agents.
>
> The danger of ambition is well described; and I know not whether it may not be said in defense of some parts which now seem improbable, that, in *Shakespeare's* time, it was necessary to warn credulity against vain and illusive predictions.
>
> The passions are directed to their true end. *Lady Macbeth* is merely detested; and though the courage of *Macbeth* preserves some esteem, yet every reader rejoices at his fall.
>
> (VI, 484)[9]

[9] Arthur Sherbo considers this addition the only important difference between the 1745 and 1765 texts; see "Dr. Johnson on *Macbeth*: 1745 and 1765," *RES*, n.s. II (1951), 40-47.

Johnson's notion of sameness in the characters is at first disturbing, but we should see that his judgment is a relative one. His point is that Shakespeare chose to follow a kind of Aristotelian emphasis on the primacy of action, whose proliferation left him no leisure for "nice" discrimination among the characters. Certainly Johnson did not mean that Macbeth and his wife are not well discriminated; his reference must be a general one, to all the characters of the drama. The comment echoes Guthrie's earlier defense of imputed flatness in the supporting characters of the play, but Johnson troubles to provide a precise reason. The events in *Macbeth* are made to control the actions of the characters, whereas—he implies—in other plays the interaction of characters precipitates the course of events. This is true of *King Lear*, where, Johnson observes, "the artful involutions of distinct interests" and "the striking opposition of contrary characters" contribute greatly to the effect of the play (VI, 158). Evidently reflecting the transition in current critical interests, Johnson's discussion of *Macbeth* constitutes an apology for its lack of varied characters and implies that a de-emphasis in favor of plot requires explanation.

Johnson's shift of interest toward dramatic characters appears also in his terse account of their moral effect. Perceiving an emphasis on the danger of ambition, he dismisses Lady Macbeth as completely detestable, but is significantly less severe with Macbeth. We rejoice at his fall, but our esteem for his courage nevertheless softens our sense of his crimes. Johnson's reference to Macbeth's saving quality adds force to his earlier emphasis on courage. While preserving the Aristotelian method of discussing character and action in relation to one another, he leaves the way open for subsequent critical concentration on character alone. Johnson is the last major critic until modern times to point out the controlling force of the supernatural in the play on both the course of action and the development of character. Critics after Johnson perceive the patterned events in a play as negligible in themselves, pertinent only as they bring about the revelation of character. After 1765 the course of criticism on *Macbeth* and *Richard III* proceeds clearly in this direction.

The move away from the structural aspects of dramatic character appears in Horace Walpole's *Historic Doubts on the Life and Reign of King Richard the Third*, first published in 1768.

Walpole's investigation proposes to relieve the historical Richard of accusations brought against him by early historians. Although Shakespeare reflects the Tudor retention of Lancastrian prejudice, his technique of character creation was influenced by a more pressing dramatic requirement. Assuming that Shakespeare began with an idea of the curses vented against the house of York by Queen Margaret, Walpole observes that the weight the playwright gives these curses establishes the need for a villain black enough to embody all Yorkist transgressions.[10] Walpole's assumption, then, is that objective history is irrelevant to Shakespeare's purpose. A playwright, he implies, deals with character as a dramatic expression of historical event. The influence of one character on the individuality of another overrules the prerogatives of history. Clearly, Walpole has substituted for the Johnsonian concept of the influential structure of events a notion of the way Shakespeare subordinates events to the dramatic creation of character.

With respect to this transmutation, Elizabeth Montagu's unjustly neglected *Essay on the Writings and Genius of Shakespear* (1769) is a conservative work. Heavily influenced by Johnson, her essay offers a new idea within the context of Johnson's view of dramatic structure in *Macbeth.* The witches, she perceives, set up a framework of superstitious forces in operation, yet never appear "but in their allotted region of solitude and night, nor act beyond their sphere of ambiguous prophecy, and malignant sorcery" (p. 153). From their vantage point outside the human action they weave a web of fatality and so become artificers of the catastrophe (p. 196). Turning to the human characters, Mrs. Montagu defends Macbeth as less particularized because his example is thus more universal. Shakespeare has placed him "on that line on which the major part of mankind may be ranked, just between the extreams of good and bad; a station assailable by various temptations . . ." (pp. 195-196). Having pursued Johnson's idea, Mrs. Montagu reduces his emphasis on the justness of Macbeth's fall by reaffirming the courage of the character. Shakespeare fused into Macbeth's constitutional fortitude a certain quality of kindness and a strong sense of honor, she observes, so as "to make the most violent perturbation, and pungent

[10] *The Works of Horatio Walpole, Earl of Orford* (1798), II, 172.

remorse, naturally attend on those steps to which he is led by the force of temptation" (p. 183).

By employing a Johnsonian precedent Mrs. Montagu thus arrives at her own original contribution to the study of Macbeth's character. Within the atmosphere created by the witches' prophecy, Shakespeare, she says, "exhibits the movement of the human mind, and renders audible the silent march of thought" (p. 183). This statement is the first in *Macbeth* criticism to put in precise language the premise of psychological criticism: words are external signs of mental events. The complex nature of Macbeth's mind is for Mrs. Montagu the most fascinating aspect of the play. Exploring a topic already suggested by Guthrie and Upton, she perceives a delicate balance between the force of courage in Macbeth's character and the mental disturbances to which he falls victim. Typically, her perspective includes both the man and his mind:

> The man of honour pierces through the traitor and the assassin. His mind loses its tranquillity by guilt, but never its fortitude in danger. His crimes[,] presented to him, even in the unreal mockery of a vision, or the harmless form of sleeping innocence, terrify him more than all his foes in arms. (p. 195)

The balance of courage and mental distress is especially delicate in Mrs. Montagu's criticism because of her great emphasis on Macbeth's increasing anguish over his crimes. This fact is clearest in her comparison of Macbeth with Richard III. Although Guthrie anticipated her in this, his purpose was limited to defining the varied qualities of their guilt. Mrs. Montagu offers a more comprehensive assessment of their differences. "The bad man is his own tempter," she asserts. Since Richard's own heart prompts him to his great crimes, supernatural forces would have been "only an idle wonder," Lady Macbeth's advice superfluous. All Richard requires to effect his projects is the ready agency of Buckingham. In contrast, Macbeth's "generous disposition" and his "good propensities" combine with strong passions and high hopes to make him open to seduction by "splendid prospects" and "ambitious counsels." The activity of these warring elements clearly reveals the nature of Macbeth's mind:

> So much inherent ambition in a character, without other vice, and full of the milk of human kindness, though obnox-

ious to temptation, yet would have great struggles before it yielded, and as violent fits of subsequent remorse.

(pp. 176-177)

Mrs. Montagu's detailed comparison sets the terms for discussion of these characters up to Hazlitt's analysis of Kean in the two roles. Published over fifteen years before Whately's much better-known treatment of the subject, her contribution to the history of this comparative critical idea merits fuller recognition than it has found. Her curious defense of Macbeth's universality as a moral lesson does not prevent her adding significantly to the study of this character as a type of human agonizing over guilt. Her correlating of mental vacillation with objective events paves the way for further penetration into mental processes in the writings of Richardson and Whately. Like her distinguished predecessor, she is both a preserver of tradition and a prophet of change.

Authors after Mrs. Montagu continue to find fascination in the agonies of the guilt-ridden mind. The decade and a half that separates the publication of Mrs. Montagu's and Thomas Whately's works on Shakespeare shows repeated efforts to reconcile morality, psychology, and the "rules" of art. The breakdown of the more homogeneous philosophy of criticism dominant in the earlier years of the century is evident in the variety of approaches, many of them heavily unbalanced, found in the writers of this later age. Obviously, the relationship of moral purpose, psychological reality, and emotional response in the presentation of dramatic character is now undergoing considerable debate.

An eminent example of such imbalance appears in Mrs. Griffith's *The Morality of Shakespeare's Drama* (1775). Her book poses but does not really solve the central problem incipient in the development of sentimental criticism: if, through sympathy for his circumstances, we palliate the guilt of a criminal character, how can we take his remorse as an object lesson to avoid his crimes? Mrs. Griffith offers only half an answer. Her strategy consists partly of an attack on Shakespeare for betraying an ignorance of human nature in making Richard smile and smile in the midst of villainy. "No designing or determined villain was ever chearful," she affirms, implying the moral imperative that a criminal must exhibit remorse (p. 317). Inconsistently, however, she praises the playwright for zealously guarding human honor by having Richard's wickedness arise from resentment over his deformed body and from jealousy of others for their more pleasing forms and graces. In this way Shakespeare "moves us to a sort of compassion for the misfortune, even while he is raising an abhorrence for the vice, of the criminal" (p. 312). Mrs. Griffith's concern with the necessity for guilt after crime runs at odds with her sympathetic interest in Richard's sense of causes external to his own volition that have made him what he is. The problems raised but imperfectly solved by such writers as Mrs. Griffith illustrate the sense of tradition and the search for new standards which together characterize post-Johnsonian criticism.[11] Throughout the remaining years of the century, interest in the psychology of the vicious mind runs a rough course parallel with moral concerns. While the sentimental movement created a need to discover essential human goodness behind even the worst of crimes, the sentimental moralist continued to see the representation of vice as a salutary lesson for the conduct of life.

iii. Sentiment and Imagination: Richardson, Whately, and Their Followers

No writer of this age found himself more fundamentally divided by these issues than William Richardson. "Professor of Humanity in the University of Glasgow," as his title pages loftily announce, Richardson first issued *A Philosophical Analysis and Illustration of Some of Shakespeare's Remarkable Characters* in 1774, then spent much of his subsequent life augmenting its already considerable bulk in a series of editions up to 1812.[12] The

[11] For example, William Cooke's highly derivative *The Elements of Dramatic Criticism* (1775) holds in common with Mrs. Griffith's work a close dependence on Kamesean verisimilitude. As in the case of Mrs. Griffith's censure of Lady Ann's conversion by Richard (p. 312), Cooke's condemnation of Queen Elizabeth's reaction to the murder of the princes in the Tower comes almost word for word from their predecessor—an indication of the widespread influence of Kames's sentimental critical ideas (compare Cooke, pp. 66-67 and 76 with Kames, *Elements*, II, 189-191 and 227).

[12] For a bibliographical analysis of these editions see R. W. Babcock, "William Richardson's Criticism of Shakespeare," *JEGP*, XXVIII (1929), 117n. References are to Richardson's 6th edn. (1812), containing all the essays previously published and embodying the author's final corrections. Babcock's work in late eighteenth-century criticism is indispensable; I am particularly indebted to the bibliography appended to his *The Genesis of Shakespeare Idolatry*

essays which appear piecemeal over this period form a history of Richardson's weakening grasp on moral certainty.

In what appears to be a conscious effort to synthesize the various approaches to dramatic character current in his day, Richardson began with an essay on Macbeth. Like all the essays which follow, it reflects an archetypal conception of Shakespearean character. Using Shakespeare's plays as perfect data for understanding man,[13] he builds on this novel foundation an analysis of the relationship between desire and satisfaction. Richardson's purpose is not to examine the character of Macbeth but, employing Macbeth as illustration, to examine the way the human mind changes in different situations according to the nature of the ruling passion. Macbeth is first shown as valiant, dutiful, and ambitious—but without guilt; yet it soon appears that the principles underlying his constitution have undergone a sudden and complete change (pp. 36-37). His ambition, far from diminishing, seems to have suppressed every virtuous quality. The key to Macbeth's transformation, Richardson explains, lies in "the power of fancy, aided by partial gratification, to invigorate and inflame our passions" (p. 38) and so to effect a total change insidiously, by degrees:

> Excursions of the imagination . . . are commonly governed by the probability of success. They are also regulated by moral considerations; for no man indulging visions of ideal felicity, embrues his hands in the blood of the guiltless, or suffers himself in imagination to be unjust or perfidious. Yet, by this imaginary indulgence, harmless as it may appear, our passions become immoderate. (pp. 39-40)

Richardson's explanation lays the groundwork for understanding Macbeth's individual reaction to any stimulus. Directly anticipating Hazlitt's analysis of imaginative response, Richardson points out that "minds, differently fashioned, and under the influence of different passions, receive from the same objects dissimilar impressions" (pp. 40-41). Through the reciprocal action of as-

---

1766-1799: *A Study in English Criticism of the Late Eighteenth Century* (Chapel Hill, 1931), pp. 245-265, previously printed (with some differences) in *SP*, extra ser. 1 (1929), 58-76.

[13] Earl R. Wasserman, "Shakespeare and the English Romantic Movement," in *The Persistence of Shakespeare Idolatry*: *Essays in Honor of Robert W. Babcock*, ed. Herbert M. Schueller (Detroit, 1964), p. 85.

sociated ideas, the thoughts aroused by passion nourish it and aid its growth, and so "imaginary representations, more even than real objects, stimulate our desires; and our passions, administering fewel [sic] to themselves, are immoderately inflamed" (p. 42).

This, however, is not the whole matter for Richardson, who now undertakes a lengthy analysis of Macbeth's vacillation at the prospect of murder and his mental turmoil after the crime. Macbeth demonstrates for us the truth that our moral faculties are the chief obstacle to our selfish desires. Following the text closely, Richardson illustrates how Macbeth, "distracted with contending principles" (p. 47), alternately takes up and abandons his wicked designs. The mind influenced by strong passions becomes disturbed and so reason functions only at intervals, heightening the horror of the disorder. Then, once Macbeth has attained the summit of his desires, contrition overwhelms him and his life becomes divided between illicit desire and despondent repentance (pp. 54-58). The lesson of Macbeth's moral disintegration is now clear:

> Sensibility is in itself amiable, and disposes us to benevolence: but, in corrupted minds, by infusing terror, it produces hatred and inhumanity. So dangerous is the domination of vice, that being established in the mind, it bends to its baneful purposes even the principles of virtue. (p. 65)

That Richardson places the essay on Macbeth at the beginning of his book suggests the priority of this character as an example of virtuous human nature in the grip of vicious passion. Notwithstanding the relentless moralizing that disfigures his writing, Richardson's essay is important as the first large-scale attempt to reconcile the study of mental processes with the practical necessity of discovering a suitable guide to human conduct. The student of literary criticism must come to terms with the encroachment of Shakespeare's plays at this time on the role of the sermon and religious tract as sources for principles of conduct, a phenomenon well illustrated by works like Mrs. Griffith's *The Morality of Shakespeare's Drama*. The idea that Shakespeare in his chief characters presents a human nature fallible like our own created for many critics a bridge to sympathetic involvement. Richardson, Mrs. Griffith, and others simply crossed the bridge the other way. Beginning with a notion of the universality of the central character, they abstracted from the circumvolutions of his mind a detailed map of the moral pitfalls awaiting emotional commitment.

Ten years later, in his essay on Richard III, Richardson launched another, even less successful attempt to reconcile objective morality and sympathetic involvement.[14] His approach constitutes a marked departure from his earlier view of Macbeth. Finding the play entirely an exhibition of guilt but acknowledging high interest in its chief character, he tries to reconcile this apparent inconsistency by adapting an idea from Hume's essay on tragedy.[15] Interest is produced, Richardson says, by the union of offensive and agreeable qualities. We admire Richard's intellectual powers even while we abhor the ends to which he puts them, so that our response is a mixed one, "compounded of horror, on account of his guilt; and of admiration, on account of his talents." The concurrence of these two emotions in the mind creates an unusual agitation which he can describe only as "strangely delightful." Almost desperate for a label, he terms these mixed feelings "indignation"—a word that belies the pleasurable reactions to which he admits (pp. 200-203). Richardson plainly lacks the control he brought to his earlier essay, where no question intruded of admiration for Macbeth's positive qualities. Noticeably uncomfortable at having to deal with Shakespeare's portrait of blunt, straightforward villainy, he wishes that Richard had given "obscure hints and surmises" instead of open declarations of guilt (pp. 208-209). Yet his admiration for Richard's abilities consistently turns up in examining individual scenes, and he provides a surprisingly perceptive account of Richard's approach to Lady Ann and her ruling passion of vanity.[16] In reconciling what he feels with what he thinks he should feel, Richardson's only recourse is to lay heavy emphasis on the role of conscience

[14] *Essays on Shakespeare's Dramatic Characters of Richard III, King Lear, and Timon of Athens* (1784).

[15] See David Hume, "Of Tragedy," in *Four Dissertations* (1757), Pt. II. For a useful explanation of Hume's ideas about tragedy, consult Walter J. Hipple, Jr., "The Logic of Hume's Essay 'Of Tragedy,'" *PhQ*, VI (1956), 43-52, and also Hipple's chapter on Hume in *The Beautiful, The Sublime, and The Picturesque*.

[16] Pp. 209-218; this portion of the essay was published separately, Richardson notes, in *The Mirror*, No. 66 (1779).

in the play. We are pleased at Richard's downfall because we have lost our admiration for him through our shock at his cruelty. Richard's end is not provoked by external causes but incurred by the natural progress of his viciousness, whose last horrible state appears in the tent scene, the night before his death. Here we see fully how the vicious person "is rendered the prey of his own corruptions: fosters those snakes in his bosom that shall devour his vitals; and suffers the most condign of all punishment, the miseries intailed by guilt." This scene, Richardson goes on, is in effect a summary of the way Shakespeare has constructed his chief character (pp. 231-235).

Common to Richardson's two essays is his preoccupation with the manifestation of remorse for guilt, a phenomenon which occupies an increasingly vital place in late eighteenth-century criticism of dramatic villains. The shift of emphasis in the latter piece is, however, revealing. Richardson in discussing Richard III has somewhat belatedly taken up the interest of previous critics in the sympathetic response to a guilty character—and has failed to adjust to it his requirement of moral purpose. Such imperfect synthesis places Richardson in the mainstream of contemporary critical writing.

A year after Richardson's latter essay there appeared a striking new departure from the limitations of the moral approach to art. Thomas Whately's posthumous *Remarks on Some of the Characters of Shakespeare* (1785) is a major work both for its own ideas and its extensive influence on later writers.[17] Like Maurice Morgann's notion of Falstaff,[18] Whately's concept of dramatic character grows out of a careful review of the principles of human con-

[17] Published by his brother, the Rev. Joseph Whately, at least fifteen years after its composition, the book consists only of an essay comparing Macbeth with Richard III. The advertisement in the first edition explains that Whately died before he could proceed further in examining eight or ten of Shakespeare's principal characters. What in fact happened was that, after writing only one essay, Whately set aside his project and composed a treatise, *Observations on Modern Gardening*; other concerns intervened, and he died (in 1772) before he could return to his earlier work. D. Nicol Smith has dated the composition of the Shakespeare essay as no later than 1770, while George Winchester Stone prefers a date somewhere in the 1760's—Smith, ed., *Eighteenth Century Essays on Shakespeare*, Intro., p. xxxv; Stone, "David Garrick's Significance in the History of Shakespearean Criticism: A Study of the Impact of the Actor Upon the Change of Critical Focus during the Eighteenth Century," *PMLA*, LXV (1950), 193.

[18] *An Essay on the Dramatic Character of Sir John Falstaff* (1777).

duct. Morgann's argument is rooted in an identification of Shakespearean and human character which allows him to examine portions of Falstaff's "life" not presented in the *Henry IV* plays and thus leads him to conclusions about Falstaff's "natural courage" which controvert the apparent cowardice of his behavior. Whately also assumes the fundamental humanity of Shakespearean character, but his interests are wholly dramaturgical. Whereas Morgann concerns himself with vindicating the essential goodness of the human being, Whately simply proposes to demonstrate Shakespeare's remarkable distinction and preservation of character. Because he sees the drama as the only form of art in which character can be "perfectly exhibited" (p. 3), Whately feels no compulsion to extrapolate from the text; instead he limits his examination to what the play itself reveals. In approaching the play, however, Whately comes already armed with a basic notion of human individuality. Like many of the "empirical" writers of his day, Whately does not infer a theory of human personality from his subject matter but instead seeks in it a corroboration of a previously formulated idea. Whately's theory is that human individuality is a product of the interaction of some predominant principle with other subsidiary qualities that check the principle but are at the same time controlled by it. "The force of character is so strong," Whately explains, "that the most violent passions do not prevail over it; on the contrary, it directs them, and gives a particular turn to all their operations" (p. 5). Proceeding on this principle, Whately analyzes Macbeth and Richard III, in his view the two most striking instances of Shakespeare's ability to discriminate character. Their circumstances are remarkably similar:

> Both are soldiers, both usurpers; both attain the throne by the same means, by treason and murder; and both lose it too in the same manner, in battle against the person claiming it as lawful heir. Perfidy, violence, and tyranny are common to both. . . . (pp. 9-10)

Shakespeare nevertheless discriminates between them by ascribing opposite principles and motives to the same plans and actions. Their differences are rooted in the opposite nature of their dispositions; and this in turn sets them in a contrasting relationship to the world. Macbeth is presented as a naturally good man whose temper would have deterred him from his crimes had he not been inordinately tempted by the witches. But Richard's disposition naturally inclines toward evil; he seems to have brought with him at birth the signs of cruelty and ambition. While Richard needs no external agency to spur him on to crime, Macbeth's softness and susceptibility to domestic affection require Lady Macbeth's insistence that he stifle his better feelings on so great an occasion. Macbeth's crime is the product of occasion, Richard's a manifestation of his own natural savageness. He delights in crimes, while Macbeth writhes in agony at the thought of his (pp. 9-18).

Shakespeare's dramaturgical genius, Whately continues, extends even beyond these well-defined contrasts to a discrimination between qualities both characters possess:

> Ambition is common to both; but in Macbeth it proceeds only from vanity, which is flattered and satisfied by the splendor of a throne: in Richard it is founded upon pride; his ruling passion is the lust of power. . . . Nothing less than the first place can satiate his love of dominion. . . . But the crown is not Macbeth's pursuit through life: he had never thought of it till it was suggested to him by the witches. (pp. 25-27)

Again, both possess courage to an eminent degree, but

> in Richard it is intrepidity, and in Macbeth no more than resolution: in him it proceeds from exertion, not from nature; in enterprise he betrays a degree of fear, though he is able, when occasion requires, to stifle and subdue it. (p. 29)

Macbeth's imagination dwells on the surrounding circumstances of horror, his agitation a direct opposite to Richard's serenity in parallel circumstances (p. 34). Macbeth's subsequent murders occur only through his need for security, whereas all of Richard's crimes are designed for his advancement (pp. 39-45). After a long, detailed exposition of Macbeth's vacillation and Richard's determination and unerring sense of purpose (pp. 57-80), Whately concludes that the character of Macbeth is the more satisfying of the two. Essentially a more complex creation, it is also the more highly finished through the greater variety and delicacy of Shakespeare's painting (p. 81).

Whately's comparison of Macbeth and Richard III offers a

comprehensive summary of previous thought. The motives behind ambition, the differing qualities of courage, the opposite disposition toward good and evil, and the contrasting stimulus to crime are all ideas which have occurred before. His originality lies in their successful synthesis within his embracing concept of individuality. Whately has managed to avoid the inconsistencies of Richardson's moralistic psychology by simply assuming that the human mind is autonomous and that an understanding of its workings leads to an understanding of dramatic character. Unconcerned with the relationship of literature to life either as a stimulus of healthy emotions or as a guide to ethical conduct, he offers a method for approaching a play as a work whose significance is self-contained. Guided by this purpose, he presents the view that human individuality is the most fascinating subject in art and that its manifestation in dramatic character follows a law universal in human nature. Mrs. Montagu's contrast of Richard's and Macbeth's impulses to crime, and Richardson's notion of the changing human mind, are both subsumed within Whately's idea that one directing principle underlies the entire range of individual conduct. His essay is the first to argue that the events of a play and the actions of its chief character are meaningless if not referred to a single organizing force within a wholly integrated personality. It remained for Coleridge and Hazlitt to develop this idea further through their concept of imagination as the orienting power which drives the human being and the dramatic character alike.

In the fifteen years of the century that remained after the publication of Whately's *Remarks,* no important new criticism appeared to challenge his comprehensiveness and authority. Although in the last decade Walter Whiter published his original work on the subject of Shakespeare's imagery—a study consciously based on the Lockean association of ideas[19]—most writers who follow Whately simply bear substantial witness to his influence on the study of dramatic character. Implied in this subservience, however, is the ever-increasing attention paid to sympathetic involvement in the plight of the hero, and of the villain

[19] *A Specimen of a Comentary on Shakespeare. Containing I. Notes on As You Like It. II. An Attempt to explain and illustrate various Passages, on a new Principle of Criticism, derived from Mr. Locke's Doctrine of the Association of Ideas* (1794).

as well. Far from attacking his theory of personality, critics after Whately find interest largely in debating the validity of his view of courage.

The most notable of these critics is John Philip Kemble, a young actor rapidly achieving preeminence at Drury Lane. The orientation of Kemble's pamphlet on the subject is immediately clear from the purpose announced in its subtitle. *Macbeth Reconsidered; An Essay: Intended as an Answer to Part of the Remarks on Some of the Characters of Shakspeare* bears the date 1786, only a year after Whately's *Remarks* appeared. Kemble takes Whately's view of Macbeth's lack of natural courage as almost a personal affront (perhaps because Kemble in fact emphasized this quality in acting the character).[20] Whately had observed that courage amounts to intrepidity in Richard but to mere resolution in Macbeth. Kemble takes strong exception to this distinction and finds that in effect Whately is calling Macbeth a coward. For proof that Macbeth is every bit as intrepid as Richard, Kemble examines the first scenes of the play. Assuming that the circumscribed nature of dramatic exposition requires a true initial picture of the principal character (p. 6), he quotes several passages to show the reputation "brave Macbeth" enjoys, and deduces that "the impetuosity of Glamis is the decision of intrepidity" (p. 10). Somewhat encumbered by his infelicitous phrasing, Kemble goes on to quibble over Whately's distinctions. He points to Macbeth's supposed personal fear of Banquo and flatly rejoins that the same ambition which impels him to murder Duncan urges the destruction of Banquo and Fleance (p. 19). After raising a number of similar points, Kemble arrives at a final statement of his views. "Macbeth and Richard are each of them as intrepid as man can be," yet each is at times "agitated with apprehensions." The only valid distinction between the two, he concludes, is that

> Richard's character is simple, Macbeth's mix'd. Richard is only intrepid, Macbeth intrepid, and feeling. Richard's mind not being diverted by reflection from the exigencies of his situation, he is always at full leisure to display his valour; Macbeth, distracted by remorse, loses all apprehension of danger in the contemplation of his guilt; and never recurs to his valour for support, till the enemy's approach rouzes his

[20] See the discussion of Kemble's interpretation in Chap. X below, pp. 253-269.

whole soul, and conscience is repell'd by the necessity for exertion. (pp. 35-36)

The more important value of Kemble's response to Whately lies in its indication of how the actor interpreted the role of Macbeth on the stage.[21] Yet it merits attention here for its demonstration of how vital the question of courage has become in late eighteenth-century discussions of dramatic character. Morgann in his essay on Falstaff goes to extreme lengths to rescue his anti-heroic hero from the charge of cowardice, and at least four earlier critics of *Macbeth* as early as 1746 raise the topic.[22] Discussions of honor in sentimental criticism also involve some notion of courage. Mrs. Montagu, as we have seen, observes that in Macbeth "the man of honour pierces through the traitor and the assassin" and that "his mind loses its tranquillity by guilt, but never its fortitude in danger" (p. 195). There is in fact a strong possibility that the emphasis these and later critics place on courage is connected with the concern of the sentimental movement, from its beginnings in Shaftesbury, to demonstrate the innate goodness of man.[23] Courage was the obvious mark of the dramatic hero long before Dryden's Almanzor epitomized that virtue. But it is nevertheless likely that efforts to free Macbeth from the onus of cowardice have the more specialized purpose of establishing a sentimental basis for sympathetic involvement in his plight.

Undeniably, Macbeth and Richard III rapidly become objects of sympathy in the later criticism of this century. Nowhere is this tendency more obvious than in another commentator after Whately, Richard Cumberland—well known to theater audiences as the author of *The West Indian* and other sentimental plays—whose series of four essays comparing Richard and Macbeth appeared in his *Observer* in 1788.[24] Cumberland follows Whately

[21] The augmentation of his essay which Kemble brought out in 1817 caused one reviewer to observe with restraint that "the present volume may be classed among those which it might be held unnecessary to publish"—*Blackwood's Edinburgh Magazine*, I (1817), 455.

[22] Upton (1746), Guthrie (1747), Johnson (1765), and Richardson (1774) all refer specifically to this quality.

[23] See the succinct summary of this idea in R. S. Crane, "Suggestions towards a Genealogy of the Man of Feeling," *ELH*, I (1934), 205-230; see also the discussion of sentimentalism above, Pt. II, Chap. V, pp. 96ff.

[24] Nos. LV-LVIII. References are to *The Observer*: *Being a Collection of Moral, Literary and Familiar Essays*, 3rd edn., 5 vols. (1790), II, 225-265—a reprint of the 2nd edn., 5 vols. (1788).

26. Garrick as Richard III, "Tent Scene"

27. Garrick as Macbeth: "Is this a dagger which I see before me . . . ?"

28. Garrick as Macbeth

29. Mrs. Pritchard and Garrick in *Macbeth*, the murder scene

30. Garrick as King Lear, on the heath

closely in the details of his comparison but adds his own emphasis on sympathy. He begins by noting the marked discrimination of the two characters in parallel circumstances. Having a disposition not prone to evil, Macbeth requires the agency of supernatural forces to involve him in murder, and so we see from the first that "Macbeth meditates an attack upon our pity as well as upon our horror. . . ." In contrast, Richard's heart feels no remorse. With ambition as his ruling passion, he needs no prompter to evil deeds. Macbeth's character grows in the course of the drama, but Richard's is fully formed for all his savage purposes from the moment he announces, "I am determined to be a villain" (pp. 228-229). This basic distinction leads Cumberland to decide that *Macbeth* is by far the more interesting play. In Richard cruelty "flames forth at once," but in Macbeth it seems to dawn gradually in his soul. Macbeth has a moral advantage in this distinction, and so the play as a whole is more interesting and affecting: "The struggles of a soul, naturally virtuous, whilst it holds the guilty impulse of ambition at bay, affords [sic] the noblest theme for the drama . . ." (pp. 230-231).

In the next essay Cumberland takes up the character of Lady Macbeth. Within the scheme of several influences preying upon Macbeth's virtue, she is the auxiliary of the witches; but because of the great force of her influence as a natural agent of evil, the witches are in effect only secondary in precipitating the action of the play. Cumberland's emphasis on cruelty in Lady Macbeth allows greater sympathy with her husband, whose principle is "honour" and whose rejoinder to his wife—"I dare do all that may become a man, Who dares do more is none"—makes "every feeling spectator lament that a man should fall from virtue with such an appeal upon his lips!" (p. 239).

Echoing in this way many now-familiar critical ideas, Cumberland devotes the succeeding essay to the middle sections of each play. He is evidently thinking here in terms of a series of impassioned scenes, an interest clearly related to his general concern with sympathy. The spectacle of a character caught in "the very whirl and eddy of conflicting passions" (p. 258) has a moral value that excites the pity and hence the sympathy of every spectator. But sympathy can arise out of admiration as well as pathos. Cumberland concludes his four essays with a description of Richard III in his final moment, a scene which evidently more than compensates for his flatness as a single-minded villain. Nothing can be more brilliant than Richard's conduct on Bosworth Field:

> He exhibits the character of a perfect general, in whom however ardent courage seems the ruling feature. . . . His gallantry is of so dazzling a quality, that we begin to feel the pride of Englishmen, and, overlooking his crimes, glory in our courageous king: Richmond is one of those civil, conscientious gentlemen, who are not very apt to captivate a spectator, and Richard, loaded as he is with enormities, rises in the comparison, and I suspect carries the good wishes of many of his audience into action, and dies with their regret. (pp. 263-264)

The unsteady balance Cumberland has contrived to maintain between concern with morality and interest in character topples in this concluding description. And the more he involves himself in the manifestation of character in the dramatic moment, the closer he moves toward the theatrical qualities of drama. Like the other writers discussed in this chapter, he quotes either from memory or from a standard literary edition of Shakespeare, not from a text based on performance, but his last essay is more specifically an estimate of an audience's reaction than a reader's. This theatrical interest is probably inevitable, given Cumberland's direct connection with the theater as a practicing playwright. Yet he attends to dramatic qualities which, he implies, pertain both to the reading and performance of Shakespeare. Cumberland's four essays, along with Kemble's pamphlet, provide evidence that a significant connection exists between theatrical and closet criticism of Shakespeare in this age. Cumberland's importance as a periodical essayist influenced by Whately requires his presence in this chapter, but he belongs with equal right to a discussion of theatrical criticism. In both traditions he exemplifies the growing preoccupation with the dramatic moment and with the villain as an object not only of terror but of sympathy.

After Kemble and Cumberland, Whately's influence continues to spread. The more pervasive his ideas become, the less significant it is to protract their discussion. By 1790 the way is completely clear for Romantic criticism to describe the sympathetic response of imagination to the dramatic situation, a response shared equally by the dramatic character and the critic.

In the first decade of the nineteenth century, glimmerings of this notion in dramatic criticism break forth in the youthful writings of Leigh Hunt and the more mature deliberations of Coleridge. At exactly the same time, in his *Analytical Inquiry into the Principles of Taste* (1805), the aesthetician Richard Payne Knight summarized the late eighteenth-century remaking of Macbeth into a sympathetic innocent which was even then giving rise to Romantic ideas. Knight compares the *Iliad* and *Macbeth* for the purpose of defending unity of action by demonstrating its basis in the unity of associated ideas. In each work, he explains, all the actions arise from a single cause: the anger of Achilles, the ambition of Lady Macbeth. Knight's view of the play is a triumph of originality over fact,[25] but it demonstrates with unmistakable clarity the change in critical notions of Macbeth's accountability for his crimes. According to Knight, it is Lady Macbeth's ambition, assisted by the witches' prophecies, that rouses Macbeth's hopes and urges him on to crime. The consciousness of his transgression makes him bitter, suspicious, and cruel enough to commit subsequent atrocities, from which naturally follows his destruction. In this way all of the events "spring, in their natural order of succession, from one source" and "the sentiments of sympathy, which they excite, will all verge to one centre, and be connected by one chain" (pp. 271-272). The center of sympathy is the character of Macbeth himself. Tears are the ultimate effect of all sublime impressions on the mind, Knight observes. We sympathize, and then weep, to see the pressure of turbulent passions on a great and elevated mind. We view with interest the struggle of contending affections, from which emanate "the most striking flashes of glowing, pathetic, sublime, and vigorous sentiment," and we sympathize with them in proportion to their truth, spirit, and energy. Macbeth in Knight's eyes loses little of his viciousness, but the blame for his sad transformation lies squarely on his wife, whose irremediably evil nature illustrates by contrast her husband's essential goodness:

> The character of an ungrateful traitor, murderer, usurper, and tyrant, is made, in the highest degree, interesting, by the

[25] But see the discussion of Mrs. Siddons' Lady Macbeth below, Chap. X, pp. 253-268. It is not unlikely that Mrs. Siddons' interpretation of Lady Macbeth's dominance over her husband influenced Knight, who could easily have seen her in the role at Drury Lane.

> sublime flashes of generosity, magnanimity, courage, and tenderness, which continually burst forth in the manly, but ineffective struggle of every exalted quality, that can dignify and adorn the human mind, first against the allurements of ambition, and afterwards against the pangs of remorse, and horrors of despair. Though his wife has been the cause of all his crimes and sufferings, neither the agony of his distress, nor the fury of his rage, ever draw from him an angry word or upbraiding expression towards her: but even when, at her instigation, he is about to add the murder of his friend, and late colleague, to that of his sovereign, kinsman, and benefactor, he is chiefly anxious that she should not share the guilt of his blood. (pp. 350-352)

Knight's analysis clearly shows what has happened to notions of dramatic character by the end of the century. As dramatic types Richard III and Macbeth have come to represent extreme opposites. Macbeth is completely malleable by outside forces and manifests his individual nature only through reaction. Richard, however, tolerates no influence from without; his identity as a villain is simple and complete from the moment he speaks. Macbeth is controlled by his world; Richard controls his. As archetypes of human nature, these characters share a similar distinction. Macbeth emerges as a man of feeling, extremely sensitive to assaults upon his inherent courage and devotion, highly susceptible to imaginative stimulus, guilty in spite of himself. Richard becomes a man of adamant, revealing human sensibilities only in his last moments, guilty through his own evil designs, admirable only in displaying undaunted courage. Yet, despite their crimes and their opposing natures as dramatic characters and human beings, both Richard and Macbeth elicit sympathy in abundance. Macbeth as a true man of sensibility, however, is the more compelling character. In his impassioned response to momentary perceptions he becomes a figure of man as hero, valiantly but unsuccessfully struggling against mental processes he cannot control and exterior forces he cannot understand.

As often as not, it is the moral or psychological philosopher (or even the aesthetician) who contributes to these widespread views, for critics and philosophers alike were hard pressed to see moral responsibility attached to a momentary act of passion by a man whose mind had lost the sovereignty of reason over will. As late as 1812 Archibald Alison still firmly believed that scientific inquiry into the phenomena of matter or of mind will never be satisfied until it ends in the discovery of "benevolent design."[26] Yet a basic, unresolvable contradiction remained in the example of pitiable, erring human beings. When a man of honorable purpose and humane instincts could awake to find himself a murderer of king and fellow subject, no solid island of virtuous conduct seemed able to stand against the tidal onslaughts of passion. If innocent beings were thus to fall victim to the irregular tendencies of their own good nature, how judge the vicious? Where compassion is aroused, cool moral judgment must abdicate.

So felt many writers of this day, although their feeling was seldom conscious enough for explicit statement. What one reads in their works is not an explanation, in objective moral terms, of man's fall from grace, but a highly subjective account of that fall as the essence of tragic human experience. For critics of the drama, as well as for many of their more rigorously philosophic contemporaries, Shakespeare's record of Macbeth's encounter with his world and Richard's encounter with himself summed up the variety of this experience. By the end of the eighteenth century, the histories of these two characters had come to epitomize the progress of the human mind in its vain quest for felicity at the expense of self-knowledge. Between human nature and its expression in dramatic form there appeared no real difference, for the experience of Shakespeare's characters might be the experience of any man. Each had become a mirror to the other.

[26] *Essays on the Nature and Principles of Taste*, 2nd edn. (Edinburgh, 1812), II, 424.

CHAPTER IX

Garrick's Shakespeare and Subjective Dramatic Character

> The present writer well remembers being in conversation with Dr. Johnson near the side of the scenes during the tragedy of King Lear: when Garrick came off the stage, he said, "You two talk so loud you destroy all my feelings." "Prithee," replied Johnson, "do not talk of feelings, Punch has no feelings."
>
> —Arthur Murphy, *An Essay on the Life and Genius of Samuel Johnson, LL.D.* (1792)

i. Punch's Feelings: The Problem of Acting Theory in the Eighteenth Century

EIGHTEENTH-CENTURY Shakespearean criticism, explored in the previous chapter, provides a valuable point of vantage from which to examine the treatment of Shakespeare on the stage of this period. The discoveries of psychological critics and moral philosophers, although theoretical and general in tenor, bear directly on the practice of contemporary actors; for in each case the sense of experience is the same. But there is another body of theory, observation, and opinion whose relationship, not nearly so easy to define, cannot be neglected. One of the most interesting (and sometimes annoying) characteristics of the age of Doctor Johnson was its increasing predilection to impose order on the chaos of life by writing treatises to explain, or explain away, its inconsistencies, contradictions, and mysteries. Among the most ponderable are the numerous theoretical forays into the vaguely charted country of the actor's mind. From that day to this, a multiplicity of books, pamphlets, periodical essays, interviews, and first-hand commentaries have attempted to define or at least to illustrate the actor's ways and means. Other writings of a secondary nature have attempted in their turn to resolve the contradictions of their predecessors by placing them within "camps" in a historical period or by setting them afloat in the stream of the history of ideas.

The work accomplished by Alan Downer, George Winchester Stone, and Earl Wasserman has added much to our knowledge of what texts appeared on the subject and of ways in which they may be grouped for study.[1] These scholars have also speculated on the extent to which acting theory relates to practice, and they have discovered that, despite the apparent heterogeneousness of writings on the actor's preparation and execution, enough consistency emerges to substantiate generalizations about declamation, rant, "naturalism," "formalism," and the host of other characteristics from grace to the use of the "claptrap" which put one party of actors on other than speaking terms with another. For such information we must be grateful. But the fact remains that it is often easier to describe contradictions than to resolve them. Some theories manifest admirably extensive efforts to present the tyro with a consistent approach to his craft, yet they offer very little of interest to the scholar who wishes to correlate theory with the practice as observed by audiences and critics. Other theories are of greater interest for their incidental illustrations describing performance than for anything else they say. Nevertheless, because acting theory in this age sometimes does present information of interest to those who desire to reconstruct performance, it is important to assess the general relevance of this large and weighty body of writing.

Despite the chaotic variety apparent in acting handbooks and other relevant documents of the period, two major "schools" may be discerned. The thesis of the first is that the careful imitation of the exterior forms of emotions (a look, a gesture, an attitude) will invariably convey that emotion to an audience. Such imitation will in turn release the inner springs of that emotion in the actor himself and so confer believability upon his presentation of

[1] See Alan S. Downer, "Mr. Dangle's Defense: Acting and Stage History," *English Institute Essays, 1946* (New York, 1947), pp. 159-190; "Nature to Advantage Dressed: Eighteenth-Century Acting," *PMLA*, LVIII (1943), 1002-1037; and "Players and Painted Stage: Nineteenth-Century Acting," *PMLA*, LXI (1946), 522-576; George Winchester Stone, Jr., "David Garrick's Significance in the History of Shakespearean Criticism: A Study of the Impact of the Actor upon the Change of Critical Focus during the Eighteenth Century," *PMLA*, LXV (1950), 183-197; and Earl R. Wasserman, "The Sympathetic Imagination in Eighteenth Century Theories of Acting," *JEGP*, XLVI (1947), 264-272.

it. An actor's training, then, must consist of studying and learning the various gestures, attitudes, and facial expressions whose conventional meanings provide him with a universal language of the passions, acquired like all other languages by imitation. In contrast, the thesis of the second school is that the imitation of exterior form has no value in itself. Like any language, it holds no meaning apart from the ideas to which it gives expression. On the contrary, it is the "ideas"—that is, the emotions experienced by the actor—which seek meaningful expression and so give rise naturally and inevitably to the forms (a look, a gesture, an attitude) *through* which they are conveyed. Hence an actor's training must consist of learning to feel. He must be able to call up in his mind the emotion that the character's particular circumstances suggest, letting the actual expression of emotion follow of itself.

It will be noticed that each of these "schools" assumes a close correlation between inner disposition and outer form. Believability is the end of both; but the means, or at least their order, differ fundamentally. The question becomes, in effect, Where does the actor begin, outside or inside? Associated with this question is its corrollary, raised by Diderot in his *Paradox sur le Comédien*: in giving expression to the emotion of the character, must the actor identify himself with the character? Do the two really become one through an act of conscious sympathy, or does the actor remain "outside" the character, detached, paring his fingernails, while only *seeming* to be the person he represents?[2] According to Charles Gildon, to represent "a choleric, hot and jealous Man" the actor "must be throughly [sic] acquainted with all the Motions and Sentiments productive of those Motions of the Feet, Hands, and Looks of such a Person in such Circumstances."[3] According to Aaron Hill, "To act a passion, well, the actor never must attempt its imitation, 'till his fancy has conceived so strong an image, or idea, of it, as to move the same impressive springs within his mind, which form that passion, when

[2] See Walter Herries Pollock, trans., *The Paradox of Acting* (1883), esp. p. 8, as well as William Archer's important inquiry into the subject, *Masks or Faces? A Study in the Psychology of Acting* (London, 1888).

[3] Charles Gildon, *The Life of Mr. Thomas Betterton, The late Eminent Tragedian* . . . (1710), p. 34. Gildon says he is quoting from some loose papers in Betterton's own hand (p. 18), although no outside authority supports his contention.

'tis undesigned, and natural."[4] Presumably an accomplished actor such as Betterton could follow a system like Gildon's—if he followed any at all—and make his character believable on the stage. Similarly Macklin could do the same by taking the opposite sort of approach described by Aaron Hill.[5] But the exact impression of their stage performances is, after all, the important thing. Betterton and Macklin differed notably in style, and this difference may well have produced variation in meaning. But the relationship of style and meaning to the actor's preparation is exceedingly difficult, and hazardous, to state. Perhaps we can be certain only that we have placed Betterton and Macklin in mutually exclusive theoretical categories.

Outside the more systematic approaches characteristic of writers like Gildon and Aaron Hill, other, fragmentary pieces of evidence appear which are sometimes used to prove or disprove an actor's sympathetic identification with his role. Evidence relating to Garrick's performances illustrates the difficulty of the question. Obvious value placed on technique and sure control appears in the opinion of Doctor Johnson, recorded (or, more likely, put into the mouth of Johnson) by Joshua Reynolds in his *Two Dialogues.* Reynolds presents Gibbon and Johnson in conversation about the nature of Garrick's acting:

> GIB. But surely he feels the passion at the moment he is representing it.
>
> JOHNS. About as much as Punch feels. That Garrick himself gave into this foppery of feelings I can easily believe; but he knew at the same time that he lied. He might think it right, as far as I know, to have what fools imagined he ought to have; but it is amazing that any one should be so ignorant as to think that an actor will risk his reputation by depending on the feelings that shall be excited in the presence of two hundred people, on the repetition of certain words which he has repeated two hundred times before in what actors call their study. No, Sir, Garrick left nothing to chance; every gesture, every expression of countenance, and variation of

[4] "An Essay on the Art of Acting," in *The Works of the Late Aaron Hill, Esq.* (1753), IV, 355.

[5] See Downer's discussions of these actors and theoreticians in "Nature to Advantage Dressed," pp. 1005-07, 1012-17, and 1029-31.

voice, was settled in his closet before he set his foot upon the stage.[6]

In contrast, a letter written by Garrick himself appears to value momentary inspiration above premeditated plan: "I pronounce that the greatest strokes of genius have been unknown to the actor himself, till circumstances, and the warmth of the scene has sprung the mine as it were, as much to his own surprise, as that of the audience. Thus I make a great difference between a great genius and a good actor. The first will always realize the feelings of his character, and be transported beyond himself. . . ."[7] Faced with such open contradictions, we may well decide it impossible to correlate Garrick's approach to character with what emerged in performance. Perhaps we may wish to say as William Archer said in his classic *Masks or Faces?* that Garrick "accepted the inspirations of the moment" but "did not rely upon them" (p. 209). Perhaps, finding some subtle significance in Johnson's comment, "He knew at the same time that he lied," we may even acknowledge as Archer did in disagreeing with Diderot that the real paradox of acting "resolves itself into the paradox of dual consciousness" (p. 150). But, having made these admissions, we are probably well advised to let them remain as they are, inconclusive, and to begin with such general ideas as Johnson's less petulant observation about Garrick: he was a universal actor; he could play any part convincingly.[8]

It seems futile, then, if not irrelevant, to offer a theoretical or historical solution to a problem that admits only to being described, not solved. Earl Wasserman has gone perhaps as far in this direction as it is possible to go with authority. He concludes that "through its development of a theory of the sympathetic imagination in acting, . . . the eighteenth century not only contrib-

[6] "Two Dialogues by Sir Joshua Reynolds," in *Johnsonian Miscellanies*, ed. George Birckbeck Hill (Oxford, 1897), I, 248.

[7] *The Private Correspondence of David Garrick with the Most Celebrated Persons of his Time* [ed. James Boaden] (1831-32), I, 359. Thomas Wilkes provides an instance of the idea in its most extreme form: the actor "must put on the character with the habit, and assume the air, look, language, and action of the person he represents, till his imagination, quite absorpt in the extensive idea, influences his whole frame; is visible in every glance of the eye, every air of his countenance"—*A General View of the Stage* (1759), p. 92.

[8] John Philip Kemble's record of a visit to Johnson, quoted by James Boswell, *Life of Johnson*, ed. G. B. Hill, IV (Oxford, 1934), p. 243.

uted to the growing importance of the imagination and an understanding of its functioning as the creative faculty, but also charted the major approaches to the dispute over the significance of conscious artifice and emotionally inspired imaginative insight into acting."[9] The acting theory of this century no doubt manifests these characteristics, and its importance for the history of ideas is, as Wasserman indicates, considerable. Curiously, however, those writings least concerned with general and theoretical ideas often tell us most about the notions underlying what contemporary men took to be a common, everyday activity—the entertainment of a nation. Theatrical reviews, letters from interested members of an audience, prompters' diaries, anonymous and pseudonymous pamphlets, and the host of other ephemera which inevitably collect around the activities of players, managers, and their associates, reveal precisely those things that writers concerned with theory often neglect or dismiss. Scholars have shown the value to be derived from such documents in reconstructing the styles of individual actors and actresses and the characteristics of individual performances.[10] In this chapter and the following I propose to show how closely this information relates to dominant intellectual, philosophical, and critical concerns of the day.

For it is evident, from an examination of records spread over the period from David Garrick to Edmund Kean, that acting in the eighteenth century and after became increasingly subjective in its presentation of dramatic character. Some actors of this time appear to have been heavily influenced by the theoretical tendencies toward sympathetic identification, others remained resolutely of the "old school," and still others seemed to combine both approaches, somehow, in unpredictable permutations. Yet, de-

[9] Wasserman, "Theories of Acting," p. 272.

[10] In addition to the articles by Downer and Stone cited above and below, see especially Arthur Colby Sprague, *Shakespeare and the Actors* (Cambridge, Mass., 1944) and *Shakespearian Players and Performances* (Cambridge, Mass., 1953); Kalman Burnim, *David Garrick: Director* (Pittsburgh, 1961); Alan S. Downer, *The Eminent Tragedian: William Charles Macready* (Cambridge, Mass., 1966) and Downer, ed., *King Richard III: Edmund Kean's Performance* . . . (London, 1959); Charles H. Shattuck, ed., *Mr. Macready Produces As You Like it; A Prompt-Book Study* (Urbana, 1962) and *William Charles Macready's King John: A facsimile prompt-book* (Urbana, 1962); and various articles collected in *Studies in English Theatre History In Memory of Gabrielle Enthoven* (London, 1952).

spite this eclecticism, the ideas developed by British empirical philosophers were becoming sufficiently popular to effect important changes in the concepts of human nature that actors invariably reflect in their performances. The new psychology which had a part in transforming the drama was also transforming the nature of the actor's interpretation of character. Garrick, Kemble, Siddons, and Kean each had highly individual styles; nevertheless, their performances of dramatic characters held in common the fundamental view that the essence of human nature appears, not in action, but in reaction. Gildon, summarizing Betterton's style, maintained that "*Action* is *Motion*, and Motion is the Support of Nature, which without it would again sink into the sluggish Mass of Chaos. Motion in the various and regular Dances of the Planets surprizes and delights: Life is Motion."[11] But Henry Siddons, a century later, preferred an emphasis opposite to Gildon's. To Siddons it is *reaction* that counts. Characters "present themselves to our regards, in each situation, under the forms proper to their characters, with the most slight modifications of the soul, and with those impressions feeble or fugitive, which, during the developement of an intrigue, the continual re-action of the one upon the other produces alternately, and without any interruption; their sentiment, always conformable to the situation, constantly shews itself just as it is:—feeble or impetuous at its birth; imperious in its progress; mastered sometimes, or half extinguished; hid for a moment, to re-appear with greater force hereafter."[12]

These two passages together suggest the changes in emphasis which took place over the hundred years that separate them. They also reveal an equally fundamental change in the view of the relationship of the characters to the play in which they appear. The passage from Gildon suggests that an actor's motion, or movement, reflects an explicit regularity in the universe, an orderliness mirrored in all its well-planned variety in the "garden plot" of a Restoration play. Siddons, on the other hand, has no thought for the *design* of a play, in which the actions of characters unite within a purposeful structure to form a thematic or at any rate essentially integral whole. Instead, he emphasizes the isolated moment of the characters' responses. "For them," he says,

[11] Gildon, *Life of Betterton*, p. 25.

[12] Siddons, *Practical Illustrations of Rhetorical Gesture and Action . . .* (1807), p. 204.

"the present moment is real—the future uncertain." The only coherence to be found in the play appears in the psychological make-up of the characters themselves. They "communicate their ideas at the moment they receive them; and their affections, at the instant they are affected by their impressions," so as to "tend to a determined mark, and constantly break forth, by the thought, into the future, continually experiencing modifications and changes, often contrary in their interior and exterior situations, whether by their own proper actions, or by foreign impulsions" (pp. 302-303).

And so, while there is little point in devoting an essay to the details of a controversy that has already been so fully documented, there is much to be gained by attempting to show how psychological analysis transformed the art of individual actors—Garrick, Kemble, Siddons, Cooke—so that it came to demonstrate with as much fidelity as ever the concepts of human nature and human experience mirrored in dramatic character.

ii. Shakespeare, Cibber, and Garrick's Richard III

The theatrical presentation of *Macbeth* and *Richard III* in the eighteenth century rested on a concept of Shakespeare's text quite different from that of literary critics and editors. It is not difficult to see why. The structure of the theater and the interests and values of its audience had undergone radical changes since Shakespeare's day. Dryden's remaking of Shakespeare's plays is only one of many indications that a playgoing aristocratic society was exerting pressures to which Shakespeare's text as it stood could not be made to respond. Sir William Davenant's "operatized" *Macbeth* and Colley Cibber's rewritten *Richard III* reflect common Restoration—and eighteenth-century—theater practice, while the literary texts edited by Nicholas Rowe and his successors reflect a theater that had ceased to exist. Editors could hope they were offering the reading public what Shakespeare himself wrote. Theater managers could only hope that Shakespeare had been "improved" sufficiently to suit the tastes of audiences on whom their existence depended. For these reasons, reconstruction of eighteenth-century performances of *Richard III* and *Macbeth* must take into account the disparity between the literary texts employed by non-theatrical critics and the texts players used in creating their roles. Yet the remarkable fact about this disparity is that it did not prevent actors and critics from making virtually identical interpretations of character.

Study of Richard and Macbeth as characters on the late eighteenth-century stage logically begins with Garrick, whose debut as Richard in 1741 was followed three years later by his own production of *Macbeth.* Acting texts used well into the nineteenth century derive from his performances of these two characters, but their previous history differs considerably. Garrick's *Macbeth* replaced Davenant's operatic spectacle with a play much closer to Shakespeare's, while his *Richard* depended on the extensively revised version Cibber had introduced some forty years before.

Produced at Drury Lane around December of 1699,[13] Cibber's *The Tragical History of King Richard III* was patently designed to exploit the talents of a particular leading actor. Samuel Sandford—"the best Villain in the World," as Charles II had called him[14]—had around 1690 played the title role in a King's Company production of Shakespeare's *Richard III.*[15] It is possible that Cibber saw his performance and certain that he rewrote Shakespeare's play with this actor in mind. Cibber played the title role himself, he explains in his *Apology,* only because Sandford was then engaged at Lincoln's Inn Fields, and he modeled his performance on the way he thought Sandford would have played the part. Cibber gives no details of his interpretation, but his description of Sandford's characteristic style suggests how he went about it:

> This Actor, in his manner of Speaking, varied very much from those I have already mentioned. His Voice had an acute and piercing Tone, which struck every Syllable of his Words distinctly upon the Ear. He had likewise a peculiar Skill in his Look of marking out to an Audience whatever he judg'd worth their more than ordinary Notice. When he deliver'd

[13] See Allardyce Nicoll, *A History of English Drama 1660-1900,* Vol. I: *Restoration Drama,* 4th edn. (Cambridge, Eng., 1952), I, 397. The play was first published in London in 1700 as *The Tragical History of King Richard III. As it is Acted at the Theatre Royal.*

[14] Anthony Aston, *A Brief Supplement to Colley Cibber, Esq; His Lives Of the late Famous Actors and Actresses* [1748], p. 11. See Robert H. Ross, Jr., "Samuel Sandford: Villain From Necessity," *PMLA,* LXXVI (1961), 367-372.

[15] See William Van Lennep's notes in *TLS* for 30 April 1938, p. 296, and 18 June 1938, p. 418.

a Command, he would sometimes give it more Force, by seeming to slight the Ornament of Harmony. In *Dryden*'s Plays of Rhime, he as little as possible glutted the Ear with the Jingle of it; rather chusing, when the Sense would permit him, to lose it, than to value it.

Had *Sandford* liv'd in *Shakespear*'s Time, I am confident his Judgment must have chose him, above all other Actors, to have play'd his *Richard the Third*: . . . he had sometimes an uncouth Stateliness in his Motion, a harsh and sullen Pride of Speech, a meditating Brow, a stern Aspect, occasionally changing into an almost ludicrous Triumph over all Goodness and Virtue: From thence falling into the most asswasive Gentleness, and soothing Candour of a designing Heart.[16]

Cibber's play is a peerless vehicle for an actor of these qualities. Behind every scene lies the intention of presenting a figure of protean variety and commanding presence, a character constantly in view, constantly in control. To this end Cibber borrowed greatly from Shakespeare's Richard, but he converted Shakespeare's history play into something more purely a character drama. By cutting the original drastically, by borrowing lines and even whole scenes from other Shakespearean histories, and by reworking Shakespeare's language and adding lines and scenes of his own invention, Cibber produced a remarkably viable theatrical property whose endurance on the stage exceeded its model's.[17] The success of Cibber's version was due in part to the rigid dramatic economy he imposed on a less shapely original, but more directly to the fascinating blackguard whose spirit informs the entire play and its clean-limbed structure.

Cibber establishes his central figure swiftly and effectively. The

[16] *An Apology for the Life of Colley Cibber*, ed. B. R. S. Fone (Ann Arbor, 1968), pp. 80-81.

[17] A late-century comment praises Cibber's version for giving Shakespeare's method and manner an "immortality, which probably would have sunk almost into oblivion, for want of some such care . . ."—*The Theatrical Review; or, New Companion to the Play-House* (1772), I, 81-82. For a succinct analysis of Cibber's borrowings see Beecher Hogan, *Shakespeare in the Theatre*, I (Oxford, 1952), 378. Christopher Spencer provides the most extensive study to date of the text and meaning of the play—*Five Restoration Adaptations of Shakespeare* (Urbana, 1965), pp. 24-28, 415-421, and 448-464. Although my interpretation of Cibber's Richard differs from Spencer's in certain respects, his point (pp. 27-28) that Cibber changed the *concept* of the character is the basis for any adequate understanding of the play.

first scene presents a pathetic king in a pathetic situation: King Henry VI, whose soul "was never form'd for Cruelty" (p. 3), discovers that Gloucester has been instrumental in killing his son. The dramatic contrast of pious ineffectuality and relentless villainy is heightened at Richard's entrance. Dropping the first four lines of Richard's soliloquy (history is only a peripheral concern) and condensing the rest, Cibber notably omits the line "I am determined to prove a villain." The result is a picture, pathetic unlike Shakespeare's, of a self-pitying deformed misfortunate. The second scene is just as brief and sure in establishing Richard's determination to possess the throne. He stabs King Henry to death and, disclaiming all ties of human affection, announces, "I am—my self alone" (p. 10). These two scenes together make up a first act reduced to the bare bones of action, almost all the display of Shakespearean rhetoric excised. Richard quickly emerges a barbarous, conscienceless villain singlemindedly plotting his way to the throne but at the same time dropping hints for sympathy which an audience can hardly fail to acknowledge. Subsequent acts develop structurally along lines suggested by the two aspects of Richard's character. His unrelenting determination to seize supreme power results in a single, straightforward action, while individual scenes are remade or invented to exploit the pathetic response of an audience. At the same time, Cibber's revisions indicate a general concern for increasing the verisimilitude of action, situation, and character. The omission of the long rhetorical periods that partly characterize Shakespeare's Richard points to a more "natural" concept of his reality on the stage, as does the tailoring of the play to emphasize Richard at the expense of other characters. Cibber's amplification of the pathetic qualities of his material also helps to create theatrical illusion by drawing the audience's emotions into direct involvement with the characters.

The scenes with Lady Ann reflect these various purposes. The first, shorter than its counterpart in Shakespeare, makes its effect through the technique of sudden reversal common to the heroic play. Holding Richard's sword poised in mid-air, Lady Ann stops abruptly for an aside interpolated by Cibber with clearly pathetic intent:

> What shall I say or do? Direct me Heaven;
> When stones weep sure the tears are natural,

31. Garrick as Richard III, on Bosworth Field

32. Kemble as Richard III

33. Kean as Richard III

34. Spranger Barry as Macbeth

35. John Henderson as Iago

36. Kemble as Macbeth

And Heaven it self instructs us to forgive,
When they do flow from a sincere Repentence.
(p. 14)

Richard's next line—"Nay, do not pause"—is much more literally obvious here than in Shakespeare. But the effect of this brief moment modifies our sense of Richard's control over Ann. In Shakespeare, his "Nay, do not pause" is a well-calculated attempt to *make* her pause, while in Cibber the pause is independently motivated by the playwright's intent to combine admiration with pathos. Similarly pathetic is the second scene, where Cibber titillates his audience's tastes by augmenting the love interest in his plot. As melancholy music sets the atmosphere, Lady Ann laments her rash capitulation to Richard—who suddenly interrupts and summarily tells her she has committed "the worst of Crimes, out-liv'd my liking." In an aside he tells us that "the fair *Elizabeth* has caught my Eye, My heart's vacant . . ." (p. 26). What is strictly a political maneuver in Shakespeare becomes a personal amour in Cibber. Nevertheless this interpolated scene is not quite the excrescence it may appear. Cibber is using a tested method for heightening interest in character; at the same time he is doubling his opportunities for rendering Lady Ann an object of pathos and for emphasizing the illusion of real life. Wherever pathos is possible, Cibber exploits it—unless it may slow down the action. The smothering of the young princes, executed off-stage in Shakespeare, comes in for quick but effective on-stage treatment in Cibber,[18] while the earlier drowning of Clarence in the malmsey butt is, like the character of Clarence himself, omitted. Clarence would have impeded the swift development of Act I, just as he does in Shakespeare, and the princes seem more likely to elicit a pathetic response.

Strangely enough, however, Cibber takes care to remove most of the self-questioning that makes Shakespeare's Richard a more complex creation. At the end of Act III Cibber interpolates a soliloquy ending "Conscience, lie still—More lives must yet be drain'd, Crowns got with Blood must be with Blood maintain'd"

[18] For some unaccountable reason, however, Cibber later excised the scene and wrote another, more brief, to cover its loss; the original scene is missing from the second (1718) and all subsequent editions. See Arthur Colby Sprague, "A New Scene in Colley Cibber's *Richard III*," *MLN*, XLII (1927), 29-32.

(p. 31) which seems to derive from the soliloquy in Shakespeare's Act IV, but with the important difference that, there, Richard reflects on the uncertainty of his position and the repeated sins it requires. In addition, Cibber rewrites this same soliloquy for his version of the "presence" scene, where Shakespeare's five lines become

> No matter what's the way—For while they live
> My goodly Kingdom's on a weak Foundation.
> 'Tis done: My daring heart's resolv'd—they're dead.
> (p. 37)

The distinctly suave tone contrasts with that of Shakespeare's Richard, who at this point feels himself too deeply embroiled in sin even to think of backing out. Again, Shakespeare's later scene with Richard, Catesby, and Ratcliffe, where Richard's unsureness and distraction are heavily emphasized, becomes in Cibber another instance of the usurper's swift decisiveness.

Cibber's purposes of focusing attention on Richard, exploiting the pathetic qualities of his material, and enhancing the illusion of reality reach their climax in the tent scene, one of the most inherently theatrical episodes in the play. Cibber establishes atmosphere with some lines from the Chorus in *Henry V*, then quickly proceeds to the main action of the dream sequence. Shakespeare had achieved a notable effect by adapting the convention of opposing camps to simultaneous setting, so that the ghosts of those Richard has slain speak first to him and then to Richmond as each warrior lies asleep in his tent, presumably on opposite sides of the stage. Cibber narrows the focus and at the same time increases verisimilitude simply by cutting out Richmond and his retinue altogether, so drawing undivided attention to Richard. Moreover, Cibber carefully pares down the number of ghosts to those whose characters have previously appeared on stage, and, not content with this, he drops Buckingham. The four who remain—King Henry, the two young princes, and Lady Ann—suggest that Cibber had the structure of this scene in mind from the beginning of the play, since he presents here the most pathetic of all Richard's unhappy victims. By judicious cutting, he adds to the effect by pointing up the quality of pathos in their speeches. The economy of Cibber's operation is preserved in Richard's speech on awakening, distilled from Shakespeare's twenty-nine lines of inner debate over sin and of momentary despair to nine lines in which Richard calls his conscience a tyrant, decides it is terrible to retreat, and concludes that he dare not repent (p. 52).

The final scenes on Bosworth Field show again what has been obvious throughout the play, that history is of interest only to the extent that it provides moments for the display of fascinating character. The Folio stage direction "Enter Richard and Richmond; they fight; Richard is slain" is scaffolding enough for Cibber to build a scene composed of ten lines in which the two characters challenge each other, another line while Richard is wounded, nine more for a death speech, and for good measure seven lines of moral-drawing from Richmond. The crowning of Henry VII provides a brief moment of spectacle, and then a truncated version of his closing speech ends the play (pp. 54-56).

Where Shakespeare has filled out a panoramic view of political chaos during the Wars of the Roses, Cibber has provided a neat and simple drama of villainy avenged. But there is more to it than this. One reader has observed that Cibber's character lacks the intellectual malignity of Shakespeare's,[19] and this is certainly the case. But, if Richard is an outrageous monster as Cibber presents him, he still retains characteristics of Shakespeare's subtle, ingenious machiavel which fascinate as well as offend. More important, as the subsequent acting tradition reveals, the adapter's brief hint at the beginning of the play of a wronged man beneath a villainous exterior becomes the cue for actors after Cibber[20] to portray a sympathetic figure disproportionate to Cibber's portrait. The liberties later actors took in playing this text show that what may be Cibber's momentary aberration becomes the key to the character he, and Shakespeare, drew.

The actor who above all others effected this change was David Garrick. When Garrick chose this role for his London debut, the weight of stage tradition apparently precluded the use of any save Cibber's version. Although Garrick later might have restored Shakespeare's original play, he did not do so, probably because audiences had come to identify him with Cibber's character and also because the lengthy restored version would have left something to be desired that Cibber's economical and eminently

[19] Hazelton Spencer, *Shakespeare Improved: The Restoration Versions in Quarto and on the Stage* (Cambridge, Mass., 1927), p. 338.

[20] Cibber was still playing the role as late as 1739; see Hogan, *Shakespeare in the Theatre*, I, 388.

playable script, written for proscenium staging, could provide. These circumstances would seem unfavorable for discovering any significant tie between the Richard Garrick played and the Richard familiar to literary critics. Yet, notwithstanding the difference in character reflected in the diverse texts, assessments of Garrick's appearances in the role show a remarkable similarity to the interpretations of later critics who supposedly had no inclination to go to the theater or even to consider that Shakespeare's plays were written for stage presentation. By Garrick's retirement in 1776, these critics were only beginning to discover independently what had been apparent on the boards of Drury Lane for over thirty years.

"He restor'd Nature to her lawful Empire upon the Stage, and taught us by the Conviction of our sympathizing Souls, that Kings themselves were *Men,* and *felt* like the rest of their Species."[21] So goes a typical mid-century comment on Garrick, echoing the praise of captivated audiences from his first performance as Richard. Garrick's ability to grip his public rested on his attention to varied, expressive features and on an unconventional pantomimic style he had worked out in place of the formality of traditional declamation. The character of Richard was visible on his face from the moment he entered, his biographer Arthur Murphy observed of the debut. The power of his imagination, Murphy thought, transformed him into the very man, and the passions, rising in rapid succession, were apparent in every feature before he uttered a word.[22] When Garrick spoke the truncated soliloquy provided by Cibber, it was clear that a new interpretation of Richard had appeared. Wherever this character speaks of his own imperfections, wrote Thomas Wilkes in 1759, he is galled and uneasy. Seeing himself unequal to the rest of mankind, he determines on villainy. Wilkes explains how new and striking Garrick's innovation was. By acting "the cross-grained splenetic turn" of Richard, he shows how the survey pains him, whereas other actors smile as if pleased with their own appearance.[23] That this prince was a man, and felt like a man, was certain to Garrick's audiences. Yet he left no doubt that he could feel and feel and be a villain still. His ability to act the dissembling passion required

[21] [J. G. Cooper], *Letters Concerning Taste* (1755), p. 109. For a more detailed assessment of Garrick's acting, see *Champion* No. 455, quoted in *Gentleman's Magazine,* XII (1742), 527.

[22] Murphy, *The Life of David Garrick* (1801), I, 22-23.

[23] Wilkes, *General View,* p. 237.

in the scene with Lady Ann was high enough to persuade her of his sincerity,[24] and when Garrick's Richard flung away his prayer book after dismissing the deputation that would have him king, the audience, according to his biographer Percy Fitzgerald, lost all hesitation and "found relief for their emotions in rapturous shouts of applause."[25]

These "moments" were consistently marked with the combination of ease, propriety, and great variety that Garrick brought to his roles. There is no better evidence of this ability in *Richard III* than the tent scene, where Garrick reinforced the interpretation established in his opening speech. The scene represented Garrick's most extended effort at total "naturalness," complete with the starts and pauses of a man under tremendous mental strain. The effect of his pauses is described in a handbook of theatrical expression, published in 1755, which chooses this scene as an example of the technique. Garrick, observes Roger Pickering, its author, "wakes all the Terrors of an Imagination distracted by conscious Guilt." In the brief sequence "Give me a Horse—bind up my Wounds! Have Mercy, Heav'n!"[26] Garrick presents the incoherence suggestive of the guilty confusion of his senses, then pauses at the end of the first line before seeking, for the first time in his life, forgiveness. The pause, Pickering explains, must be long because terror retards the motion of the blood, and "to bring a remorseless Wretch to *Feeling*, and from *Feeling* to *Pray*, requires a PAUSE *indeed*," one which demonstrates the justness and beauty of Garrick's action "in so small a *Compass!*"[27] Wilkes also

[24] *The Theatrical Review; or, Annals of the Drama* ([1763]), I, 79.

[25] Fitzgerald, *The Life of David Garrick*, rev. edn. (London, 1899), p. 41. Fitzgerald's distance from his subject offers little interference with the accuracy of his summaries; my general reading makes it apparent that, despite his lack of documentation, Fitzgerald bases his accounts on an exhaustive examination of contemporary sources. See the general description of these sources in his Introduction, pp. xiii-xiv.

[26] Throughout this chapter and those that follow I have given the text presented by the writer quoted rather than arbitrarily choosing some one version as standard.

[27] [Roger Pickering], *Reflections Upon Theatrical Expression in Tragedy* (1755), pp. 50-51. A member of the audience at one of the performances in 1741, however, preferred an even longer pause when Richard lies down upon the couch and then starts up and blurts out, "Ha! what means that dismal voice!"—Letter from the Rev. Thomas Newton, dated 16 December 1741, in Boaden, ed., *Private Correspondence*, I, 3-4. Again, another correspondent would have Garrick "lie asleep some little time after the disappearing of the ghosts, and give signs of farther commotions in his mind . . ."—Undated, unsigned letter in Boaden, ed., *Private Correspondence*, I, 10.

makes a point of the terror Garrick evoked in this moment and contrasts it with the calmness of his soliloquy before retiring to his couch.[28] Fitzgerald's summary of Garrick's innovations in this scene and in the play as a whole is representative:

> What struck all present was that before there had been only one broad conventional delineation of "the wicked tyrant," who was savage and furious, and nothing more, merely raging like a maniac. Even at his opening speech, something new and characteristic was presented; for instead of "chuckling" over his own deformity, and taking pleasure in being so odious to his fellow-creatures, he showed himself pained and uneasy when he dwelt on these defects. . . . In his love-making to *Lady Anne,* his ardour was so earnest and passionate that the audience for the moment forgot it was mere hypocrisy. Here, again, what a contrast to the mouthing, scornful advances of the older school. . . . The famous tent scene, which was much talked of, and which Hogarth painted, seems to have deserved all this admiration. When he started from his sleep, his face, attitude, everything was a picture of horror and terrors. He called out boldly, as if in the battle, "Give me another horse!" then paused, and, with dismay in his face, came forward, crying out in misery, "Bind up my wounds!" then dropping on his knee, prayed in the most piteously tender accent—
>
> "Have mercy, Heaven!"[29]

[28] Wilkes, *General View,* p. 239.

[29] Fitzgerald, *Life of Garrick,* p. 250. A poem published late in Garrick's career almost certainly reflects his business in the tent scene:

> And mark where Richard near his tent,
> Tastes the cool fragrance of the air,
> Remorse within his bosom pent,
> And deadly hate, and black despair;
> Yet once again behold, he sleeps,
> Hark! on his ear the low groan creeps;
> He shudd'ring starts, convulsive shakes,
> He heaves, he turns, he leaps, he wakes,
> Each feature seems with wild amazement hung,
> The sudden pray'r to heav'n drops fault'ring
> from his tongue.

For the complete text see Andrew Erskine, "Ode to Fear," *Gentleman's Magazine,* XXXIII (1763), 196.

Although forced for various reasons to use Cibber's text, Garrick seems to have brought to it an interpretation of character suggestive of Shakespeare's. Cibber minimized the Shakespearean qualities of disturbed inner ruminating and momentary remorsefulness; Garrick, as if to compensate for the omission, played what Cibber had left of these qualities with an impassioned emphasis out of proportion to their meagerness in the script. His success in the tent scene in exhibiting the tortured soul beneath kingly garments fixed this interpretation in the minds of his audience. The epitome of Garrick's Richard was the moment when he awoke to the full and terrible realization of the consequences of his crimes. Hogarth's justly famous painting of this moment, together with the many illustrations it inspired—more numerous than of any other scene in *Richard*[30]—indicates its new meaning beyond doubt. [see Plate 26]

iii. Garrick's "Restored" *Macbeth*

Three years after his debut in Cibber's *Richard,* Garrick, although not yet manager of Drury Lane, produced a *Macbeth* for which he himself was wholly responsible. The ample scholarship on this production obviates a detailed comparison of Garrick's text with his source. Scholars have demonstrated that the young actor bravely abandoned the Davenant version which had held the boards for almost three quarters of a century in favor of the text "as written by Shakespeare."[31] The fidelity to Shakespeare is not complete, since Garrick retained two of Davenant's musical scenes with the witches, cut some 269 lines from his "restored" text including Lady Macbeth's in the discovery scene, and added a death speech of his own devising.[32] Nevertheless Garrick managed to preserve substantially intact the spirit and language of the original in a text that faithfully reflects the identity of Shakespeare's central character.[33] Garrick was now free to build a pro-

[30] See, for example, *Catalogue of Dramatic Portraits in the Theatre Collection of the Harvard College Library*, ed. Lillian Arvilla Hall (Cambridge, Mass., 1931), II, 102-104.

[31] See George Winchester Stone, "Garrick's Handling of *Macbeth*," *SP*, XXXVIII (1941), 609-628, and Burnim, *Garrick*, pp. 103-126.

[32] See Stone, "*Macbeth*"; Robert E. Moore, "The Music to *Macbeth*," *Musical Quarterly*, XLVII (1961), 22-40; and Roger Fiske, "The 'Macbeth' Music," *Music and Letters*, XLV (1964), 114-125.

[33] As the reader's own comparison will easily reveal, Garrick's text is the

duction and an interpretation based on the essential dramatic contrast in Shakespeare's play between Macbeth's hesitation and Lady Macbeth's inveteracy. Records of *Macbeth* performances at Drury Lane during the Garrick period provide full evidence of this intention.

Fully aware that carping criticism might destroy what he had taken such pains to create, Garrick anticipated his opening performance with a delightful satirical pamphlet entitled *An ESSAY on ACTING: In which will be consider'd The Mimical Behaviour of a Certain fashionable faulty ACTOR, and the Laudableness of such unmannerly, as well as inhumane Proceedings. To which will be added, A Short CRITICISM on His acting MACBETH* (1744). Although scholars have established its bearing on the *Macbeth* production,[34] it has not been extensively examined for the light it sheds on Garrick's interpretation of his role.[35] Garrick adopts the tone and verbal mannerisms of the typical critic whose attack he intends to forestall, offering such excellent comic ironies as a suggested emendation of "*Goary Locks*" to "*Goary* TYE" or "Goary *Wig*" in deference to accepted costume (p. 20). But beneath the satirical veneer it is possible to discover some precise indications of how he intends to play the part. Turning a serious description upside down by adding one patent absurdity after another, he comments:

> When the *Murder* of *Duncan* is committed, from an immediate *Consciousness* of the Fact, his *Ambition* is *ingulph'd* at that Instant, by the Horror of the Deed; his *Faculties* are intensely rivited to the *Murder* alone, without having the least Consolation of the *consequential Advantages*, to comfort him in that Exigency. He should at that Time, be a *moving Statue*, or indeed a *petrify'd Man*; his Eyes must *Speak*, and his *Tongue* be *metaphorically Silent*; his *Ears* must be *sensible* of *imaginary* Noises, and *deaf* to the *present* and *audible* Voice of his Wife; his *Attitudes* must be *quick* and *permanent;* his Voice *articulately trembling*, and *confusedly intel-*

basis, as Stone shows, for the Bell editions beginning in 1773; see Stone's detailed examination of Garrick's text in "*Macbeth*," pp. 611-622.

[34] See Stone, "*Macbeth*," pp. 609-610, and Burnim, *Garrick*, pp. 105-106.

[35] Alan Downer has shown that this pamphlet contains important clues to Garrick's interpretation; see "Nature to Advantage Dressed," p. 1016.

> *ligible;* the Murderer should be seen in *every Limb,* and yet every *Member,* at that Instant, should seem *separated* from his *Body,* and his *Body* from his *Soul:* This is the Picture of a compleat *Regicide,* and as at that Time the *Orb below should be hush as death;* I hope I shall not be thought *minutely circumstantial,* if I should advise a *real* Genius to wear *Cork Heels* to his Shoes, as in this Scene he should seem to *tread on Air. . . .* (pp. 8-9)

The inordinate use of rhetorical paradox and italics for emphasis does not obscure the impression that Garrick will play the scene for its possibilities of horror and will portray a Macbeth almost rooted to the ground with hesitancy over the projected crime. Again, employing the advice of his anonymous critic to play in a manner opposite to his own conception, Garrick describes the dagger scene:

> *Macbeth,* as a Preparation for this Vision, is so prepossess'd, from his Humanity, with the Horror of the Deed, which by his more prevailing Ambition he is incited to, and for the Perpetration of which, he lies under a promissary Injunction to his Lady, that his Mind being torn by these different and confus'd Ideas, his Senses fail, and present that *fatal Agent* of his Cruelty,—the *Dagger,* to him:—Now in this visionary Horror, he should not rivet his Eyes to an *imaginary* Object, as if it *really* was there, but should shew an *unsettled Motion* in his Eye, like one not quite awak'd from some disordering Dream; his *Hands* and *Fingers* should not be *immoveable,* but *restless,* and endeavouring to disperse the Cloud that over shadows his optick Ray, and bedims his Intellects; here would be Confusion, Disorder, and Agony! *Come let me clutch thee!* is not to be done by *one* Motion only, but by several *successive Catches* at it, first with one Hand, and then with the other, preserving the same Motion, at the same Time, with his Feet, like a Man, who out of his Depth, and half drowned in his Struggles, *catches* at *Air* for *Substance:* This would make the Spectator's Blood run cold, and he would almost feel the Agonies of the Murderer himself.
>
> (pp. 17-18)

One infers that Garrick will rivet his eyes on the imaginary object,[36] that eyes and hands will be equally immovable, and that he will reach for the visionary dagger with a single motion. [see Plate 27]

Garrick uses the same techniques of ironic advice and inverted description in speaking of the banquet scene, where Macbeth's reaction to the ghost of Banquo sitting in his chair is to stare fixedly at him while crying out, "Which of you have done this?"[37] On the ghost's second appearance Macbeth is to become "quite lost in the present Guilt and Horror of his Imagination" (p. 21), yet holding his ground and finally summoning courage enough to follow the ghost out, his hand upon his sword (p. 19). The combination of guilt-stricken horror and fortitude indicated in the description of this scene tallies with Garrick's general concept of Macbeth's character. "He is an experienc'd General," he says, "crown'd with Conquest, *innately Ambitious*, and religiously Humane, spurr'd on by *metaphysical* Prophecies, and the *unconquerable Pride* of his *Wife*, to a Deed, *horrid* in *itself*, and *repugnant* to his Nature . . ." (p. 13).

Shortly after the opening of his new *Macbeth*, Garrick received a letter criticizing his performance and offering suggestions. Its anonymous author objects to the excessive dejectedness of Macbeth's mind, a contradiction to Shakepeare's "bold and daring fellow."[38] Granting that Macbeth is not naturally malicious and

[36] Arthur Murphy offers support for this inference in his comment, "I cannot help starting with him at the visionary DAGGER, and partake of his amazement"—Charles Mercury, pseud., in *The Entertainer*, No. 11 (12 November 1754), reprinted in *New Essays by Arthur Murphy*, ed. Arthur Sherbo (n.p.: Michigan State University Press, 1963), p. 66.

[37] Pp. 18-19. Andrew Erskine's "Ode to Fear" corroborates Garrick's business at this point:

> See at the regal banquet curst *Macbeth*
>   Secure of empire secretly rejoice;
> The fiend seems smiling at the work of death,
>   And hears, with pleasure hears, the murderer's voice;
> When lo! at once Fear's dreadful pow'r is felt,
>   As injur'd *Banquo* points the livid wound,
> Cold chilling dews upon his forehead melt,
>   Fades the gay scene of splendor all around,
> Drops from his nerveless hand the rosy bowl,
> While sluggish thro' his veins life's purple torrents roll.
>
> —*Gentleman's Magazine* (1763), p. 212.

[38] Letter endorsed "Upon my acting Macbeth, Jan, 1743 [1744 n.s.]," in Boaden, ed., *Private Correspondence*, I, 19-20.

so, after the murder, feels the stings of conscience, he censures Garrick for giving his passion here "more the appearance of grief than horror: and all those long pauses, those heart-heavings, and that melancholy countenance and slack carriage of body, were by no means proper to express remorse in a man so warm and full of courage." Since Macbeth is by nature intrepid, he ought to behave with a certain greatness even when most stung by guilt; his penitent face and lowly gestures, however consonant with his temper of mind, are incompatible with his character. Such a person would naturally say, "I dare do all that may become a man" with rough tones, indignant at imputed cowardice, not in a voice that speaks remorse. Again, in the banquet scene, Garrick was wrong in not playing boldness as a dominant quality. The faintness of his line "Avaunt and quit my sight!" was unbecoming a brave man, and similarly Macbeth should have followed the slowly receding ghost of Banquo with more resolution, step by step, thus relieving the spectators of much painful suspense.

Painful suspense, of course, was almost certainly what Garrick was after. His sense of what would best catch up an audience in the tensions of the moment stood him in good stead throughout the course of the tragedy, and he continued to emphasize the horror and grief of Macbeth's desperate agonies as long as he played the role. Thomas Wilkes in 1759 found his performance of the character unusually satisfying. In observing Macbeth's progress in guilt from intention to act, he says, "How his ambition kindles at the distant prospect of a crown, when the witches prophecy! and with what reluctance he yields, upon the diabolical persuasions of his wife, to the perpetration of the murder! How finely does he shew his resolution staggered, upon the supposed view of the air-drawn dagger. . . ." Wilkes enumerates the great moments of Macbeth's agonies: the horror of his looks on returning from Duncan's chamber [see Plate 28], his confusion and anguish at the knockings from without, the self-condemnation in his muttering " 'Twas a rough night."[39] If Garrick was paying heed to Shakespeare's indications of Macbeth's courage, there is little doubt that he preferred to concentrate on what seemed greater opportunities for theatrical effectiveness in the portrayal of horror.

[39] Wilkes, *General View*, pp. 248-249.

Yet, toward the end of his career in the role, Garrick began to place more emphasis on qualities of resourcefulness and intrepidity. The letter written shortly after his first performance objects to his lack of warmth and courage in the role; a later correspondent objects precisely to the presence of these qualities. "H. H.,"[40] writing in 1762, took exception to Garrick's banquet scene, where, after the second appearance of Banquo's ghost, Garrick had spoken the lines beginning "Dare me to the desert with thy sword" with resolution and in a firm tone of voice as he advanced on the ghost. H. H. explained his preference for a fixed attitude of horror and amazement, since Shakespeare intended Macbeth to be overpowered by Banquo's supernatural appearance.[41] Garrick found the letter worth answering but politely disagreed with his critic:

> Should Macbeth sink into pusillanimity, I imagine that it would hurt ye Character, & be contrary to the intentions of Shakespear— The first appearance of ye Spirit overpow'rs him more than ye 2^d^— but before it vanishes at first, Macbeth gains strength— *If thou can'st nod, Speak too*— Must be spoke with terror, but with a recovering Mind— and in the next Speech with him— He cannot pronounce *Avaunt & quit my Sight*! without a Stronger Exertion of his Powers under the Circumstance of Horror— the *Why so— being gone*— &c means, in my opinion,— I am returning to my Senses, wch were before Mad & inflam'd with what I have Seen— I make a great difference between a Mind sunk by Guilt into Cowardice, & one rising with Horror to Acts of Madness & desperation; which last I take to be the case of Macbeth— I certainly (as you say) recollect a degree of Resolution— but I never advance an *inch*, for notwithstanding my Agitation, my feet are immoveable.[42]

Garrick had apparently come to think that the desired effect of horror could be better achieved by portraying Macbeth consciously struggling against his mental terrors instead of letting

[40] Possibly Hall Hartson, poet, dramatist, and associate of Garrick in later years; see *The Letters of David Garrick*, ed. David M. Little and George M. Kahrl, 3 vols. (Cambridge, Mass., 1963), I, 352n.

[41] Boaden, ed., *Private Correspondence*, I, 133-134.

[42] Little and Kahrl, eds., *Letters of Garrick*, I, 351.

himself be possessed by them.[43] He perhaps sensed that such a shift in emphasis would allow greater opportunity to display physical energy and that the resulting higher tensions would increase the theatrical effect.[44] His greatest emphasis, however, still remained on portraying the agonies of a remorseful conscience. Thomas Davies, in his *Dramatic Miscellanies,* recognized the quality of courage as present but quite subordinated. Doctor Johnson, he says, held that Macbeth's courage preserves some esteem, but, Davies objects, this quality he holds in common with Banquo and others, whereas his extreme reluctance before the crime, his mental affliction afterwards, and the continual revolt of conscience at each subsequent act of cruelty render Macbeth, "though not worthy of our esteem, yet an object not entirely unmeriting our pity, in spite of his ambition and cruelty." Although Shakespeare has deviated from history in reducing the fierceness of the character, the change is for the good, since the spectator's delight proceeds "from the sensibility of the murderer, from his remorse and agonies, and from the torments he suffers in the midst of his successful villainy."[45] As Garrick's biographer, Arthur Murphy also found the quality of horror predominant, although he allowed that, despite the presentation of "*the torture of the mind in restless extacy,*" his natural courage gives him support through all his trials.[46]

Garrick's portrayal of virtuous reluctance in Macbeth offered

[43] Writing to Arthur Murphy in 1768, Garrick thanked him for his description of the way his Macbeth "affects chearfullness to Banquo"—Little and Kahrl, eds., *Letters of Garrick,* II, 593.

[44] Other comments indicate Garrick's overall concern with evoking terror. A letter from Arthur Murphy praises his conversation with Banquo just before going to commit the murder: "You dissembled indeed, but dissembled with difficulty. Upon the first entrance the eye glanced at the door; the gaiety was forced, and at intervals the eye gave a momentary look towards the door, and turned away in a moment. This was but a fair contrast to the acted cheerfulness with which this disconcerted behaviour was intermixed"—undated letter in Boaden, ed., *Private Correspondence,* II, 363; in view of its obvious precedence to the letter from Garrick to Murphy quoted above, note 43, this letter may with certainty be dated 1768. Another writer offered unconstrained praise for the banquet scene: "When the ghost of Banquo rises, how repeatedly astonishing his transition, from the placidly merry, to the tremendously horrific!"—*The Theatrical Review; or, Annals of the Drama,* I (1763), 79.

[45] Thomas Davies, *Dramatic Miscellanies* (1783-84), II, 191, 148.

[46] Murphy, *Garrick,* I, 79-86. For further details of Garrick's Macbeth, see Burnim, *Garrick,* pp. 103-126.

possibilities for a strong contrast in his wife. The unrelenting, remorseless woman Shakespeare created found a more than adequate impersonater in Mrs. Pritchard, who became almost as closely associated with the role as did Garrick with Macbeth. Thomas Davies in 1780 remembered her ability to present "an image of a mind insensible to compunction, and inflexibly bent to gain its purpose." In taking the daggers from Macbeth as if despising "the agitations of a mind unaccustomed to guilt and alarmed at the terrors of conscience," she conveyed a sense of "the most consummate intrepidity in mischief."[47] In his *Dramatic Miscellanies* Davies again emphasized the balanced playing of Garrick and Pritchard, his mental distraction and horrible agony a contrast to "her seeming apathy, tranquillity, and confidence" [see Plate 29]; and Davies repeated his praise of her business in the banquet scene, where she tries to draw the guests' attention away from Macbeth's frenzy and then at last, seizing his arm, whispers, "Are you a man!" with an unsurpassed look of anger, contempt, and indignation.[48]

In the latter years of the eighteenth century this scene, and this line, become one of the high points of the even more explicitly psychological portrayal of Macbeth and his lady by Kemble and Mrs. Siddons. Beginning with his revolutionary Richard, Garrick had singlehandedly established a tradition of subjective acting which became both a model and a license to his followers. Whether acting opposite the severely emotional Mrs. Pritchard or holding center stage by himself, Garrick made a reputation for presenting the variety of inner response to circumstances which lies so close to the surface of Shakespearean tragic character. Thomas Wilkes's praise of him at once echoes Dryden's fascination with the individuality of Shakespearean character and sug-

[47] Thomas Davies, *Memoirs of the Life of David Garrick* [1st edn., 1780], new (2nd) edn. (1808), II, 188-189.

[48] Davies, *Dramatic Miscellanies*, II, 148, 167. The contradictions of journalistic "puffing" make it difficult to synthesize a consistent notion of Mrs. Pritchard's qualities as an actress, but there is general agreement that she combined dignity of mien, grace of manner, and commanding presence with a certain easy naturalness probably derived from Garrick's tutelage. See *The Theatrical Examiner: An Enquiry into the Merits and Demerits of the Present* English *Performers in General* (1757), pp. 49-51; *The Theatrical Review* (1758), pp. 16-17; Wilkes, *General View*, p. 284; Tate Wilkinson, *Memoirs of His Own Life* (York, 1790), I, 140 and III, 103; and Charles Dibdin, *A Complete History of the Stage* ([1800]), V, 207, 353.

gests Garrick's unique ability to underscore its responsiveness. "I am of the opinion," said Wilkes, "that he excels all his predecessors, as he does all his cotemporaries in the power of shewing the distinguishing touches that separate passion from passion; thence is he able to unite in his performance the greatest spirit and exactest truth."[49] A less well-known commentator was even more explicit. Garrick's Lear was most noteworthy, he observed, for its "violent starts of amazement, of horror, of indignation, of paternal rage, excited by filial ingratitude the most prodigious; such a perceptible, yet rapid gradation, from these dreadful feelings to the deepest frenzy; such a striking correspondence between the tempest in his mind, and that of the surrounding elements."[50] [see Plate 30]

Although no evidence exists to show specific influence of Lockean psychology on Garrick's study of his roles,[51] there is no doubt that his interpretations of Richard III, Macbeth, and other Shakespearean and non-Shakespearean tragic characters anticipated the critical views of late eighteenth-century writers who were obviously indebted to the psychology of a century before. Attempts have been made, but it is difficult to define direct lines of influence here.[52] In any case specific debts are not as important as the inescapable fact that philosophy, psychology, dramaturgy, acting, and criticism during the eighteenth century follow the same tendencies toward concern with the sensitive response of the individual human mind. Mrs. Montagu came close to the mark in suggesting how important Garrick's innovations in Shakespearean acting were to her and to others who dug in that rich mine. "All the labours of the critics," she declared, "can do noth-

[49] Wilkes, *General View*, pp. 262-263.

[50] Letter from "J. Forfyce" [sic, for James Fordyce?] to Garrick, dated 13 May 1763, in Boaden, ed., *Private Correspondence*, I, 158.

[51] George Kahrl's work-in-progress on the contents of Garrick's library may perhaps reveal the same kind of connection shown in Kemble's; see Chap. X below, pp. 246-248.

[52] I share George Winchester Stone's view that Garrick exerted considerable influence on the criticism of his age, especially through his contact with literary editors of the period like Johnson and Steevens; see Stone, "Garrick's Significance," pp. 183-197. Stone sees this influence exemplified in Whately's essay on Macbeth and Richard III, where he finds an analysis of Richard that "agrees in every point with the interpretation which Garrick presented" (p. 193). But direct connections are often so difficult to establish that I prefer to view coincident interpretations of Shakespeare's characters on the stage and in the closet mainly as a general indication of the temper of the age.

ing by the dead letter of criticism against the living force of Mr. Garrick's representation."[53] Wilkes, although less precise, had similar views of his centrality. "If he has his faults," he said, "they are like spots in the sun. . . ."[54]

[53] Letter to Garrick, dated 13 May 1770, in Boaden, ed., *Private Correspondence,* I, 385-386. This letter provides one of the few unquestionable instances of the actor's direct influence on the philosophical critics of his day.

[54] Wilkes, *General View,* p. 263.

37. George Henry Harlow, Mrs. Siddons as Lady Macbeth, "Letter Scene"

38. Mary Hamilton, Mrs. Siddons as Lady Macbeth: "Hark! Peace!" (12 July 1802)

39. Mrs. Siddons as Lady Macbeth, sleepwalking

CHAPTER X

Shakespearean Character on the Early Romantic Stage

> It is even here within the province of the moral alchemist to . . . decompose, combine, or transmute; and if in the process any latent good should be elicited, or any superficial evil obliterated, the labour will not have been in vain.
>
> —*The Port Folio* (1814)

i. Kemble and the "Science" of Shakespearean Acting

THE PRECEDENTS of Shakespearean acting established by Garrick in the middle years of the eighteenth century influenced later actors to an extraordinary degree. As late as 1813-14, when Edmund Kean rose to triumph almost overnight, comparisons with Garrick seemed so inevitable that Kean has since been often thought of as his legitimate heir. Yet Kean's own originality, especially his cultivation of grotesque posturing and idiosyncratic mannerisms, marked him as an actor much unlike his graceful predecessor. Kean shared with Garrick a high proficiency in revealing a character's mental processes, but his method of giving them theatrical substance was all his own. The point is an important one, not only because it serves to differentiate two similar actors but because it raises a crucial issue involved in the study of acting: the distinction between an actor's individual style and the aesthetic effect which that style produces in the theater. This distinction in turn suggests a basic but neglected truth about acting: there are "schools" based on similarities in personal styles, and other "schools" which reflect dominant aesthetic tendencies of their age. When scholars designate a "Garrick school" or a "Kemble school" they refer to a certain homogeneity in style,[1] and in

[1] See Alan Downer's use of "school" in this sense to classify eighteenth-century acting—"Nature to Advantage Dressed: Eighteenth-Century Acting," *PMLA*, LVIII (1943), 1002-1037.

placing Kean with Garrick instead of with Kemble they add to our knowledge of the history of acting. But it is also possible to describe a "school" to which all three of these actors conform. Despite wide differences in their personal styles, Garrick, Kemble, and Kean belong with equal right to the "Romantic school" because their emphasis on interpreting character was oriented toward the presentation of subjective response.[2] The aesthetic impression derived from such an emphasis is that a character is by nature individual and so his response in a given situation is necessarily unique. Consequently the audience identifies sympathetically with the character, sees the world through his eyes, and ultimately finds the meaning of the play inseparable from, and in fact the same as, the meaning of that character's responses. Modern scholars like Arthur Colby Sprague have justly devoted efforts to defining the styles of major English actors. Clearly, our sense of innovation in acting depends to a great extent on the knowledge these scholars provide of attitudes, gestures, "business," costumes, and other aspects of performance.[3] But such knowledge, valuable in itself, should not be allowed to obscure the fact that the aesthetic response of an audience is as much a part of an actor's contribution to his art as the innovationary gesture that draws plaudits from audiences and paragraphs from critics.

The preceding chapter on Garrick should make clear that this study seeks a correlation between the characteristic style of an individual actor and those tendencies connected with it which serve to identify the significance his acting held for his age. I do not wish to slight the importance of gestures, attitudes, and other particularities, but at the same time I do not see how these things can be fully meaningful outside a discussion of the actor's interpretation of character. And once this context is brought in, the audience is brought in also. The actor interprets for better or for

[2] By employing the term "Romantic" to designate a phenomenon characteristic of the period from Garrick to Kean (about 1740 to 1820), I mean simply to emphasize the homogeneousness of aesthetic norms in the theater of this age. The sense of the word as used in the title of this book and at other points in the discussion is a combined one, suggesting the importance of the early nineteenth century but at the same time implying continuity over a longer span of development.

[3] See the books and articles by Burnim, Downer, Shattuck, Sprague, and Stone cited in Pt. III, Chap. IX above, notes 1 and 10.

worse with regard to his character, but inescapably *for his audience.* His use of the oratorical right forefinger, for example, may interest students of oratory and of acting alike, but for the student of theatrical and dramatic history and even of general culture that finger points unerringly toward meanings of which the actor himself may not be aware. To find indications of such meanings, and of their connection with the details of an actor's style, one need only study for a brief time the theatrical reviews in late eighteenth-century English newspapers. Following the course of players and productions day by day, or even eclectically over the years, one quickly discovers that reviewers habitually notice two things: the innovations actors introduce into traditional approaches to the roles of the repertory theater, and the effect that these innovations have on an audience. The rapport that an actor like Garrick, Kemble, Mrs. Siddons, or Kean establishes with his audience is the measure of his success, and the means whereby he achieves it are rooted in his individual style. Yet it is an inescapable fact, which reviews and other records show, that actors of this period with styles as different as those of Kemble and Kean contrived to produce essentially the same effect on their audiences.

This effect, which I have described as the product of the "Romantic school" of acting, distinguishes the period of the late eighteenth and early nineteenth centuries as an age fascinated both with heroism and with the irreducible uniqueness of the hero's reaction to an uncertain world and to his own elusive nature. Sheridan, knowingly or not, found in Rolla a hero of this sort, and in addition he managed to form the imaginary world of *Pizarro* into an emblem of the "Romantic" world of uncertainty, of fatal chance. The casting of Kemble in the role of the Peruvian warrior-hero simply brought the emblem to life. For at the time (1799) when Sheridan's tragedy appeared, Kemble was enjoying a reputation as the most eminent portrayer of subjective tragic character of his day. However unlikely it may seem that an actor so "neoclassic," so formal in attitude and measured in cadence, could produce such an extensive display of subjective states of mind, of mental processes and of the emotional reactions they prompted, the fact remains that he did—to the immediate interest and involvement of his audiences. Perhaps no style has ever been so deliberate, so calculated, as his, and therefore so different from the mental and physical leaps and bounds of Kean and from the graceful rapidity and controlled variety of Garrick. [see Plates 31, 32, and 33] And yet the surviving records of Kemble's performances, especially of Macbeth, leave the certain impression that his acting was as essentially subjective as Garrick's before him or Kean's after him. In fact, if one wished to find a single actor who might be claimed the abstract and brief chronicle of his time, one could hardly do better than to turn, as did Sheridan, to Kemble.

When John Philip Kemble made his debut as Hamlet at Drury Lane in 1783-84, it was clear that the London stage had once more an actor potentially Garrick's equal in popularity but one who would by no means depend on imitations of Garrick to achieve his own measure of success. A survey of the contents of Kemble's library, sold at auction after his death, adds weight to the impression given by his performances that his approach to a role was an extraordinarily informed, conscious, and systematic one. Among the authors listed in the sale catalogue are many that would naturally have filled the shelves of any late eighteenth-century gentleman's library: Aristotle, Cicero, Demosthenes, Longinus, Mandeville, Quintilian, Shaftesbury. But there are others, even aside from the editions of plays and volumes of theatrical ephemera, which indicate Kemble's peculiar interests not only as a gentleman but as the renowned scholar-actor of his day. In addition to treatises on rhetoric and manuals of acting, works by seventeenth- and eighteenth-century philosophers, psychologists, and aestheticians evidently formed an important part of Kemble's reading. A selected list of such works includes Bailey's *Etymological Dictionary* (1764), Beattie's *Essays on Poetry and Music* (1779), Blair's *Lectures on Rhetoric and Belles Lettres* (1787), *Recherches sur les Costumes et les Théatres de toutes les Nations* (10 volumes, 1790), Carter's *Specimens of Ancient Sculpture and Painting* (1787), and so on down the alphabet through Diderot, Du Bois, Hartley, Hayley, Hobbes, Hume, Knight, Le Brun, and Locke, to Paley, Price, Reynolds, Rousseau, Rymer, Adam Smith, and Thomas Warton.[4]

[4] *A Catalogue of the Valuable and Extensive Library, Choice Prints, and Theatrical Portraits, of John Philip Kemble, Esq. . . .* (1821). *Biographia Dramatica* refers to his "unrivalled" collection of plays and books relating to the theater—ed. David Erskine Baker, Isaac Reed, and Stephen Jones (1812),

For most actors of his day (or any other) such a library would be almost unthinkable. But not for Kemble, who, when not convivial with his many friends, might very likely do the sort of thing recorded in his diary for 16 January 1798: "Sat at home. . . . I read Lessing's Critique on Diderot's Pere de Famille. . . ."[5] Kemble's reputation in his own day was such that he was held to be, through his superior learning and devotion to art, the one man who could restore correctness to the British stage. Thomas Campbell summarized this view in his "Ode on the Retirement of Mr. J. P. Kemble":

> At once ennobled and correct,
> His mind survey'd the tragic page,
> And what the actor could effect,
> The scholar could presage.[6]

A decade before the actor's retirement he received similar praise from Gilbert Austin, author of a now little-known but important treatise on rhetorical gesture that Kemble himself owned. Kemble's art, said Austin, "is no doubt consummate; his various learning with most laudable propriety is made to bear with its full effect on all his theatrical characters." Kemble devoted his reading and deep knowledge of costume to illustrate these characters, Austin continues, and he employed "the truth, the precision, the grandeur and significancy of his action" to emphasize their sentiments.[7] The "intellectual endowments, the extent of his mind, and the perseverance of his nature" that his close acquaintance Michael Kelly observed in him[8] were equally evident in Kemble's efforts as producer. "To be critically exact was the great ambition of his life," observed his biographer James Boaden, and to that end he studied "the antiquities of his own and other countries," their architecture, dress, weapons, and manners, bending every

I, ii, 425. Herschel Baker has described the disposal of the library after Kemble's retirement: about four thousand plays and forty volumes of playbills were sold to the Duke of Devonshire and now reside in the Huntington Library in San Marino, California; the remainder, some 1,677 titles, were sold at auction—see *John Philip Kemble: The Actor in His Theatre* (Cambridge, Mass., 1942), pp. 220-223.

5 "Memoranda of J. P. Kemble," Vol. II: 1796-1800, British Museum Add. MS. 31,973.

6 Printed in the *Annual Register* (1817), p. 606.

7 *Chironomia; or A Treatise on Rhetorical Delivery* . . . (1806), p. 494n.

8 *Reminiscences* (1826), I, 345.

nerve to make his productions "perfect, beyond all previous example."[9]

Kemble's antiquarian interests, although perhaps susceptible to ridicule, were much different from those of a leisurely collector of oddments from the past. With the aid of William Capon, his chief scene painter,[10] Kemble realized those efforts toward unity of style in production which characterized his own concern for integrity as an actor. His innovations in atmospheric scene design, introduced over the course of his career as manager of Drury Lane and later of Covent Garden, had behind them the same concern for unity of effect fundamental to the landscape gardening and Gothic architecture of his day.[11] The new stage lights introduced at Drury Lane in 1785 enhanced the possibilities of achieving this unity, as a reviewer in that year implicitly suggested. The flame of the patent lamp, he observed, "is bright without dazzling, strong and vivid, yet at the same time so perfectly clear and steady, that the eye can bear to dwell upon it, not only without pain, but even with some degree of peculiar satisfaction."[12] Lighting such as this obviously repaid the added labor necessary to surround the acting area with scenery whose architectural detail and style were of a piece with the historically correct costume worn by the actors.[13] Although financial considerations usually required scenery designed for general atmospheric qualities rather than for special relevance to a particular play, a definite degree of unity of effect proved possible within these limits. And, in any case, as Sir Walter Scott observes, it would have been foolish and pedantic to insist on literal accuracy. The

[9] *Memoirs of the Life of John Philip Kemble* (1825), I, 157-158.

[10] Capon's important contributions are described in Sybil Rosenfeld and Edward Croft-Murray, "A Checklist of Scene Painters Working in Great Britain and Ireland in the 18th Century," *TN*, XIX (1964), 13-15; see also W. J. Lawrence, "The Pioneers of Modern English Stage Mounting: William Capon," *Magazine of Art*, XVIII (1895), 289-292, and Sybil Rosenfeld, "Scene Designs of William Capon," *TN*, X (1956), 118-122 and plates.

[11] See above, Pt. I, Chap. III, pp. 66-68.

[12] *The Gazeteer and New Daily Advertiser*, 9 February 1785; see the discussion of this new lighting in Pt. I, Chap. III above, pp. 66-67 and note 25.

[13] An adequate history of this important subject has yet to be written. I have summarized some of the information already available in "John Hamilton Mortimer and Shakespearean Characterization," *Princeton University Library Chronicle*, XXIX (1968), 193-207. See also Lily B. Campbell's pioneer investigation, "A History of Costuming on the English Stage Between 1660 and 1823," *University of Wisconsin Stud. in Language and Literature*, No. 2 (1918), 187-223.

painted and tattooed pagans of King Lear's time could not very well be made to appear so before the eyes of decorous eighteenth-century audiences. Productions on the modern stage, Scott explains, may convey a consistent sense of history without dwelling on detail for its own sake:

> As the poet, carrying back his scene into remote days, retains still to a certain extent the manners and sentiments of his own period, so it is sufficient for the purpose of costume if every thing be avoided which can recall modern associations, and as much of the antique be assumed as will at once harmonize with the purpose of the exhibition and in so far awaken recollections of the days of yore as to give an air of truth to the scene.[14]

Not literal fact, but the illusion of reality, was evidently the great requirement. The reality was, of course, not that of the early Jacobean stage but the even further remove of Shakespeare's dramatic setting. Never doubting that the playwright's sense of history was fully as sharp as his own, Kemble proceeded to introduce the innovation in staging that remains his chief contribution to the English theater. With the fullest realizable detail Kemble dressed out his stage in the settings and special effects called for in the new texts accepted for production as well as those implicitly suggested by plays in the repertoire which carried over from Garrick's time and before. Shakespeare was mounted with such propriety in Kemble's later years as manager of Covent Garden that Kemble exceeded the reputation he himself had earned earlier as the guiding director of Drury Lane. However much he found it necessary to satisfy unruly audiences' demands for spectacle, his activities as a man of the theater demonstrated his sense of the subtler unity to be found by correlating visual effects with the equally apprehensible qualities manifested by his subjective approach to character. The suggestion in late eighteenth-century drama and graphic art that landscape may reflect individual states of mind was embodied in Kemble's artistic practice both as manager and actor.

If one word could summarize the striking innovations in Kem-

[14] Scott, review of Boaden, *Life of Kemble, Quarterly Review*, XXXIV (1826), 225-226. See also Harold Child, *The Shakespearean Productions of John Philip Kemble* (London, 1935).

ble's acting, that word must be *pace*. From the time of his debut as Hamlet, Kemble became famous—or, perhaps, infamous—for a technique that combined frequent pauses with habitual grace and dignity. Conservatives of the Garrick school attacked him, ignoring for the moment the earlier actor's reputation for "heart-heaving" pauses while citing Garrick's characteristic display of rapidity and passion. Kemble was obviously a much more studied, much less "spontaneous," actor. Gilbert Austin singles Kemble out for attaining "the perfection and the glory of art, so finished, that every look is a commentary, every tone an illustration, every gesture a model for the statuary, and a study for the painter."[15]

Kemble's emphasis on grace also irritated those who preferred a less restrained show of passion.[16] But his scholarly, "scientific" approach, no doubt the offspring of an unusual temperament, may also be traced in no small measure to physical limitations. In a perceptive summary of his acting Sir Walter Scott says that Kemble often sacrificed energetic action to grace because his physical shortcomings demanded restraint. Kemble possessed a nobility of person, a grace of demeanor, and features "decidedly heroic," Scott recalls, but, unlike Garrick's commanding and melodic voice, Kemble's was affected with an asthmatic tendency which made it essential to reserve his efforts for "those bursts of passion to which he gave such sublime effect."[17] A taxing role like Macbeth or King Lear could apparently leave Kemble gasping toward the finish if he did not keep close rein on his energies. Of his Lear in a performance of 1788 one reviewer observed that its great defect arose "from a want of bodily powers; for the character is drawn with such a variety of emotions that it really demands considerable vigour to sustain it with proper energy; and

[15] *Chironomia*, p. 279.

[16] One disaffected writer commented that the sentiments of a burdened heart and the scarcely audible voice of inward agony appear to Kemble merely as an opportunity for "raising his voice, displaying his figure, and *deploring* his last new robe"—*The Times*, 19 September 1811.

[17] Scott, *Quarterly Review* (1826), p. 215. Boaden notes that Kemble's acting seems to follow Sir Joshua Reynolds' view that "the expression of violent passion, is not always the most excellent in proportion as it is the most natural," because such extremeness may depart from "the deliberate and stately step, the studied grace of action, which seems to enlarge the dimensions of the actor, and alone to fill the stage"—Reynolds' Thirteenth Discourse, quoted in Boaden, *Life of Kemble*, I, 178.

therefore in the 'whirlwind of the passion,' Kemble was obliged to sink into softness, when the text obviously required the most choleric effusions of rage." The reviewer went on to describe what had already become Kemble's characteristic method, although not yet well under control. The imbecility of the monarch, a product of age and agony, "was not managed with judgment, as it either came before, or immediately succeeded the excesses of vehemence that were expressed with too juvenile an animation."[18] Even when Kemble came to learn how to husband his unequal energies—a control Leigh Hunt later described with annoyance as "that frigid reservation of himself for particular passages"[19]—his voice could on occasion fail him. But compensations made up for this defect, John Taylor explains:

> Oft when the hurricanes of passion rise,
> For correspondent tones he vainly tries,
> To aid the storm no towering note combines,
> And the spent breath th'unequal task declines:
> Yet, spite of Nature, he compels us still
> To own the potent triumph of his skill;
> While with dread pauses, deepen'd accents roll,
> Whose awful energy arrests the soul.[20]

"No actor," said John Williams, looking back over Kemble's career, "manages his utterance more admirably, or could conceal such a defect better than he does."[21]

Understandably, Kemble attempted to make a virtue of deficiency by concentrating on passages where sudden bursts of energy would produce the most telling results. Meanwhile, between these intermittent bursts of power, his method of acting was much different. Scott says that Garrick seized and expressed with passion the first and most obvious quality of a scene, while Kemble relied on a minute examination of the text for its hidden subtleties of meaning, which he then with much labor transformed into highly refined and steadily paced speech and action. The unfortunate result, in Scott's opinion, was that sometimes

[18] *Morning Post,* 25 January 1788.

[19] Lawrence Huston Houtchens and Carolyn Washburn Houtchens, eds., *Leigh Hunt's Dramatic Criticism 1808-1831* (New York, 1949), p. 103.

[20] Taylor, *The Stage,* quoted in John Ambrose Williams, *Memoirs of John Philip Kemble . . .* (1817), p. 60.

[21] *Memoirs of Kemble,* p. 74.

the part appeared too precisely studied. Emphasis on almost every word vitiated what should have been a unified, vehement effect; and in the meantime the action hung suspended.[22] James Boaden, however, found Kemble's method far from unsatisfactory. He held that the actor's great originality consisted in providing new philosophical grounds for the grace and deliberateness of posture and action that linked him to many of his predecessors. Kemble's "academic or critical style of acting," he observed,

> is built on a metaphysical search into our nature, and a close attention to all the minutiae of language. It deals, therefore, in *pauses,* which were not before made; for the unlearned actor cared little about the transitions of thought. He never examined, of the associations of our ideas, how much in dramatic dialogue is suppressed—and never dreamt that the rapid junction of ideas totally unconnected is violent and unmeaning. It lays a peculiar *stress* upon words, which before received no emphasis; because it analyses every thing by which meaning is conveyed, and can leave nothing to chance, which ought to be settled by reason. In short, what philosophical criticism had discovered to be properties of Shakespeare's characters, the actor now endeavoured to shew. To be a just representative of the part, he was to become a living commentary on the poet.[23]

Boaden's perceived connection between psychology, philosophical Shakespearean criticism, and theatrical performance affords an unusually full glimpse of values that grow out of individual acting style. Equally important is the context of traditional stylistic pauses within which Boaden places Kemble's innovation. Garrick's use of the technique is well known, especially at the end of the tent scene in *Richard III,* and his example undoubtedly influenced other actors.[24] Spranger Barry, for example, who performed Macbeth at Covent Garden in the 1750's and

[22] *Quarterly Review* (1826), pp. 215-216.

[23] Boaden, *Life of Kemble,* I, 175-176.

[24] See Pt. III, Chap. IX above, pp. 231-232, and compare Garrick's comment on the use of pauses in soliloquy to avoid "running the different parts of a Monologue togeather," which results in monotony and a lack of spirit and sense—*The Letters of David Garrick,* ed. David M. Little and George M. Kahrl (Cambridge, Mass., 1963), II, 559-560.

then later took over the role at Drury Lane after Garrick gave it up, drew admiration for his vocal "breaks," those "most sudden and most difficult transitions, from one passion to another" where the stifling weight of emotions prevents "their utmost and loudest exertion."[25] [see Plate 34] This kind of momentary pause appears more extemporaneous than studied, but Garrick's precedent also allowed for pauses more consciously premeditated. Richard Cumberland in a late letter to Garrick praised John Henderson for "the most marking pauses (next to your own) I ever heard. . . ."[26] W. C. Oulton's assessment of Henderson, on the other hand, suggests a certain synthesis of premeditation and spontaneity in "his sudden transition from one passion to another" and his "strong colouring, in broken and abrupt speeches, especially in parts of tragic horror."[27] Boaden's analysis of Henderson unearths the same significance he finds in Kemble's methods. Henderson's power was analytic and revealed philosophical ingenuity, Boaden said. Unsatisfied with the light of common meaning, "he shewed it you through a prism, and refracted all the delicate and mingling hues, that enter into the composition of any ray of human character."[28] [see Plate 35] Kemble, then, was working in the Garrick tradition of effective pauses but chose, perhaps partly with regard to his own physical limitations, to minimize the sudden transition in favor of a slower and more elaborate technique designed to reveal the hidden workings of a mind in the grip of passion.

ii. Kemble and Mrs. Siddons in *Macbeth*

Kemble's interpretation of Macbeth carries on tendencies observable in Garrick's portrayal, but it is fully understandable only with reference to Mrs. Siddons' strong and definite view of her character. This actress held an unrivaled claim to Lady Macbeth from her first appearance in the part at Drury Lane on 2 February 1785. By the time Kemble joined her as heir to the title role, she had established the authority of an interpretation in some twenty-five performances.[29] The fact that Kemble's interpretation

25 *The Theatrical Review* (1758), pp. 23-24.

26 Boaden, ed., *Private Correspondence of Garrick*, II, 367.

27 *History of the Theatres of London* (1796), I, 150-151.

28 *Life of Kemble*, I, 76-77.

29 See the calendar of performances in Charles Beecher Hogan, *Shakespeare in the Theatre, 1701-1800*, II (Oxford, 1957), 387-389.

of Macbeth was subordinate to his sister's approach to the chief female character cannot be ignored, for it underlies the development of two of the most representative characterizations in the English Romantic theater. Because Shakespeare's two characters are complementary in the fullest dramatic sense, Kemble's and Mrs. Siddons' cooperative approach to them holds unusually high theatrical interest. But their interpretations are otherwise of importance as well, since they present in dramatic form the essence of human nature and its relationship to the outside world as the Romantic age consistently viewed it, and in so doing they epitomize ideas about tragic experience which pervade the literary criticism and philosophical enquiry of the time.

The eighteenth-century critical debate over Lady Macbeth, discussed in an earlier chapter, appears also in the theatrical commentary of the age. Although Lord Kames had voiced the fervent hope that no such wretch was to be found,[30] other writers found her character consonant with nature. In 1759 the theatrical historian Thomas Wilkes argued that, after all, since the character is drawn from history we may suppose it to exist in the world; and even the arch-conservative moralist and theatrical "censor" Francis Gentleman reluctantly concluded her a "detestable, though a possible, picture of the fair sex."[31] The contradiction reflected in the views of Kames and his antagonists figures importantly in Mrs. Siddons' interpretation of the role, for the two most extensive records of her playing present openly conflicting accounts. About 1807 Professor G. J. Bell of Edinburgh—solicitor, expert on mercantile law, and devoted follower of Mrs. Siddons —made a series of notes on her Lady Macbeth subsequently edited and studied in detail by H. C. Fleeming Jenkin. At about the same time or possibly later Mrs. Siddons herself wrote a lengthy analysis, "Remarks on the Character of Lady Macbeth," which Thomas Campbell printed in his *Life of Mrs. Siddons.*[32]

[30] Kames, *Elements of Criticism* (1762), II, 189-191.

[31] Wilkes, *A General View of the Stage* (1759), p. 29; [Gentleman], *The Dramatic Censor; or, Critical Companion* (1770), I, 84-85.

[32] Jenkin, *Mrs. Siddons as Lady Macbeth and as Queen Katharine*, Publications of the Dramatic Museum of Columbia University, 2nd. ser.: Papers on Acting, III (New York, 1915), subsequently cited as "Bell"; Campbell, *The Life of Mrs. Siddons* (1834), II, 10-34, subsequently cited as "Remarks." Campbell says Mrs. Siddons showed him her commentary "some nineteen years ago" (II, 44) but does not offer to date it exactly.

Jenkin, comparing the two documents, found that Bell recorded a central impression of "turbulent and inhuman strength of spirit" (p. 36), but that Mrs. Siddons insisted on a "fair, feminine, nay, perhaps, even fragile" woman (II, 11). Baffled by these opposing views, Jenkin decided that the actress had formed "two distinct conceptions: for no one can believe that if Mrs. Siddons had been able to appear the fair and fragile beauty she conceived, she would have used a single gesture or one inflexion similar to those employed when she was representing turbulent inhuman strength" (p. 37). I have elsewhere resolved this contradiction by observing that, far from writing conventional literary criticism, Mrs. Siddons was instead describing an independent image helpful in creating her role. The extensive evidence of Mrs. Siddons' performances shows clearly that she had discovered in this fair, feminine beauty an initial concept of the character *against* which she could play from the moment she stepped on stage.[33] Furthermore, James Boaden's latter-day assessment of her interpretation, while seeming to conflict with those of Bell and Mrs. Siddons herself, actually reveals how the character evolved in the course of performances in the 1780's. Bell had observed that, when the role of Macbeth is in the hands of an inferior actor, Mrs. Siddons' Lady Macbeth "becomes not the affectionate aider of her husband's ambition, but the fell monster who tempts him to transgress, making him the mere instrument of her wild and uncontrollable ambition" (p. 38). Boaden's reconstruction of early performances refers explicitly to a Macbeth played not by Kemble but by his predecessor, William "Gentleman" Smith.[34] Among the many reviews of Smith's acting as Macbeth opposite Mrs. Siddons, one is especially succinct in suggesting Smith's deficiencies. A critic of their first performance together found Smith "a very passable tyrant" whose efforts were far from mawkish and never wanting "in a shew of *importance*," but he unfortunately lacked "subtile discriminations, and aetherial energies which are needful to realize the '*rapt* partner' of Banquo. . . ."[35] From such com-

[33] See my article, "Kemble and Mrs. Siddons in *Macbeth*: The Romantic Approach to Tragic Character," *TN*, XXII (Winter 1967-68), 65-86. The present account of their performances is in part a summary of the detailed reconstruction provided there.

[34] *Memoirs of Mrs. Siddons* (1827), II, 136, 147.

[35] *Morning Chronicle*, 5 February 1785. For similar accounts of Smith's acting see the evidence gathered in the article cited above, note 33.

ments it is easy to infer that, when Mrs. Siddons was playing opposite an actor who did not cooperate with her by realizing the varied qualities of Macbeth's vacillating purpose, she could hardly have played the affectionate aider of her husband's designs.

On 16 October 1788, after Smith's retirement, Kemble took over the role of Macbeth at Drury Lane. He had played the part there once before, for his benefit on 31 March 1785, when the critic for the *Morning Chronicle* noted with pleasure that "his endeavours were extremely various" and expressed the hope that Kemble would possess the role for the future.[36] When this event took place a little over three years later, a Macbeth appeared whose cooperative playing opposite Mrs. Siddons was to become one of the most impressive features of a singular career. Essentially, Kemble's Macbeth combined an extensive and detailed display of conscience-stricken agony with intermittent bursts of great physical courage and energy. Boaden explains how Kemble succeeded in combining these two varied aspects into a coherent interpretation of Shakespeare's intention. Any actor of strong imagination can convey the sort of terror one expects in a murderer, he observes, but this is not necessarily a Macbeth. The question is, "Does the actor . . . exhibit to us a noble nature absolutely sunk and depraved by that act, or a base one losing its very cunning in the fear of detection? Is he a hero, who descends to become an assassin, or a common stabber, who rises to become a royal murderer?" Kemble succeeds in presenting nobility, Boaden continues, through the inspiration he feels in the moral progression of the part. Keeping in his mind at all times the influence of "*spirits who know all mortal consequences,*" he fuses what would otherwise be mere external demonstrations into a unified, consistent character.[37] [see Plate 36]

Kemble's answer to Thomas Whately's *Remarks* helps to document his heavy emphasis on courage when he performed the role. He finds that Whately's analysis imputes cowardice to Macbeth and so automatically destroys opportunities for sympathy. We are unable to enjoy a virtuous satisfaction in Macbeth's repugnance to guilt if it arises from mere cowardice, and can gain no instruction from his remorse if it comes from mere imbecility. As

[36] *Morning Chronicle, and London Advertiser,* 1 April 1785.
[37] *Life of Kemble,* I, 173-174.

a coward Macbeth is only despicable, since "we cannot feel for him."[38] Despite the imperfect logic and misinterpretations evident in Kemble's pamphlet, his conclusion that both Macbeth and Richard III are "as intrepid as man can be" but that Macbeth is a more complex character, "intrepid, and feeling" (pp. 35-36), underscores the dual emphasis on courage and agonized remorse in his performance. Reviewing Kemble's answer to Whately, Boaden asserts that Whately made the basic mistake of not taking Macbeth as a thoroughly virtuous character before the witches' temptation. He explains Macbeth's apparent diminution of strength and courage in the play by pointing to the strong fatalism in the character: when a man once believes in the predominance of external agency, he necessarily loses personal and mental energy. Mildly censuring Kemble's reply to Whately for finding more courage in Macbeth than is really present, Boaden nevertheless observes that in performance Kemble achieved a better balance between courage, the obvious mark of a noble man, and remorse, "the last expiring glimmer of his original virtue."[39]

Placed within the developing tradition of English dramatic criticism, Kemble's pamphlet on Macbeth sums up the almost unanimous view that the fundamental attractiveness of the character derives from his moral disintegration—a process in which his wife plays the crucial role. Once Kemble took over the part, his acting gave Mrs. Siddons as Lady Macbeth an opportunity to exercise a great hold on Macbeth's natural instincts of conjugal love and to turn them unwittingly to his destruction and her own. Given the close bond of their affection, Mrs. Siddons could compound the preternatural villainy she first brought to the role with qualities more pitiably human, while Kemble at the same time could play a good and valorous man who disintegrates under the onslaught of his wife's insults to his manhood. The curious result of this cooperative interpretation is that it elicits a great amount of sympathy from the audience despite the overt evil of the characters' actions. The moral problem implicit in the play is to decide where the responsibility lies for Duncan's murder and the subsequent atrocities. If the interaction of the two characters as Shakespeare presents them makes the solution a complex one,

[38] Kemble, *Macbeth Reconsidered* (1786), p. 4. See the discussion of this pamphlet in Pt. III, Chap. VIII above, pp. 209-210.

[39] *Life of Kemble*, I, 262-264.

their extremely sympathetic portrayal makes it ultimately impossible. Preoccupation with character for its own sake obscures the ethical values on which judgment must depend. The result is that an audience neglects the moral concerns of the play as a whole in favor of involvement in the plight of two essentially virtuous persons, victimized by exterior forces and interior passions against which their natural goodness has no defense.

This idea of tragic hero and heroine as innocent victims provides the key to an understanding of Kemble and Mrs. Siddons' cooperative venture. At the same time, the complementary nature of the two characters appears in the notably different styles that actor and actress brought to their roles. Kemble's innovations in the delivery of his lines are among the many indications of his effort to delineate the complex workings of Macbeth's mind.[40] The audience is invited to respond, not merely to the murder of Duncan and the cruel actions it precipitates, but to the subtle, labyrinthine ways of a mind which tends to turn inward upon itself but which is now and again shocked into response by the sudden impingement of forces in the outside world. To such an approach as Kemble's Mrs. Siddons' constituted a foil of high dramatic intensity. From the beginning of her career this "Mirror of a polish'd Age"[41] combined qualities of grace and statuesque dignity with an ability to summon up strong and violent passion. Describing the varieties of beauty in the human countenance, the contemporary aesthetician Archibald Alison observed that, when Mrs. Siddons plays one of her tragic roles, "the Forms and Proportions of every Feature vary with the Passions which they so faithfully express" and that almost every conceivable variety of form appears in the space of a few hours.[42] In contrast with Kemble's intricate presentation of Macbeth's vacillating mind, Mrs. Siddons brought to the role of Lady Macbeth a style notable for frequent impassioned outbursts of ever-shifting variety but constant power.

This approach is manifest from her first moment on stage. Professor Bell found that, as soon as the letter scene begins, we see her mind "wrought up in high conception of her part, her eye

[40] See the examples assembled in the article cited above, note 33.

[41] *The Theatrical Portrait, A Poem, on the Celebrated Mrs. Siddons, in the Characters of Calista, Jane Shore, Belvidera, and Isabella* (1783), p. 1.

[42] *Essays on the Nature and Principles of Taste*, 3rd edn. (1812), II, 261-263.

never wandering, never for a moment idle, passion and sentiment continually betraying themselves" (p. 38). Close attention to the text enabled Mrs. Siddons to achieve a unity of idea as well as a unified emotional impression. As she begins to read Macbeth's letter, the coherence of the lines beginning "They met me in the day of success . . ." is evident in her careful choice of emphasized words to sum up the underlying notion of Lady Macbeth's belief in the potency of preternatural beings. Moreover, in this brief sequence appears the transformation Mrs. Siddons effects in the character from the "feminine, nay, perhaps, even fragile woman" described in her "Remarks." In the phrase "and *shalt be* what thou art promised," her emphasis on the verb was uttered, according to Bell, in an "exalted prophetic tone, as if the whole future were present to her soul" (p. 39). [see Plate 37] As Lady Macbeth attempts to shed all vestiges of womanly frailty, two complementary aspects of interpretation become clear. The actress takes pains to associate the fateful nature of the witches' predictions with the role Lady Macbeth is to play in bringing them to fruition. But this association leads to the inevitable perversion of Lady Macbeth's inherent feminine instincts. Exhorting her spirits to "unsex me *here*,"[43] the actress employs a special emphasis which almost certainly reflects a gesture accompanying the line "Come to my woman's breasts. . . ." In turn, these lines sum up the central interpretative idea that Mrs. Siddons brings to this crucial first scene: she establishes a dramatic tension between impulsive, masculine strength of purpose and qualities more naturally feminine, even maternal.

The dominance that Lady Macbeth is now prepared to exert upon Kemble's Macbeth emerges in their first scene together. Bell in fact states that Macbeth as Kemble plays it "is only a co-operating part" (p. 35), but it must be understood that Macbeth's subordination is precisely the relationship that made possible the originality of Kemble's own interpretation. An extended example of "co-operating" acting occurs in the murder scene, a long sequence which in the hands of Kemble and Mrs. Siddons affords a detailed panorama of the terror and guilt attendant on the murder of a king. In the dagger soliloquy, with which the

[43] Marked 2nd edn. of Kemble's text in the Garrick Club; see the discussion of this valuable document in note 37 of the article cited above, note 33.

murder sequence begins, Kemble used one of those infrequent bursts of great physical energy that, together with the subtle explorations of the character's mind, constituted his manner of approach. Charles Bell, the well-known surgeon and brother of Professor Bell, thought instead that "he should stand or sit musing, his eye fixed on vacancy, then a more piercing look to seem to see what still is in the mind's eye only, characterised by the bewildered look which accompanies the want of a fixed object of vision; yet the eye should not roll or start" (Bell, p. 50). Another viewer, in 1811, registered a similar objection to Kemble's technique—perhaps with accounts of Garrick's "natural" acting in mind:

> The true actor would have seen the dagger slowly and reluctantly,—he would have fixed his eye upon a particular spot of the scene, until the image grew, as such an image might, on the eye of a bewildered, terrified, and brain-sick man;—he would have shrunk from the belief of its reality, and returned to it only with a struggling conviction until it obtained full possession of him. Mr. *Kemble*'s conception was otherwise; he stretched his arms, yawned, and at once started at the dagger; all after this was *palpability*: he made no doubt of its existence; he followed it with his eyes steadily in all its evolutions through the air, and walked after it composedly to *Duncan*'s door.[44]

Boaden records a like disappointment in commenting that Kemble was here "too explosive, too much in action. . . ."[45] But Kemble's behavior is not without its merits and certainly reveals the studied approach to character always apparent in his performances. E. H. Seymour's *Remarks, Critical, Conjectural, and Explanatory, upon the Plays of Shakspeare* (1805) provides for Kemble's outburst a theoretical basis such as the actor himself may have discovered. Kemble's initial start reveals Macbeth's terror at the apparition, but Seymour points out that the dominant effect is "confidence and animation, and he tries to lay hold of the dagger; and, indeed, upon what principle of reason, or on what theory of the human mind, can it be presumed, that the appearance of supernatural agency, to effect the immediate object of our wish, should produce dread and not encouragement?" (I, 196).

[44] *The Times,* 19 September 1811. [45] *Life of Kemble,* I, 416.

Later in the murder sequence, when Macbeth has returned from Duncan's chamber leaving the two attendants still alive, Kemble and Mrs. Siddons make capital out of Shakespeare's momentary postponement of this discovery. A series of horrifying whispers punctuates the silence as he re-enters, Mrs. Siddons' character behaving "as if her inhuman strength of spirit" is "overcome by the contagion of his remorse and terror" (Bell, pp. 52-53). [see Plate 38] When at last Lady Macbeth observes that her husband has unthinkingly brought the murder instruments away with him (Bell, p. 55), she seizes them in a sudden burst of purpose—"Give ME the daggers"—which, Boaden recalls, "excited a general start from those around me."[46] The consistency of Mrs. Siddons' interpretation is again clear in this moment. As she herself describes it in her "Remarks," "Instantaneously the solitary particle of her human feeling is swallowed up in her remorseless ambition, and, wrenching the daggers from the feeble grasp of her husband, she finishes the act which the infirm of purpose had not courage to complete, and calmly and steadily returns to her accomplice with the fiend-like boast, 'My hands are of your colour; But I would scorn to wear a heart so white' " [sic] (II, 20-21).

Percy Fitzgerald, in an unpublished summary of English acting tradition, says that there are three "grand scenic points of attraction" in the play which "exhibit Macbeth under different views." The first is the murder scene, "where he is interesting from his hesitation & remorse"; the second, the banquet scene, "where he is conscience stricken and cowed"; and the last, "the scenes with the witches & in the Battle where he is desperate and defiant." Of these, the banquet scene "is the grandest of all & from its opportunity for show & crowds & the dramatic, ought to be the CENTRAL POINT."[47] Kemble's lavish production of the play in April 1794 at the new Drury Lane demonstrates that this actor, following precedents established earlier in the century by Garrick, did indeed make the banquet scene the focal point of his production. Its centrality was not limited, however, to scenic display, although this contributed largely to the success of the production. As Fitzger-

[46] *Life of Siddons*, II, 137.

[47] Notes made by Fitzgerald in an unidentified copy of *Macbeth* tipped in to a workbook now in the Folger Shakespeare Library (Folger Prompt Mac 48), note opp. p. 1.

ald observes, the scene offers extensive opportunities for "the dramatic." It is hardly surprising to find that Kemble as producer integrated the scenic splendor of a medieval banquet with the equally "dramatic" presentation of a character caught in the snares of his own guilt.

Records preserved in the Garrick Club combine with other materials to show how Kemble staged the banquet and arranged its effects. The chief playing areas numbered four: a platform with two thrones somewhere near the center of the stage; the banqueting tables at stage right; an open area downstage center and leading up to the thrones; and the area by the left proscenium door, where the hired murderer makes his entrance.[48] It is possible to plot the positions of Kemble and Mrs. Siddons at every point in this scene.[49] Their lines of movement fix Kemble exclusively in the downstage area, playing alternately near the tables and near the left proscenium door, while Mrs. Siddons remains most of the time sitting or standing upon the raised platform but occasionally moving off of it to relate more closely to Kemble or to the guests at the tables. The aesthetic effect of this series of positions suggests the thematic importance that Kemble and Mrs. Siddons discovered in the scene. Kemble uses the downstage area, left to right, for hesitant, rambling but sometimes frantic movement, so to convey more graphically the sense of a man trapped by his own unwitting connivance. Meanwhile Mrs. Siddons continues for the most part immobile but raised above the heads of the other actors, so that her increasing unease and actual terror at Macbeth's self-incrimination may be evident to all the audience. The growing divisiveness between Macbeth and his wife implicit in this staging is emphasized over the course of the scene with sure and mounting effect. As the action progresses, the disintegration of Lady Macbeth from her former solid position of dominance is set forth by Mrs. Siddons in a series of meaningful gestures and facial expressions. These are especially evident when, having explained that Macbeth is sometimes given to momentary fits, she leaves her regal position to move downstage, catches Macbeth's hand, and with "smothered terror" pro-

[48] Unless otherwise indicated, the source for the details of the staging of this scene is the marked second edition in the Garrick Club, in which the conventional shorthand for indicating movement is clear and consistent.

[49] As I have shown elsewhere in greater detail; see note 33 above.

nounces the line "Are you a man?"[50] At this moment her "well-conceived attentions, smiles, nods" to the amazed guests create a "conflict of courtesy and inquietude" which her "*mute* acting impressed on the auditors with an unusual degree of power."[51]

Meanwhile Kemble plays the entire sequence with the combination of terrifying fear and gradually increasing courage reminiscent of Garrick's approach and dominant in Kemble's own characterization as a whole. Here his interpretation throws into even greater relief Lady Macbeth's dwindling influence upon her husband. Although Kemble could hardly have seen Garrick play the role, he appears to have exploited Garrick's combination in this scene of initial terror followed by rising fortitude.[52] But Kemble, never a mere imitator, let alone a slavish one, also introduced one of his striking innovations in staging whose precedent lies in theatrical verse and dramatic criticism, not in stage tradition. It is now well known that, on the occasion of his *Macbeth* produced at the new Drury Lane in 1794, Kemble did away with the actual presence of an actor playing the ghost of Banquo. The text, carefully prepared by Kemble himself,[53] shows no stage direction for an entering ghost, and it is clear from reviews of the performance that what the audience saw was Macbeth's reaction to a wholly imagined presence undoubtedly meant to illustrate the tortured state of the usurper's guilty mind. In eliminating the ghost of Banquo Kemble may have been responding to a suggestion in Robert Lloyd's poem *The Actor* (1760). The contemporary historian W. C. Oulton asserts that this was Kemble's source and quotes the relevant lines:

> When chilling horrors shake th'affrighted King,
> And guilt torments him with her scorpion sting;

[50] Bell, p. 61; "Remarks," II, 26.

[51] *Morning Chronicle*, 14 February 1785; *Morning Herald, and Daily Advertiser*, 31 October 1785.

[52] For example, a reviewer in 1794 refers to "the tremor, the assumed energy in the struggle with *Banquo* . . ."—*The World*, 23 April.

[53] *Macbeth, Written By Shakspeare, As Represented By Their Majesties Servants, On Opening The Theatre Royal Drury Lane, On Monday, April 21st. 1794. Printed by C. Lowndes, No. 66, Drury-Lane, Next The Stage Door, And Sold In The Theatre* [1794]. Kemble's text follows Garrick's ("Bell's Shakespeare," Vol. I, 1774) with some minor additions and omissions but with much greater heaviness in punctuation. For a complete analysis of scenes and lines see Hogan, *Shakespeare in the Theatre*, II, 363.

When keenest feelings at his bosom pull,
And fancy tells him that the seat is full;
Why need the ghost usurp the monarch's place,
To frighten children with his mealy face?
The king alone should form the phantom there,
And talk and tremble at the vacant chair.[54]

Lloyd himself may have derived the idea from Bonnell Thornton, to whom *The Actor* is addressed, since it was undoubtedly Thornton who asserted in 1752 that "our surprise would be much greater, and our terror more alarming, while the imagination of MACBETH conjur'd up an airy form before him, though he were really looking only on a chair."[55]

The omission of the ghost may appear inconsistent with Kemble's concern at other points in the production to give substantial form to the imaginary presences of Shakespeare's play.[56] Yet it is understandable that Kemble might have wished to avoid what was often a ludicrous source of amusement to spectators. "The Ghost of Banquo (*like a man turned out of a meal sack*) no longer offends the eye," observed one grateful reviewer. "The guilty fancy of Macbeth is left to fill the vacant chair," he explained, echoing Lloyd's phrase.[57] Very likely Kemble was responding to a tendency of his age, prompted partly by increasing scepticism toward belief in spirits, to prefer the imaginary agonies of the mind to their personified representation on the stage. An American writer offered a compromise typical of this tendency. The ghost of Banquo, he suggests, ought to exchange his earlier costume for the same design dyed several shades lighter, and the same attention should be given to his hair, so that the more aetherial figure would contrast imaginatively with the living persons.[58] With regard to Kemble's even more imaginary ghost, the actor's rising vehemence at its repeated appearance suggests an effect different from that of Garrick's similar interpretation.

[54] *History of the Theatres*, II, 141.

[55] *Have At You All: Or, The Drury-Lane Journal*, No. X (19 March 1752), p. 22. Arthur Colby Sprague, in *Shakespeare and the Actors*, p. 255, identifies its author as Thornton.

[56] See my discussion of Kemble's innovations in "Kemble's Production of *Macbeth* (1794): Some Notes on Scene Painters, Scenery, Special Effects, and Costumes," *TN*, XXI (1966-67), 63-74 and Plate 3.

[57] *London Packet*, 21-23 April 1794.

[58] *The Theatrical Censor*, No. XV (1806), p. 88.

Although difficult—and perhaps hazardous—to describe in detail, the response elicited from the audience by this behavior may well have been admiration for Macbeth's determination and courage in daring to confront a creature far less substantial than any actor, however well made up, could represent. At least, the absence of any objective presence on the stage can hardly fail to suggest that Macbeth is here the victim of an overwrought imagination rather than the object of some palpable accuser.[59]

By the end of the scene Mrs. Siddons' Lady Macbeth gives the impression of total nervous exhaustion (Bell, p. 65). In contrast, Macbeth's strident tones at the second "appearance" of the ghost introduce the more vigorous line of action that Kemble follows in the concluding half of the play. After the guests have departed and Lady Macbeth has tottered from the throne, the chasm that now gapes between the two characters is given a brief but sure dramatic statement by Kemble's cross to the right on the lines ". . . should I wade no more, Returning were as tedious as go

[59] Banquo's corporeal reality had disturbed even the tradition-minded Francis Gentleman, who called the ghost "the raw-head-and-bloody-bones of tragedy"—*Dramatic Censor*, I, 95. The compromise suggested by the American writer above is analogous to Boaden's description of Henry Fuseli's painting of the ghost in *Hamlet*: "It has what seems person [sic], invested in what seems to be armour; it bears the regal sceptre; its countenance is human in its lineaments, though it inspires more awe than mere humanity can excite"—*Life of Kemble*, II, 98. Oulton says that Kemble's innovation was generally approved—*History of the Theatres*, II, 142—but by the turn of the century a controversy was running intermittently in the periodicals. Some writers cited Shakespeare's apparent intention to have the ghost actually appear on stage, and others ingeniously refined the idea by suggesting *two* ghosts—Banquo's and Duncan's. Most, however, preferred an imaginary Banquo, and their criterion was clearly that of added terror. "Nothing real," said one critic, "can approach in horror what the imagination can conceive—to attempt, indeed, to realize what is horribly conceived by the mind, is to deprive it of half its horror"—*Monthly Mirror*, n.s. II (1807), p. 436; see also *Monthly Mirror*, V (1798), 112-113, 170-171, and 301; XV (1803), 333-334; XVI (1803), 413-414; XVII (1804), 188-189; and *The Times*, 19 September 1811, where the reviewer objects to the *presence* of the ghost, which by this time for some unknown reason had been restored. Richard Payne Knight, who did not share Kemble's sense of the ethereal, could nevertheless describe the problem Kemble was attacking: "In dramatic representations, there can be nothing left indeterminate for the imagination to work upon; whence, I believe, every person, who, after having been a reader, has become a spectator of the witches in Macbeth, has felt how totally they lose their grandeur by being exhibited on the stage in distinct forms"—*An Analytical Inquiry into the Principles of Taste* (1805), p. 291.

o'er." Mrs. Siddons is left by herself at the center of the stage. In contrast to the earlier scene in which she had led Macbeth away to don his night-gown, clapping him on the shoulder to bolster his courage (Bell, pp. 56-57), she can now only follow Kemble off in silence as he delivers Macbeth's cynical observation, "We are yet but young in deed."

The isolation from one another of Macbeth and Lady Macbeth, moulded into an overt dramatic statement in the banquet scene, is carried out in the construction of the remaining scenes in the play. So, suitably, the contrasting qualities of courage, born of despair, in Macbeth and mental disintegration in his wife become the themes of Kemble's and Mrs. Siddons' interpretations of the last act. In her famous sleep-walking scene, Mrs. Siddons established the essence of her interpretation early in her career simply by entering in a dress of white satin, which in the "language" of eighteenth-century costume indicated a heroine gone mad.[60] But this was only one of a series of innovations that Mrs. Siddons introduced. As early as her first performances in 1785 she set down upon a table the taper that previous actresses had carried throughout the scene. The result, obviously, was an added freedom for the pantomimic washing of hands.[61] But certain perceptive critics detected a more subtle advantage as well in the added psychological realism that resulted. James Boaden sums up the psychological basis for Mrs. Siddons' actions in explaining Shakespeare's purpose in this scene:

> When the force of volition is withdrawn, the fancy becomes a dreadful victim to the images of past guilt: and she who waking can dispel her husband's terrors and her own, in sleep beholds her bleeding victims for ever present. . . . [see Plate 39] Mrs. Siddons seemed to conceive the fancy as having equal power over the whole frame, and all her actions had the wakeful vigour; she laded the water from the imaginary ewer over her hands—bent her body to listen to the sounds presented by her fancy, and hurried to resume the taper where she had left it, that she might with all speed drag her pallid husband to their chamber.[62]

[60] See *Morning Post,* 3 February 1785, and *Public Advertiser,* 4 February 1785.

[61] She "sets down the light and rubs her hand, making the action of lifting up water in one hand at intervals"—Bell, pp. 66-67.

[62] *Life of Siddons,* II, 143-144. See also Mrs. Siddons' "Remarks," II, 32,

Subsequent scenes, finishing out the now well-established contrast between the two characters, send Kemble's Macbeth rapidly toward his courageous end. The only interruption in the sustained activity of the final moments occurs when Macbeth hears the news of his wife's death, and even here Kemble used the announcement to motivate one of those judicious bursts of energy he reserved for special effect. At the news of the queen's death, after a long pause of abject despair, Kemble broke into frenetic action, building the "Tomorrow and tomorrow" speech "to a climax of desperation that brought down the enthusiastic cheers of the closely-packed theatre." This outburst, according to William Charles Macready, who saw Kemble act the part just before the "noblest Roman of them all" retired, initiated a sustained display of energy that lasted to the very end. At his death, Macready recalled, Macduff (Charles Kemble) "received him in his arms, and laid him gently on the ground, his physical powers being unequal to further effort."[63]

Kemble's emphasis on qualities of courage and endurance in these last scenes gives full expression to the notion of sympathetic response explained in the answer to Whately at the beginning of his career. In fact, when the strength and purposiveness of Mrs. Siddons' Lady Macbeth are set alongside Kemble's approach to his character, there appears a high concentration on military qualities. Mrs. Siddons' emphasis on "the *valour* of my tongue"[64] suggests a Lady Macbeth who has assumed the role of a general, systematically attacking Kemble's Macbeth at the weak point of his supposed unmanliness and taking advantage of his ineffectual soul-searching to dominate him completely. At the same time, deliberately assaulting the fortress of her own femininity, Mrs. Siddons' character conquers the natural frailty of womankind in order to gain the monarchy for her spouse. But ironically her love for him and its attendant selflessness prompt her to hide her own wretchedness out of regard for her husband's misery. In so doing

---

and the critical praise for her emphasis on realism which occurs as early as *Morning Chronicle*, 14 February 1785, and as late as Bell, pp. 67-68.

[63] *Macready's Reminiscences, and Selections from His Diaries and Letters*, ed. Sir Frederick Pollock (1875), I, 148. An impressive instance of the continuity of English stage tradition may be seen by comparing the present reconstruction of Kemble's Macbeth with Alan Downer's reconstruction of Macready's; see *The Eminent Tragedian: William Charles Macready* (Cambridge, Mass., 1966), pp. 318-338.

[64] Boaden, *Life of Siddons*, II, 134.

she destroys their intimate relationship and precipitates their tragic end. Kemble's share in this approach was to allow Macbeth an extensive exhibition of those qualities of moral perspicacity which made him more a man than a warrior. But as the unwholesome effects of their inverted relationship become progressively more clear, Kemble infuses into the character the old and familiar attribute of almost barbaric valor in war which initially set him on the road to preferment and which, at the end, predominates over his remorse and despair. And so each actor presents just that sort of psychologically credible character which the moralists and philosophical critics of the eighteenth and early nineteenth centuries describe: a naturally virtuous person whose innate sensibilities ironically bring about his own downfall.

If, as William Richardson might protest, Lady Macbeth's last moments suggest to audiences of this period an object lesson to avoid the indulgence of the passions, the lesson is effectively blurred by the fact that, as Mrs. Siddons plays it, the "passion" which led to her destruction was conjugal love. The same complexity is apparent in Kemble's Macbeth. His extensive reading in the philosophical criticism of his age and in the Lockean psychology that came down to him was apparently of great service in detailing, with almost Richardsonian explicitness, the process by which a hero becomes a villain in spite of himself. At the end of the century Charles Dibdin, the prolific playwright and stage historian, analyzed the progress of Macbeth in a passage that well sums up the Romantic view of tragic character and at the same time the essence of Kemble's own interpretation:

> He is first timid, then wavering, then determined, then guilty; and what is masterly, even to wonder, he neither sees his actual danger, nor questions the ambiguity of his tempters, till he has atchieved the end of his ambition. Thus he hurries from desperation to desperation; yet, still retaining some faint colour of his original nature through his numerous and sanguinary villanies, he deplores his wickedness with philosophy, and holds his courage to the last.[65]

Undeniably, Kemble's relentless penetration into the springs of human passion and his illustration of mental processes on the stage place him in a significant relationship to the philosophical

[65] Dibdin, *A Complete History of the Stage* (1800), III, 328.

and critical tendencies of his age. Where Garrick's performances had anticipated critical views of Macbeth and Richard III, Kemble's contribution was to epitomize ideas about dramatic character which now dominated the thought of his day.

iii. Kemble, Cooke, and Transition in Richard III

When Kemble assumed the role of Richard III at Drury Lane in the season of 1788-89, he brought to it the inherent nobility and grace displayed in Macbeth. The resulting interpretation was much different from Garrick's but nevertheless consonant with certain aspects of the tradition. Scott observed in retrospect that Kemble's qualities were inconsistent with the ludicrous or comic aspects of his roles, and the author of the introduction to the play in *Cumberland's British Drama* found Kemble also deficient in portraying Richard's cunning, artful trickery.[66] Kemble attempted to make up for these shortcomings with a vigorous emphasis on courage. Forgetting his strictures, the writer of *Cumberland*'s introduction saw definite majesty in Kemble's Richard: although he struggles with dissimulation in the early part of the play, he becomes on the field of battle a "daring and aspiring monarch" illustrating his bloody maxims with "terrific energy" (I, 8). H. Martin, writing in 1802, went even further, remarking that Kemble does not condescend to play the hypocrite villain but instead portrays a "sublime being."[67]

As in Macbeth, moreover, Kemble's emphasis on courageousness in Richard elicited both admiration and sympathy. "Alas!" lamented Martin, "why must we rejoice when such a spirit is vanquished?" (p. 37). The question echoes a perennial concern among critics of the Garrick-Kemble period. Despite Francis Gentleman's record of "eager applause" habitually accompanying the tyrant's fall,[68] critics were increasingly inclined to make ex-

[66] Scott, *Quarterly Review* (1826), p. 215; London: John Cumberland, 1826, I, 8.

[67] [H. Martin], *Remarks on Mr. John Kemble's Performance of Hamlet and Richard the Third* (1802), p. 37.

[68] Gentleman, notes to Bell edition, III (1774), p. 65n. The motives for such applause are not always clear, however. George Steevens, in a letter to Garrick, observes that "those who die on stage either in single combat or by suicide generally meet with applause" since "an Englishman loves a spirited, but abhors a phlegmatic exit"—Boaden, ed., *Private Correspondence*, I, 452.

ceptions for Richard on account of his admirable valor. William Hodson found him a perfectly vicious character but allowed that the general prohibition of such parts as central characters on the stage is lifted for the sake of his "daring spirit, and ambition."[69] Thomas Davies contrasted Richard with the King in *Hamlet*. In Garrick's adaptation, Davies observes, Claudius is given courage and so becomes a less mean character than Shakespeare intended; but the inherently brave villain like Richard III, although justly hated, cannot be despised.[70] The natural result of such admiration, however qualified, was a degree of sympathy for the villain. Richard Cumberland, writing a few years after Davies, reflected the rising tendency toward sympathy when he described how Richard at the moment of death, "loaded as he is with enormities, . . . carries the good wishes of many of his audience into action, and dies with their regret."[71] It is not surprising, then, to find Martin asserting that Richard in Kemble's performance is not really vanquished at all:

> His fall produced an effect that cannot be described. He had faced death as one resolved to conquer—but, victory fled, he would not be subdued—he would not sink to earth. When he felt his death-wound, he seemed rather to throw life away, than to wait till it was wrested from him. He bounded ere he fell, as if to leap into eternity, and there seize the renown he had won in spite of fate or fortune. (p. 38)

The cooler-headed writer for the *Cumberland* edition also found that, when justice demands Richard's death, "his better qualities inspire a momentary regret, which is not diminished by the reflection that he falls by the hand of a meaner adversary" (I, 6).

Kemble's eminence in conveying nobility of spirit and in eliciting favorable audience response established him as a legitimate successor to Garrick, but there was one quality of his predeces-

---

Again, Thomas Davies describes the effect of Garrick's death scene in his debut performance of Richard: "The death of Richard was accompanied with the loudest gratulations of applause"—*Memoirs of the Life of David Garrick*, new (2nd) edn. (1808), I, 41. Such applause, one suspects, owes more to Garrick's acting than to virtuous approval of a tyrant's fall.

[69] Hodson, *Zoraida, . . . To Which Is Added . . . Observations on Tragedy* (1780), pp. 87-88, 88n.

[70] Davies, *Dramatic Miscellanies* (1783-84), III, 146-147.

[71] *Observer*, 3rd edn. (1790), II, 264.

sor's which he could not hope to equal: as Scott found, Kemble simply could not look like a villain. [see Plate 40] Himself sensible of this, Kemble argued that Richard as a man of aristocratic breeding should not descend to low cunning and vulgar cruelty.[72] But in 1800 there appeared on the London stage an actor whose performance of Richard III was hailed as superior to Kemble's precisely because of his success in portraying these characteristics. [see Plate 41] George Frederick Cooke returned to London as Richard at Covent Garden on 31 October, his reputation already high from twenty years of acting villains in provincial theaters. The qualities Cooke manifested in the role so eclipsed Kemble's interpretation in popular opinion that, although Kemble's prerogatives as manager and chief tragedian at Drury Lane assured him the role, he stepped aside in deference to the new actor. Cooke's swift victory in wresting the role from Kemble is evident in the calendar of performances through the end of the year. Kemble played Richard once in September and again in October, but after Cooke's return the only performances are his—eight in all, from late October up through December.[73] Genest's summary of Cooke's season demonstrates his success. He acted Richard twenty-two times, Shylock ten, Iago ten, Macbeth seven, Kitely ten, The Stranger two, Sir Giles Overreach five, and Sir Archy MacSarcasm an uncertain number.[74] One third, then, of a total of more than sixty-six performances was of Richard III.

Cooke's qualities of originality and variety were apparent from the first. One reviewer, in a lengthy and detailed analysis for the *Monthly Mirror*, praised his knowledge of the "science" of acting, the result of his capacious intellect. Cooke's readings and emphases are to so great a degree his own that he is a kind of mannerist, but these eccentric habits go far toward supporting his interpretation of Richard. The actor's interpolation of several lines from *3 Henry VI* comprises an index to his general approach:

> Why I can smile, and murder while I smile,
> And cry content to that which grieves my heart;
> And wet my cheeks with artificial tears,
> And frame my face to all occasions.

[72] Scott, *Quarterly Review* (1826), p. 218.
[73] Hogan, *Shakespeare in the Theatre*, II, 575.
[74] John Genest, *Some Account of the English Stage* (Bath, 1832), VII, 520.

Cooke's subtlety, sarcasm, and ludicrous turns are unparalleled, the reviewer finds: "We have seen *Richard* rendered more awful and terrific, but never more thoroughly detestable." Adding to this another implicit comparison with Kemble, he observes that Cooke is somewhat deficient in the kingly and heroic aspects of the character and lacks a certain vivid impressiveness, but he more than makes up for this fault in his malignant cruelty. When Cooke delivered the first of his interpolated lines, "it conveyed the idea of a man, sensible of his personal deformities, and the barriers which separated him from the rest of his brethren, *hugging himself up*, and enjoying a horrible satisfaction in the possession of a faculty by which he hoped to overreach the rest of mankind, and secure the grand object he had in his eye."

This was the dominant quality of the first few acts, but there was also present another aspect of the character. His soliloquies revealed with utter naturalness "the secret deliberations of the soul, forming themselves into words as they arose in the mind." Connected with these inner musings were Cooke's momentary misgivings, especially during the murder of the princes and later, just before the tent scene. Here, "his hesitation and *walking to and fro*, . . . with some admirable *bye-play*, . . . finely denoted the misgivings of his mind as to the event of the approaching battle, and suitably prepared the audience for the awful visitation that was at hand, when the ghosts of those he had murdered were *to sit heavy on his soul*. . . ." But Richard's courage recalls him to himself at the end of the play:

> The conflict might be more desperate and protracted, but the ineffectual struggle to catch, in his expiring moments, at his fallen sword, was well conceived, and in the true spirit of Richard, whom even his enemies affirmed to have been "a noble knight, who defended himself to the *last breath*, with eminent valour."

These last moments, the reviewer finds, precipitate a change in the audience. Through most of the play a detestable villain, Richard becomes in the last act "an object of deeper interest—as his fate approaches, commiseration of his sufferings, and admiration of his valour, are blended with our disgust at his crimes."[75]

The points raised in this early review receive repeated critical

[75] *Monthly Mirror*, x (1800), 318-321.

attention over the course of Cooke's brief subsequent career. The anonymous author of *Remarks on the Character of Richard the Third; as played by Cooke and Kemble* (1801) finds that, since the key to Richard's character lies in a series of varied and sudden changes, an actor must bring to the role quick feelings, a capacity to express them, and consequently a variety of voice and feature. Kemble's "stern, gloomy, unalterable face" is inadequate to the task. His unwavering austerity and monotonous voice are totally out of place in a character of such "fire and cruel facetiousness" (pp. 9-11). Cooke, on the other hand, produces a sense of the variety of familiar life in his speech and actions through the modulation of voice and the rapid variation of movements. Unlike Kemble, who in his soliloquies talks with the pit, Cooke appears arguing with himself in such a way that his thoughts rise naturally to his face. Beyond these points Cooke displays similar virtuosity, especially in elucidating the subtle shades of remorse. Richard's personal deformity offers a continual subject for lamentation—rightfully so, the author points out, since the playwright intended to offer "some excuse for his hero's actions . . ." (pp. 16-19).

These moments of mental turmoil prepare for the major change that overcomes Richard in Act IV, reflected in Cooke's discriminating alterations. No more the smiling, vain hypocrite, he has become almost another person (p. 24). By the fifth act, before the battle, Richard's melancholy has increased. Cooke's manner of presenting it in a "still, small," and deliberate voice suggests "a great mind bowed down by gloomy reflections" (pp. 34-36). Because of the "poetical" nature of the tent scene, Kemble appears in it to advantage, exhibiting "the horrors of a dreadful vision,"[76] [see Plate 42] but in the subsequent minutes of the play he is clearly outdone. Beginning with the scroll scene, Cooke elicits admiration both as actor and character. Kemble, reading over the missive addressed to "Jockey of Norfolk," merely throws it away in disdain. Cooke, in contrast, reads slowly, with increasing attention, and pronounces ". . . is bought and sold" in a low tone of consideration:

[76] P. 15. A Birmingham reviewer recalled that Cooke as Richard "was never so effective in the *fifth* as in the preceding acts, and in the tent scene his falling off was extreme"—*The Theatrical Looker-on,* I (1 July 1822), p. 21.

> Richard perceives, or at least fears, that he is betrayed. His great mind surveys, in a few moments, the whole occurrence. He sees that the most expedient course is an affectation of reliance on those who now form his only support. He slowly throws aside the scroll, and says it is merely "an invention of the enemy," with such a voice and in such a manner as lets us into his whole soul, and leaves us suspicious of those about him, and in admiration of his prudence and ability. (pp. 39-40)

Finally, in the battle scene, Cooke energetically displays the vehemence born of despair which moves the proud tyrant. Although the thick, low tone of his last words—"and darkness be the burier of the dead"—mingles with his "characteristic malignity," the scene elicits an unmistakable response from the spectator, "the channel to whose heart lies through his eyes" (pp. 44-45). Whereas Kemble in general acts with formality and severe coldness, Cooke, in his bustling natural manner and changeable countenance, succeeds in presenting "*a portrait of the human mind under the vicissitudes of accident and passion.*"[77]

Cooke's variety continued to draw the attention of reviewers, who never tired of praising his manner as "natural," faithful to the behavior of real men. When Cooke left England for an American tour, he took with him a reputation for "unstudied" actions and responses that captured the imaginations of American critics. A New York reviewer unhesitatingly praised "the force and comprehension of his genius, the boldness and originality of his manner, the significance of his gestures, the astonishing flexibility of his countenance, and the quick and piercing expression of his eye. . . ."[78] Many comments, like this one, smack of puffery, but in fact they are often substantiated with precise descriptions of individual scenes and lines. The standard praise of natural vari-

[77] Pp. 51-52. Macready recalls that "there was such significance in each inflexion, look, and gesture, and such impressive earnestness in his whole bearing, that he compelled your attention and interest"—*Reminiscences,* ed. Pollock, I, 66. James Boaden viewed the contrast as one between the "academic" and "vulgar" styles of acting and found Kemble and Cooke "the *best* of each by infinite degrees"—*Life of Kemble,* II, 289. On the same points see Thomas Gilliland, *The Dramatic Mirror* (1808), II, 712.

[78] Unidentified source, quoted in *The Mirror of Taste,* III (Philadelphia, 1811), p. 23. For a general survey of Cooke's success at the Park Theater, New York, see George C. D. Odell, *Annals of the New York Stage,* II (New York, 1927), 353-362.

40. Kemble as Richard III

41. George Frederick Cooke as Richard III

42. Kemble as Richard III, "Tent Scene"

43. Kean as Shylock

ety reserved for Cooke's Richard often explained this attribute as a product of his energy and powers of intellect. A twenty-page article in the Philadelphia *Mirror of Taste* in 1811 found these new qualities of energy and intellectual power pre-eminent. Summarizing many of the current critical ideas about Richard's character, the author makes a point of Cooke's success in epitomizing them. Shakespeare's object, he says, was

> to exhibit in the strongest colors the unlimited powers of stupendous intellect when united with stupendous courage. To this end he forms a monster who, to the pollution of every crime that can make man noxious to man and offensive to God, adds the most disgusting personal deformity, and yet renders him terribly great, and admirable and sublimely attractive, by the mere force of valor, which nothing can dismay, and of intellect capacious of every thing. These are the fundamental parts of the composition which a true philosophic actor like Cooke will take for his guide. . . .[79]

From this review may be inferred a shift of emphasis in Cooke's interpretation: his earlier pointing of simple melancholy has become subordinate to a greater and more consistent presentation of strength, mental and physical. Where earlier accounts of his soliloquies describe Richard's lamentation over his deformities, the present review finds that his first speech elicits admiration for his complete disregard of external beauty and that he treats "his own manifold deformity" with actual levity (p. 185). According to this reviewer, Cooke is still playing the fundamental change that overcomes the villain in Act IV; he is predictably good in the meditation scene before retiring[80] and predictably inferior in the tent scene that immediately follows. But the essential character newly manifested in the earlier part of the play remains at the end. Cooke, the critic observes, often varies the particulars of his action, yet stays the same impressive character who died as he had lived:

[79] *Mirror of Taste*, III (1811), pp. 183-184.

[80] "Doubt—confidence—apprehension—disregard—defiance—and yet misgiving of the event of the next day, are successively displayed and sent home to every eye and heart by his restlessness, and walking backwards and forwards,—by his sticking the point of his sword in the ground, and then recovering and flourishing it,—by his sighing and silent attempts to speak,—by his unequalled by-play, and by the matchless expression of his countenance . . ."—pp. 195-196.

One time in the dying scene Richard makes an ineffectual effort to rise, and failing in it dashes away his sword in despair; another time he drops his sword, and, in making a vain effort to recover, falls again; both equally characteristic of the intrepid furious Richard. But that which gives the finishing stroke to the picture is the look which, raising himself on his elbow, he darts at Richmond. It was terrible, it had soul in it; it looked a testamentary curse, and made the death exactly correspond to the life and living character of the monster Richard. (p. 196)

iv. Summary: The Man of Feeling in a World of Horror

Cooke's combination of the familiar change in Richard in Act IV with the newer qualities of sublime spirit reflects the same transformation in dramatic character evident in early nineteenth-century drama, where the villain-hero is quickly becoming the Byronic man of melancholy grandeur. Reviews of Cooke for the length of his later career record impressions of almost preternatural energy and power, and consistently comment on the admiration Richard elicits despite his monstrous cruelty. Particularly during the period of Cooke's London success, the fine line between admiration and sympathy is continually crossed, as in the anonymous *Remarks* of 1801, where Richard's announcement, "I am—myself alone," spoken by Cooke in tones of pitiable dejection, is taken to show that the tyrant "is calling to mind his imperfections of form, for a bad purpose, but still he is viewing them as the afflictions of his destiny" (p. 20). The description in the *Monthly Mirror* in 1800, quoted above, indicates the moral ambivalence implicit in Richard's fall: "As his fate approaches, commiseration of his sufferings, and admiration of his valour, are blended with our disgust at his crimes."[81]

The development of this complex response in philosophical Shakespearean criticism, discussed earlier, parallels a similar

[81] P. 319. Compare Boaden: ". . . the unsparing ambition of Richard has something of an immoral effect upon the audience; and their proper sympathy with his victims is blunted by the *certainty* of his success, and the daring intrepidity with which he hurries them on from one atrocity to another. There is something in triumphant villany against which the moral sense is never sufficiently guarded"—*Life of Kemble*, II, 59.

growth in theatrical criticism. Many conventionally moral comments extending into the nineteenth century exist side by side with a less well explained fascination with evil presented sympathetically on the stage. Francis Gentleman, always careful to protect young persons from the insidious attractiveness of vice, declared that *Macbeth* is not distinguished for its moral tendencies and found Macbeth's character difficult to describe because, notwithstanding his pernicious villainy, he impresses an audience more strongly than any other character in English drama. In hearing Garrick's interpolated death speech, Gentleman asks, who "but trembles at the idea of future punishment, and almost pities the expiring wretch, though stained with crimes of the deepest die?"[82] The writer on Lady Macbeth in *The Port Folio* in 1814 attempts to palliate her guilt by pointing out that, in the relationship of husband and wife, conjugal affection ran parallel to ambition: "It was not that she loved Duncan less, but Macbeth more" (III, 342). His purpose of extenuating Lady Macbeth's guilt by adducing her benevolent human instincts, the writer confesses, has a deep emotional need behind it. "Whatever items we can fairly deduct from individual guilt," he explains, "we so far diminish that aggregate which weighs so heavily on our common race" (p. 344). We sympathize with the servant of Joanna Baillie's poor De Monfort who pronounces his dead master too good to do a cruel deed; yet De Monfort murdered a fellow man.

> Does not the character of lady Macbeth authorize the same conclusion, since her offence received the same awful expiation? It is even here within the province of the moral alchemist to . . . decompose, combine, or transmute; and if in the process any latent good should be elicited, or any superficial evil obliterated, the labour will not have been in vain.
>
> (p. 345)

It was surely no accident that led Coleridge to manifest the same response to moral complexity when, in discussing the experiential basis of Maturin's *Bertram,* he said: "Love *me,* and not my qualities, may be a vicious and insane wish, but it is not a wish wholly without a meaning."[83]

With such compelling reasons for offsetting the guilt of dra-

[82] *Dramatic Censor,* I, 106-108.

[83] *Biographia Literaria,* ed. J. Shawcross (Oxford, 1907), II, 188.

matic character and human being alike, it is not surprising that this aspect of the sentimental movement created profound changes in the drama and theater of the late eighteenth and early nineteenth centuries. The pervasive—and, to some observers, pernicious—effect of sentimental standards of human behavior transformed the image of Shakespearean character inherited from the sixteenth and seventeenth centuries. The intimate connection between new interpretations of Richard III and Macbeth, documented in this chapter, and the drama being written in this age is suggested implicitly in James Boaden's assessment of the influence of "modern" and especially of German plays on English morals. The reader, he comments,

> will have remarked with surprise, and I hope with disgust, that they were most of them built upon moral paradox. He will remember to have heard . . . that *all* VICE had a contagious influence; that any *single* enormity, long indulged, from the natural operation of our self love, begot a specious sanction that satisfied the conscience; and by the extension of similar palliation to kindred crimes, the whole mind became irrecoverably tainted, and the BEING obnoxious and to be avoided. The *German* secret of interest tended to strengthen the self-delusion in actual life; it laid the "flattering unction to the soul," that any one vice might maintain its power in the most amiable minds; and exhibited the *adultress*, and the *seducer*, and the *robber*, and even the *murderer*, as the most generous of the species. The sort of thing became popular, from the *passion* it set in motion, as well as the balm it infused into the festering wounds of memory. The *most* guarded had some imperfections, which they would fain hope to be venial; they were now systematically taught, that even GOODNESS might consist with errors far more criminal than their own. Thus sympathy usurped the place of censure, and a door was opened to that fatal fallacy, of making a *compromise* with morals, and setting the vices to which we were *not* inclined, as a sort of balance to those in which we were determined to indulge.[84]

Boaden sees no connection between the doubtful morality of the new drama and the presentation of Shakespeare's plays by

[84] *Life of Kemble*, II, 252-253.

actors whose abilities to elicit admiration and sympathy are described in so many of his pages. But the connection exists all the same, reflecting the profound change in notions of dramatic character taking place in this age. The framework of a moral order in Shakespeare's plays, within which a character's speech and actions are made relevant to objective standards of good and evil, has in this new era disappeared or at least been transmuted out of recognition, leaving the dramatic character itself as the only source of meaning. The character's manifestation of great energy and power and his conscious awareness of the nature of evil, if not referable to a code of moral behavior implicit in the structure of the play itself, become exclusively expressions of his unique and therefore fascinating personality. The significance of a character's life now centers on the history of his emotional responses, which in turn are the product of inner conditions and outward circumstances that operate, for better or worse, on human passion. Under these new assumptions, sympathy is inevitable for the plight of a man who must act in a somehow unverifiable universe. Since the meaning of the play comes from inside his character rather than from the moral pattern implicit in the interplay of character and event, performances of *Macbeth* and *Richard III* could hardly avoid presenting notions about human experience that simply do not accord with the text. The great actors from Garrick to Cooke (and beyond), however unwittingly, were important agents in effecting this transformation of Shakespeare. In addition to their revolutionary interpretations, the star system created a focus on central character which accelerated its phenomenal distortion by the end of the century. Although exact lines of influence are difficult to trace, it is certain that Garrick's novel interpretations of heroic villains in *Richard* and *Macbeth* strikingly anticipate the views of psychological criticism. It is equally certain that Kemble, Mrs. Siddons, and Cooke exemplify these same views, now fully matured, on the stage. Together, the disparate activities of contemporary dramaturgy, closet criticism, and theatrical performance form a significant body of thought, attitude, and supposition which helps define an age and its radical concept of dramatic character.

CHAPTER XI

Coleridge, Lamb, and the Theater of the Mind

> I know that I rebel against most performances of Shakespeare's plays because I want a direct relationship between the work of art and myself, and I want the performance to be such as will not interrupt or alter this relationship any more than it is an alteration or interruption for me to superpose a second inspection of a picture or building upon the first. I object, in other words, to the interpretation. . . .
>
> —T. S. Eliot, "Four Elizabethan Dramatists"

i. Innovation in the Early Nineteenth Century

THE NOTIONS of dramatic character that emerge in eighteenth-century criticism and performance of Shakespeare become the heritage of the early nineteenth century. Critics and actors in this later period stand in obvious debt to the two traditions that, developing independently, reached identical views of dramatic character by the end of the former age. Nineteenth-century critics derive from their predecessors the fundamental assumptions that character is the essence of drama and that the meaning of a play is the meaning of a particular character's experience. And they carry on the ambivalent attitudes of genuine sympathetic involvement in the plight of the character and uneasy moral awareness of his guilt. Like previous writers, they cannot reconcile in rational ways their interest in characters they find immoral and actions they consider evil, and so they either dismiss the problems of ethical conduct altogether or justify their interest as the analysis of motive in the human mind. Similarly, the actors of the early nineteenth century perform in a tradition dating from Garrick which assumes the centrality of the star actor and emphasizes both his impassioned response to the stimulus of the moment and his revelation of the motives which make that response unique. The "Romantic" tradition of acting not only is an outgrowth of the eighteenth century but involves many of the same actors, notably Kemble, Mrs. Siddons, and Cooke, all of whose careers bridge the period between Garrick and Kean.

But meanwhile an idea had developed whose influence on early nineteenth-century notions of dramatic character is of paramount importance. Closet criticism in the eighteenth century had established the notion that Shakespeare's plays could exist completely independent of theatrical performance. In this view, Shakespeare's characters had somehow taken on a certain immediacy that differed from their flesh-and-blood embodiment on the stage. Even in the theater itself the attitude was evident. Kemble's attempt to etherealize the ghost of Banquo represents a general dissatisfaction with the unavoidably palpable "reality" of performance. Such dissatisfaction caused an increasing preference for experiencing Shakespeare's characters unencumbered by the translation of image into substance. By the early nineteenth century this preference, having gone beyond the point of simple negative reaction, emerged as a positive ideal. The description of an ideal actor and an ideal production became such an important phenomenon that many dramatic critics and theatrical reviewers may be classed according to their awareness of the concept and their reactions to the gap between it and actual performance. Of these writers, the two most significant are Samuel Taylor Coleridge and William Hazlitt, who display the most profound notions of ideal production and who at the same time present opposite reactions to the difference they perceive between the actual theater and the theater of the mind. Consequently they provide convenient standards against which may be compared the view of Charles Lamb, who like Coleridge is wholly concerned with ideal performance, and the views of Leigh Hunt and a less important commentator such as Thomas Barnes, who like Hazlitt point toward a union of the actual and the ideal. Coleridge and Hazlitt are most notable for their ability to fuse eighteenth-century notions of dramatic character with their original ideas of sympathetic imagination; but all of these writers hold in common a concept of human nature and its embodiment in dramatic character that marks the distinct significance of their age.

ii. Lamb, Closet Criticism, and the Sense of the Dramatic

The conventional view of Charles Lamb as a critic of the drama derives from two works, the essay "On the Tragedies of

Shakspeare, Considered with Reference to Their Fitness for Stage Representation" and the *Specimens of English Dramatic Poets*. In 1924 T. S. Eliot looked back at the *Specimens* and decided that its publication had established the accepted attitude toward Elizabethan drama. "Lamb," he observed, "set in motion the enthusiasm for poetic drama which still persists, and at the same time encouraged the formation of a distinction which is, I believe, the ruin of modern drama—the distinction between drama and literature. For the *Specimens* made it possible to read the plays as poetry while neglecting their function on the stage."[1] That Lamb's *Specimens* indicated a flowering, rather than an initiation, of a tradition should require no further documentation. The point at issue is that Eliot has in effect labeled Lamb a closet critic as the term is commonly used, and it must be admitted that Lamb's essay on Shakespeare's tragedies is the most familiar example of this attitude in the corpus of English criticism. Lamb's comment on the Kembles' *Macbeth* in this essay expresses the notion succinctly. Their performances, he observes,

> seemed to embody and realize conceptions which had hitherto assumed no distinct shape. But dearly do we pay all our life after for this juvenile pleasure, this sense of distinctness. When the novelty is past, we find to our cost that instead of realizing an idea, we have only materialized and brought down a fine vision to the standard of flesh and blood. We have let go a dream, in quest of an unattainable substance.[2]

It is no wonder Lamb felt that "the plays of Shakspeare are less calculated for performance on a stage, than those of almost any other dramatist whatever," that "there is so much in them, which comes not under the province of acting, with which eye, and tone, and gesture, have nothing to do" (*Works*, I, 99). Yet, to apologize for Lamb's judgment by explaining it as a reaction to the deplorable tendencies of the theater of his day—"the contemptible machinery by which they mimic the storm" in *King Lear*, for ex-

[1] Eliot, "Four Elizabethan Dramatists," *Selected Essays*, new edn. (New York, 1950), p. 92.

[2] *The Reflector*, IV (1812), reprinted in *The Works of Charles and Mary Lamb*, ed. E. V. Lucas (New York and London, 1903), I, 98, subsequently cited as *Works*.

ample (*Works*, I, 107)—would be to mislead.[3] If the building of huge theaters and the presentation of lavish spectacle in this age contributed to the enervation of serious drama and to the disgust of its critics, the fact remains that Lamb and others depended for their views on a concept of the nature of drama larger than that encompassed in the mere reading of the plays as "poetry." Lamb neglected their function on the stage, as Eliot implies, in the sense that he felt actual production destroyed the reality of his "dream." He did not neglect their function on the imagined stage of his mind.

In this sense Lamb's criticism is closely allied to that of Coleridge, who shared with his fellow student of Christ's Hospital a blatant dislike of the scenes and machines that invariably dressed out the plays of Shakespeare on early nineteenth-century stages. The usual view is that Coleridge's distaste for theatrical performance moved him to "withdraw" into the solitude of his study where he could meditate undisturbed on the complex characters of the great Elizabethan. And certainly, in reading through the impressive body of lectures, notes, and marginal jottings that comprise Coleridge's Shakespearean criticism, one is struck with the penetration of his insights, with his high sensitivity to the obscure springs of motive in the human mind, and, perhaps most of all, with the pervasive sense of a great intellect brooding over the complexity of human personality profoundly illustrated in the figures of Shakespeare's plays. In no other writer since Maurice Morgann appears such an unclouded sense of the profound reality of the Shakespearean dramatic character. Notwithstanding the clarity and comprehensiveness of his theories of dramatic illusion,[4] Coleridge found no divisive distinction necessary between real human beings and the "*genera* intensely individualized" in Shakespeare.[5] But from this sense of the immediate reality of the dramatic character one derives the impression that

[3] René Wellek thus disposes of Lamb's view; see *A History of Modern Criticism: 1750-1950*, Vol. II: *The Romantic Age* (New Haven, 1955), p. 192.

[4] See J. R. deJ. Jackson's dissertation, "The Influence of the Theatre on Coleridge's Shakespearean Criticism" (Princeton, 1961), pp. 114-122, and Jackson's article, "Coleridge on Dramatic Illusion and Spectacle in the Performance of Shakespeare's Plays," *MP*, LXII (1964), 13-21.

[5] *Coleridge's Shakespearean Criticism*, ed. Thomas Middleton Raysor, 2 vols. (London, 1930), I, 137; subsequent references to this edition are abbreviated *SC*.

Coleridge, while deeply influenced by the theatrical qualities of his subject, often chooses to ignore their relevance because they interfere with the direct perception of psychological reality. This apparent predilection generates a curious atmosphere which pervades his criticism. It has, I believe, been one of the reasons why much Coleridge scholarship has presupposed him, like Lamb, a "closet" critic.

J. R. deJ. Jackson has endeavored to show that "whatever leanings [Coleridge] may have had in the direction of the closet were based on his dissatisfaction with the contemporary methods of producing Shakespeare's plays and not on either the conviction that they should not be acted or that the stage was an unworthy medium."[6] Jackson's work offers abundant evidence in support of this thesis; but, in his concern to disembarrass Coleridge of the pejorative implications of the term "closet critic," Jackson seems to have ignored a pressing need to qualify the usual meaning of this phrase. As commonly employed, the term suggests a critic who not only deplores the alleged debasement of the drama by unenlightened theatrical performance but furthermore denies the validity of placing the drama within its original (or traditional) theatrical context. A closet critic, in short, is one who prefers to read a poetic drama as a dramatic poem, one who like T. S. Eliot feels that any attempt to set a play on the stage almost certainly imposes unjustifiable "interpretation" and so robs the work of its universality. The actor, no matter how accomplished a performer, is no more than an imperfect human barrier that interferes with the direct and immediate enjoyment of "pure" poetry. I have put this definition, perhaps unfairly, in its most extreme form. But, curiously, even so eminently "theatrical" a critic as Hazlitt can fall within its general limits. "We do not like to see our author's plays acted," he once asserted, "and least of all, HAMLET. There is no play that suffers so much in being transferred to the stage. Hamlet himself seems hardly capable of being acted."[7]

The revealing word in this passage is *transferred*, implying that the text exists as a separate entity—as a "poem"—apart from its realization in theatrical production. Coleridge himself evinced

[6] Jackson, "The Influence of the Theatre on Coleridge's Shakespearean Criticism," p. 96.

[7] *The Complete Works of William Hazlitt*, ed. P. P. Howe, 21 vols. (London, 1930-34), IV, 237. Subsequent references to this edition are cited by volume and page number.

exactly the same attitude when, in one of his Bristol lectures, he is reported to have said that "he never saw any of Shakespeare's plays performed, but with a degree of pain, disgust, and indignation. He had seen Mrs. Siddons as Lady, and Kemble as Macbeth:—these might be the Macbeths of the Kembles, but they were not the Macbeths of Shakespeare" (*SC*, II, 278). Here, as in Hazlitt, there is more to Coleridge's dismay than a mere repugnance at the shortcomings of contemporary acting and production. Another factor is involved: that of the ideal performance. Judged by this standard, *all* actual performances, not only contemporary ones, are bound to fail in some respect. Since Lamb, Coleridge, and Hazlitt seem to hold this ideal in their minds as they write, the usual distinction between closet criticism and theatrical criticism must be set aside. The ostensible anti-theatrical bias in the passages just examined grows out of an assumption these writers share about the nature of the drama itself and the qualities it manifests to an intelligent and sympathetic observer. The fact that Lamb, Coleridge, and Hazlitt approach the drama and its characters with this ideal in mind is an important indication of the homogeneity of their critical writings. Their essential difference is simply that Lamb and Coleridge are descriptive critics wholly concerned with the ideal performance, while Hazlitt is a judicial critic concerned with assessing the failure of most actors and most productions to measure up to this same ideal.

Poetry in general is always ideal, Coleridge insisted and Lamb everywhere implied; nevertheless a distinction is necessary between dramatic and non-dramatic forms of the ideal. Unfortunately no clear discrimination of this sort appears in Romantic writing—witness Coleridge's reference to those poems of Wordsworth "in which the author is *more or less* dramatic"[8]—and the problem is compounded by our lack of an adequate vocabulary. Still, Coleridge's implied distinction may have use, for it seems likely that by "dramatic" poems he means those in which a character exists to some immeasurable extent independent of the poet's own personality. I suggest that the presence of this character must add importantly to Coleridge's definition of poetry in terms of felt emotion (*BL*, II, Chap. XIV), because his presence requires an imaginative effort to *see* as well as to feel. The requirement of

[8] *Biographia Literaria*, ed. J. Shawcross, 2 vols. (Oxford, 1907), II, 31, italics added; subsequent references to this edition are abbreviated *BL*.

visualizing seems to be implied whenever this character is introduced, for along with the character comes the situation in which he appears. Wordsworth's "Resolution and Independence" is a "dramatic" poem in this sense, a kind of confrontation scene. Given this notion of the dramatic as the discovery of character in situation, it is possible to make a connection between Shakespeare's poetry and poetry as defined by Coleridge. Both are forms of the ideal—the pleasurable experience of emotion in the mind through a direct response to the words, unhampered by any intermediary "substance." Shakespeare's poetry, however, like certain poems by Wordsworth, presents an imagined reality of character in situation. Hence it is dramatic: it requires visualizing in the imagination, a response not only to the emotion expressed by the language but to human figures independent of their creator presented in a context of action or reaction. The place where this larger response takes place is the theater of the imagination, and the drama performed there is what I call the ideal production. For Lamb, as for Hazlitt and Coleridge, Shakespeare's plays present a mode of reality fuller and more satisfying when directly imagined than when seen performed on stage. The most significant purpose of dramatic criticism in the age is to describe this ideal production and, sometimes, to contrast it with actual production through an analysis of the ideal actor as dramatic character. Being completely one with the character, this actor has no name or separate identity, yet he fills out the skeletal text of speech with an imaginary vitality that transcends all "mere acting" and corresponds, in manner and in essence, to human nature itself.

An early review of Cooke's Richard III typifies Lamb's critical approach and its underlying assumption of an ideal actor. Writing for the *Morning Post* of 8 January 1802, Lamb contrasts Cibber's "compilation," still serving as the players' text, with the Shakespearean original and indicates the course that an actor playing Richard should follow. "In this chaos and perplexity," Lamb observes, ". . . it becomes an Actor to shew his taste, by adhering, as much as possible, to the spirit and intention of the original Author, and to consult his *safety* in *steering* by the *Light*, which Shakespeare holds out to him, as by a great *Leading Star*." Cooke fails to observe this principle, Lamb goes on to say, since he presents us with a monster, not a man. His hypocrisy is "too glaring and visible": "It resembles more the shallow cunning of a mind which is its own dupe, than the profound and practised art of so powerful an intellect as *Richard's*" (*Works*, I, 37). In a letter to Robert Lloyd written the previous summer, Lamb described even more specifically Richard's intellectual powers and Cooke's complete lack of imagination in portraying them. "Shakespeare's bloody character," he remarks, "impresses you with awe and deep admiration of his witty parts, his consummate hypocrisy, and indefatigable prosecution of purpose." But Cooke's portrayal is too coarse for this: "The lofty imagery and high sentiments and high passions of *Poetry* come black and prose-smoked from his prose Lips."[9]

Lamb's unmistakable preference for experiencing the play "directly," in his study, matches his preference for character at the expense of the events of the play. The continuous linear development of character in situation which engrossed Coleridge was lost upon Lamb, who felt himself unable to "grasp at a whole" (*Letters*, I, 362). Of greatest value for him were the opportunities for reflection that Shakespeare's characters afforded. They are, he said in the essay on the tragedies, "so much the objects of meditation rather than of interest or curiosity as to their actions, that while we are reading any of his great criminal characters,—Macbeth, Richard, even Iago,—we think not so much of the crimes which they commit, as of the ambition, the aspiring spirit, the intellectual activity which prompts them to overleap those moral fences" (*Works*, I, 106). Like Coleridge and many eighteenth-century critics, Lamb finds fascination in the psychology of motive, not in the objective representation of an act. In Shakespeare, he observes, "so little do the actions comparatively affect us, that while the impulses, the inner mind in all its perverted greatness, solely seems real and is exclusively attended to, the crime is comparatively nothing" (*Works*, I, 106).

We should hesitate, nevertheless, before deciding that for Lamb the drama has left off being drama and has become only an aid to reflection. Lamb's supposition is that the presentation of character on the stage must of necessity emphasize actions and not the motives for actions, and so the theatrical production in-

[9] Letter dated 26 June 1801 in *The Letters of Charles Lamb: to which are added those of his sister Mary Lamb*, ed. E. V. Lucas (London, 1935), I, 259.

terferes with his perception of the inner mind of the character. It is only this that "seems real." For Lamb the drama has become not so much an aid to reflection as a proving ground for an ideal actor who involves himself sympathetically with Shakespeare's character and so brings to light those motives or causes for action by which we recognize in him a unique individual.

Lamb's impression of the ideal performance merits attention for several reasons. His notions because of their extreme nature provide a helpful contrast with the more enlightened and complex sense of this idea in the writings of Hazlitt and Coleridge. In addition, Lamb's views aid in demonstrating that the reading of a play in the closet represents for these critics something more than a negative reaction to the grossness of much contemporary theatrical production. Towards the end of the essay on the tragedies he objects to elaborate scenery and costume because it "positively destroys the illusion" and explains that, in contrast, "the reading of a tragedy is a fine abstraction," that "it presents to the fancy just so much of external appearances as to make us feel that we are among flesh and blood, while by far the greater and better part of our imagination is employed upon the thoughts and internal machinery of the character" (*Works,* I, 111). Without putting a burden it will not bear upon Lamb's distinction here between fancy and imagination, we may observe that his ideal production is one in which the fancy through association presents vivid images of reality to the mind, while the imagination, like Coleridge's penetrating and unifying faculty, organizes these phantoms of imagined flesh and blood in order to see within them the inner reality of the ideal dramatic character. One departs from Lamb's extreme and somewhat fleshless notion of the ideal performance with increased respect for the abilities of Hazlitt and Coleridge, who endow this ideal with a fullness and vitality that approximates the nature of the real human being whose qualities they saw mirrored so completely in Shakespeare's plays.

iii. Coleridge and the Problem of Criticism

Lamb's criticism, modest as it is in comprehensiveness and bulk, presents few difficulties to the student of Romantic prose. The critical writings of Coleridge, on the other hand, continue to elicit fresh attempts to achieve a just and balanced view of their significance. René Wellek, the most denigrating of recent commentators, sees little in Coleridge apart from his interest as an eclectic plagiarist of German ideas, and that little he thinks unsuccessful as either a philosophical or critical system of thought.[10] Others like R. H. Fogle and W. J. Bate, however, find that the fragmentary and sometimes apparently haphazard jottings and notes which form the record of Coleridge's critical endeavors take on a certain wholeness if seen as his continuing efforts to bring the critical act into meaningful relationship to life.[11]

The way to make criticism at once valid and relevant, Coleridge observes, is to refer to "fixed canons of criticism, previously established and deduced from the nature of man . . ." (*BL,* I, 44). Man's nature, or the "idea" of man, as Coleridge would put it, rests on a notion of the subordination of intellect and passion to the moral sense, the ideal felt relationship of the subjective human consciousness to the outer world. Coleridge's "coadunating" habit of mind led him to express this relationship in terms derived from analysis of that combining faculty he called *imagination,* a power shared by all human beings, not just by superior poets and critics. Because human nature is constructed in this way, Coleridge says, the products of hand and mind must reflect the moral relationship between subject and object expressed in the act of perception itself. Art, therefore, must have some essential unity; otherwise it presents no more than a group of objects collected in the ragbag of the fancy. In the exercise of his imaginative faculties, the poet, and consequently the critic as well, must follow human nature in seizing upon the *idea* which brings together the multitudinous variety of the world and unites it within the meaningful perspective of the human consciousness. Yet, at the same time, he must remain faithful to multiplicity in all its contradictoriness. To simplify is to falsify. To be true to the characteristic variety of the world, the poet must unremittingly hold fast to his sense of *the other.* In addition he must see that

[10] Wellek, *History of Modern Criticism,* II, 151ff.

[11] See the discussion of the problem of Coleridge's criticism in Richard Harter Fogle, *The Idea of Coleridge's Criticism* (Berkeley and Los Angeles, 1962), Pref., pp. vii-xiv; see also Walter Jackson Bate, "Coleridge on the Function of Art," *Perspectives of Criticism,* ed. Harry Levin (Cambridge, Mass., 1950), pp. 125-159, and Bate, ed., *Criticism: the Major Texts* (New York and Burlingame, 1952), pp. 357-364. My debt to Fogle and Bate, as to other scholars and critics too numerous to mention here, will be evident in the following discussion. The sources on which I have drawn are indicated in the Bibliographical Note.

this fundamental act of discrimination between the self and what lies outside it takes place as a *process* of apprehension, a seizing upon *parts* whose growth and development correspond to the gradually increasing awareness characteristic of mental effort. The idea of unity, then, is the idea of a growing organism whose basic quality is vitality and whose characteristics, like those of a full-blown flower, all refer to the seed from which it springs. The idea of criticism, consequently, is of the perceptive act that discovers the seed beneath the flower, the flower within the seed. Not seldom, it reflects as well on the mind of the gardener and the quality of his tools.

Upon these "fixed canons of criticism . . . deduced from the nature of man" Coleridge erected a body of writing whose influence on subsequent thought has been almost incalculable. In no area more so than in his Shakespearean criticism has this influence been felt, sometimes to the detriment of his reputation, sometimes to its enhancement, and sometimes simply to the obfuscation of the reader. For the question, even after so many years of scholarly commentary, may still be legitimately raised: what are we to make of Coleridge as a critic of Shakespeare? Thomas Middleton Raysor's conviction of his greatness is familiar to all students of the subject, who must inevitably base their own judgments on Raysor's two editions of Coleridge's Shakespearean writings.[12] Yet it is sobering to reflect that, aside from the marginalia, what we have consists largely of lecture notes of varying, second-hand authority, the remainder in Coleridge's own hand representing only an uncertain fraction of his total work. The return of recent scholarship to his philosophy of art as the only means of finding coherence within the fragmentary body of ideas and *apperçus* that have survived has done much to clarify his thought and practice as a critic. Strangely, however, little attempt has been made to describe the particular philosophy of dramatic character which grows out of his general philosophy and lies implicit in his studies of individual Shakespearean characters. Plainly, scholarship must seek some method of arriving at Coleridge's essential notions of dramatic character without being bound by the all-too-

[12] Raysor's 2nd edn. (Everyman Library, 2 vols., London, 1960), essentially a reprint of the 1st (London, 1930), contains a valuable preface (pp. x-xi) summarizing recent discoveries and in addition presents more correct texts of some of the lectures of 1808. For Raysor's assessment of Coleridge's importance see *SC*, Intro., p. xvii.

obvious limits of individual marginal scribblings and elliptical notes.

A return to Coleridge's philosophy of art certainly helps, but a second avenue lies open too. It is universally known (and almost as universally ignored) that Coleridge was a practicing playwright as well as a practicing poet, critic, lecturer, and would-be philosopher. In addition to his translation of Schiller, adaptation of *The Winter's Tale* (*Zapolya*), and early collaboration with Robert Southey on *The Fall of Robespierre,* Coleridge spent considerable effort to become a provider of serious plays for Drury Lane, early and unsuccessfully with *Osorio* (1797) and later, with temporary success, as author of *Remorse* (1812-13).[13] The labor Coleridge expended intermittently over some dozen years in revising *Osorio* for eventual production as *Remorse* has gone neglected in accounts of his life and works—a regrettable omission, since an examination of his revisions provides an unusual chance to see how Coleridge, in attempting to master the techniques of a difficult craft, gradually developed a sense of the theater that uniquely complements his earlier and already well-developed notions of human nature. In addition, study of *Remorse* repays whatever temporary discomfort it entails because the central character, Ordonio, epitomizes ideas about tragic character which elsewhere receive extensive treatment in Coleridge's analyses of Richard III and Macbeth. If it seems unjust to compare the playwright Coleridge with Shakespeare, it is nevertheless fair to approach *Remorse* as an imitation of the *idea* of Shakespearean character and drama as this latter-day dramatist, poet, and critic conceived of it.

iv. Coleridge's Ordonio and the Revisions in *Remorse*

"I tried to imitate [Shakespeare's] manner in the Remorse," Coleridge acknowledged in 1833, "and, when I had done, I found I had been tracking Beaumont and Fletcher, and Massinger instead."[14] Coleridge's distinctions between Shakespeare and other dramatists of his day are worth considering for the light they

[13] Coleridge's plays are collected in Vol. II of *The Complete Poetical Works of Samuel Taylor Coleridge,* ed. E. H. Coleridge (Oxford, 1912), subsequently abbreviated as *CPW.*

[14] *Specimens of the Table Talk of the Late Samuel Taylor Coleridge,* 2 vols. (1835), entry for 17 February 1833, II, 121-122.

shed on notions of dramatic character and structure evident also in his own practice as a playwright. The basic difference Coleridge perceives between Shakespeare and his fellows emerges well expressed from his comments on Massinger's *Maid of Honour*. The dramatis personae in this play, he observes, "were all planned *each by itself*," whereas a Shakespearean play presents a "*syngenesia*." Drawing his metaphor from Linnaeus' classification of sexual systems, Coleridge explains that the Shakespearean character has "a life of its own and is an *individuum* of itself, but yet an organ to the whole—as the heart, etc., of *that* particular whole." Shakespeare, he concludes, was "a comparative anatomist."[15] Always fond of botanical and especially floral metaphors, Coleridge consistently uses them to suggest ideas of growth and organic coherence fundamental to his critical views as well to his sense of the unity of art and life. Perhaps the most revealing use of such figures occurs in his contrast of Fletcher's *Bonduca* with Shakespeare's *Richard II*. In Fletcher, he says, one finds "a well arranged bed of flowers, each having its separate root, and its position determined aforehand by the *will* of the gardener—a fresh plant, a fresh volition." In Shakespeare, on the contrary, "all is growth, evolution, each line, each word almost, begets the following—and the will of the writer is an interfusion, a continuous agency, no series of separate acts" (*MC*, pp. 88-89).

The basic inadequacy of Massinger and Fletcher is, then, their inability to make parts conform to an idea of the whole. Their characters have no inner consistency and no lived relationship to other characters in the same play, but are merely functionaries of the moment. Such playwrights care only "to pitch a character into a position to make him or her talk. . . ."[16] When placed in the context of Coleridge's confession that *Remorse* turned out as a Fletcherian and not a Shakespearean imitation, these strictures offer revealing commentary on his own attempt to create vital characters and at the same time to fuse them, through "irremissive" artistic control, into a powerful structural unity. Moreover,

[15] *Coleridge's Miscellaneous Criticism*, ed. Thomas Middleton Raysor (London, 1936), p. 95, subsequently abbreviated as *MC*. *Syngenesia* according to the *Oxford English Dictionary* refers to "the nineteenth class in the Linnaean Sexual System, comprising plants having stamens coherent by the anthers, and flowers (florets) in close heads or *capitula*; corresponding to the Natural Order *Compositae*."

[16] *Table Talk*, II, 119.

his noticeable awareness that non-Shakespearean playwrights deal merely with fragments underscores his own less than successful endeavor as a playwright to resist the magnetic attraction of autonomous "poetic" passages. Scarcely a single speech in Beaumont and Fletcher is "exclusively tragic," he observes, "that is not in a higher degree poetic—i.e., capable of being narrated by the poet in his own person in the same words, with strict adherence to the character of the poet" (*MC*, p. 84).

If Coleridge found difficulty in avoiding the kind of writing from which Charles Lamb might have delighted to excerpt "specimens," an even greater obstacle presented itself in the moral orientation of character. Shakespeare's ability to keep "*at all times the high road of life*" appears in his constant refusal to render "amiable" those qualities which reason and religion teach us to detest. He "never clothed vice in the garb of virtue, like Beaumont and Fletcher, the Kotzebues of his day . . ." (*SC*, II, 266). Nevertheless, Coleridge admits, certain Shakespearean characters pose almost insuperable problems in this respect. In creating Edmund in *King Lear*, for example, Shakespeare faced the need to control the moral anarchy which might otherwise result from portraying a character totally unscrupulous in his lust for power over others. Shakespeare knew that "courage, intellect, and strength of character" were power's most impressive forms. Yet, as in the foam and thunder of a cataract, power in itself compels inevitable admiration. The issue is both dramaturgically and ethically of the highest importance:

> For such are the appointed relations of intellectual power to truth, and of truth to goodness, that it becomes both morally and poetic[ally] unsafe to present what is admirable—what our nature compels us to admire—in the mind, and what is most detestable in the heart, as co-existing in the same individual without any apparent connection, or any modification of the one by the other. That Shakespeare has in one instance, that of Iago, approached to this, and that he has done it successfully, is perhaps the most astonishing proof of his genius, and the opulence of its resources. (*SC*, I, 58)

Shakespeare's success, according to Coleridge, lies in his amazing ability to hold moral contraries in suspension. We admire the qualities of Iago's mind even as we detest the uses to which he puts them. Yet, oddly enough, Coleridge's analysis of Kotzebue ("the German Beaumont and Fletcher") uncovers the presence of this same technique—a "trick," he calls it, which brings "one part of our moral nature to counteract another—as our pity for misfortune and admiration of generosity and courage to combat our condemnation of guilt, as in adultery, robbery, etc. . . ." (*SC*, I, 60). Presumably the difference between Shakespeare and Kotzebue is that Shakespeare elicits complex response by presenting two contraries existent in one individual "without any apparent connection," while Kotzebue so arranges things that our admiration and awareness of guilt battle one against another for supremacy. But this does not really explain satisfactorily the difference between the moral concerns of the two dramatists. If anything, it explains Coleridge's deep concern with the moral issues attendant on the creation of dramatic character. In addition it suggests that he found singular difficulty in working out his ideas on the subject. His comment on Iago appears in a signed note dated 1 January 1813, sent from the London address where he stayed during rehearsals for *Remorse*. It is not at all fanciful to consider that Coleridge at this time found himself drawn to the moral issues involved in the presentation of near-monstrous villainy on the stage, and that concern for his villain-hero Ordonio manifests itself in musings on a similar problem encountered by Shakespeare in creating the amoral character of Iago.

Ordonio, like Hamlet, is the central character of the play in which he appears. Obvious enough, but for Coleridge the point is a crucial one. No greater indication exists of his concept of dramaturgy than the idea that the dramatist begins with a notion of his central character. Shakespeare, Coleridge observes in his criticism of *Hamlet*, creates his characters "out of his own intellectual and moral faculties, by conceiving any one intellectual or moral faculty in morbid excess and then placing himself, thus mutilated and diseased, under given circumstances . . ." (*SC*, I, 37). Such a technique, then, concentrates on some fundamental imbalance or inversion of the hierarchical relationship of moral, intellectual, and physical powers. Beginning with this imbalance as the seed, the dramatist moves on to illustrate its pernicious growth by providing a series of dramatic events. So did Coleridge conceive of the original character of Osorio, whose name in revision he changed to Ordonio but whose characteristics remained unalloyed:

> A man, who from constitutional calmness of appetites, is seduced into pride and the love of power, by these into misanthropism, or rather a contempt of mankind, and from thence, by the co-operation of envy, and a curiously modified love for a beautiful female . . . into a most atrocious guilt. A man who is in truth a weak man, yet always duping himself into the belief that he has a soul of iron. (*CPW*, II, 519)

In both the early and later versions of his drama Coleridge sought to create a character fundamentally inclined to self-deception and easily impelled on a course of action by any suitable agency. To achieve this end, he drew from Schiller's *Die Geisterseher*[17] a series of events ending in both the death and the spiritual salvation of his central figure. It appears through exposition that, before the time at which the play begins, Osorio had commissioned Ferdinand, a Moresco chieftain, to murder Osorio's brother Albert and thus pave the way for Osorio's marriage to Maria, Albert's beloved. Osorio rests easy in the belief that the assassination has been accomplished, but in the first act we see that Albert has clandestinely returned from his long journey. In this return lies the guiding force behind the chain of events to follow, for Albert's purpose throughout the play is not only to reclaim Maria but to bring his younger brother to true remorse for his attempted crime. In order to keep this dramaturgical device operative for the length of five acts, Coleridge depends on the familiar convention of disguise—Albert appears in Moorish clothing—but he gives this convention a naturalistic underpinning by having it explained that Albert's long absence and hardships have changed his outward appearance. So Coleridge establishes for the structure of his play the fundamental dramatic device of the disguised and purposive brother who will act as the agent of destiny. But in working out the relationship between the apparent passivity of Osorio and the therapeutic activity of his brother Albert, Coleridge confused the functions of these two characters in a way that demonstrates clearly his intention to let Osorio predominate. The play is indeed so much

[17] See John Livingston Lowes, *The Road to Xanadu* (Boston and New York, 1927), p. 243 and the excellent note, pp. 540-541.

Osorio's that virtually everything, including his own actions, conduces to laying bare the tortured mind he attempts to hide by misanthropic comments and a generally iron-clad behavior.

No similar sureness, however, psychological or otherwise, appears in Coleridge's treatment of the other characters. One sometimes feels they are there only to give Osorio objects on which to vent his spleen. Particularly in the early version of the play, little coherent relationship exists between the stated purposes of the subordinate characters and their eventuation in acts which might goad Osorio into response. Significantly, a felt tension emerges between human psychology and dramatic form. In the theater the presentation of events must have a recognizable beginning, but Coleridge's intense interest in the psychology of his characters presupposes that they have each a "life" anterior to the beginning of the play. Coleridge himself was uncomfortably aware of this problem. He had carefully worked out the complex plot, only the latter part of which is enacted in the play, and consequently felt he had a clear view of the backgrounds and relationships of his characters. But he found it distressingly difficult to work the exposition of prior events into the fabric of his opening scenes. "This long story," he confessed in the preface of the manuscript of *Osorio* sent to Drury Lane in 1797, "which yet is necessary to the complete understanding of the play, is not half told." An even more important failure, he thought, lay in his delineation of the chief character, whose growth "is nowhere explained—and yet I had most clear and psychologically accurate ideas of the whole of it . . ." (*CPW,* II, 519).

"The thing is but an embryo," he concluded (*CPW,* II, 519). Over the next fifteen years after its rejection by Drury Lane—on the "*sole* objection," said Coleridge with unaccountable naïveté, to "the obscurity of the three last acts"[18]—the poet labored to bring his embryo to full form and birth. Granted that Coleridge seemed temperamentally unsuited to the activity required of a dramatist (*Osorio* "is done," he wrote to Bowles in 1797, "and I would rather mend hedges & follow the plough, than write another"[19]), a comparison of the texts of *Osorio* and *Remorse* may

[18] Letter to Thomas Poole [endorsed 2 December 1797], in *Collected Letters of Samuel Taylor Coleridge,* ed. Earl Leslie Griggs, 4 vols. (Oxford, 1956-59), I, 358, subsequently cited as *Letters.*

[19] Letter to William Lisle Bowles, dated 16 October 1797, in *Letters,* I, 356.

convince even the disbelieving reader that he had in considerable measure overcome his difficulty in reconciling a display of the complete human psyche with the limits imposed by dramatic form. Perhaps Arnold, the manager of Drury Lane, and the actors cast in the play deserve a large share of credit for the changes evident in the text of *Remorse*; but it was nevertheless Coleridge himself who gave form to whatever suggestions were made during rehearsals in early January of 1813.

Close comparison of *Osorio* and *Remorse* reveals alterations that range from new names for the same characters and other incidental verbal adjustments to the wholesale rearrangement, expansion, and curtailment of entire scenes and acts. Among the most revealing changes is that in Act II connected with the portrait of herself which the young girl Maria (Teresa in *Remorse*) gave to Albert (Alvar in *Remorse*) when he departed some time before the stage action begins. Osorio plans to have Albert masquerade as a sorcerer and through magic reveal the portrait to Maria, so convincing her that Albert is dead. Albert's counterploy is to substitute for the portrait a picture he himself painted of the supposed assassination and so make Osorio aware that his nefarious scheme to get rid of his brother is somehow mysteriously known. But at this point, already enmeshed in psychological subtleties, Coleridge left the audience to guess which picture is actually introduced during the incantation scene. Consequently Osorio's misconception of its nature offers no dramatic irony and indeed creates pointless confusion.

The revision of the scene for *Remorse*, however, shows unmistakably that Coleridge had grasped the need for strong theatrical enhancement of Ordonio's misapprehension. His cry of "Duped!" when the portrait is revealed is a direct, amazed response which at once clarifies both Alvar's own intention and Coleridge's dramatic aim of showing Ordonio's failure to respond with true remorse. This tightening of essential dramatic purpose was augmented by the scenic resources of Drury Lane. The first edition of *Remorse*, rushed with such speed to the press that Coleridge apologized to his readers in his preface for the inordinate "number of directions printed in italics" (*CPW*, II, 815), suggests how effective the moment of revelation proved in the theater. As music "*clashes*" into a chorus,

> *The incense on the altar takes fire suddenly, and an illuminated picture of* ALVAR'S *assassination is discovered, and having remained a few seconds is then hidden by ascending flames.* (*CPW*, II, 851)

With this new impetus the scene now builds to a sure dramatic climax. Where Osorio had remained in a stupor throughout the revelation sequence, here Ordonio first reacts violently and then lapses into a stupor as if from shock. At this very moment Monviedro and his familiars of the Inquisition burst in, "*fill the stage,*" and seize Alvar. Ordonio, recovering from his fit of mental absence, calls on them to drag Alvar off to the dungeon, and as "*All rush out in tumult*" the scene closes.

Combined with other important but less extensive revisions, this scene and those which follow in Act III indicate that a more consistent dramatic emphasis has replaced the vagueness and uncertainty of the first three acts of *Osorio*. Coleridge has given additional thematic weight to the elicitation of remorse from the adamant soul of Ordonio, an emphasis also clear in the rearranged scenes of Act I as well as in the change in title from the name of the chief character to the name of the chief emotion. It is much more obvious now that the basic dramatic strategy is to introduce a series of events which will bring Ordonio to his knees—or, more exactly, which will *fail* to bring Ordonio to his knees until very late in the play. Probably with major assistance from experienced professionals at Drury Lane, Coleridge has reconstructed the haphazard plot of *Osorio* to effect a clarification of the dramatic action, a greater psychological individuation of the main characters, an increased cohesiveness between the characters and the plot, and, added to all this, a surer setting of atmosphere through the use of dramatically appropriate language.

Similar attainments discernible in the fourth and fifth acts clear the way for the quick resolution of the play, still to be centered on the mental disposition of Ordonio himself. Adding to the smoothness of the dramatic action, Coleridge introduces an important revision apparently calculated at once to clarify Ordonio's end and to provide the thematic resolution left so uncertain at the conclusion of *Osorio*. His revision is the simple one of allowing Ordonio to be killed *on stage* by Alhadra, the vengeful widow of the murdered henchman Isidore, instead of having him merely carried off stage, unprotesting, by the Moorish rebels who accompany her. This not only provides clear retribution for the base slaughter of Isidore (who had refrained from killing Alvar when he learned that Alvar was the brother of Ordonio) but allows for the *moment à faire,* so to speak, in which Ordonio, about to die, sees his death as "Atonement!" (*CPW,* II, 879) and pleads earnestly for forgiveness. The entrance of Valdez and his men, dramatically purposeless in *Osorio,* now serves to unite Alvar and Teresa, the two virtuous lovers who have survived the horrendous course of events into which Ordonio's vicious derangement has drawn them. The patriarchal Valdez blesses them, Alvar concludes with a thematic summary of the "dire Remorse" that results from the stifling of conscience, and the play is done.

The principal trend observable in Coleridge's revisions of *Osorio,* then, is the placing of human emotions more securely within a well-conducted dramatic action. The petulant critic for the *Times* maintained that the plot was "singularly involved and laboured" and that the author had failed to manifest "a vigorous and combing [sic, for *combining*?] mind, that muscular grasp of understanding, capable by its force of compressing the weak and the scattered, into a firm and vigorous solidity" (25 January 1813). Hazlitt's review in the *Morning Chronicle,* much more sympathetic in its approach, sensed Coleridge's purpose and evaluated the play on that basis. Coleridge keeps interest alive, Hazlitt observes, by providing "a succession of situations and events, which call forth the finest sensibilities of the human breast. . . ." Hazlitt, like Coleridge, concentrates on Ordonio, his description remarkably close to the one Coleridge himself provided in the manuscript preface.[20] Coleridge, who considered the *Times* review a fine specimen of "infernal Lies,"[21] was convinced that the play had such merits as Hazlitt had praised. In an important letter to Southey he set down what he considered its most significant quality—"the simplicity and Unity of the Plot, in respect of that which of all the Unities is the only one founded on good sense, the presence of a one, all-pervading, all-combining,

[20] 25 January 1813. Howe (XVIII, 463) identifies the author of the review as Hazlitt.

[21] Letter to Sarah Coleridge, [27 January 1813], in *Letters,* III, 430.

Principle." "As from a circumference to a centre," he concluded, "every Ray in the Tragedy converges to Ordonio."[22]

Those critics who accuse Coleridge of having no sense of the structure of a play would do well to read this letter. Much confusion has been caused by setting twentieth-century discoveries about the nature of Shakespearean structure against Coleridge's criticism of that dramatist and then concluding that Coleridge, despite his notion of organic unity, did not really understand dramatic technique.[23] His letter to Southey provides incontrovertible testimony to his understanding of the structure of *Romantic* drama. To say that he did not grasp the nature of Shakespearean dramaturgy may be true, up to a point, but misses the fact that Coleridge had perhaps as much knowledge of Fletcherian structure and its latter-day offspring as any writer of his time. A less irrelevant stricture might suggest that Coleridge's critical excesses relate more to Joanna Baillie's complex development of single emotions than to the fragmentary bias of Lamb or the "historical" bias of Morgann. Allowing for the fact that *Remorse* belongs to a convention of poetic drama which died in the course of the nineteenth century despite repeated attempts to prolong its life, we may nevertheless see in it one of the most ambitious attempts in English drama to give new life to time-worn theatrical traditions by infusing them with the spirit of a fundamental conviction of man's nature, both in its ideal and its regrettably real aspects. Bertrand Evans has demonstrated how Coleridge took over the conventions of the Gothic play to work out his scheme of reclaiming his villain-hero, and in so doing "raised the Gothic above itself through finer poetry."[24] It should also be pointed out that this "finer poetry," undramatic or merely atmospheric as it sometimes is, reveals Coleridge's attempt to reconcile the inevitable (and, perhaps to him, lamentable) necessity for dramatic economy with a full explication of those characteristics of the human mind so subtle that exterior event has little relevance to them.

[22] Letter to Robert Southey, dated [9] February 1813, in *Letters,* III, 433-434.

[23] See the discussions of this issue in Barbara Hardy, " 'I Have a Smack of Hamlet': Coleridge and Shakespeare's Characters," *EIC,* VIII (1958), 238-255, and M. M. Badawi, "Coleridge's Formal Criticism of Shakespeare's Plays," *EIC,* X (1960), 148-162.

[24] *Gothic Drama from Walpole to Shelley* (Berkeley and Los Angeles, 1947), p. 224.

v. Coleridge on Richard III and Macbeth

Coleridge's effort to write a viable dramatic tragedy, then, ultimately falls within the scope of his more generally philosophical notion of the reconciliation of opposites. This notion is in fact the guiding idea behind the creation of dramatic character, both as Coleridge himself practiced it and as he saw it emerge in the deeply individual characters of Shakespeare's plays. The vitality of such character depends on the dramatist's sense of *the other*. Far from making his speeches mere echoes of the poet's own voice—producing the "wordsworthian or egotistical sublime," as Keats devastatingly phrased it[25]—the dramatist must, through a species of sympathy, transform himself into the character he means to represent, letting his own experiential knowledge of the imbalances common to human nature guide him in placing himself, as Shakespeare did in the case of Hamlet, "thus mutilated and diseased, under given circumstances." And yet this sense of otherness is saved from becoming simply a vacating of oneself by the co-directing principle of organic unity, here essentially a dramatic principle by which everything becomes referable to everything else and the whole in turn referable to the psychological reality manifested by the mind of the chief character. This is the principle upon which Coleridge sees dependent the nature of dramatic art: an imitation, a willed illusion; not a mere copy, not a fraudulent deception. According to Coleridge the true relationship of the drama to life is the same as that of the individual human being's. It consists in

> one great principle . . . common to all, a principle which probably is the condition of all consciousness, without which we should feel and imagine only by discontinuous moments, and be plants or animals instead of men. I mean that ever-varying balance, or balancing, of images, notions, or feelings (for I avoid the vague word, idea) conceived as in opposition to each other; in short, the perception of identity and contrariety, the least degree of which constitutes *likeness*, the greatest absolute difference; but the infinite gradations between these two form all the play and all the interest of our intellectual and moral being, till it lead us to a feeling and an

[25] *The Letters of John Keats*, ed. Hyder Edward Rollins, 2 vols. (Cambridge, Mass., 1958), I, 387.

object more awful than it seems to me compatible with even the present subject to utter aloud. . . . (*SC*, I, 204-205)

The theater, then, affords opportunity to do what our very nature as human beings moves us to do: to enrich moral awareness through subjective perception. The special feature of a theatrical performance is that it effects in its beholders a kind of neutral state characterized by a dual consciousness that we see something artificially contrived and yet that we are under no necessity to disbelieve in it (*SC*, I, 128-130). But this feature is only a heightened form of the same act of perception carried out in common life, in which subject and object are taken as contraries and yet are reconciled into the wholeness conferred by the very act in which the "I" perceives them as they are.

So, in this same way, do we as audience penetrate into the mind of the central dramatic character. We ourselves justify the danger of presenting gross immorality in the character of Ordonio by the interest we take in his mental problems. His imbalance produces the tragic action of the play, while his very imperfection leads us to see his thoughts and acts as analogous to our own. Because the illusion, to which we voluntarily submit, has been effected through the exercise of the "irremissive" will of the artist (*BL*, II, 12), a mutual sympathy is produced, a kind of circularity which proceeds from the poet through the dramatic character to the audience and then back to the poet. Perhaps it is some sort of near-ultimate unity like this at which Coleridge hints when he describes the effect of a theatrical performance as one which "leads us to a feeling and an object more awful than it seems to me compatible with even the present subject to utter aloud"—in brief, to a sense of what must be the divinely inspired coherence of all things.

It cannot be claimed that the dramatic apprenticeship Coleridge served over the years between 1797 and 1813 was in effect the preparation necessary for his criticism of Shakespeare, since much of what he had to say, both as a lecturer and marginal commentator, was said during these same years. Yet, precisely because these two periods of critical and dramaturgical practice coincide, it is useful to view the one in light of the other. Coleridge's criticism of Shakespeare's plays and characters yields additional meaning when placed in the context of his attempts to create a drama in which a vital character emerges distorted and scarred by encounters with the world and with himself. Coleridge's letter to Southey holds evidence of the close analogy between the character of Ordonio and two of Shakespeare's characters pre-eminent both for criminal deeds and for the remorse that eventually overtakes them. Coleridge's extended foray into the jungle of Ordonio's guilt should not be ignored in examining his views of Shakespeare's Richard III and Macbeth. At the same time, Coleridge's efforts to define Ordonio's entire dramatic milieu suggest that we must relate his supposedly fragmentary psychological analyses of these Shakespearean characters to a notion of integral artistic form. His idea of the structure of *Remorse* as a circumference of rays converging on his central character provides the imaginative perspective from which his comments on Shakespearean character may be viewed.

Deriving much of importance from the eighteenth-century critical commentary that came down to him, Coleridge brought to this tradition his original sense of the way imagination works in the mind of the poet and in the analogously "human" mind of the dramatic character. In his *Literary Remains* Coleridge speaks of "that pleasurable emotion" which poetry affords—"that peculiar state and degree of excitement, which arises in the poet himself in the act of composition;—and in order to understand this, we must combine a more than ordinary sympathy with the objects, emotions, or incidents contemplated by the poet, consequent on a more than common sensibility, with a more than ordinary activity of the mind in respect of the fancy and the imagination" (repr. in *SC*, I, 163-164). Attuning his mind to the sensibility characteristic of the poet himself, the critic must make an act of conscious sympathy. Coleridge is generally prepared for such an act even when it involves the analysis of Shakespeare's villains. "It was," he says, "in characters of complete moral depravity, but of first-rate wit and talents, that Shakespeare delighted . . ." (*SC*, II, 29-30), and he makes a conscious effort to duplicate Shakespeare's sympathetic approach. As one might expect, the analysis Coleridge offers is oriented toward the presentation of moral depravity, not toward Shakespeare's delight in presenting it; but his observations nevertheless form a carefully reasoned attempt to describe in imaginative terms the psychological basis for the villain's actions and not the mere immorality of the actions themselves.[26]

Although no record remains of the eleventh lecture in Coleridge's 1811-12 series, it appears from Collier's report of the twelfth that Coleridge had in the previous instance devoted attention to those characters of Shakespeare "in which pride of intellect, without moral feeling, is supposed to be the ruling impulse, such as Iago, Richard III., and even Falstaff." In Richard, he proceeded to observe,

> ambition is, as it were, the channel in which this impulse directs itself; the character is drawn with the greatest fulness and perfection; and the poet has not only given us that character, grown up and completed, but has shown us its very source and generation. The inferiority of his person made the hero seek consolation and compensation in the superiority of his intellect; he thus endeavoured to counterbalance his deficiency. This striking feature is pourtrayed most admirably by Shakespeare, who represents Richard bringing forward his very defects and deformities as matters of boast. (*SC*, II, 181)

Coleridge places emphasis not so much on Richard's assertion, "I am determined to prove a villain" as on those personal characteristics which actually move him to crime. Richard's predominant trait is not cruelty but pride, "to which a sense of personal deformity gave a deadly venom" (*SC*, II, 209). His villainy, moreover, does not emerge through the absence or ignorance of moral scruple but through his willful abjuration of it. Richard is one of those men who

> reverse the order of things, who place intellect at the head. . . . No man, either hero or saint, ever acted from an unmixed motive; for let him do what he will rightly, still conscience whispers "it is your duty." Richard, laughing at conscience, and sneering at religion, felt a confidence in his intel-

[26] Sylvan Barnet has suggested that Coleridge's tendency to seek the reconciliation of opposites relates to a fear of meeting unmitigated evil head-on. He points out that Coleridge's explanation of the psychological motives for villainy, as in his analysis of Richard III, may have been his way of avoiding a direct confrontation with the evil nature of villainous acts themselves. See "Coleridge on Shakespeare's Villains," *SQ*, VII (1956), 9-20.

lect, which urged him to commit the most horrid crimes, because he felt himself, although inferior in form and shape, superior to those around him; he felt he possessed a power that they had not.[27]

Coleridge provides here, in effect, a psychological explanation for the familiar conventional type, the "single-minded" villain. At the same time he gives this traditional figure a generic identity by citing Richard's pride of intellect and its emergence in the ruling passion of ambition. Much like the Ordonio of *Remorse* as Hazlitt found him, a man "whose pride finds consolation for its vices in its contempt for the dull virtues, or perhaps hypocritical pretenses of the generality of men," Richard impresses Coleridge as a character who feels superior through his possession of extraordinary mental power. No hint of imagination appears in Richard's character as Coleridge views it. His mental superiority is a quality not of imagination but of intellect and will. We recognize in Richard the broad outlines of a theatrical stereotype, but we also understand him as a human being because we see that his motives have arisen from a sense of his own physical inadequacy. In turn these motives urge him to invert the balance of morality and intellect which regulates human behavior. Nevertheless, Richard has no chance of being misled by the operations of fancy and imagination. His intellect and will alone are sufficient to accomplish his deeds, and so his fullness as a character is limited by his lack of "human" complexity.

Such an approach to Richard is plainly allied to the late eighteenth-century critical emphasis on the motives that impel Richard to crime. In each case the sympathetic understanding of

[27] *SC*, II, 286-287. Hartley Coleridge's transcription of his father's notes for this lecture includes the comment that the play deals with "the dreadful consequences of placing the moral in subordination to the intellectual"—*SC*, I, 232. Coleridge is quite clear about the moral consequences resulting from the diseased imagination: "When once the mind, in despite of the remonstrating conscience, has abandoned its free power to a haunting impulse or idea, then whatever tends to give depth and vividness to this idea or indefinite imagination increases *its* despotism, and in the same proportion renders the reason and free will ineffectual. Now fearful calamities, sufferings, horrors, and hairbreadth escapes will have this effect far more than even sensual pleasure and prosperous incidents. Hence the evil consequences of sin in such cases, instead of retracting and deterring the sinner, goad him on to his destruction. This is the moral of Shakespeare's Macbeth . . ."—*MC*, p. 293.

Richard is predicated upon the assumption that his acts, however criminal on first inspection, present no adequate evidence of his nature as a "human being." To be sure, Coleridge's analysis applies a more explicit moral notion of imbalance in his view of Richard's subordination of morality to intellect. But, curiously, the resulting idea of Richard's great intellectual power elicits a fascination from Coleridge that goes unreconciled with his sense of Richard's moral deformity—and that links him even more closely with his predecessors. It is evident that his view of Iago, an instance of Shakespeare's ability to present the total disjunction of moral and intellectual powers, has much in common with his unresolved admiration for Shakespeare's hump-backed usurper and, not incidentally, with his notion of the character of Ordonio. Coleridge's theory of dramatic illusion reconciles the contrary forces of attraction and repulsion by referring them to the audience's interest in the mentality of a "man" like themselves. In practice, however, Coleridge, like his forebears, often fails to point out the moral purpose underlying the admittedly dual response of an audience to a character at once a villain and a hero.

Coleridge's analysis of the character of Richard is unfortunately not accompanied, here or elsewhere in his criticism, by any full account of his relationship to the play in which he appears. In two instances, however, comments occur which reveal how Coleridge's ideas on the subject developed. In his lectures of 1808 he is reported to have said that Shakespeare wrote no part of *Richard III* except the character of Richard himself ("doubtless," said Crabb Robinson, "with a silent reference to the disgusting character of Lady Anne") (*SC,* II, 16). Yet, in making notes for the lectures delivered at Bristol in 1813, Coleridge planned to show in the play "*Growth* as in a plant. No ready cut and dried [structure]; and yet everything *prepared* because the preceding involves or was the link of association"; and he proposed to follow this by elucidating "the one idea which gives the tone" to the play (*SC,* I, 233). Here appears one of the few instances in Coleridge's criticism where the evolution of his ideas on a play can be tracked down. Far from contradicting themselves, these two remarks show clearly that Coleridge had come to see in *Richard III* the same consistency he had attempted to infuse earlier that same year into his own dramatic composition.

44. Kean as Shylock

45. Kean as Othello

46. Kean as Richard III

47. Kean as Macbeth: "Stars, hide your fires"

48. Kean as Macbeth

49. "Terror," in Siddons' *Practical Illustrations . . .*

Fortunately, the detailed analysis missing from Coleridge's discussions of *Richard* exists in relative abundance in his criticism of *Macbeth*. In contrast to his view of Richard, Macbeth emerges as a character who embodies the complete array of mental faculties—will, intellect, fancy, and imagination—and so offers Coleridge the opportunity to present a more complete idea of character and of its complex development within Shakespeare's intricate dramatic structure. Directly concerned with the presence of evil in the human psyche, Coleridge consistently applies himself to the hidden origin and growth of things as much as to their manifestation in human conduct. His subtle technical analyses of the first scenes of plays form a fascinating analogue to his equally astute examinations of the mental beginnings of human viciousness. One might expect that his analysis of Macbeth would focus on the seed of unlawful ambition growing secretly in Macbeth's mind and that it would place perhaps less emphasis on his intense response to the stimulus of situation. But in fact Coleridge reconciles these two apparently diverse interests by applying his theory of sympathetic imagination to the dramatic character and to the play as a whole.

Coleridge's notion of the way imagination operates in the play complements his initial concern with the hidden sources of guilt in Macbeth's breast. Turning to the opening scenes, Coleridge points out Shakespeare's dramatic contrast of Banquo's "*unpossessedness*" of mind with the mind of Macbeth, "rendered *temptable* by previous dalliance of the fancy with ambitious thoughts" (*SC*, I, 68). Intending to show "how Macbeth became early a tempter to himself" (*SC*, II, 270), Coleridge singles out Macbeth's attempt to halt the departure of the witches ("Stay, you imperfect speakers"): "all that follows is reasoning on a problem already discussed in his mind, on a hope which he welcomes, and the doubts concerning its attainment he wishes to have cleared up" (*SC*, I, 68-69). Macbeth's "recurrence to the *self-concerning*" in his discussion with Banquo after the witches depart is highly revealing to Coleridge. "So truly," he says, "is the guilt in its germ anterior to the supposed cause and immediate temptation" (*SC*, I, 69). Despite extensive attention to the dramaturgy of the first scenes, Coleridge has established here a notion of the character by ignoring, for the moment, the limitations inherent in the dramatic presentation of direct causes for action. Not satisfied with the *dramatic* causes which ostensibly arouse ambition in Macbeth and impel him along the road to eventual ruin, Coleridge seeks an anterior state of mind, one that exists before the play begins, in which the fancy dallies with images of ambition and so becomes unwittingly a prey to them.

In escaping the limitations placed on psychological analysis by dramatic structure, however, Coleridge does not really violate the structural integrity of the play. His use of the word *fancy* in describing Macbeth's anterior state of mind immediately suggests his fundamental distinction between fancy and imagination, a concept that serves him in adjusting his fascination with the psychological complexities of character to his consideration of the play as a dramatic form. The reconciliation of these two apparently conflicting interests lies in his analysis of the way Shakespeare imposes imagination upon fancy once the play begins. Speaking of Macbeth's ambition as hope, Coleridge relates the character of Macbeth to "the superstition natural to victorious generals." Immediately we recall that the prowess of Macbeth as Duncan's general supplies the underlying dramatic context of the first scenes. Macbeth's victory in battle becomes for Coleridge a dramatic analogue to Macbeth's desire for another sort of conquest, and he explains the way in which Macbeth's ambition develops dramatic focus through the influence of the victory he has just won. Hope, he says, is "the master element of a commanding genius, meeting with an active and combining intellect, and an imagination of just that degree of vividness which disquiets and impels the soul to try to realize its images" (*SC*, I, 81).

"Combining intellect" is, of course, a phrase Coleridge often applies to the imaginative process. Just as the primary imagination is "the living Power and prime Agent of all human Perception," so the secondary imagination echoes the former and co-exists with the conscious will: "It dissolves, diffuses, dissipates, in order to re-create; . . . at all events it struggles to idealize and to unify" (*BL*, I, 202). Macbeth, under the influence of "the superstition natural to victorious generals," ignores the element of chance in his present victory. Through the combining power of his imagination, Coleridge implies, he associates his present success with what he hopes to achieve in the future. Highly excited by his victory, Macbeth's imagination easily responds to the stimulus of the witches' prophecy, and so provides the dramatic impulse which in turn generates everything to come.

Coleridge carefully explains that the initial situation offers a sure and effective spur to Macbeth's imaginative powers. In the first scene, where the witches appear alone, "the invocation is made at once to the imagination, and the emotions connected therewith" (*SC*, I, 67). It is hence both logical and dramatically appropriate that Macbeth should respond to their prophecy when they re-enter. Coleridge's view of Macbeth's activity in this scene forms a striking analogue to the description in the *Biographia* of the poet's "synthetic" power of imagination:

> This power, first put in action by the will and understanding, and retained under their irremissive, though gentle and unnoticed, controul . . . reveals itself in the balance or reconciliation of opposite or discordant qualities: of sameness, with difference; of the general, with the concrete; the idea, with the image; the individual, with the representative; the sense of novelty and freshness, with old and familiar objects. . . . (*BL*, II, 12)

Almost a poet himself in this sense, Macbeth calls for the witches to stay as he seeks a reconciliation of discordant qualities, reasoning on "a hope which he welcomes, and the doubts concerning its attainment he wishes to have cleared up" (*SC*, I, 69). Macbeth's interest in the "old and familiar objects" of his fancy has been heightened and sharply focused by the "novelty and freshness" his imagination finds in them after the witches' prophecy. The confirmation of the prophecy matches Macbeth's hopes for the moment. He swiftly begins to act as a "usurper in intention" (*SC*, I, 70), and the stage is set for what follows.

Moving beyond the eighteenth-century notion of an ambitious but virtuous man suddenly accosted by the insidious evil of the witches' predictions, Coleridge has established Macbeth as neither predominantly good nor evil but as simply a human being whose fancy makes him a tempter to himself and whose imagination prompts his unique response to the dramatic stimulus he encounters at the beginning of the play. Through the use of his concept of imagination as an instrument for analysis, Coleridge has produced a subtle, cogent view of the way sinful desires grow within the recesses of the human mind and, in addition, has reconciled human psychology and dramatic character by focusing on Macbeth's imaginative response to stimuli presented theatrically in the structure of the opening scenes. The success of Coleridge's analysis depends in great measure on his ability to visualize this process on the stage of his mind and to convey intensely to his reader a sense of the visually perceived. It is difficult, Coleridge said in his notes to *Romeo and Juliet*, to think that Shakespeare wrote "for any stage but that of the universal mind" (*SC*, I, 4). The theatrical quality in Coleridge's visualizing eludes close analysis, yet it acts as continued assurance that his criticism is of an ideal production, replete with sights and sounds, not of an abstract construct based solely on a reading of the words.

In fact one infers that the theater of the mind, so to speak, has a double sense for Coleridge. It is, fundamentally, the place where the imaginative response to Shakespeare's plays occurs. But, because throughout his writings Coleridge emphasizes relationships between actual and imaginary theaters, and analogues between real human beings and dramatic characters, it is likely that he came to consider the mind of the dramatic character as itself a "theater" where primary conflicts engage, where the act of perception both conditions and is the product of subjective individuality.

For the individual human mind is, after all, the subject closest to Coleridge's interest. His enduring attraction to the drama seems to have grown from his conviction that it replaces the shapelessness of common life and ordinary mental habit with integral form which lends vitality and meaning to the "dead" objects of the exterior world. Coleridge's difficulty in reconciling the recognition of extreme evil in the dramatic character with admiration for his power and intellect seems ultimately rooted in a sense of the dichotomy between subject and object, between the lifeless world of things by themselves and the attempt of the human consciousness to create vitality in what is dead through an act of sympathy which paradoxically attempts to draw all things to itself.

Consequently it is in these moments of perception, more so than in the structure of the play as a whole, that Coleridge finds most evidence of the activity natural to poet, character, and audience alike. One critic has observed that scholarly emphasis on Coleridge's character criticism has unjustly minimized his merits as a critic of dramatic form. He argues persuasively that Coleridge's analysis of first scenes is based on his doctrine of organic growth, that he sees the individual scene as having "an implied past, a present and a future," and that the value Coleridge places on an early scene exists "in proportion to its contribution towards the total effect of the whole play." In his ability to discover dramatic irony, moreover, Coleridge manifests a necessary ability "to hold in mind the *whole* of a play, to perceive the subtle meaning of one part in relation to another, as well as to the whole."[28] Yet the fact remains that Coleridge is consistently drawn to the investigation of first scenes as if to imply that they constitute the most striking examples of organic growth to be found in the play. Again, although Coleridge's analysis of the formal qualities of the beginning is unfailingly adequate to his notion of the organic connection of parts, the fact also remains that the focal point of this structural analysis lies in the response of the central dramatic character to the stimulus of the individual situation. It is true that these responses fall into a temporal developmental organization but also true that the discrete moments in which the character reacts are the foundation upon which Coleridge builds his larger generalizations.

Perhaps sufficient evidence of Coleridge's emphasis on these "moments" lies in the fragmentary form of his criticism itself. Dealing with the responses of the dramatic character as well as with the psychological propensities underlying them, he consistently gives the impression that the keys to the nature of character are to be found in short speeches or even in single lines. Similarly, his analysis of opening scenes is founded on the assumption that the initial interactions of characters and events are significant structural fragments that illuminate the central human dilemma of the play. He does not concern himself in detail with the structure of the drama as a whole, with themes, or with imagery reiterated throughout the play, but with the intense response of the individual character to a set of stimuli which elicit a full demonstration of his nature as a human being. His brief comment on Edmund Kean (often quoted out of context) offers a useful example of both his own method of sympathetic critical penetration and his distaste for the inadequacies of theatrical production:

[28] Badawi, "Coleridge's Formal Criticism," pp. 151-155.

> KEAN is original; but he copies from himself. His rapid descents from the hyper-tragic to the infra-colloquial, though sometimes productive of great effect, are often unreasonable. To see him act, is like reading Shakspeare by flashes of lightning.[29]

For Coleridge, the brilliancy of human acts is referable to the darkness of the human psyche. Although he spent considerable effort in illuminating the areas left black between Kean's "flashes," his method still retains its fundamental emphasis on these moments of vivid clarification.

[29] *Table Talk,* I, 24.

CHAPTER XII

Hazlitt, Kean, and the Lofty Platform of Imagination

> The next year, the next hour, the next moment is but a creation of the mind; in all that we hope or fear, love or hate, in all that is nearest and dearest to us, we but mistake the strength of illusion for certainty, and follow the mimic shews of things and catch at a shadow and live in a waking dream. —Hazlitt, "A Letter to William Gifford"

i. Leigh Hunt and Thomas Barnes: Common Life and Tragedy

DESCRIBING the cultural context of Crabb Robinson's early comments on the theater, a modern editor observes that a shift in early nineteenth-century taste away from formalism toward naturalism was outdating Kemble's studied approach to his art and preparing the way for the triumph of Edmund Kean.[1] As surely as Hazlitt's championing of that actor represents the emergence of this new taste, the theatrical reviews of his contemporary Leigh Hunt provide an index to the shift as it occurred. The student who seeks a frame of reference for the mid-nineteenth-century domestic dramas of Boucicault, Tom Taylor, and Robertson would hardly do better than begin by studying Hunt's dramatic criticism. Replete with analyses of the "natural" and the "everyday," his theatrical commentaries document many of the extensive changes that distinguish high Romantic Art from the Victorian domesticity to which it gave way. As early as 1807 Hunt published his *Critical Essays on the Performers of the London Theatres,* a collection of youthful but nonetheless distinguished pieces culled from his and his brother's short-lived periodical the *News,* and as late as 1832 he was still contributing to the *Tatler*. The span of his reviews thus includes the later per-

[1] Eluned Brown, ed., *The London Theatre 1811-1866: Selections from the diary of Henry Crabb Robinson* (London, 1966), p. 29.

formances of John Philip Kemble and Sarah Siddons, the meteoric latter days of George Frederick Cooke's career, and the immediate success of Kean. If it is true that the writer of second rank reflects most explicitly the cultural tendencies of his age, Leigh Hunt's writings on the theater present a valuable background against which may be viewed the uncommon achievements of Coleridge and Hazlitt. Hunt shared the enthusiasm of Coleridge and Lamb for Shakespeare's characters and their "perverted greatness," yet never tired of seeing Shakespeare's plays on the stage. His reviews and dramatic essays reveal an endless appetite for the inadequacies his better judgment told him existed in theatrical performance. And, like Hazlitt, Hunt developed out of his many disappointments a concept of the ideal actor which places him, if uneasily, in the company of his two critical betters. Although he never connected this concept with a theory of ideal performance, Hunt's developing notions of dramatic character are unusually helpful in relating the views of Coleridge, Lamb, and Hazlitt to one another and to the cultural life from which they sprang.

A single criterion underlies Hunt's early analyses of tragic characters. The actor, he believed, must combine a thorough awareness of the artificiality of serious drama with an equally thorough ability to appear natural in the effusions of passion. This requirement is not so much a contradiction as may at first appear. In the essay on tragedy which introduces his *Critical Essays*, Hunt calls the drama "the most perfect imitation of human life," since "by means of the stage it represents man in all his varieties of mind, his expressions of manner, and his power of action . . ." (p. 1). Such imitation is not the mere copying of "real and simple manners" but of "our habitual ideas of human character. . . ." The popular idea of a great man is that he is somehow more dignified than ordinary men; hence the playwright in presenting heroism on the stage must be conscious of a decided need for artifice. "The loftier persons of tragedy," Hunt explains, "require an elevation of language and manner, which they never use in real life. . . . A tragic hero, who called for his follower or his horse, would in real life call for him as easily and carelessly as any other man, but in tragedy such a carelessness would become ludicrous: the loftiness of his character must be universal . . ." (pp. 2-3). Here, in sum, is the notion of aesthetic distance that explains the calculated artificiality of romantic heroes like Sheridan's (and Kemble's) Rolla. Yet, says Hunt, the actor in achieving this loftiness must follow a middle course between "too natural a simplicity of manner" and "a ridiculous elevation by pompousness and bombast" (p. 3). Hunt frankly admits that only an actor with natural genius can hope to portray the higher passions effectively, and even this may not be enough: "Where there is strong natural genius, judgment will usually follow in the developement of great passions, but it may fail in the minute proprieties of the stage: where there is not a strong natural genius, the contrary will be generally found. For the common actions of great characters he must study the manner of the stage, for their passions nothing but nature" (p. 4).

The achievement of this delicate balance between two extremes was a commodity Hunt rarely found, but he persisted in analyzing the failure of most actors to purchase it. Hunt's *Critical Essays* deserve attention, partly because they establish ideas on which his subsequent reviews are based, and partly because they present a contrast with what Hunt will later say about Edmund Kean, an actor who to a great extent destroyed the assumptions of reviewers that had existed up until his day.

In assessing the talents of Kemble and Mrs. Siddons, Hunt pays careful obeisance to the measured artificiality of the great actor-manager but nevertheless decides conclusively in favor of his sister. Kemble's diligent study, he observes, allows him great success "in the expression of impressive seriousness." Able to attach importance to a speech of any interest or length, Kemble also possesses "an exact knowledge of every stage artifice local and temporal" (pp. 8, 9)—he has studied "the manner of the stage," as Hunt requires in his introductory essay. But this completeness and correctness, somewhat ironically, define Kemble's limits as an actor. Hunt concludes his analysis with a general judgment whose assumptions point directly forward to the views Hazlitt expresses in his assessment of Kean:

> He does not present one the idea of a man who grasps with the force of genius, but of one who overcomes by the toil of attention. He never rises and sinks as in the enthusiasm of the moment; his ascension though grand is careful, and when he sinks it is with preparation and dignity. (p. 15)

The ideal actor, this passage implies, is one who responds intensely and passionately to the stimulus of the isolated situation, one whose forceful genius enables him to seize, *to grasp*. Hunt's emphasis is characteristic of his developing approach to theatrical performance. The grandness of the moment appears to outweigh the more sober consistency of the presentation as a whole.

Hunt's essay on Mrs. Siddons supports this inference. Like Kemble she combines noble conceptions of nature with a detailed knowledge of art, propriety, and effect, but does so in a significantly different way—"with that natural carelessness, which shews it to be the result of genius rather than grave study. If there is a gesture in the midst, or an attitude in the interval of action, it is the result of the impassioned moment; one can hardly imagine, there has been any such thing as a rehearsal for powers so natural and so spirited" (p. 20).

Hunt's assessment of Kemble and Mrs. Siddons accompanies another essay which prepares for his later analysis of Kean as Richard III. Still concerned with his required conjunction of artifice and mirrored nature in the actor, Hunt brings his *Critical Essays* to a close with a balanced account of George Frederick Cooke. This "MACHIAVEL of the modern stage" can subordinate all passions to one passion and one purpose, Hunt finds, but he can do nothing "without artifice" (p. 216). Making an important distinction, Hunt discriminates between the artifice pertaining to the role of the tragic hero and accompanied by dignity (an appeal to the hoary principle of decorum) and the artifice natural to a particular kind of non-tragic hero and accompanied by what Hunt subsequently praises as "carelessness."[2] Nowhere in his essay does he discuss Cooke's ability to capture the essence of an individual scene. Instead he analyzes the actor's noticeable lack of grace and dignity as ultimately an asset in the portrayal of a certain restricted type of character. He notes Cooke's "fits of thoughtfulness so inimitably familiar" in his Iago, his "artlessness of tone" as Sir Pertinax MacSycophant, "accompanied with such a dragged smile and viciousness of leer, that he seems as if he had lost his voice through the mere enjoyment of malice"

[2] See p. 219, and note the changing use of this word in the *Critical Essays* from disapprobation—"in tragedy such a carelessness would become ludicrous" (pp. 2-3)—to strong approval—"that natural carelessness, which shews it to be the result of genius" (p. 20).

(pp. 219-222). In this type of role, Hunt observes, Cooke exceeds all his contemporaries despite his rough and undignified ways. Although his faults include monotonous gestures and an awkward manner of walking, his "shrinking rise of the shoulders" suggests "that contracted watchfulness, with which a mean hypocrite retires into himself" (p. 222). Cooke's shortcomings somehow become virtues. His success at portraying villainy is so complete that he actually gives the impression of being a villain himself.

Having begun his *Critical Essays* by demanding a decorous balance of artifice and natural response, Hunt concludes by revitalizing this somewhat bloodless ideal, allowing his taste for natural genius and indecorous manner to outweigh his admiration of dignified, studied art. So, unwittingly, he develops a critical disposition which only seven years later will lead him to a careful appreciative estimate of these same qualities in the acting of Edmund Kean.

Hunt's tendency to emphasize an actor's vitality and response to the moment remains pronounced in subsequent reviews. Comments in the *Examiner* up to the time of his imprisonment for libel in 1813 indicate the direction of his ideas. Early in 1809 he reviewed the Macbeth of Charles Mayne Young, the leading contender for tragic honors before Kean appeared. Typically Hunt observes that Young avoided the extremes of Kemble's "methodistical artifices" and of Robert William Elliston's natural picture of the tyrant's "noisy despair."[3] Young is "more harmonious in his colouring, more skilful in the dispositions of his lights and shades . . ."; his dagger scene was nevertheless unsuccessful for its lack of "a variety of countenance approaching to delirium." Again, although Young was impressive in the banquet scene, he evidently lacked the power for "a various and preternatural agitation." Having fastened on the idea of *variety,* Hunt stresses it again and again as an important criterion for dramatic effectiveness. Young and tragedians in general do not use the lower part of the face well; they open their mouths in astonishment but "never chase the expression about with fugitive variety. . . ." Actors, he finds, are slaves to tradition where it is easily upheld,

[3] *The Examiner,* 15 January 1809, reprinted in *Leigh Hunt's Dramatic Criticism 1808-1831,* ed. Lawrence Huston Houtchens and Carolyn Washburn Houtchens (New York, 1949), p. 22. Unless otherwise indicated, subsequent criticism by Hunt is quoted from this edition, abbreviated *DC.*

but "why preserve the easy passages only, the mere starts, stamps, and strides? Or why preserve only single expressions? Why not give us the variety, the combination, the ever-shifting genius?" Hunt sums up with his notion of the ideal actor's expressiveness:

> I think of the lightning which a true actor flashes from *all* corners of his mind and face, and of the thunder that follows such flashes and such only. . . . (*DC*, pp. 22-25)

It is easily observed that in the space of a few years Hunt has significantly shifted emphasis in his conception of the ideal actor. Gradually abandoning his theoretical notion of a balance between artificial and natural extremes, he now favors a response to the individual scene and its requirements of great variety, forcefulness, vitality, and striking imaginative quality—lightning and thunder, to use his metaphor. Hunt's comments on Mrs. Siddons during these years follow the same shift of interest. In a review of her farewell performance as Lady Macbeth in 1812, Hunt noted that she brought perhaps too much "domestic familiarity" to the business of washing her hands, but "the deathlike stare of her countenance, while the body was in motion, was sublime; and the anxious whispering with which she made her exit, as if beckoning her husband to bed, took the audience along with her into the silent and dreaming horror of her retirement . . ." (*DC*, p. 72). [see Plate 39]

Following his release from prison early in 1815, Hunt resumed the writing of his "Theatrical Examiner" column for the *Examiner,* a task his friend Thomas Barnes had performed during Hunt's incarceration.[4] Barnes had written ecstatically of Kean during that actor's first year on the London stage, his enthusiasm particularly strong for Kean's first performance of Richard III. "To go through all his excellencies," Barnes exclaimed, "would be to write a pamphlet. . . ."[5] But Barnes's highly favorable reaction did not distract him from presenting a well-considered view of the character itself. He points out that "the great characteris-

[4] Edmund Blunden ascribes "almost all" the theatrical notices for 1814 in this periodical to Barnes, with the obvious exception of Hazlitt's own pieces which appeared there and are collected in Howe's edition of Hazlitt's works. See Blunden, *Leigh Hunt's "Examiner" Examined* (New York and London, [1928]), p. 36.

[5] *The Examiner,* 27 February 1814, p. 138.

tics of *Richard* are a daring and comprehensive intelligence, which seizes its objects with the grasp of a giant,—a profound acquaintance with the human soul, which makes him appreciate motives at a glance,—a spirit immoveably fearless. . . ." Although Richard is a villain we are not repelled by his actions, for he belongs to "a class above mankind: he is the destroying demon whom we regard with awe and astonishment," not a "mere murderer." Barnes approves of Kean's having "made it all probable and perfectly natural." Anticipating the drift of Hunt's remarks the following year, he was especially struck with "that sure test of a superior mind, his daring to adopt the simplicities and familiarities of the commonest every-day life." His acting contained "no mock-heroic" (p. 138). Like most reviewers, Barnes analyzed the moments of unusual success, singling out the familiar examples of the courting of Lady Anne, the "chop-off-his-head" sequence, the tent scene, and the death scene. More important, his description lays heavy emphasis on the qualities of power and strength of will that Coleridge had fixed on as Richard's essential characteristics and that early nineteenth-century critics emphasize more than the agonized remorsefulness central to earlier notions:

> His death-scene was the grandest conception, and executed in the most impressive manner; it was a piece of noble poetry, expressed by action instead of language. He fights desperately: he is disarmed, and exhausted of all bodily strength: he disdains to fall, and his strong volition keeps him standing: he fixes that head, full of intellectual and heroic power, directly on his enemy: he bears up his chest with an expansion, which seems swelling with more than human spirit: he holds his uplifted arm in calm but dreadful defiance of his conqueror. But he is but man, and he falls after this sublime effort senseless to the ground. (p. 139)

Barnes's view parallels exactly Hunt's concept of preternatural power expressed consummately in the naturalness of every-day manner.

Early in 1815, Hunt with high expectations went for the first time to see Kean as Richard. In his review for the *Examiner* of 26 February 1815 he recorded a signally important assessment of the new actor, whom he carefully measured against his now explicit ideal concept. Frankly disappointed with Kean's Richard, Hunt felt that his unhappiness was due to something other than his perhaps inordinate anticipation of Kean or to his position fairly well back in the house. During the greater part of the performance Kean seemed to be "nothing but a first-rate actor of the ordinary, stagy class, and to start only occasionally into passages of truth and originality" (*DC*, p. 112). What Hunt wanted to see in Kean, he explains, was a distinct departure from the artificial:

> We expected to find no declamation, no common rant, no puttings forth of the old oratorical right hand, no speech-making and attitudinizing at one, no implication, in short, of a set of spectators; but something genuine and unconscious, something that moved, looked, and spoke solely under the impulse of the immediate idea, something as natural in its way, with proper allowance, of course, for the gravity of the interests going forward, as the man who enters his room after a walk, takes off his hat, pinches off one glove and throws into it [sic], then the other glove and throws into it, gives a pull down to his coat or a pull up to his neckcloth, and makes up the fire-place with a rub of his hands and a draught of the air through his teeth. If this should be thought too much to demand in tragedy, it is only because we have been accustomed to the reverse—to art instead of nature. (*DC*, p. 113)

Hunt goes on, however, to allow that Kean in certain moments achieved this complete anti-theatrical naturalness:

> Nothing, for example, can take leave, with better effect, of the usual solemn pedantry of the stage than that action of rubbing his hands, to which he gives way occasionally in his part when he thinks his views are succeeding. . . . His other gestures too, now and then, and the turns of his countenance, tend in a very happy manner to unite common life with tragedy—which is the great stage-desideratum; and it would be impossible to express in a deeper manner the intentness of *Richard's* mind upon the battle that was about to take place, or to quit the scene with an abruptness more self-recollecting, pithy, and familiar, than by the reverie in which he stands drawing lines upon the ground with the point of his

sword, and his sudden recovery of himself with a "Good night."[6]

Within eight years after the publication of his *Critical Essays,* Hunt has reversed the position he first took in favor of a distinct separation of tragic art from life. To be sure, he had formerly classed *Richard III* as other than tragedy. But here, referring to the definite "gravity" of the play, he uses the straightforward generic term and obviously takes Richard as a serious character capable of great heights of villainy. Nor could he have been more explicit in commending Kean for having united "common life with tragedy. . . ." Clearly, Kean's electrifying performance, fulfilling at least at some points the "great stage-desideratum," more greatly satisfied Hunt's aesthetic sensibilities (despite his avowed disappointment) than anything Kemble had been able to do in the way of dignified and studied artifice. Just as important as Hunt's shift to this new criterion of naturalness is his reiterated emphasis on the intensity of the individual moment. He had evidently come to feel that the actor's response in this moment belonged inseparably to the thorough naturalness he had come to require.

In working out his notion of the ideal actor, Hunt followed a line of development opposite to that of Lamb and Coleridge. However familiar Hunt may have been with the text of Shakespeare, his concept of ideal acting was not derived from reading but from performance. For this reason it is not surprising that added experience of plays in the theater led him to abandon his early theoretical view of the distinctness of dramatic art from life and to require instead their imaginative synthesis in the person of an ideal actor. In "An Answer to the Question 'What is Poetry?' "—an essay prefaced to his anthology *Imagination and Fancy* (1844)—he listed some seven varieties or degrees of imagination, the first, "that which presents to the mind any object or circumstance in every-day life," and the third, "that which combines character and events directly imitated from real life, with imitative realities of its own invention."[7] Instead of turning his back, as Lamb did, on the "gross" substance of makeshift nature

[6] *DC,* p. 114. One should note, as Arthur Colby Sprague observes, that Kean has improved on Cooke's business at this point; see *Shakespeare and the Actors* (Cambridge, Mass., 1944), p. 102.

[7] *Imagination and Fancy: with an essay in answer to the question 'What is Poetry?'* (New York, 1845), p. 5.

on the stage, Hunt found a way of reconciling reality with the equally distinct outlines of life imitated imaginatively in the theater. But since he could hardly hope to find this ideal fully realized throughout a performance, even one of Kean's, he came to expect it only in the brief moments when actors like Kean and Siddons responded with a pantomimic spirit indistinguishable from the particularities of actual human behavior.

Similarly Hunt's fellow critic Thomas Barnes, less important than Hunt but just as representative, reveals an interest in erecting ideal critical standards for theatrical performance. Significantly close to Hunt in suggesting a relationship between tragedy and common life, Barnes is important also for the evidence he provides of the destructive impact of Kean's performances on conventional critical approaches to the actor's art. Kean's Macbeth apparently threw him back unprepared on his own immediate responses, forcing him to redefine his notion of dramatic heroism in the light of Kean's new interpretation. The review published in the *Examiner* on 15 November 1814 gives an ambitious but unsatisfactory description of Macbeth that sets in relief Hazlitt's profound and well-delineated archetype of imaginative human nature.[8] Barnes's theoretical outline of consistent character disintegrates, in the course of the review itself, under the influence of Kean's emotional response to situation. His description of that actor's combination of everyday nature and intellectual power in Richard should have better prepared him for his discovery of Kean's similar presentation of spirited volition in the death scene of *Macbeth.* Yet, in that final scene, Kean's conjunction of ferocious rage and "the agony of apalling doubts" (p. 735) impressed Barnes as a kind of summary of the anguish and horror which, despite his own theory, characterized Kean's interpretation of the role. Like Hunt, Barnes finds himself abandoning theoretical constructs and their vocabulary, preferring the more immediate appeal of a character's impassioned response to the impinging situation. Although neither of these writers approaches the significance of Hazlitt's and Coleridge's notions of ideal performance, they demonstrate an important emphasis in the Romantic concept of dramatic character. The general tendency of poets like Wordsworth to concern themselves with the language and behavior of common men is reflected in the high praise

[8] See the discussion below, pp. 338-343.

awarded to actors like Cooke and Kean for their fidelity to the details of ordinary life. When these are presented in a particular dramatic situation, the vivid impression takes on an imaginative quality through the momentary connection of theatrical "unreality" with real life. For Barnes and Hunt, as for Hazlitt and numerous reviewers before and after, this imaginative leap on the actor's part comprised an impassioned response that sums up the nature of dramatic character and defines the essential humanity for which it stands.

ii. Hazlitt and the Sense of the Dramatic

Lord Byron's connection with the management of Drury Lane and his habit of frequent playgoing afforded him an intimacy with the contemporary theater denied to other poets of his day, but his many activities—and his own eccentric ways—prevented him from recording the fruits of that intimacy to any important extent.[9] For such a record, the historian and critic alike necessarily turn to William Hazlitt, whose accounts of his unfortunately brief period as a theatrical reviewer present the most extensively documented concept of dramatic character available in the writings of his day.

"She is a Unitarian in poetry," Hazlitt said of Joanna Baillie in 1818. "With her the passions are, like the French republic, one and indivisible: they are not so in nature, or in Shakspeare."[10] A gathering of frequently recurring subjects in Hazlitt's criticism—poetry, passion, nature, Shakespeare—the comment reflects an attitude which drew him to the theater again and again. "For I am nothing if not critical," Hazlitt reminded his readers (who scarcely needed reminding) on the title page of *A View of the English Stage*. The words out of Iago's mouth suggest Hazlitt's perennial concern with Shakespeare's plays and their chief characters; persistently critical, he sought time and again for the best in Shakespeare that London's two patent theaters could, but rarely did, provide. Between 1813 and 1817 he regularly reviewed theatrical productions at Covent Garden and Drury

[9] Interesting comments on Kean may be found in *The Works of Lord Byron: Letters and Journals*, ed. Rowland E. Prothero (London, 1898), III, 81, 385-387 and n., IV, 339-340.

[10] *The Complete Works of William Hazlitt*, ed. P. P. Howe, 21 vols. (London, 1930-34), V, 147, subsequently cited by volume and page number.

Lane, and in writing the notices which appeared in the *Morning Chronicle*, the *Champion*, the *Examiner*, and the *Times* the failed painter and amateur philosopher belatedly found his real calling as a journalist. At the age of thirty-five Hazlitt had come upon a near-perfect opportunity for the clear formulation and display of ideas which had long been in his mind. A close and constant reader of Shakespeare, Hazlitt brought to his reviews the experience of seasoned playgoing and wide, if eclectic, familiarity with the literary monuments of western culture. He was no "expert" but he knew what he liked, and when he found it he could record his gratification in the most explicit way. Immediate and total response was what Hazlitt had to give, and he frequently gave it best under the pressure of an impending deadline.

Of the works usually thought to constitute Hazlitt's contribution to English criticism, *The Characters of Shakespeare's Plays* comes as close as any to exemplifying the uniqueness of his legacy. And chiefly in *A View of the English Stage*, together with the additional reviews Hazlitt omitted from it,[11] does one find fully expressed the total involvement in the passionate experience of art which epitomizes Hazlitt's greatness as a Romantic critic. Unlike Coleridge and Schlegel, who wrote their criticism from the study or composed it *extempore* at the lectern, and unlike Lamb and Leigh Hunt, whose reviews are not matched by large-scale extra-theatrical criticism, Hazlitt holds the singular position in the Romantic age of being an important writer of criticism who was equally at home in the study or in the pit—who in fact could include the accumulated impressions of repeated readings within the galvanized complex of the theatrical experience. In a period when almost no play of lasting value was written, when Shakespeare was produced as altered (mangled, some would have it) by Cibber, Tate, and others, Hazlitt recorded the disappointment of his ideals in language that describes a major concept of the dramatic. In an age when the star actor far outshone the play in which he appeared, Hazlitt was able to wed his fascination with the Shakespearean character to his fascination with the chief actors of his day. In so doing, he achieved a singular vision of the romantic hero in his encounter with evil and self.

An acute sense of the immediate colors almost everything Hazlitt wrote about the theater. This sense of confronting the actual

[11] Collected by Howe in Vol. XVIII of the *Works*.

developed early enough to form the basis for his first work, *An Essay on the Principles of Human Action* (1807).[12] Subtitled *An Argument in Defence of the Natural Disinterestedness of the Human Mind,* the essay bears a close relationship to Hazlitt's later criticism, particularly to his theatrical reviews, for in it he sets forth concepts of human individuality and volition which underlie his response to dramatic character on the stage.

The basic assumption of the *Principles* is Hazlitt's notion of a strong feeling of future good as the foundation of all human action. Hazlitt transforms the Shaftesburian notion of benevolence into the *exstasis* of sympathetic imagination. "The imagination," he begins, "by means of which alone I can anticipate future objects, or be interested in them, must carry me out of myself," and he explains how, by its force, he is thrown forward into his future being (I, 1-2). Hazlitt emphasizes the orientation of action toward the future and then goes on to develop his idea of the stimulus which prods the human being to act:

> The direct primary motive, or impulse which determines the mind to the volition of any thing must therefore in all cases depend on the *idea* of that thing as conceived of by the imagination, and on the idea solely. . . . We are never interested in the things themselves which are the real, ultimate, practical objects of volition: the feelings of desire, aversion, &c. connected with voluntary action are always excited by the ideas of those things before they exist. (I, 8)

[12] The importance of this essay for understanding Hazlitt's thought has been indicated in J. M. Bullitt, "Hazlitt and the Romantic Conception of the Imagination," *PQ*, XXIV (1945), 343-361; Walter Jackson Bate, *From Classic to Romantic: Premises of Taste in Eighteenth-Century England* (Cambridge, Mass., 1946), pp. 176-178; W. P. Albrecht, "Hazlitt's Principles of Human Action and the Improvement of Society," in *If by your art: Testament to Percival Hunt* (Pittsburgh, 1948), pp. 174-190; Bate, ed., *Criticism: the Major Texts* (New York and Burlingame, 1952), pp. 281-292; and Albrecht, "Hazlitt's Preference for Tragedy," *PMLA*, LXXI (1956), 1042-51; see also Sylvan Barnet and Albrecht, "More on Hazlitt's Preference for Tragedy," *PMLA*, LXXIII (1958), 443-445. Herschel Baker sets the *Principles* in its full biographical and historical contexts in *William Hazlitt* (Cambridge, Mass., 1962), pp. 139-152. More recently, Albrecht has reworked his earlier treatments of the subject in *Hazlitt and the Creative Imagination* (Lawrence, 1965), pp. 1-28. My summary of the *Principles* here is prompted by the fact that no analysis yet exists of the direct relationship between Hazlitt's essay and his theatrical criticism.

Our primary interest in a future good, then, says Hazlitt, arises through its striking us as an unattained desire in the present. The importance of direct stimulus in Hazlitt's notion is great. His emphasis is not on the future good, but on the individual's present conception of it, and this conception is directly a result of outside stimulus (I, 13). Here is Hazlitt's sense of the immediate—a "practical" bias for seeing human desires as non-existent in the abstract, existent in fact only as propensities roused and brought into sharp focus by an impinging external force. Time, for Hazlitt, consists partly in these moments of stimulation in which the individual responds with the whole force of his person. The totality that represents his past being gathers itself in a huge movement toward the future, so that he seems to be already identified with his future being and to feel a "necessary sympathy" with it. The imagination in this way, following an "unbroken line of individuality," endows his desires with a reality and a connection with his present feelings which they can in fact never have (I, 41).

At this point Hazlitt introduces the notion of appetite as a partly selfish principle. What moves the human being to act, Hazlitt says, is primarily the high degree of vividness and force which the appetite gives to the idea of a particular object. For this reason "we find that the same cause, which irritates the desire of selfish gratification, increases our sensibility to the same desires and gratification in others, where they are consistent with our own . . ." (I, 45). In passages like these Hazlitt betrays his great fascination with the selfish motives of individuals. Despite his purpose in the *Principles* to show the natural disinterestedness of the human mind (I, 1), Hazlitt never resolved the unstated contradiction that exists between his theory of the disinterestedness of human motives and his view of tragic character as dramatically fascinating because of its fundamental egotism. In 1820 he made a statement that reflects his thinking for years before. "Within the circle of dramatic character and natural passion," he observed, "each individual is to feel as keenly, as profoundly, as rapidly as possible, but he is not to feel beyond it, for others or for the whole." On the contrary, each character must be "a kind of centre of repulsion to the rest"; we must see their conflicting interests "brought into collision. . . ."[13] Hazlitt did allow the pref-

[13] "The Drama: No. IV" (XVIII, 305).

erence of self as a human motive, but in his concluding statement he attempts to apologize for it:

> The only reason for my preferring my future interest to that of others must arise from my anticipating it with greater warmth of present imagination. It is this greater liveliness and force with which I can enter into my future feelings, that in a manner identifies them with my present being. . . . (I, 49)

Here, at the end of the *Principles*, Hazlitt summarizes what becomes a touchstone in his subsequent criticism. The notion that the imagination carries one out of the present self and into the future being applies directly to the tragic hero's vivid conception of his immediate desires. This is the motivating force that impels him to action. The impulse depends directly on the *idea* of what is essentially a non-entity as it is entertained *presently* in the mind. The imagination is drawn, not to the thing itself, since it does not yet exist, but to its own conception of it in the present; and the impulse is so strong and vivid that it outweighs all other considerations.

Hazlitt's later concept of the tragic hero, then, may logically be expected to emphasize the dramatist's ability to present his hero in the act of experiencing an invincible desire for what he conceives to be an unattained good. In turn, one may expect to find that the actor as he interprets the role of the tragic hero will succeed in proportion to his ability to convey to his audience an impassioned dramatic moment. A strong implication can in fact be found in Hazlitt's *Principles* of an idea which later becomes overt in his reviews. Hazlitt's criticism, confined largely to the success or failure of the star actor, rests on the assumption that a play is composed of a series of "moments," crises in which the chief character is called upon to respond imaginatively to strong external influences by conceiving, or revising his conception, of some ultimate future good. Moreover, tragic irony as Hazlitt thinks of it depends on this same notion of sympathetic imagination. Since it is a present idea, not an actual future good, which motivates the heroic character, tragic irony arises from the potential illusoriness of his idea. Its great warmth and vividness belie the fact that it is a phantom.

The notion that human impulses toward good are essentially disinterested, or at least not based exclusively on selfishness, reappears in Hazlitt's later writings. The notion of the tragic hero in his reviews appears as a negation of the disinterested impulse to action propounded in the *Principles*. In this view, the hero is tragic to the extent that certain blind spots or tendencies toward perverse willfulness impel him to disregard the balance between selfishness and selflessness which Hazlitt sees at the root of all human action. The individual personality arises from "the peculiar connection" that exists between a man's faculties and perceptions, so that "the same things impressed on any of his faculties produce a quite different effect upon *him* from what they would do if they were impressed in the same way on any other being. Personality seems to be nothing more than conscious individuality . . ." (I, 36). The uniqueness of a given man's reaction to common stimuli explains the imbalance of the tragic character, who is driven to great and passionate extremes in his impulse toward future good. In short, the hero ultimately becomes the victim of the vividness of his own unique imagination. The figures, or ideas, which the appetite moves the imagination to conjure up bear to such a great degree the stamp of reality that, given his own propensities, the hero is irresistibly drawn to them and seeks to fulfill the desires they arouse.

But man, in Hazlitt's view, does more than merely fall beneath the crushing force of his own emotions. Since he has the power to reason he remains a moral agent, responsible for his actions. At a future time, Hazlitt observes, he may regret the folly of a past action, and so "I ought as a rational agent to be determined now by what I shall then wish I had done when I shall feel the consequences of my actions most deeply and sensibly." The continued consciousness of his own feelings gives him an immediate interest in whatever relates to his future welfare and makes him always accountable to himself for his conduct (I, 47). The character of Macbeth as Hazlitt later describes it is morally accountable in just this way. Before turning to his discussions of this and other Shakespearean characters, it remains only to observe that the moral basis of tragedy inferred from the *Principles* provides a framework for the more immediate and consuming interest in the great "moments" of response of which, to Hazlitt's mind, tragedy is largely composed. If the morality of tragedy remains always a minor issue for him, however, it is nevertheless always there—at least in Shakespeare, of whom Hazlitt once said that he was the most moral of playwrights because he never let "morality" intrude upon his faithfulness to nature. Morality itself is negative—it dissects, whereas Shakespeare is the great synthesizer. All the passions are found complex in his plays, just as they exist in nature (IV, 346-347). "In the world of his imagination," Hazlitt said in an early review, "every thing has a life, a place and being of its own" (V, 185).

The timing of Hazlitt's four years of theatrical reviewing could not have been more appropriate. The period from 1813 to 1817 witnessed the last days of John Philip Kemble and Mrs. Siddons and the spectacular appearance of Edmund Kean—the three most renowned actors of his day. Hazlitt's distinction between the acting styles of Kemble and Kean indicates the bias of his ideals of acting. He became a Kean aficionado from the first and now famous performance of that actor in 1814 on the stage of the Drury Lane, and against the intensely individual style of Kean's acting he henceforth measured the success or failure of other actors. "In Hamlet," Hazlitt observes, "Mr. Kemble in our judgment unavoidably failed from a want of flexibility, of that quick sensibility which yields to every motive, and is borne away with every breath of fancy, which is distracted in the multiplicity of its reflections, and lost in the uncertainty of its resolutions"; instead, Kemble "played it like a man in armour, with a determined inveteracy of purpose, in one undeviating straight line . . ." (V, 377). Yet Hazlitt was not unappreciative of Kemble's talents. In the same review, devoted to the actor's farewell performance in June 1817, Hazlitt summed up his admiration by describing Kemble's excellence as an ability to seize upon a single idea or feeling and, with prodigious intensity, develop it "to a very high degree of pathos or sublimity." Nevertheless, Kemble's style was essentially classical, since, "if he had not the unexpected bursts of nature and genius, he had all the regularity of art . . ." (V, 379).

It is clear in the context of Hazlitt's reviews that what he observes lacking in Kemble he finds present in Kean—and conversely. The essential review of Kean is the first one, of his London debut. Subsequent descriptions of his acting do little more than amplify. With commendable insight Hazlitt predicted that Kean would do better in other parts. However well he did as Shylock,

> there was a lightness and vigour in his tread, a buoyancy and elasticity of spirit, a fire and animation, which would accord better with almost any other character than with the morose, sullen, inward, inveterate, inflexible malignity of Shylock. The character of Shylock is that of a man brooding over one idea, that of its wrongs, and bent on one unalterable purpose, that of revenge. In conveying a profound impression of this feeling, or in embodying the general conception of rigid and uncontroulable self-will, equally proof against every sentiment of humanity or prejudice of opinion, we have seen actors more successful than Mr. Kean; but in giving effect to the conflict of passions arising out of the contrasts of situation, in varied vehemence of declamation, in keenness of sarcasm, in the rapidity of his transitions from one tone and feeling to another, in propriety and novelty of action, presenting a succession of striking pictures, and giving perpetually fresh shocks of delight and surprise, it would be difficult to single out a competitor. (v, 179) [see Plates 43 and 44]

The undisguised admiration Hazlitt feels for Kean does not limit the accuracy with which he assesses his talents. The passage can in fact bear extensive analysis, not only for the quality of its perceptions but as an archetype of Hazlitt's habitual approach to the actor's performance of an established dramatic role. Often this is a Shakespearean role, and Hazlitt judges the performance against a pre-established and well-defined concept of the central character. Long familiarity with Shakespeare's plays had apparently led Hazlitt to definite decisions about the nature of Shakespeare's characters even before he began reviewing, for no evidence emerges from his theatrical criticism of any major change. He is quite apt to tell his readers that the character of Shylock, or whomever, *is* this or that, and then proceed to measure the actor's success against his own prior conception.

Moreover, if Hazlitt's comparative judgment is taken as an evaluation of the actor's ability to become the character, the review of Kean's debut can be richly glossed in the terms Hazlitt first elucidated in the *Principles of Human Action.* At the center of the passage appears Hazlitt's notion of the sympathetic imagination, and it applies in three distinct ways. First there is the character of Shylock himself, "brooding over one idea" and "bent on one unalterable purpose." In Hazlitt's eyes a precise correlation exists between the insults Shylock suffers in his early encounter with Antonio and Bassanio and the *idea* that this external stimulus presents to Shylock's mind. Shylock acts under the principle of the sympathetic imagination as he projects himself forward into the future, conceiving of revenge as a good to pursue with all the energy of will at his command. He thus abandons the disinterestedness at the root of normal human behavior, falls under the power of "uncontroulable self-will," and so becomes "proof against every sentiment of humanity."

Kean is not ideally suited to such a role, Hazlitt observes. His analysis of Kean's shortcomings suggests a second way in which the sympathetic imagination may function. Sympathetic identification with one's future being, as described in the *Principles,* also explains the actor's task of completely becoming the character he represents. In a subsequent review Hazlitt criticizes Kean for failing to meet the "highest conception of an actor, . . . that he shall assume the character once for all, and be it throughout, and trust to this conscious sympathy for the effect produced" (v, 184). Kean proves not so good as other actors in conveying a profound impression of Shylock's fixed idea. But on the other hand he is incomparable in projecting himself into the character as he confronts a series of situations, each unique—incomparable "in giving effect to the conflict of passions arising out of the contrasts of situation."[14] Although Kean remains deficient in Kemble's forte of conveying a consistent impression, he shows an unequalled capacity to present "a succession of striking pictures." Hazlitt admires in Kemble the talent for embodying profound consistency, but he finds irresistible in Kean the ability to catch up his audience in the great intensity of the "moment."

Still a third way exists in which Hazlitt's notion of sympathetic

[14] Hazlitt appears to distinguish between disinterested sympathy and a personal involvement of the actor in the plight of the character. In a review of Eliza O'Neill as Belvidera in *Venice Preserv'd,* he noted how she had changed for the worse: "Her pathos is less simple, less touching, and her action more outrageous and violent. Perhaps the reason of this change may be, that, acting in such parts from an impulse of real sympathy with the heroine, as she repeats the character, her immediate interest in it becomes gradually diminished, and she is compelled to make up for the want of genuine feeling by the external vehemence of her manner" (XVIII, 265).

imagination may apply: the involvement of the spectator. A practice existed in the theater of Hazlitt's time which most modern playgoers would find odious—the habit of applauding a star actor at his first appearance on stage and at every point where he made a "hit."[15] Hazlitt notices how Kean's delivery of well-wrought Shakespearean passages "was received with equal and deserved applause." It is hard to imagine how such constant interruption could co-exist with any considerable degree of audience involvement, but it must in fact have been so. Hazlitt indicates how great such involvement must have been when, in an essay on "Whether Actors Ought to Sit in the Boxes" when they attend a performance, he objects to their doing so on the grounds that it destroys the audience's identification of them with their theatrical roles (VIII, 272ff). Later, in 1820, in the first of a series of important articles for the *London Magazine*, Hazlitt explains his concept of audience identification. In the theater, he observes, humanity is presented in "the reality of persons, of tones, and actions" and is "raised from the grossness and familiarity of sense, to the lofty but striking platform of the imagination." The stage, he continues, "at once gives a body to our thoughts, and refinement and expansion to our sensible impressions. It has not the pride and remoteness of abstract science: it has not the petty egotism of vulgar life."[16]

To the reader familiar with the *Principles* it is apparent that Hazlitt's ideas and their vocabulary have not changed over the

[15] A "hit" is Hazlitt's term for an enlightening moment in which the actor fully realizes the potential of the passage he is delivering; or it may refer to an especially apt or original bit of pantomime. See V, 223, and compare Hazlitt's phrase "fresh shocks of delight and surprise" in the Shylock review above, p. 330.

[16] XVIII, 272-273. Yet a fourth aspect of sympathy may be detected in Hazlitt's scheme, one which involves the poet as creator. Hazlitt discusses Shakespeare in these terms: "That which distinguishes the dramatic productions of Shakespear from all others, is the wonderful variety and perfect individuality of his characters. Each of these is as much itself, and as absolutely independent of the rest, as if they were living persons, not fictions of the mind. The poet appears for the time being, to be identified with the character he wishes to represent, and to pass from one to the other, like the same soul, successively animating different bodies. By an art like that of the ventriloquist, he throws his imagination out of himself, and makes every word appear to proceed from the very mouth of the person whose name it bears." See V, 185, and compare Coleridge's notion of Shakespeare's method in creating the character of Hamlet, discussed above, Pt. III, Chap. XI, p. 294.

course of fifteen years. If Hazlitt assumes an undeniably bourgeois audience, it is also true that its response is obviously not conventionally Aristotelian, for it partakes as much of the "perpetually fresh shocks of delight and surprise" that Kean brought to the role of Shylock as it does of the incitement to pity and terror. Yet this is what Shakespeare meant to the audiences of Covent Garden and Drury Lane. If Shakespeare meant something more significant to Hazlitt himself—and there is no doubt he did—Hazlitt as a practicing journalist recognized the necessity of writing for the common reader. As a critic he also recognized a responsibility for the education of his audience and the improvement of its taste. In the preface to *A View of the English Stage* (reviews collected for publication in 1818), he set forth his impression of the critical task. We all have an interest in the stage, he says, because it tells us of ourselves, and he goes on to relate an anecdote about Garrick's command of an audience's sympathies. "The knowledge of circumstances like these," he explains, "serves to keep alive the memory of past excellence, and to stimulate future efforts" (v, 174). But the essential task of the critic, Hazlitt felt, was to combine the exercise of careful and earnest judgment with the impassioned imaginative response to the "moment" which he had described in the *Principles.*

> My opinions have been sometimes called singular: they are merely sincere. I say what I think: I think what I feel. I cannot help receiving certain impressions from things; and I have sufficient courage to declare (somewhat abruptly) what they are. (v, 175)

The tenor of Hazlitt's reviews, then, is wholly theatrical. His response is to the powerful immediate stimulus of the performance itself, and his position in the pit is one of close relationship to the whole audience. From this intimate point he can both see and feel. His reviews of Shakespearean tragedy for the four years of his office comprise a full and vivid record of his experience of the imaginative moment—and of those unfortunately frequent moments when imagination fails.

iii. Hazlitt on Kean as Richard III and Macbeth

Remarkable for its richness and scope and for its consistently high standards, Hazlitt's theatrical criticism proved unfailingly adequate to the talents, and deficiencies, of Edmund Kean. By the end of that actor's first season in London, Hazlitt had analyzed in incisive detail Kean's Shylock, Richard III, Hamlet, Othello [see Plate 45], and Iago, as well as certain non-Shakespearean roles.[17] But it was not until his second season, on 5 November 1814, that Kean finally essayed the role of Macbeth and so moved Hazlitt to the extended comparison which documents most fully his concept of dramatic character. Writing in the *Champion* for 13 November, Hazlitt followed the general pattern of previous reviews, first by summarizing the character Shakespeare had written and then continuing with an estimate of Kean's success in the role. He varied the format to a significant extent, however, by introducing a comparison of two characters whose similarities and differences had struck him with great force. In placing Macbeth side by side with Richard III, Hazlitt was continuing the now well-established critical tradition already described in this study.[18] More important, Hazlitt managed to employ familiar comparative techniques to set down in explicit terms the most fundamental distinction found in Romantic criticism of dramatic character.

Undoubtedly, part of Hazlitt's incentive to compare Macbeth with Richard III had come from Kean's success in the role of Richard. On 12 February of the previous season Kean had performed the role for the first time before a highly expectant audience.[19] In his review for the *Morning Chronicle* three days later,

[17] See *A View of the English Stage*, v, 179-190.

[18] It is certain that Hazlitt had read Whately's essay on Macbeth and Richard III. A footnote to this review in the *Champion* refers the reader to "an admirable analysis of the two characters by the author of an Essay on Ornamental Garden"—see v, 405 (n. to p. 205), where Howe explains Hazlitt's inaccurate citation of the title of Whately's work on gardening. In any case, the unusually close similarity of Hazlitt's phrasing of the details of the comparison to Whately's language makes Hazlitt's debt obvious; see the analysis of this debt below, p. 341.

[19] For an account of the performance and the reactions it elicited, consult H. N. Hillebrand, *Edmund Kean* (New York, 1933), pp. 114ff. See also Brown, ed., *The London Theatre*, p. 56, for Crabb Robinson's lucid explanation of his disappointment with Kean's Richard as performed on 7 March. Robinson's subsequent viewings of Kean's roles caused him to modify his initially unfavorable impression of the actor's abilities; two months later he praises Kean's Othello for its unsurpassed "bursts of passion" and finds that he "could hardly keep from crying" at Othello's "exquisite farewell" to his occupation—it was "pure feeling," a "masterpiece" (p. 57). Keats's reaction to

Hazlitt followed the reviewer's usual practice of describing the moments in the performance where the actor particularly shone. But Hazlitt, no ordinary reviewer, embodied these specific points within an essentially philosophical analysis of character. For Hazlitt, the basis of Richard's actions lies in the great forcefulness of the usurper's will. Hazlitt begins by observing that Kean's manner of acting was peculiarly his own and that, "as the character of Richard is the most difficult"—that is, more so even than Shylock—"so we think he displayed most power in it" (v, 181). Hazlitt then moves quickly to a description of the character itself:

> The Richard of Shakespear is towering and lofty, as well as aspiring; equally impetuous and commanding; haughty, violent, and subtle; bold and treacherous; confident in his strength, as well as in his cunning; raised high by his birth, and higher by his genius and his crimes; a royal usurper, a princely hypocrite, a tyrant, and a murderer of the House of Plantagenet.
>
> 'But I was born so high;
> Our airy buildeth in the cedar's top,
> And dallies with the wind, and scorns the sun.'
>
> The idea conveyed in these lines . . . is never lost sight of by Shakespear, and should not be out of the actor's mind for a moment. The restless and sanguinary Richard is not a man striving to be great, but to be greater than he is; conscious of his strength of will, his powers of intellect, his daring courage, his elevated station, and making use of these advantages, as giving him both the means and the pretext to commit unheard-of crimes, and to shield himself from remorse and infamy. (v, 181)

Hazlitt now proceeds to employ this notion of Richard's strength of will as the criterion for estimating Kean's success in the role. Although there were some minor failures on Kean's part,

> his courtship scene with Lady Anne was an admirable exhibition of smooth and smiling villainy. The progress of wily adulation, of encroaching humility, was finely marked

---

Kean has been studied in detail by Bernice Slote in *Keats and the Dramatic Principle* (U. of Nebraska, 1958), pp. 86-96.

> throughout by the action, voice, and eye. He seemed, like the first tempter, to approach his prey, certain of the event, and as if success had smoothed the way before him. . . . Richard should woo not as a lover, but as an actor—to shew his mental superiority, and power to make others the playthings of his will. Mr. Kean's attitude in leaning against the side of the stage before he comes forward in this scene, was one of the most graceful and striking we remember to have seen. It would have done for Titian to paint. [see Plate 46]

Swiftly drawing to his conclusion, Hazlitt emphasizes once more his impression of Kean's great vitality in the role and his ability to project the essence of the character's immensely strong-willed nature:

> He gave to all the busy scenes of the play the greatest animation and effect. He filled every part of the stage. The concluding scene, in which he is killed by Richmond, was the most brilliant. He fought like one drunk with wounds: and the attitude in which he stands with his hands stretched out, after his sword is taken from him, had a preternatural and terrific grandeur, as if his will could not be disarmed, and the very phantoms of his despair had a withering power. (v, 182)

When Hazlitt came to review Kean in his newest role as Macbeth, the actor's manner of playing Richard III was still fresh in his mind. Kean had returned from Dublin to do Richard at Drury Lane early in October of 1814, a scant month before his first performance of Macbeth. Hazlitt had then noted with chagrin that the performance was not up to the standard Kean had set the previous season. Generally objecting to the variations Kean had newly introduced, Hazlitt leveled his heaviest criticism at the actor for changing the original death scene:

> He at first held out his hands in a way which can only be conceived by those who saw him—in motionless despair,—or as if there were some preternatural power in the mere manifestation of his will:—he now actually fights with his doubled fists, after his sword is taken from him, like some helpless infant. (v, 202)

Crabb Robinson found this pantomimic ending Kean's "best conception" of "an intense love of life and power."[20] But Hazlitt clearly would not relinquish his notion of Richard as essentially a character of consummate will, and for Hazlitt this quality was epitomized in Kean's "motionless despair."

It must be remarked here that Hazlitt's view of the character of Richard is in a sense unfair to Kean. Hazlitt's Richard derives from Shakespeare's text, whereas Kean's depends on the character radically altered by Colley Cibber, whose version of Shakespeare's play ran uninterrupted and unchallenged from 1700 until after Hazlitt had ceased to review.[21] Moreover, Hazlitt's notion of the ideal performance erects standards so high that the actor is almost bound to fail. He is, to begin with, at the mercy of the play's adapter, who has significantly altered the role he must play. At the same time, he is at the mercy of the reviewer who grants him unrestricted license in the creation of a role and then demands that he approach the character as Shakespeare wrote it and fix this interpretation once and for all in a permanence as complete as the ideal text itself (v, 202). No actor can prevail for long in this frustrating, exacting contest.

But before dismissing Hazlitt as an impossible idealist who refuses to accept the ordinary limitations of theatrical performance, we must remember that something of great significance remains in these reviews. Hazlitt's fundamental assumption as a reviewer is, it would seem, that if failure is inevitable, critical analysis of it is still both fascinating and profitable. The great actors of Hazlitt's day were all failures—but in a comparative sense only. Their acting remained for Hazlitt the highest possible embodiment of ideal character in an ideal performance. If a philosophical consciousness emerges from his reviews, it is certainly an awareness that human failure must receive the most sympathetic and detailed inspection that can be brought to bear upon it. This notion applies equally to Shakespeare's characters and to the actors and actresses who attempted to portray them. Only through this profound sense of failure and missed opportunity in Hazlitt's reviews do we properly arrive at his notion of the heroic attempt of both actor and character to achieve the imaginary ideal. The complete felicity of situation, the perfection of the mo-

[20] Brown, ed., *The London Theatre*, p. 60.

[21] See the discussion of this alteration above, Pt. III, Chap. IX, pp. 224-229.

ment, are at once their goal and their despair. Upon this philosophical assumption Hazlitt's concept of dramatic character is firmly based.

When Kean finally appeared as Macbeth in November of 1814, Hazlitt went to the theater unwittingly doomed to disappointment. In the review of Kean's Richard a few weeks before, he had called upon the theater managers to give Kean opportunity to display the versatility Hazlitt thought his chief excellence by bringing him out in *Macbeth* (v, 203). It was perhaps to be expected that Hazlitt would be frustrated in his hopes. Fortunately, however, he documented his impression of Kean's failure precisely and profoundly. Beginning with a comparison of the characters of Richard III and Macbeth, Hazlitt's review provides a rich source for his notion of sympathetic imagination in dramatic character and its relationship to the performance of the ideal actor.

The terms of the comparison are simple. Hazlitt discusses the essential difference between a character impelled by imagination, as explained in *The Principles of Human Action*, and a supposedly similar character whose motives are in reality quite different. After a pair of introductory paragraphs on the general theme of Shakespeare's subtle discrimination of characters, Hazlitt turns at once to the details of his intended comparison. With "powerful and masterly strokes," he observes, Shakespeare

> has marked the different effects of ambition and cruelty, operating on different dispositions in different circumstances, in his Macbeth and Richard the Third. Both are tyrants and usurpers, both violent and ambitious, both cruel and treacherous. But, Richard is cruel from nature and constitution. Macbeth becomes so from accidental circumstances. He is urged to the commission of guilt by golden opportunity, by the instigations of his wife, and by prophetic warnings. "Fate and metaphysical aid," conspire against his virtue and loyalty. Richard needs no prompter, but wades through a series of crimes to the height of his ambition, from ungovernable passions and the restless love of mischief. He is never gay but in the prospect, or in the success of his villanies: Macbeth is full of horror at the thoughts of the murder of Duncan, and of remorse after its perpetration. Richard has

> no mixture of humanity in his composition, no tie which binds him to the kind; he owns no fellowship with others, but is himself alone. Macbeth is not without feelings of sympathy, is accessible to pity, is even the dupe of his uxoriousness, and ranks the loss of friends and of his good name among the causes that have made him sick of life. He becomes more callous indeed as he plunges deeper in guilt, "direness is thus made familiar to his slaughterous thoughts," and he anticipates his wife in the boldness and bloodiness of his enterprises, who, for want of the same stimulus of action, is "troubled with thick-coming fancies," walks in her sleep, goes mad, and dies. Macbeth endeavours to escape from reflection on his crimes, by repelling their consequences, and banishes remorse for the past, by meditating future mischief. This is not the principle of Richard's cruelty, which resembles the cold malignity of a fiend, rather than the frailty of human nature. Macbeth is goaded on by necessity; to Richard, blood is a pastime.—

These distinctions alone are not enough, however, and Hazlitt concludes in more explicitly imaginative terms:

> There are other essential differences. Richard is a man of the world, a vulgar, plotting, hardened villain, wholly regardless of every thing but his own ends, and the means to accomplish them. Not so Macbeth. The superstitions of the time, the rude state of society, the local scenery and customs, all give a wildness and imaginary grandeur to his character. From the strangeness of the events which surround him, he is full of amazement and fear, and stands in doubt between the world of reality and the world of fancy. He sees sights not shewn to mortal eye, and hears unearthly music. All is tumult and disorder within and without his mind. In thought, he is absent and perplexed, desperate in act: his purposes recoil upon himself, are broken, and disjointed: he is the double thrall of his passions and his evil destiny. He treads upon the brink of fate, and grows dizzy with his situation. Richard is not a character of imagination, but of pure will or passion. There is no conflict of opposite feelings in his breast. The apparitions which he sees are in his sleep, nor

does he live like Macbeth, in a waking dream. (v, 205-206) [see Frontispiece]

Macbeth is for Hazlitt the essential romantic hero implicitly described in the *Principles,* whose volition depends on the *idea* conceived by the imagination in response to "certain accessory objects or ideas" whose "extraordinary degree of force and vividness . . . irritates the desire of selfish gratification . . ." (I, 8, 13, 45). The immorality of Macbeth's actions is clear in terms of the *Principles,* where Hazlitt observes that man's rational nature requires him to determine his actions by what he will in the future wish he had done (I, 47). But Macbeth, in contrast to this moral ideal, tries to avoid reflecting on his crimes by ridding his mind of their consequences; he "banishes remorse for the past, by meditating future mischief." Macbeth's uniquely imaginative personality, his "conscious individuality" (I, 36), impels him to pervert the natural disinterestedness of the human mind, and so in responding to the goads of his own ambition he is unable to maintain moral vision and stands doubtfully between two worlds, one real, one illusory. What Hazlitt has done is to take the traditional view of Macbeth's vacillation and, employing the vocabulary of sympathetic imagination developed in the *Principles,* to describe that fundamental imbalance of the tragic character which makes him dramatically fascinating. The "petty egotism of vulgar life," as he called it in the *London Magazine,* has been raised through the medium of the dramatic character "to the lofty but striking platform of the imagination" (XVIII, 272-273). Macbeth is ultimately a compelling character to the extent that he departs from disinterested moral behavior. Having encountered the stimulus of the weird sisters' prophecy, he is carried out of himself and thrown forward into his future being through continued encounters with the phantasms of his own imagination. [see Plates 47 and 48]

Although Hazlitt's emphasis in this review naturally falls on the imaginative basis of Macbeth's character, it is clear that the notion of Richard as a character not "of imagination, but of pure will or passion" is completely consistent with Hazlitt's earlier and more detailed view. These two characters thus represent for him a fundamental opposition which defines his notion of the nature of dramatic character. The varying success of Kean in these two roles was the closest human approximation to the ideal response of character to situation which, to Hazlitt's mind, summed up the essence of dramatic art. Kean's ability to endow the dramatic moment with life contributed more to Hazlitt's notion of the ideal actor than any other single influence. Yet, ironically, it was Kean's "failure" in Macbeth which inspired Hazlitt to adapt Whately's comparison of two oppositely motivated characters to his own notion of sympathetic imagination. Beginning with Whately's central idea of comparing a self-sufficient character with one completely dependent on external stimulus, and borrowing closely from Whately's detailed exposition, Hazlitt worked out a fundamental distinction between a character narrowly bound by the strong forces of will and passion alone and a contrasting character whose vacillation between good and evil motives was the result of his vivid imagination. When set in its historical context, Hazlitt's achievement was to transform the late eighteenth-century view of Macbeth as a man of sensibility into his own view of the character as an archetype of imaginative human nature. His view of Richard, however, involved no such radical change. George Frederick Cooke (whom Hazlitt had seen and mentions in this review) had introduced a change in emphasis in his interpretation of Richard from guilt-stricken agony to the diabolical power of will. Hazlitt, prompted by Kean's performances, took over this same idea unchanged—except in one important respect. Although Richard was not a character of imagination, Hazlitt found him possessed of preternatural power which elicited great admiration despite the cruelty of the tyrant's acts. Kean's ability to present this power was for Hazlitt an indication of his great sympathetic abilities.

But Kean was not a success as Macbeth. The "tenseness of fibre," the "pointed decision of manner," the general tightness and compactness that Kean brought to the role of Richard were carried over to his Macbeth with unhappy effect. "He was deficient in the poetry of the character," Hazlitt found, for "he did not look like a man who had encountered the Weird Sisters." Kean was particularly disappointing in Act V, where "there was not that giddy whirl of the imagination—the character did not burnish out on all sides with those flashes of genius, of which Mr. Kean had given so fine an earnest in the conclusion of his Richard." Only in the scene after the murder did Kean preserve the "fierce, impetuous, and ungovernable" qualities characteristic of Macbeth's mental condition:

> The hesitation, the bewildered look, the coming to himself when he sees his hands bloody; the manner in which his voice clung to his throat, and choaked his utterance; his agony and tears, the force of nature overcome by passion—beggared description. (v, 206-207)

Despite Kean's overall inadequacy in the role, his success in this one scene afforded Hazlitt the opportunity to complete his most detailed description of a character acting under the impulse of imagination. It is plain that the result of this influence is to deprive the character of his sure grasp of exterior reality and render him the prey of illusory forces, so that he walks as if in a "waking dream." Since Hazlitt's view of Macbeth's mental processes and actions follows the laws of general human behavior set down in the *Principles*, the implication in this review is that Macbeth is a type of human nature itself, traduced by its own faculties into committing an act whose moral effect is vividly summed up in Hazlitt's description of Kean's acting after the murder.

In this moral context, Hazlitt's comparison of the two characters and his analyses of their embodiment in Kean's acting synthesize the two traditions of criticism and performance which Hazlitt had inherited to his own advantage. Proceeding on the assumption that what happens to Macbeth comprises the entire meaning of the play, Hazlitt describes what we must take as an archetype of tragic human experience. Aroused by the stimulus of the witches' prophecy, Macbeth's imagination is perverted from exercising its ordinary salutary effect on the conduct of a sensitive and honorable man. No longer able to reflect on the moral consequences of his ambitious plans, he proceeds in them —only to be abruptly awakened to the horrors of a remorseful conscience after he has committed the act. The philosophical and moral implications of Macbeth's descent from virtue have not changed between Richardson and Hazlitt. Once it is admitted that a man's acts are determined by the sensitivity of his mental faculties to the influence of forces in the exterior world, objective judgment of his guilt in falling victim to them is no longer possible. In the absence of standards, the "spectator"—whether a reader or a member of a theater audience—can only contemplate the struggles of the dramatic character which illustrate and stand for his own.

Hazlitt's original notion of imaginative response operates within this context in two ways. On the one hand, it provides a sympathetic explanation of the relationship between the private mental world of the human being and the world in which he must act. On the other, it provides a guide for the actor who must impersonate this human being on the stage. The extent to which the actor becomes the character reveals the depth of the actor's sympathetic response. But, for Hazlitt, the almost inevitable breach between attempt and accomplishment marks the difference between the real and the ideal actor. As Macbeth, Kean achieved only momentary success in embodying the imaginary ideal. That moment, set against the actor's lapses throughout the rest of the play, epitomizes Hazlitt's sense that the confrontation of reality and imagination suggests both human aspiration and human failure. The imaginative response that reveals the nature of actor, character, and human being alike produces merely a temporary synthesis. Such periods, as Coleridge said of Kean's acting, bring flashes which only for the moment illuminate the surrounding darkness.

Conclusion

> Now it is part of the ideality of the highest sort of dramatic poetry that it presents us with a kind of profoundly significant and animated instants, a mere gesture, a look, a smile, perhaps—some brief and wholly concrete moment—into which, however, all the motives, all the interests and effects of a long history, have condensed themselves, and which seem to absorb past and future in an intense consciousness of the present.
>
> —Walter Pater, "The School of Giorgione," in *The Renaissance*

THE OUTCOME of late eighteenth-century notions in the writings of Hazlitt, Coleridge, and their contemporaries is effectively summarized in a now little-known work which appeared early in their day. In 1807 Henry Siddons, actor and eldest son of Mrs. Siddons, brought out his adaptation of a German treatise he entitled *Practical Illustrations of Rhetorical Gesture and Action, Adapted to the English Drama.* The dramatic poem, Siddons says, presents figures that, in each important situation, find themselves

> in the real embarrassment of persons who communicate their ideas at the moment they receive them; and their affections, at the instant they are affected by their impressions; so that, far from being solely occupied in expressing these sentiments and these ideas, they always tend to a determined mark, and constantly break forth, by the thought, into the future. . . . For them the present moment is real—the future uncertain. . . . Their sentiment, always conformable to the situation, constantly shews itself just as it is:—feeble or impetuous at its birth; imperious in its progress; mastered sometimes, or half extinguished; hid for a moment, to re-appear with greater force hereafter. . . . All the characteristical traits which distinguish the personages of a dramatic poem from those of every other poem, may be presented to the mind in one single idea, which is that of their actual presence and reality before our eyes; and it is the imposition of this magic

> upon our imagination which constitutes the sole effect of the dramatic poem. (pp. 302-305)

Although Siddons is describing the characteristics of a play performed on stage, his idea of its impressions reflects the notions of ideal actor and ideal performance that Coleridge, Hazlitt, and others were developing at this same time. Whether the character is ideal or "real," his nature is the same. Plunged into the immediate situation, he has no time to meditate on his reactions; they burst forth at the instant they are formed in the mind, impelling him into the future. Subsequent moments, drawing forth repeated demonstrations of his responsive nature, reveal the struggle of the mind with the varying forms of passion. Only these moments, as they occur, are real. Siddons' idea of the magical illusion of reality on the stage presupposes that this reality consists entirely of a sequence of "moments," each revealing the character's nature by eliciting a reaction "conformable to the situation."

The sixty-eight plates together with the accompanying discussions provided by Siddons reinforce his idea that the momentary situation holds the key to an understanding of human response. These "practical illustrations" of gesture and attitude reflect a conventional visual language; each plate immediately conveys the intended emotion and so constitutes its symbol. Of Siddons' many examples, one will suffice to show the relevance of his notions. Plate 17, representing "Terror" [see Plate 49], presents a statuesque woman dressed in a flowing robe. The conventional form of terror represented in her attitude is indisputably mirrored in Mrs. Siddons' response to Kemble's Macbeth when he returns from Duncan's chamber. When Kemble speaks the line "There's one did laugh in his sleep, and one cried 'Murder!' " Mrs. Siddons, according to Professor Bell—whose elliptical syntax suggests the intensity of actual performance—

> displays her wonderful power and knowledge of nature. As if her inhuman strength of spirit overcome by the contagion of his remorse and terror. Her arms about her neck and bosom, shuddering.[1]

Here is Henry Siddons' notion of immediate reality. In this moment of intense response, the actress allows the womanly nature

[1] Jenkin, ed., *Mrs. Siddons as Lady Macbeth*, p. 53n.

of Lady Macbeth to break through the hard veneer of fiendish ambition and so epitomizes, in an instant, the character's essential humanity.

The tradition behind graphic emblematization of this sort forms a fascinating and largely unexplored area of interest. It seems fitting to conclude the present study of persistence and change in dramatic character by exploring an instance of that tradition. A convenient summary of the ideas I have attempted to define, this analysis may also perhaps suggest the potential fruitfulness of further investigation.

In 1806 Charles Bell, the brilliant surgeon and brother of G. J. Bell, the annotator of Mrs. Siddons' performances, brought out his *Essays on the Anatomy of Expression in Painting*. Offering vivid examples of *despair* from poetry and drama, Bell quotes the description of the hero Beverley's despair in Edward Moore's tragedy *The Gamester* (1753): "When all was lost, he fixed his eyes upon the ground, and stood sometime with folded arms stupid and motionless: then snatching his sword that hung against the wainscot, he sat him down, and with a look of fixed attention drew figures on the floor" (p. 150). This gesture strikingly prefigures Kean's business as Richard just before the tent scene. Leigh Hunt's depiction of the moment, already quoted above, is perhaps the most pictorial:

> It would be impossible to express in a deeper manner the intentness of *Richard's* mind upon the battle that was about to take place, or to quit the scene with an abruptness more self-recollecting, pithy, and familiar, than by the reverie in which he stands drawing lines upon the ground with the point of his sword, and his sudden recovery of himself with a "Good night."[2]

In 1820 the *Theatrical Inquisitor* suggested that Kean derived the idea for this business from a speech of Young Norval (a role Kean himself played) in Act IV of Home's *Douglas*:

> To help my fancy, in the smooth green turf
> He cut the figures of the marshalled hosts;
> Described the motion, and explained the use

[2] *Hunt's Dramatic Criticism*, ed. Houtchens and Houtchens, p. 114.

> Of the deep column, and the lengthened line,
> The square, the crescent, and the phalanx firm.[3]

Just as likely a source, and far more appropriate, is the description of despair from *The Gamester* (in which Kean appeared often as Beverley). The possibility that Kean means to suggest Richard's sense of the hopelessness of his enterprise is enhanced by Catesby's lines immediately after his "Good night": "Methinks the King has not that pleas'd Alacrity Nor Cheer of Mind that he was wont to have."[4] Kean's Richard sketches out his battle plans on the ground, not with the sureness of an experienced and confident general, but, as Hunt describes, in "reverie." Kean's supposedly original "hit," then, may well represent in iconographic "language" an image of despair immediately recognizable as such to theater audiences. To cite the possible presence of such a tradition behind Kean's business is not at all to detract from its brilliance. Properly considered, Kean's use of his sword's point to sketch out the opposing lines of battle for the field on which his character is to die sums up the processes of tradition and change that produced both the Romantic actor and the Romantic hero.

The theory of ideal imaginative response formulated by Hazlitt, Coleridge, and Lamb grows naturally out of the same assumptions about dramatic character and human nature that both Kean and Henry Siddons unconsciously illustrate. Siddons speaks of figures on an actual stage, but his interest in them does not derive from their objectification of human action. His view of dramatic character in situation depends on the auditor's ability to imagine the total reality represented in the human being's response. The great critics of Siddons' day share this same fascination. Their distinction is simply that they described their high interest in ways which reflect a more profound and systematic concept of the human mind and its emblem in the dramatic character.

Behind this theory of ideal human nature lies the long evolution of traditions described in the present study. Despite the apparent independence of closet criticism from theatrical performance, their mutual concern with dramatic character forms

[3] Cited in Alan S. Downer, ed., *King Richard III: Edmund Kean's Performance* (London, 1959), p. xxx.

[4] Cibber, *King Richard III,* V.iv.18-19.

a homogeneous attitude that follows the general tendency of the age to turn inward upon itself. The growth of an empirical tradition in philosophy created a need to extend understanding of the reasons why men act as they do. Literary critics, caught up in this spirited search for motives, began to suspect that a human act held no particular meaning unless referred to the state of mind that prompted it. In explicating the causes which eventuate in action, they were led to new understandings both of dramatic character and human nature; for the study of one illuminated the other. Meanwhile, actors and audiences were engaged in a similar pursuit. The psychological depth imputed to human nature by late eighteenth-century closet critics had for years been apparent on the stage. Amid the diversity of acting styles represented by Garrick and, later, Kemble, Mrs. Siddons, Cooke, and Kean, there appeared a common concern to demonstrate the essential nature of the dramatic character by exposing his motives to the common eye, so eliciting from audiences a sympathetic response to one whose humanity was indistinguishable from their own. The dramatic situation served this purpose by giving the actor an opportunity to respond, and so the sequential events of the play became merely the agencies necessary to draw forth from the character an emblematic demonstration of his inner self.

In achieving these ends, both actors and critics found that the text of Shakespeare contained the fullest available record of essential human experience. Whether they began or ended there, it was clear to them that Shakespeare's tragic heroes were the most meaningful of all analogues that might teach men of themselves. In Richard III and Macbeth they discovered two especially rich sources, for these characters represented extreme opposite cases of man's relation to the world about him and his awareness of evil and self. Eighteenth-century attention to these two figures established the view that dramatic character in its response to situation displays the full variety of human aspiration and failure. It remained for the early nineteenth century to take this dramatic moment as symbolic of man embracing in his imagination the perfect felicity he could not otherwise attain.

BIBLIOGRAPHICAL NOTE

This note differs from a straightforward alphabetical list both in its categorical grouping and its selectivity. The largest deliberate omission is of plays. To cite those mentioned in the text would serve no important purpose, and to discuss them would require pointless reiteration; all such titles are included in the Index. Also omitted, as a general principle, are newspaper and periodical reviews and other dramatic and theatrical writings of topical or otherwise limited interest; these are fully cited in the footnotes.

What remains is a compendium of primary and secondary materials arranged as much as possible in homogeneous groups. I have sought to raise into larger general categories many works that appear at one point or another in some particular context, leaving for inclusion under a chapter-by-chapter account those whose present value does not exceed such limits.

As in the text and notes above, the place of publication of works issued prior to 1850 is London unless otherwise indicated.

Bibliography and General Reference

The most useful tools for the student of eighteenth- and nineteenth-century English drama and theater are the *Cambridge Bibliography of English Literature*, ed. F. W. Bateson, 4 vols. (Cambridge, Eng., 1940), supplement ed. George Watson (Cambridge, Eng., 1957), containing many of the plays of the period as well as the best listing of dramatic histories, theatrical memoirs, and biographical and critical materials; Watson's revision, the *New Cambridge Bibliography of English Literature,* in progress, of which Vol. 3: 1800-1900 (Cambridge, Eng., 1969), has so far been issued; and Allardyce Nicoll's indispensable *A History of English Drama 1660-1900*, 6 vols. (Cambridge, Eng., rev. edns. 1952-59), whose handlists of plays exceed those of the *CBEL* in comprehensiveness and whose last volume, an alphabetical catalogue of plays, affords easy location of pertinent information. Although one may disagree with his critical judgments, Professor Nicoll's unparalleled knowledge of the range and breadth of English drama and his industry and care in putting that knowledge at the service of others have left all students of the subject permanently in his debt. A more specialized but still essential work is Robert W. Lowe's *A Bibliographical Account of English Theatrical Literature* (New York and London, 1888), a much needed revision of which by J. Arnott and J. Robinson is, at this writing, about to appear. Also helpful is James J. O'Neill, "A Bibliographical Account of Irish Theatrical Literature," *The Bibliographical Society of Ireland,* Vol. 1, no. 6 (Dublin, 1920), 57-88. For a bibliography of sources containing lists of English plays see Carl J. Stratman, C.S.V., comp., *Dramatic Play Lists 1591-1963* (New York, 1966); pp. 35-36 contain references to scholarship citing additions and corrections to Nicoll's handlists. Stratman has also edited *A Bibliography of English Printed Tragedy 1565-1900* (Carbondale and London, 1966)—very useful but limited by Stratman's omission of plays that fail (with an amateurism that is somehow charmingly English) to acknowledge their genre on their title pages. The availability of these and many other English plays has been enhanced by their appearance in microprint in the series *Three Centuries of English and American Plays*; see G. William Bergquist's *Checklist* under this title (New York and London, 1963), spanning the period 1500-1800 in England and 1714-1830 in the United States; see also Theodore Grieder's "Annotated Checklist of the British Drama, 1789-99," *RECTR*, IV (1965), 1, 21-47. With reference to the extensive collection in the Huntington Library see Dougald MacMillan's compilation, *Catalogue of the Larpent Plays in the Huntington Library* (San Marino, 1939), corrected and augmented by E. Pearce in *HLQ*, VI (1943). Other very helpful lists for the student of eighteenth-century drama and culture include R. W. Babcock's "A Preliminary Bibliography of Eighteenth-Century Criticism of Shakespeare," *SP*, extra ser. I (1929), 58-76, also to be found (with some differences) appended to his book *The Genesis of Shakespeare Idolatry 1766-1799* (Chapel Hill, 1931); and John W. Draper's comprehensive *Eighteenth Century English Aesthetics: A Bibliography* (Heidelberg, 1931), augmented by R. D. Havens in his review in *MLN*, XLVII (1932). Samuel A. Tannenbaum's *Shakspere's Macbeth (A Concise Bibliography)*, Elizabethan Bibliographies No. 9 (New York, 1939) is useful despite its early date and incompleteness.

For records directly relevant to performance consult the standard calendars: Rev. John Genest, *Some Account of the English Stage*, 10 vols. (Bath, 1832), to be superseded to 1800 on the completion of the still-in-progress *The London Stage 1660-1800*, ed. Emmet L. Avery, C. Beecher Hogan, Arthur H. Scouten, George Winchester Stone, Jr., and William Van Lennep (Carbondale, Ill., 1960-), four parts (1660-1776) of a projected five having already appeared; and Hogan's *Shakespeare in the Theatre, 1701-1800*, 2 vols. (Oxford, 1952-57). For materials on acting, production, and design consult Charles H. Shattuck, *The Shakespeare Promptbooks: A Descriptive Catalogue* (Urbana, 1965), and Sybil Rosenfeld and Edward Croft-Murray, "A Checklist of Scene Painters Working in Great Britain and Ireland in the 18th Century," *TN*, XIX (1964-65), 6-20, 49-64, 102-113, 133-145, and XX (1965-66), 36-44, 69-72, and 113-118. No catalogue of promptbooks other than Shattuck's has yet, to my knowledge, been published, but most good theater collections have either a separate catalogue of promptbooks (as do the Harvard and Princeton theater collections) or contain the makings of one in larger, more comprehensive catalogues (as in the case of the Dyce and Forster collections in the Victoria and Albert Museum). The most recent guide to such holdings is *Performing Arts Libraries and Museums of the World,* ed. André Veinstein; 2nd edn. rev. and enl. by Cécile Giteau (Paris, 1967).

Helpful reference works, in addition to Nicoll's *History,* include E. K. Chambers, *The Elizabethan Stage,* 4 vols. (Oxford, 1923); Gerald Eades Bentley, *The Jacobean and Caroline Stage,* 7 vols. (Oxford, 1941-68), and George C. D. Odell's unfortunately uncompleted *Annals of the New York Stage,* 14 vols. (New York, 1927-45). More general reference value will be found in the *Oxford Companion to the Theatre,* ed. Phyllis Hartnoll, now in its 3rd edn. (London, 1967); the profusely illustrated *Enciclopedia dello Spettacolo,* ed. Silvio D'Amico *et al.,* 9 vols. (Rome, 1954-62), and the ever-useful but sometimes biased *Dictionary of National Biography.*

In addition to Rosenfeld and Croft-Murray's checklist, a variety of graphic materials pertaining to the theater are cited in *A Catalogue of the Pictures in the Garrick Club* (London, 1936), the *Catalogue of Dramatic Portraits in the Theatre Collection of the Harvard College Library,* ed. Lillian Arvilla Hall, 4 vols. (Cambridge, Mass., 1931), and the *British Museum Catalogue of Personal and Political Satires,* Vols. Vff. ed. M. D. George (London, 1935-), in progress but already covering the period of this study.

Critical, Cultural, and Historical Background

One of the great contributions of modern scholarship to our understanding of the past has been in the area of eighteenth- and nineteenth-century critical history. M. H. Abrams' *The Mirror and the Lamp: Romantic Theory and the Critical Tradition* (Oxford, 1953) is essential reading, as are William K. Wimsatt, Jr. and Cleanth Brooks's *Literary Criticism: A Short History* (New York, 1957), René Wellek's *A History of Modern Criticism: 1750-1950,* 4 vols. (New Haven, 1955-65), and R. S. Crane's "English Neoclassical Criticism: An Outline Sketch," *Critics and Criticism: Ancient and Modern,* ed. Crane (Chicago, 1952), 372-388. Also of value are W. J. Bate's introductory essays in his edition, *Criticism: The Major Texts* (New York and Burlingame, 1952), Bate's indispensable essay "The Sympathetic Imagination in Eighteenth-Century English Criticism," *ELH,* XII (1945), 144-164, and the more recent study by George Watson, *The Literary Critics: A Study of English Descriptive Criticism* (Harmondsworth, 1962), as well as Wellek's "German and English Romanticism," in his *Confrontations:*

Studies in Intellectual and Literary Relations between Germany, England, and the United States in the Nineteenth Century (Princeton, 1965). A more specialized study is Charles Harold Gray, *Theatrical Criticism in London to 1795* (New York, 1931), useful also for its citation of little-known periodicals. See, in addition, Claude E. Jones, "Dramatic Criticism in the *Critical Review*, 1756-1785," *MLQ*, xx (1959), 18-26, 133-144.

Of many works which treat intellectual and cultural history, I found the following the most suggestive: Louis I. Bredvold, *The Intellectual Milieu of John Dryden* (Ann Arbor, 1934); Marjorie Hope Nicolson's *The Breaking of the Circle*, rev. edn. (New York, 1960), *Mountain Gloom and Mountain Glory* (Ithaca, 1959), and *Newton Demands the Muse* (Princeton, 1946); W. J. Bate, *From Classic to Romantic* (Cambridge, Mass., 1946); and Ernest Tuveson, *The Imagination as a Means of Grace: Locke and the Aesthetics of Romanticism* (Berkeley and Los Angeles, 1960), as well as Tuveson's wide-ranging article "The Importance of Shaftesbury," *ELH*, xx (1953), 267-299; see also Tuveson, "Shaftesbury on the Not So Simple Plan of Human Nature," *SEL*, v (1965), 403-434, and Basil Willey, *The Eighteenth Century Background: Studies on the Idea of Nature in the Thought of the Period* (London, 1940). Similarly important for the study of intellectual and cultural history are A. O. Lovejoy's *The Great Chain of Being* (Cambridge, Mass., 1936) and, among Lovejoy's numerous contributions, "The Supposed Primitivism of Rousseau's Discourse on Inequality," *MP*, xxi (1923), 165-186, and "Monboddo and Rousseau," *MP*, xxx (1933), 275-296. Notions of the primitive, so widespread in the thought of the period, have been extensively studied in C. B. Tinker, *Nature's Simple Plan* (Princeton, 1922); Hoxie Neale Fairchild, *The Noble Savage: A Study in Romantic Naturalism* (New York, 1928); Lois Whitney, *Primitivism and the Idea of Progress in English Popular Literature of the Eighteenth Century* (Baltimore, 1934); Lovejoy and George Boas, *Primitivism and Related Ideas in Antiquity* (Baltimore, 1935); and Edith Amelie Runge, *Primitivism and Related Ideas in Sturm und Drang Literature* (Baltimore, 1946); see also Benjamin Bissell, *The American Indian in English Literature of the Eighteenth Century* (New Haven, 1925).

In the area of dramatic character and its relation to cultural and artistic tendencies, especially helpful works include B. H. Bronson's article "Personification Reconsidered," *ELH*, xiv (1947), 163-177; R. S. Crane's deservedly famous "Suggestions Towards a Genealogy of the 'Man of Feeling,'" *ELH*, i (1934), 205-230; Mario Praz, *The Romantic Agony*, 2nd edn. (Oxford, 1951); Robert Langbaum, *The Poetry of Experience: The Dramatic Monologue in Modern Literary*

Tradition (London, 1957); and Earl R. Wasserman's two articles on Elizabethanism, "The Scholarly Origin of the Elizabethan Revival," *ELH*, IV (1937), 213-243, and "Henry Headly and the Elizabethan Revival," *SP*, XXXVI (1939), 491-502. Two suggestive studies of time, the latter extending into a later period, are Georges Poulet, "Timelessness and Romanticism," *JHI*, XV (1954), 3-22, and Jerome H. Buckley, *The Triumph of Time: A Study of the Victorian Concepts of Time, History, Progress, and Decadence* (Cambridge, Mass., 1966).

There are few good studies of the social character of the theatrical audience in the period. The best known are Harry W. Pedicord, *The Theatrical Public in the Time of Garrick* (New York, 1954), and James J. Lynch, *Box, Pit, and Gallery: Stage and Society in Johnson's London* (Berkeley and Los Angeles, 1953). Contemporary accounts include J. P. Malcolm, *Anecdotes of the Manners and Customs of London during the Eighteenth Century* (1808; 2nd edn., 2 vols., 1810); *Lichtenberg's Visits to England as described in His Letters and Diaries*, trans. Margaret L. Mare and W. H. Quarrell (Oxford, 1938), containing much material on Garrick; and, for the later period, Henry Crabb Robinson, *Diary, Reminiscences, and Correspondence*, ed. Thomas Sadler, 2nd edn., 3 vols. (London, 1869); more accessible is the edition by Eluned Brown, *The London Theatre 1811-1866: Selections from the diary of Henry Crabb Robinson* (London, 1966). See also the modern study by John A. Kelly, *German Visitors to English Theaters in the Eighteenth Century* (Princeton, 1936).

Drama and Theater

The best brief survey of English drama as a whole is Alan S. Downer's *The British Drama: A Handbook and Brief Chronicle* (New York, 1950). A number of books and articles on the drama of particular periods and on more specialized topics have served the present study, among which the following are cited in the chronological order of the period they treat. Madeleine Doran, *Endeavours of Art: A Study of Form in Elizabethan Drama* (Madison, 1954) contains a good chapter on tragicomedy. Two fine recent studies of new modes in Jacobean drama are Arthur C. Kirsch, "*Cymbeline* and Coterie Dramaturgy," *ELH*, XXXIV (1967), 285-306, and John H. Reibetanz's unpublished dissertation "The Two Theatres: Dramatic Structure and Convention in English Public and Private Plays 1599-1613" (Princeton, 1968). Still worth reading is Frank H. Ristine's early study *English Tragicomedy* (New York, 1910), the first full modern discussion. Other important works on late sixteenth- and seventeenth-century drama include Eugene Waith's *The Herculean Hero in Marlowe, Chapman, Shakespeare, and Dryden* (London, 1962) and Alfred Harbage's *Cavalier*

Drama (New York and London, 1936). Harbage deals also with the drama of the Commonwealth, both in this book and in the important article "Elizabethan-Restoration Palimpsest," *MLR*, XXXV (1940), 287-319; in addition consult two articles by Hyder E. Rollins, "A Contribution to the History of the English Commonwealth Drama," *SP*, XVIII (1921), 267-333, and "The Commonwealth Drama: Miscellaneous Notes," *SP*, XX (1923), 52-69; and see Louis B. Wright, "The Reading of Plays during the Puritan Revolution," *Huntington Library Bulletin*, No. 6 (1934), 73-108. The study of Restoration drama has recently benefited from two compact and unusually suggestive books, Arthur C. Kirsch's *Dryden's Heroic Drama* (Princeton, 1965), and Eric Rothstein's *Restoration Tragedy: Form and the Process of Change* (Madison and Milwaukee, 1967).

The complex problems presented by eighteenth-century drama have received plentiful but not always discerning treatment. Ernest Bernbaum's pioneer study, *The Drama of Sensibility* (Cambridge, Mass., 1915) should be read, in company with later works: Stanley T. Williams, "The English Sentimental Drama from Steele to Cumberland," *SR*, XXXIII (1925), 405-426; F. O. Nolte, *The Early Middle-Class Drama in England, 1696-1774* (Lancaster, Pa., 1935); Joseph Wood Krutch, *Comedy and Conscience after the Restoration*, augmented edn. (New York, 1949); Arthur Sherbo, *English Sentimental Drama* (East Lansing, Mich., 1957); and Paul E. Parnell, "The Sentimental Mask," *PMLA*, LXXVIII (1963), 529-535, an unusually perceptive study.

The basic book on the Gothic drama is Bertrand Evans, *Gothic Drama from Walpole to Shelley* (Berkeley and Los Angeles, 1947); see also Theodore Grieder, "The German Drama in England, 1790-1800," *RECTR*, III (1964), II, 39-50, a detailed introductory survey of a crucial decade. For the drama of the late eighteenth and early nineteenth centuries a variety of other works, contemporary and modern, repays attention, among them Bertrand Evans, "Manfred's Remorse and Dramatic Tradition," *PMLA*, LXII (1947), 752-773; Samuel C. Chew's early *The Relation of Lord Byron to the Drama of the Romantic Period* (Baltimore, 1914) and, also on the Byronic hero, Donald M. Hassler, "*Marino Faliero*, the Byronic Hero, and *Don Juan*," *KSJ*, XIV (1965), 55-64; see also Marlies K. Danziger, "Heroic Villains in Eighteenth-Century Criticism," *CL*, XI (1959), 35-46. Aside from major works by Hazlitt, Coleridge, and others, cited below, important contemporary studies ranging through the period include George Colman the Elder's *Critical Reflections on the Old English Dramatick Writers* (1761); an anonymous article, "The British Theatre," in the *London Magazine*, XL (1771), 262-265, 311-313; and, in the later period, two long essays of first importance by Sir Walter Scott, his review of Boaden's *Life of*

Kemble and Kelly's *Reminiscences* in the *Quarterly Review,* XXXIV (1826), 196-248, and his "Essay on the Drama" for the *Britannica,* reprinted in Scott's *Miscellaneous Prose Works* (Edinburgh, 1827), VI, 257-470. No student should neglect the incisive criticism of George Darley, pseudonymously John Lacy, in the *London Magazine*: "Letters to the Dramatists of the Day," VIII (July-December 1823), 81-86, 133-141, 275-283, 407-412, 530-538, 645-652, and IX (January-May 1824), 60-64, 275-276, 469-473; "Old English Drama—*The Second Maiden's Tragedy,*" X (1824), 133-139; and "Theatricals of the Day," X (1824), 469-473; also of interest is an essay "State of the Drama in England," an unsigned review of *Cumberland's British Theatre* (1826) in the *Monthly Review,* III (1826), 371-372. Among modern studies of the nineteenth-century drama, consult Arnold Hauser's indispensable *The Social History of Art,* 2 vols. (New York, 1952), particularly an excellent chapter serving as background to this period, "The Origins of Domestic Drama," and another, "German and Western Romanticism" (II, sec. VI, Chaps. 3 and 6); and one of the most profound studies of its kind, all the more remarkable for its early date (1909), George Lukacs' "The Sociology of Modern Drama," trans. Lee Baxandall, *TDR,* IX (1965), 146-170. Helpful brief surveys are Harold Child's "Nineteenth-century Drama," in the *Cambridge History of English Literature,* XIII (Cambridge, Eng., repr. 1961), 255-274, and U. C. Nag's article, "The English Theatre of the Romantic Revival," *Nineteenth Century and After,* CIV (1928), 384-398, containing much good material although marred by some false assumptions. On the topic of melodrama the more important recent works are Eric Bentley's discussion of the subject in *The Life of the Drama* (New York, 1964); Michael R. Booth, *English Melodrama* (London, 1965); Frank Rahill, *The World of Melodrama* (University Park, Pa., and London, 1967); Robert W. Corrigan, "Melodrama and the Popular Tradition in the Nineteenth-Century British Theatre," *Laurel British Drama: The Nineteenth Century* (New York, 1967); and Gary James Scrimgeour's unpublished doctoral dissertation, "Drama and the Theatre in the Early Nineteenth Century" (Princeton, 1968); an interesting early article of lesser importance is M. J. Landa, "The Grandfather of Melodrama," *Cornhill Magazine,* n.s. LIX (1925), 476-484, on Richard Cumberland as a precursor of melodrama. Perhaps the best general modern survey of this period is E. B. Watson's *Sheridan to Robertson* (Cambridge, Eng., 1926).

The stage history of earlier plays in this later period forms an important subject for study; see especially Donald J. Rulfs' survey "Reception of the Elizabethan Playwrights on the London Stage, 1776-1833," *SP,* XLVI (1949), 54-69, and the same author's "Beaumont and Fletcher on the London Stage 1776-1833," *PMLA,* LXIII (1948), 1245-64; perhaps the most well-known of such studies is Robert H. Ball's work on Massinger's hardy villain, *The Amazing Career of Sir Giles Overreach* (Princeton and London, 1939). See also R. G. Noyes, *Ben Jonson on the English Stage 1660-1776* (Cambridge, Mass., 1935) and the detailed and perceptive study by Aline Mackenzie Taylor, *Next to Shakespeare: Otway's* Venice Preserv'd *and* The Orphan *and Their History on the London Stage* (Durham, N. C., 1950).

The standard histories of the theater written in this period are Lewis Riccoboni's *An Historical and Critical Account of the Theatres in Europe* (1741), translated from the French, reissued in 1754 as *A General History of the Stage* and again in 1790 as *Declamation; or An Essay on the Art of Speaking in Public*; W. R. Chetwood, *A General History of the Stage* (Dublin, 1749); Thomas Wilkes, *A General View of the Stage* (1759); Benjamin Victor, *The History of the Theatres of London and Dublin*, 2 vols. (1761), a second edition appearing in 1771 as *The History of the Theatres . . . A Continuation*; Walley Chamberlain Oulton's lively and detailed *The History of the Theatres of London*, 2 vols. (1796); and Charles Dibdin's ambitious *A Complete History of the English Stage*, 5 vols. ([1800]); see also John Jackson, *The History of the Scottish Stage, From its First Establishment to the Present Time* (Edinburgh, 1793). The British Museum holds an interesting collection of source material by Richard John Smith, "Collections for a history of the English Stage down to Kemble's retirement in 1817," B.M. Add. MSS. 38,620-38,621. A useful modern gathering is A. M. Nagler, *Sources of Theatrical History* (New York, 1952), while the best pictorial assemblage is Raymond Mander and Joe Mitchenson's *A Picture History of the British Theatre* (London, 1957). Among the many modern histories see, in addition to Downer's *British Drama*, Percy Fitzgerald's useful and reliable *A New History of the English Stage*, 2 vols. (London, 1882); H. Barton Baker, *History of the London Stage and Its Famous Players* (London and New York, 1904); and A. Thaler, *Shakspere to Sheridan* (Cambridge, Mass., 1922). In addition to Nicoll's five volumes, divided by period, consult, for the Restoration era, Montague Summers, *The Playhouse of Pepys* (London, 1935); Leslie Hotson, *The Commonwealth and Restoration Stage* (Cambridge, Mass., 1928); and Eleanor Boswell, *The Restoration and Court Stage (1660-1702)* (Cambridge, Mass., 1932). A good collection of essays on special topics ranging from the Restoration to the nineteenth century is *Studies in English Theatre History in Memory of Gabrielle Enthoven*, published by the Society for Theatre Research (London, 1952). Two excellent studies of the nature and problems of theatrical monopoly are Watson Nicholson's *The Struggle for a Free Stage in London* (Boston and New York, 1906) and Dewey Ganzel, "Patent

Wrongs and Patent Theatres: Drama and the Law in the Early Nineteenth Century," *PMLA*, LXXVI (1961), 384-396, including a discussion of the now well-known *Report from the Select Committee on Dramatic Literature: With the Minutes of Evidence*, printed for the House of Commons (London, 2 August 1832). A study of theatrical architecture during the period is Rand Carter's unpublished doctoral thesis, "The Architecture of English Theatres 1760-1860" (Princeton, 1966).

Individual contemporary sources, despite great unevenness, shed light on the drama and theater of the day. A brief list, arranged by date, includes *The Dramatic Historiographer: or, the British Theatre Delineated* (1735); Theophilus Cibber's *Two Dissertations on the Theatres* ([1756]); *The Theatrical Review; or, Annals of the Drama*, Vol. I ([1763]); the widely useful reference work by David Erskine Baker, *The Companion To The Play-House*, 2 vols. (1764), augmented and reissued by Isaac Reed and Stephen Jones as *Biographia Dramatica; or, A Companion to the Playhouse*, 3 vols. (1812); Francis Gentleman's petulantly critical but well-informed *The Dramatic Censor; or, Critical Companion*, 2 vols. (1770); *The Theatrical Review; or, New Companion to the Play-House* (1772); Thomas Davies' important *Dramatic Miscellanies*, 3 vols. (1783-84); Thomas Dutton's unusually thorough *The Dramatic Censor; or, Weekly Theatrical Report*, 5 vols. (1800-01); Thomas Gilliland, *The Dramatic Mirror*, 2 vols. (1808); and Horace Foote, *A Companion to the Theatres; and Manual of The British Drama* (1829). Of less value but characteristic are Paul Hiffernan, *Dramatic Genius* (1770); *Some General Advice to Theatrical Managers* (1789); *The Wonderful Secrets of Stage Trick; or a Peep Behind the Curtain* (1794); and the anonymous pamphlet by Frederick Howard, the fifth Earl of Carlisle, *Thoughts Upon The Present Condition of The Stage, and upon The Construction of a New Theatre*, new edn. (1809). Of the uncounted pamphlets and essays that gather in the wake of Jeremy Collier, pro and con, two may be singled out for perhaps unusual interest: H. Flitcroft's *Theatrical Entertainments consistent with Society, Morality, and Religion* (1768), and the well-written attack by John Styles, *An Essay on The Character, Immoral, and Antichristian Tendency of The Stage* (1806), reissued in a second edition (1807) and yet a third (1815), with slightly varying titles—an essay useful beyond its intention for its extended analyses of individual plays. Usefulness of another sort is found in J. Brownsmith's *The Dramatic Time-Piece; or Perpetual Monitor* (1767), which lists the playing times, including the half-price times, for current pieces in the repertory. In addition several volumes of periodical essays devoted wholly or in part to the stage include W. C. Oulton's *The Busy Body; A Collection of Periodical Essays*, 2 vols. (1789), and Arthur Sherbo's edition of *New Essays by Arthur Murphy* (Michigan State Press, 1963).

Biographies and memoirs, together with modern biographical studies, form a body of writing important for the history both of acting and production and of the drama. Representative works of some importance include Charles Gildon, *The Life of Mr. Thomas Betterton, The late Eminent Tragedian* (1710); James Thomas Kirkman, *Memoirs of the Life of Charles Macklin*, 2 vols. (1799); [Thomas Davies?], *A Genuine Narrative of the Life and Theatrical Transactions of Mr. John Henderson, Commonly Called The Bath Roscius* (1777); and Edward Cape Everard, *Memoirs of an Unfortunate Son of Thespis* (Edinburgh, 1818). Of high interest are contemporary and later books about Garrick; see especially Thomas Davies, *Memoirs of the Life of David Garrick* (1780), new (2nd) edn., 2 vols. (1808); Arthur Murphy, *The Life of David Garrick*, 2 vols. (1801); Percy Fitzgerald's comprehensive *The Life of David Garrick*, rev. edn. (1899); and Kalman A. Burnim, *David Garrick, Director* (Pittsburgh, 1961), a fine example of modern theatrical scholarship; see also the extensive selection from Garrick's correspondence, *The Letters of David Garrick*, ed. David M. Little and George M. Kahrl, 3 vols. (Cambridge, Mass., 1963), as well as the detailed survey by Raymond J. Pentzell, "Garrick's Costuming," *ThS*, X (1969), 18-42. On Mrs. Siddons the best known contemporary references are James Boaden's *Memoirs of Mrs. Siddons*, 2 vols. (1827) and Thomas Campbell's *The Life of Mrs. Siddons*, 2 vols. (1834); various modern biographies, frivolous, romanticized, and serious, exist, but an adequate full study of her professional career has yet to appear; see, however, *The Reminiscences of Sarah Kemble Siddons 1773-1785*, ed. William Van Lennep (Cambridge, Mass., 1942). Mrs. Siddons' brother John Philip Kemble was the subject of James Boaden's pompous but well detailed *Memoirs of the Life of John Philip Kemble*, 2 vols. (1825) and, in this century, Herschel Baker's balanced scholarly appraisal *John Philip Kemble: The Actor in His Theatre* (Cambridge, Mass., 1942). Other memoirs and biographies, inconsistent but continually necessary to consult, are William Dunlap, *The Life of George Fred. Cooke*, 2nd edn., rev., 2 vols. (1815); Boaden's *The Life of Mrs. Jordan*, 2 vols. (1831), as well as the study by Brian Fothergill, *Mrs. Jordan: Portrait of an Actress* (London, 1965); Charles Inigo Jones, *Memoirs of Miss O'Neill*, 2nd edn. (1818); *Macready's Reminiscences, and Selections from His Diaries and Letters*, ed. Sir Frederick Pollock (London, 1875), and the recent definitive study, a model of its kind, Alan S. Downer's *The Eminent Tragedian: William Charles Macready* (Cambridge, Mass., 1966), as well as Downer's earlier article, "The Making of a Great Actor—William Charles Macready," *TA*, VII (1948-49), 59-83.

Other biographical works, contemporary and modern, on playwrights, managers, and other theatrical personages include Esther K. Sheldon's very competent assessment, *Thomas Sheridan of Smock-Alley* (Princeton, 1967); Tate Wilkinson's useful *Memoirs of His Own Life,* 4 vols. (York, 1790), perhaps the best single account of theater in the British provinces; Richard Cumberland's self-congratulatory but informative *Memoirs,* 2 vols. (1807), as well as the modern treatment by Stanley T. Williams, *Richard Cumberland: His Life and Dramatic Works* (New Haven, 1917); Eugene R. Page, *George Colman the Elder* (New York, 1935); Michael Kelly's *Reminiscences,* 2 vols. (1826), and *The Reminiscences of Thomas Dibdin,* 2 vols. (1827); Louis F. Peck, *A Life of Matthew G. Lewis* (Cambridge, Mass., 1961), containing a selection of letters; Margaret S. Carhart, *The Life and Work of Joanna Baillie* (New Haven, 1923); and the less interesting study by Willem Scholten, *Charles Robert Maturin: The Terror-Novelist* (Amsterdam, 1933).

Also taking at least a general biographical approach but not limited to single figures are Theophilus Cibber, *Lives and Characters of the Most Eminent Actors and Actresses of Great Britain and Ireland,* Pt. I (1753), and such later works as D. Terry, *British Theatrical Gallery, A Collection of Whole Length Portraits, with Biographical Notices* (1825); the helpful *Oxberry's Dramatic Biography and Histrionic Anecdotes,* William Oxberry's ambitious project brought to completion, after his death, by his wife Catherine Elizabeth Oxberry, 6 vols. (1825-27); and the much less full *Lives of the Players* by John Galt, 2 vols. (1831).

Acting, Staging, and Production

Many of the works cited in the preceding category and in the section on Shakespeare below pertain, in whole or in part, to performance. The following, however, are placed in a separate group because of their direct concern with the art, and the science, of the acted play and with its effect in the theater.

Perhaps the single best collection of first-person commentary and other close sources is the series *Papers on Acting* published early in this century in the Publications of the Dramatic Museum of Columbia University; see also *Actors on Acting,* ed. Toby Cole and Helen Krich Chinoy, 2nd edn. (New York, 1954). A useful compendium of contemporary documents on important players of the eighteenth and nineteenth centuries is *Actors and Actresses of Great Britain and the United States,* ed. Laurence Hutton and Brander Matthews (New York, 1886), new illus. edn. (Boston, 1900); see the volumes on Garrick, on the Kembles, and on Kean and Booth. The best-known first-person account, deservedly so, is Colley Cibber's *Apology* (1740), modern editions by

Robert W. Lowe, new edn., 2 vols. (London, 1889), and B. R. S. Fone (Ann Arbor, 1968); see also the modern study, Richard Hindry Barker, *Mr. Cibber of Drury Lane* (New York, 1939), as well as the contemporary Anthony Aston's *A Brief Supplement to Colley Cibber, Esq* [sic] ([1748]). Aston's is only one of numerous contemporary commentaries, fair, sane, and otherwise, that extend up into the nineteenth century. Despite wide variations in reliability and point of view, I found the following helpful (full titles are given in some cases to discriminate among similar titles and to suggest the characteristic flair of the group as a whole): *The Present State of the Stage in Great-Britain and Ireland. And the Theatrical Characters of the Principal Performers, In Both Kingdoms, Impartially Considered* (1753); *The Theatrical Examiner* (1757); *The Theatrical Review: for The Year 1757, and Beginning of 1758* (1758); George Saville Carey, *A Lecture on Mimicry* (1776), which uses passages from Shakespeare to burlesque actors and acting; and *The Green-Room Mirror. Clearly Delineating Our Present Theatrical Performers, By a Genuine Reflection* (1786)—despite its promise, a vicious personal attack on a number of actors. In this same category belong works written in verse, sometimes satirical, often highly informative, and constituting a significant minor genre of their own: Robert Lloyd's *The Actor* (1760); Charles Churchill's well-known *The Rosciad*, whose 8th edn. had appeared by 1763 and is available in a modern edition by Douglas Grant in the *Poetical Works* (Oxford, 1956); Hugh Kelly, *Thespis: or, A Critical Examination into the Merits of all the Principal Performers Belonging to Drury-Lane Theatre* (1766), Book II (1767); Sir Nicholas Nipclose (pseud., sometimes identified as Francis Gentleman), *The Theatres. A Poetical Dissection* (1772); *Propriety: A Poetical Essay. To which is added, A Poetical Epistle to a Young Gentleman, On his Determination to appear upon the Stage* (1773); *The New Rosciad: A Poem* (1786); and two works reflecting Mrs. Siddons' quick ascent to stardom in the 1780's, *The Theatrical Portrait, A Poem, on the Celebrated Mrs. Siddons, in the Characters of Calista, Jane Shore, Belvidera, and Isabella* (1783), and Thomas Young's *The Siddoniad: A Characteristical and Critical Poem* (Dublin, 1784).

Contemporary writing on the art of acting is full and, as I have indicated in Chap. IX, above, often contradictory. The following brief list is merely suggestive of a larger body of source material which must be studied in aggregate. See James Eyre Weeks, *A Rhapsody on the Stage or, The Art of Playing* (1746); the ubiquitous Sir John Hill's *The Actor; or, a Treatise on the Art of Playing* (1755); Aaron Hill's essential "An Essay on the Art of Acting," available in his *Works*, 4 vols. (1753), Vol. IV; *An Essay on the Stage; or, The Art of Acting. A*

Poem (Edinburgh, 1754); the anonymous essay by James Boswell, "On the Profession of a Player," *London Magazine* (Aug., Sept., Oct., 1770), 397-398, 468-471, 513-517, as judicious and sensitive as any in the period; *The Sentimental Spouter: or, Young Actor's Companion* (1774), one of a swelling number of books of excerpts for amateurs that kept "My name is Norval" and other elocutionary set pieces on the lips of generations of schoolboys; Henry Siddons, *Practical Illustrations of Rhetorical Gesture and Action* (1807); and the indispensable statement of the basic problem in acting, Diderot's *Paradoxe sur le Comédien*, translated by Walter Herries as *The Paradox of Acting* (1883).

Siddons' book is clearly aimed at the practicalities of acting on the stage; other works exist whose connection is more tenuous and which deserve, but have not yet received, comprehensive assessment. See, for example, John Bulwer's early *Chirologia: or the Naturall Language of the Hand . . . whereunto is added Chironomia: Or, the Art of Manuall Rhetoricke* (1644), and Rev. Gilbert Austin, *Chironomia; or A Treatise on Rhetorical Delivery* (1806); a clear case for the possible influence of rhetorical theory on acting might be based on the actor-manager Thomas Sheridan's method, detailed in *A Discourse Delivered in the Theatre at Oxford* (1759), *A Course of Lectures on Elocution* (1762), and *Lectures on the Art of Reading*, 2 vols. (1775); in a similar connection consult Joshua Steele's *An Essay Toward Establishing the Melody and Measure of Speech* (1775), 2nd edn. enl. and retitled *Prosodia Rationalis: or, An Essay . . .* (1779), well known for Steele's ingenious but ultimately unsuccessful attempt to record Garrick's delivery of "To be or not to be."

Regarding modern scholarship on the theory and practice of English acting, see, in addition to the works of A. C. Sprague listed in the section on Shakespeare below, the following: Alan S. Downer's extensive studies of the subject, "Nature to Advantage Dressed: Eighteenth-Century Acting," *PMLA*, LVIII (1943), 1002-37, "Players and Painted Stage: Nineteenth Century Acting," *PMLA*, LXI (1946), 522-576, his series of six articles on the development of the actor's art, "The Private Papers of George Spelvin," *Players Magazine*, XIX (May, 1943) - XX (Feb., 1944), and, surely the best rationale for the scholarly study of this subject as a whole, "Mr. Dangle's Defense: Acting and Stage History," *EIE*, 1946 (New York, 1947), 159-190; Earl R. Wasserman, "The Sympathetic Imagination in Eighteenth Century Theories of Acting," *JEGP*, XLVI (1947), 264-272, whose notes incorporate one of the best bibliographies of acting theory available; and other less major but useful pieces, including Brewster Rogerson, "The Art of Painting the Passions," *JHI*, XIV (1953), 68-94; Kalman A. Burnim, "Eighteenth-Century Theatrical Illustrations in the Light of Contemporary Documents," *TN*, XIV (1959-60), 45-55; and Frederick J. Hunter, "Passion and Posture in Early Dramatic Photographs," *ThS*, V (1964), 43-63. One of the best and most suggestive of all attempts to explain the art of acting is William Archer's classic, *Masks or Faces? A Study in the Psychology of Acting* (1888). The most comprehensive modern study of acting history is Edwin Duerr's *The Length and Depth of Acting* (New York, 1962), containing an excellent bibliography. Typical of less rigorous essays on the relationship of actor and audience, useful in limited ways, is William Angus's "Actors and Audiences in Eighteenth Century London," *Studies in Speech and Drama in Honor of Alexander M. Drummond* (Ithaca, 1944), 123-138.

Some of the best scholarly talent of this sort has recently been turned to the investigation of promptbooks, most notably Charles H. Shattuck's two fine reconstructions, *Mr. Macready Produces As You Like It; A Prompt-Book Study* (Urbana, 1962), and *William Charles Macready's King John: A facsimile prompt-book* (Urbana, 1962); and Alan Downer's facsimile edition, *Oxberry's 1822 Edition of King Richard III with the descriptive notes recording Edmund Kean's Performance made by James H. Hackett* (London, 1959). An earlier article on the subject is William S. Clark's "Restoration Prompt Notes and Stage Practices," *MLN*, LI (1936), 226-230. Kalman Burnim's book, *David Garrick, Director*, illustrates how well the promptbook may be employed to reconstruct production.

On the subject of stage production and scene design, Lily B. Campbell's two pioneer articles offer detailed introductions, useful despite some out-of-date assumptions: "The Rise of a Theory of Stage Presentation in England during the Eighteenth Century," *PMLA*, XXXII (1917), 163-200, and "A History of Costuming on the English Stage between 1660 and 1823," U. of Wis. Stud. in Lang. and Lit., No. 2 (1918), 187-223, both reprinted in *Collected Papers of Lily B. Campbell* (New York, 1968), 61-100 and 101-139. See, in addition, Ralph G. Allen, "The Stage Spectacles of Philip James de Loutherbourg," unpublished D.F.A. dissertation (Yale, 1960), and, on de Loutherbourg's fascinating scenic invention the Eidophusikon, the description in Ephraim Hardcastle, pseud. [William Henry Pyne], *Wine and Walnuts*, 2 vols. (1823), I, 278-304, and the discussion in George Speaight, *The History of the English Puppet Theatre* (London, 1955), pp. 127-129; W. J. Lawrence, "The Pioneers of Modern English Stage Mounting: William Capon," *Magazine of Art*, XVIII (1895), 289-292; Sybil Rosenfeld, "Scene Designs of William Capon," *TN*, X (1956), 118-122; and the standard work on the English scenic tradition, Richard Southern's *Changeable Scenery* (London, 1952).

A very interesting and suggestive study on a special subject is Kirsten

Gram Holmström's *Monodrama, Attitudes, Tableaux Vivants: Studies on some trends of theatrical fashion 1770-1815* (Stockholm, 1967).

Shakespearean Criticism and Performance

Part of my bibliography on this subject is covered in the preceding section on acting; see also the notes on individual chapters below. The following contemporary works, located either through the use of Babcock's bibliography (cited above) or in the course of my own research, are limited to those most helpful or, at least, directly relevant to the study of *Macbeth* and *Richard III*, while the modern scholarship, cited subsequently, is also in some cases suggestive of larger concerns.

Of those works dealing with Shakespeare *inter alia*, the reader would do well to consult William Guthrie, *An Essay upon English Tragedy* (1747); [Edward Taylor], *Cursory Remarks on Tragedy, on Shakespear, and on certain French and Italian Poets* (1774), if possible the well-annotated copy of Richard Grant White, now in the Folger Library; William Cooke, *Elements of Dramatic Criticism* (1775); [William Jackson], *Thirty Letters on Various Subjects*, 2 vols. (1783); and Edward Du Bois, *The Wreath . . . To Which Are Added Remarks on Shakespeare, Ec.* (1799).

A chronological list of studies dealing entirely with Shakespeare includes the following significant or characteristic works: Samuel Johnson's anonymous *Miscellaneous Observations on the Tragedy of Macbeth* (1745); John Upton, *Critical Observations on Shakspeare* (1746); Horace Walpole, *Historic Doubts on the Life and Reign of King Richard the Third* (1768), reprinted in *The Works of Horatio Walpole, Earl of Orford*, 5 vols. (1798), II, 103-184; [Mrs. Elizabeth Montagu], *An Essay on the Writings and Genius of Shakespear* (1769); *Shakespeare. Containing the Traits of his Characters* ([ca. 1774]); William Richardson, *A Philosophical Analysis and Illustration of Some of Shakespeare's Remarkable Characters* (1774), 6th edn. (1812), the most complete, entitled *Essays on Shakespeare's Dramatic Characters*; Mrs. [Elizabeth] Griffith, *The Morality of Shakespeare's Drama Illustrated* (1775); Maurice Morgann, *An Essay on the Dramatic Character of Sir John Falstaff* (1777); [Thomas Whately], *Remarks on Some of the Characters of Shakespeare. By the Author of Observations on Modern Gardening* (1785); Martin Sherlock, *Fragment on Shakspeare, Extracted from Advice to a Young Poet. Translated from the French* (1786); John Philip Kemble, *Macbeth Reconsidered; An Essay: Intended as an Answer to Part of the Remarks on Some of the Characters of Shakspeare* [by Whately] (1786), 2nd edn., enl. (1817); [George Steevens], Letter on Whately's *Remarks, European Magazine*, XI (1787), 227-229; Richard Cumberland, essays comparing Macbeth and

Richard III in his *The Observer*, 2nd edn., 5 vols. (1788) [unavailable to me], repr. in 3rd edn., 5 vols. (1790), II, 225-265, repr. also in *The British Essayists*, ed. A. Chalmers, 45 vols. (1817), XXXIX, 117-144; [Walter Whiter], *A Specimen of a Commentary on Shakspeare . . . on a New Principle of Criticism, derived from Mr. Locke's Doctrine of the Association of Ideas* (1794), 2nd edn. rev. and enl. by Whiter in interleaved copy ed. Alan Over and Mary Bell (London, 1967); E. H. Seymour, *Remarks, Critical, Conjectural, and Explanatory, upon the Plays of Shakspeare* (1805); and Henry Mercer Graves, *An Essay on the Genius of Shakespeare, with Critical Remarks on the Characters of Romeo, Hamlet, Juliet, and Ophelia* (1826). I have found it more convenient to cite the works of the major Romantic critics in the notes to Chaps. XI and XII.

Graphic illustration of Shakespeare's plays sometimes bears a relationship to stage practice, although more often it simply illustrates the developing fascination in the late eighteenth century with the pictorial suggestiveness of Shakespeare's text. See, among others, the following: *The Picturesque Beauties of Shakspeare, Being a Selection of Scenes, From the Works of that great Author* (n.d.; plates dated 1783-1787); on John Boydell's Shakespeare Gallery, [Boydell], *A Catalogue of the Pictures in the Shakspeare Gallery, Pall-Mall* (1789), the descriptive catalogue of [H. Repton], *The Bee; or, a Companion to the Shakespeare Gallery* (1789), and *The Shakespeare Gallery; Containing A Select Series of Scenes and Characters* (1792), comprising fifty plates along with "Criticism and Remarks"; and *Shakespeare Illustrated. By an assemblage of Portraits & Views*, 2 vols. (1793), something of a bibliographical puzzle perhaps fostered by S. Harding, Babcock's designated author, and apparently the basis for *The Whole Historical Dramas of William Shakspeare Illustrated, by an Assemblage of Portraits . . . and Views*, 2 vols. (1811). The artistry in these works is often of very poor, even insipid quality, as in *Illustrations of Shakespeare; comprised in Two Hundred and Thirty Vignette Engravings* (1825) and Frank Howard, *The Spirit of the Plays of Shakspeare, Exhibited in a Series of Outline Plates*, 5 vols. (1827-33).

In a class by themselves are the travesties of the age, deserving but so far ungraced by extended serious study. One of the better sort is *Macbeth Travestie; In Three Acts. With Burlesque Annotations*, 4th edn. (1813), including such stage directions as "Enter Lady Macbeth with a light, and a pail of water." Even more entertaining is *A Key to the Drama; . . . Vol. I. Containing the Life, Character, and secret History of Macbeth* (1768), a purported collection of the materials on which Shakespeare based his play but actually a Gothic novel, full of intrigue and, as the anonymous author acknowledges with some pride, passages that are "rather luxuriant," in fact, pornographic in the zestful spirit of John Cleland.

Modern history of Shakespearean criticism has been well served by the energies of several generations of scholars. Despite its dated judgments, Augustus Ralli's *A History of Shakespearian Criticism*, 2 vols. (London, 1932) is still useful for its extensive gathering and close summary of sources, while the first study of late eighteenth-century criticism, R. W. Babcock's *The Genesis of Shakespeare Idolatry 1766-1799* (Chapel Hill, 1931) should be consulted by all students of the subject. More recently, Arthur M. Eastman has succeeded in providing what every new generation of readers requires but seldom receives, a judicious and well-written reassessment of a long tradition; see his *A Short History of Shakespearean Criticism* (New York, 1968). An earlier treatment along more limited lines is David Nichol Smith's concise *Shakespeare in the Eighteenth Century* (Oxford, 1928); see also Smith's fine introduction to his collection, now in its 2nd edn., of *Eighteenth Century Essays on Shakespeare* (Oxford, 1963), and Smith's edition in the "World's Classics," *Shakespeare Criticism: A Selection 1623-1840* (London, 1916). An indispensable work, despite its brevity, is T. M. Raysor's "The Study of Shakespeare's Characters in the Eighteenth Century," *MLN*, XLII (1927), valuably supplemented by the introduction to his edition of *Coleridge's Shakespearean Criticism*, 2 vols. (London, 1930), I, xvii-lxi. Clearly the most important and influential of eighteenth-century commentators on Shakespeare is Samuel Johnson, whose criticism has been collected in W. K. Wimsatt's edition *Samuel Johnson on Shakespeare* (New York, 1960) and, more fully, in Vols. VII and VIII of the Yale Edition of Johnson's works, *Johnson on Shakespeare*, ed. Arthur Sherbo, 2 vols. (New Haven and London, 1968); see also Sherbo's article, "Dr. Johnson on *Macbeth*: 1745 and 1765," *RES*, n.s. II (1951), 40-47. Additionally consult Babcock, "William Richardson's Criticism of Shakespeare," *JEGP*, XXVIII (1929), 117-136; David Lovett, "Shakespeare as a Poet of Realism in the Eighteenth Century," *ELH*, II (1935), 267-289; and Earl R. Wasserman, "Shakespeare and the English Romantic Movement," in *The Persistence of Shakespeare Idolatry: Essays in honor of Robert W. Babcock*, ed. Herbert M. Schueller (Detroit, 1964). Fred Manning Smith, in "The Relation of *Macbeth* to *Richard The Third*," *PMLA*, LX (1945), 1003-1020, provides an appraisal of numerous parallels but advances only a tenuous and narrowly conceived argument for their connection.

Studies of Shakespeare on the eighteenth- and nineteenth-century English stage include the early but comprehensive and still useful work by George C. D. Odell, *Shakespeare from Betterton to Irving*, 2 vols. (New York, 1920). Two indispensable books, each a model of their kind, are Arthur Colby Sprague's *Shakespeare and the Actors* (Cambridge, Mass., 1944) and *Shakespearian Players and Performances* (Cambridge, Mass., 1953). On the subject of Shakespeare in the Restoration the reader should consult Hazelton Spencer's *Shakespeare Improved: The Restoration Versions in Quarto and on the Stage* (Cambridge, Mass., 1927), although in some respects this is out of date; more recently Christopher Spencer has edited *Five Restoration Adaptations of Shakespeare* (Urbana, 1965) and prefaced this with a valuable critical introduction. Similar studies for the eighteenth century include George C. Branam's *Eighteenth-Century Adaptations of Shakespearean Tragedy* (Berkeley and Los Angeles, 1956). Attention to the production history of specific plays is illustrated by Alice I. Wood, *The Stage History of Shakespeare's King Richard the Third* (New York, 1909); Sprague, "A New Scene in Colley Cibber's *Richard III*," *MLN*, XLII (1927), 29-32; William Van Lennep's pair of letters on *Richard III* in *TLS* (30 April 1938), 296, and (18 June 1938), 418; and, in unpublished material, Percy Fitzgerald's MS. notebook on *Macbeth*, comprising an unidentified copy of the play tipped in a work book (in the Folger Library). Studies whose implications are more general are G. E. Bentley's article, now basic reading on the subject, "Shakespeare and the Blackfriars Theatre," *ShS*, I (1948), 38-50; Maynard Mack, "Engagement and Detachment in Shakespeare's Plays," *Essays on Shakespeare and Elizabethan Drama in Honor of Hardin Craig*, ed. Richard Hosley (Columbia, Mo., 1962), pp. 275-296; for the eighteenth century, George Winchester Stone, Jr., "David Garrick's Significance in the History of Shakespearean Criticism: A Study of the Impact of the Actor Upon the Change of Critical Focus during the Eighteenth Century," *PMLA*, LXV (1950), 183-197; Arthur H. Scouten's two studies, "Shakespeare's Plays in the Theatrical Repertory when Garrick Came to London," *Studies in English* (Texas), 1944 (Austin, 1945), 257-268, and "The Increase in Popularity of Shakespeare's Plays in the Eighteenth Century," *SQ*, VII (1956), 189-202. A basic article for Shakespeare in the nineteenth century is Arthur E. DuBois, "Shakespeare and 19th-Century Drama," *ELH*, I (1934), 163-196; see also Carol Jones Carlisle, "The Nineteenth-Century Actors *Versus* the Closet Critics of Shakespeare," *SP*, LI (1954), 599-615, whose coverage extends beyond the Kemble period.

The study of acting texts is still, at this late date, a wide open field, despite what Sprague and, more recently, editors like Christopher Spencer have shown to be their possibilities. The problems of location and of establishing provenance are, however, admittedly complex; see in this connection M. St. Clare Byrne's discussion, "Bell's Shakespeare," *TLS* (31 January 1948), 65. The fullest bibliography to date of eighteenth-century editions of Cibber's *Richard III* is Albert E. Kalson's in *RECTR*, VII (1968), I, 7-17.

On staging, costuming, and actors' interpretations, consult, with regard to *Macbeth*, the following: M. St. Clare Byrne, "The Stage Costuming of *Macbeth* in the Eighteenth Century," *Studies in English Theatre History in Memory of Gabrielle Enthoven* (London, 1952), 52-64; my articles, "Kemble's Production of *Macbeth* (1794): Some Notes on Scene Painters, Scenery, Special Effects, and Costumes," *TN*, XXI (1966-67), 63-74, and "Kemble and Mrs. Siddons in *Macbeth*: The Romantic Approach to Tragic Character," *TN*, XXII (1967-68), 65-86; Denis Donoghue, "Macklin's Shylock and Macbeth," *Studies* (Dublin), XLIII (1954), 421-430, including an account of some interesting notes on Macbeth in Macklin's hand; and, for a minor but revealing instance of theatrical continuity, W. Graham Robertson's reference to Ellen Terry's use of Mrs. Siddons' notes on Lady Macbeth in *Life Was Worth Living* (New York and London, n.d.). Dennis Bartholomeusz' stage history, *Macbeth and the Players* (Cambridge, Eng., 1969), appeared after my own work on the play had been completed; a fine example of judicious and thorough scholarship, it provides reconstructions of performance but varies enough in purpose to leave room for both approaches. Two useful articles on the addition of music in the play are Robert E. Moore, "The Music to *Macbeth*," *Musical Quarterly*, XLVII (1961), 22-40, and Roger Fiske, "The 'Macbeth' Music," *M&L*, XLV (1964), 114-125.

Another relevant area of scholarship still full of possibilities is that of Shakespeare and the graphic arts. The basic work, covering perhaps too much but highly suggestive of what can be done with a subject of acknowledged complexity, is W. Moelwyn Merchant's *Shakespeare and the Artist* (London, 1959). One of the best scholars in this area is T. S. R. Boase; see his "Illustrations of Shakespeare's Plays in the Seventeenth and Eighteenth Centuries," *JWCI*, X (1947), 83-108. I have suggested connections between the graphic arts, theatrical staging, and cultural developments in "John Hamilton Mortimer and Shakespearean Characterization," *PULC*, XXIX (1968), 193-207. Students of this subject who have access to the British Museum should not fail to see there the copy of Shakespeare described in Boase's article, "An Extra-Illustrated Second Folio of Shakspeare," *BMQ*, XX (1955), 4-8; the work contains thirty-seven watercolors including six by William Blake, one of which is "Richard III and the Ghosts."

Aesthetics and Tragic Theory

Draper's bibliography (cited above) of eighteenth-century aesthetic theory makes it unnecessary to attempt here an extensive record of the

British mind's unbounded enthusiasm for the subject. I shall cite only those works whose applicability to my subject makes them of special interest. Similarly restricted citations follow for tragic theory of the period, again excepting the major Romantics, whose works are referred to in a subsequent section.

Alexander Gerard's *An Essay on Taste* (1759) has been edited in facsimile from the third edition (1780) by Walter J. Hipple, Jr. (Gainesville, Fla., 1963). Gerard is influential, but even more so is Henry Home, Lord Kames, whose *Elements of Criticism* appeared first in 1762 (3 vols., Edinburgh). In the same year, as interest in the new aesthetics began to mount, Richard Hurd published his *Letters on Chivalry and Romance*; see the modern edn. by Hoyt Trowbridge in the Augustan Reprint Society's series Nos. 101-102 (Los Angeles, 1963). Another herald of transformation was Henry Fuseli, who translated Winkelmann's *Reflections on the Painting and Sculpture of The Greeks* for London publication in 1765. Other works now followed, including William Duff's striking *An Essay on Original Genius; and its Various Modes of Exertion in Philosophy and the Fine Arts, particularly in Poetry* (1767), of which see the facsimile edn. by John L. Mahoney (Gainesville, Fla., 1964); Daniel Webb's *Observations on the Correspondence between Poetry and Music* (1769), and James Beattie's "An Essay on Poetry and Music, as They Affect the Mind," in his *Essays* (Edinburgh, 1776); Joseph Priestley, *A Course of Lectures on Oratory and Criticism* (1777), and Adam Smith's university lectures, now available in a modern edition by John M. Lothian entitled *Lectures on Rhetoric and Belles Lettres* (London, 1963), a title Smith posthumously shares with his late contemporary Hugh Blair, who published his lectures in 3 volumes in Dublin in 1783; see also the less important observations of "Robert Heron" [John Pinkerton] in *Letters of Literature* (1785). In the course of the next two decades the three most important aestheticians of the period make their appearance: Archibald Alison, in *Essays on the Nature and Principles of Taste* (1790), 3rd edn., 2 vols. (Edinburgh, 1812); Uvedale Price, in *An Essay on the Picturesque as compared with the Sublime and the Beautiful*, 2 vols. (1794-98); and Richard Payne Knight, in *An Analytical Inquiry into the Principles of Taste* (1805). Henry Fuseli's *Lectures on Painting, Delivered at the Royal Academy*, 2 vols. (1801-20), are among the most interesting of the period; see also the eminent surgeon Charles Bell's *Essays on the Anatomy of Expression in Painting* (1806).

Among works on tragic theory in the period the reader should consult especially the following: [Roger Pickering], *Reflections Upon Theatrical Expression in Tragedy* (1755), an essay of interest comparable to William Mason's earlier "Letters Concerning the following Drama," prefixed to *Elfrida, a Dramatic Poem* (1752), the letters themselves dated 1751, the whole reaching a sixth edn. by 1759; the best-known essay on the subject in this period, David Hume's "Of Tragedy," in *Four Dissertations* (1757), Pt. II; Horace Walpole's Postscript to his drama *The Mysterious Mother* (1768) and his "Thoughts on Tragedy: in Three Letters to Robert Jephson, Esq." in *The Works of Horatio Walpole, Earl of Orford*, 5 vols. (1798), I, 125-129 and II, 305-314 respectively; William Hodson's "Observations on Tragedy," a Postscript to *Zoraida. A Tragedy* (1780), and the interesting rejoinder in the *Monthly Review*, LXII (1780), 185-188; of first importance for its implications, Joanna Baillie's "Introductory Discourse" in the first volume of her *A Series of Plays . . .* (1798); and M. G. Lewis's various inimitable pronouncements on the theory and practice of dramatic art, especially his Preface to *Alfonso, King of Castile* (1801) and his Postscript to *Adelgitha; or, The Fruits of a Single Error* (1806). Of real significance are two general essays, J. Aikin's "On the Impression of Reality attending Dramatic Representations," *Memoirs of the Literary and Philosophical Society of Manchester*, IV, Pt. 1 (1793), 96-108, and George Walker, "On Tragedy & the Interest in Tragical Representations" in the same series, V, Pt. 2 (1802), 319-345.

Modern studies of British aesthetics and tragic theory are among the brightest examples of humanistic scholarship in this century. Christopher Hussey provided essential reading in *The Picturesque: Studies in a Point of View* (London, 1927), as did Samuel Holt Monk in *The Sublime: A Study of Critical Theories in XVIII-Century England* (New York, 1935) and Walter John Hipple, Jr. in his comprehensive and rigorously analytical *The Beautiful, The Sublime, and The Picturesque in Eighteenth-Century British Aesthetic Theory* (Carbondale, Ill., 1957). Of similar importance, although more specialized, are Rensselaer W. Lee's essay *Ut Pictura Poesis: The Humanistic Theory of Painting*, now reissued (New York, 1967); Margarete Bieber, *Laocoön: The Influence of the Group Since its Rediscovery*, rev. edn. (Detroit, 1967); Sir John Summerson's stimulating book on architecture, *Heavenly Mansions* (London, 1949); Martin Price's chapter "The Theatre of Mind" in his book *To The Palace of Wisdom: Studies in Order and Energy from Dryden to Blake* (Garden City, N.Y., 1964), on the sublime, the picturesque, and the Gothic, and Price's more detailed study, a major essay, "The Picturesque Moment," in *From Sensibility to Romanticism: Essays Presented to Frederick A. Pottle* (New York, 1965), 259-292; see also Paul Zucker, "Ruins—An Aesthetic Hybrid," *JAAC*, XX (1961), 119-130. On the subject of history painting see three widely allusive works: Edgar Wind, "The Revolution of History Painting," *JWCI*, II (1938), 116-127; Jean Seznec, "Diderot and Historical Painting," in *Aspects of the Eighteenth Century*, ed. Earl Wasserman (Baltimore, 1965); and Ronald Paulson, "The *Harlot's Progress* and the Tradition of History Painting," *ECS*, I (1967), 69-92, as well as my article on J. H. Mortimer cited in the section on Shakespeare above.

Of the numerous studies of tragic theory in Restoration and eighteenth-century English writing, the three most helpful in my case have been John W. Draper, "Aristotelian 'Mimesis' in Eighteenth Century England," *PMLA*, XXXVI (1921), 372-400, Earl R. Wasserman's essential article "The Pleasures of Tragedy," *ELH*, XIV (1947), 283-307, and Eric Rothstein, "English Tragic Theory in the Late Seventeenth Century," *ELH*, XXIX (1962), 306-323, which appears also in revised form in Rothstein's *Restoration Tragedy* (Madison and Milwaukee, 1967). Useful also are Clarence C. Greene's book *The Neo-Classic Theory of Tragedy in England During the Eighteenth Century* (Cambridge, Mass., 1934); J. Frederick Doering, "Hume and the Theory of Tragedy," *PMLA*, LII (1937), 1130-34; Baxter Hathaway, "The Lucretian 'Return Upon Ourselves' in Eighteenth-Century Theories of Tragedy," *PMLA*, LXII (1947), 672-689; W. J. Hipple, Jr., "The Logic of Hume's Essay 'Of Tragedy,'" *PhQ*, VI (1956), 43-52; Richard H. Tyre, "Versions of Poetic Justice in the Early Eighteenth Century," *SP*, LIV (1957), 29-44; and David S. Berkeley, "Some Notes on Probability in Restoration Drama," *N&Q*, CC (1955), 237-239, 342-344. A sensible modern study of Aristotelian theory is F. L. Lucas's *Tragedy: Serious Drama in Relation to Aristotle's Poetics*, rev. edn. (New York, 1958). For a study of ideas and examples of tragic language see Moody E. Prior, *The Language of Tragedy* (New York, 1947).

Philosophy and Psychology

An extensive bibliography of this subject would be out of place here, but the following selected items are cited as both representative and particularly appropriate in the present context.

John Locke's *Essay Concerning Human Understanding* (1690 *et seq.*) precedes such other essential works for the study of the human mind as George Berkeley's *An Essay towards a New Theory of Vision* (Dublin, 1709); David Hume's *A Treatise of Human Nature*, 2 vols. (1738) and the later essay *Concerning Human Understanding* (1748); and Thomas Reid's *An Inquiry into the Human Mind, On the Principles of Common Sense* (1763). With regard to the moral philosophy of the period, the most important work for my purposes has been Adam Smith's *Theory of Moral Sentiments* (1759); also of interest are such lesser works as James Beattie's *Dissertations Moral and Critical* (1783). The relevance of religious philosophy to the present study is to be found chiefly in the subject of natural religion, especially in Samuel Clark's Boyle Lectures of 1705, *A Discourse Concerning the Unchangeable Obligations of Natural Religion* (1706); Joseph Butler's widely known *The Analogy of Religion, Natural and Revealed, to the Constitution and Course of Nature* (1736); and Henry Home, Lord Kames's *Essays on the Principles of Morality and Natural Religion* (Edinburgh, 1751), a work symptomatic of changes in areas much wider than Kames's declared subject.

The application of the ideas of these writers is illustrated, in addition to Tuveson's important book *Imagination as a Means of Grace,* by such modern works as Kenneth MacLean's *John Locke and English Literature of the Eighteenth Century* (New Haven, 1936) and Gordon McKenzie's *Critical Responsiveness: A Study of the Psychological Current in Later Eighteenth-Century Criticism* (Berkeley and Los Angeles, 1949). See also R. Haven's article "Coleridge, Hartley, and the Mystics," *JHI,* xx (1959), 477-494 and, for a discussion of Smith's *Moral Sentiments,* Walter J. Ong, "Psyche and the Geometers: Aspects of Associationist Critical Theory," *MP,* XLIX (1951), 16-27.

Individual Chapters

Cited in this section are works, mostly of modern scholarship, whose present significance or usefulness does not extend to the subject as a whole. My purposes here are simply to indicate the resources I have found most useful and to suggest helpful guides to the reader considering special topics.

CHAPTERS I AND II. Many studies of Fletcherian drama are of interest, especially Lawrence B. Wallis, *Fletcher, Beaumont & Company: Entertainers to the Jacobean Gentry* (New York, 1947); Eugene M. Waith, *The Pattern of Tragicomedy in Beaumont and Fletcher* (New Haven, 1952); John F. Danby, *Poets on Fortune's Hill* (London, 1952), rev. edn. issued as *Elizabethan and Jacobean Poets* (London, 1964); William W. Appleton, *Beaumont and Fletcher: A Critical Study* (London, 1956); Clifford Leech, *The John Fletcher Plays* (London, 1962); also the articles by Arthur Mizener, "The High Design of *A King and No King,*" *MP,* XXXVIII (1940), 133-154; Eugene Waith, "John Fletcher and the Art of Declamation," *PMLA,* LXVI (1951), 226-234; Philip Edwards, "The Danger not the Death: The Art of John Fletcher," *Jacobean Theatre,* Stratford-Upon-Avon Stud., Vol. 1 (London, 1960), 159-177; and Marco Mincoff, "Shakespeare, Fletcher, and Baroque Tragedy," *ShS,* xx (1967), 1-15. On the subject of Fletcherian drama in the Restoration, see James W. Tupper, "The Relation of the Heroic Play to the Romances of Beaumont and Fletcher," *PMLA,* XX (1905), 584-621; Arthur Colby Sprague's indispensable *Beaumont and Fletcher on the Restoration Stage* (Cambridge, Mass., 1926); and John Harold Wilson, *The Influence of Beaumont and Fletcher on Restoration Drama* (Columbus, O., 1928). For Massinger see especially two articles, James G. McManaway, "Philip Massinger and the Restoration Drama," *ELH,* I (1934), 276-304, and J. Frank Kermode, "A Note on the History of Massinger's 'The Fatal Dowry' in the Eighteenth Century," *N&Q,* CXCII (1947), 186-187. The important subject of theatrical continuity has recently been added to, at least by implication, in two studies of Shakespeare's "lost" *Cardenio*: see Harriet C. Frazier, "Theobald's *The Double Falsehood*: A Revision of Shakespeare's Cardenio," *CompD,* I (1967), 219-233, and John Freehafer's excellent piece "*Cardenio,* by Shakespeare and Fletcher," *PMLA,* LXXXIV (1969), 501-513, which provides corroboration for Fletcherian co-authorship of the play.

CHAPTERS III AND IV. Most of the scholarship and other works relevant to this chapter have been cited in the sections on drama and on aesthetics and tragic theory above. Two recent articles, however, may be mentioned here: M. M. Kelsall, "The Meaning of Addison's *Cato,*" *RES,* XVII (1966), 149-162, and C. F. Burgess, "Lillo Sans Barnwell, or The Playwright Revisited," *MP,* LXVI (1968), 5-29, a badly needed reassessment of Lillo's dramaturgy.

CHAPTER V. For this chapter the essential contemporary work of comic theory is Corbyn Morris's *An Essay Toward Fixing the True Standards of Wit, Humour, Raillery, Satire, and Ridicule* (1744). Good modern scholarship on the subject may be found in John W. Draper's article, "The Theory of the Comic in Eighteenth-Century England," *JEGP,* XXXVII (1938), 207-223; Stuart Tave's study of Morris, "Corbyn Morris: Falstaff, Humor, and Comic Theory in the Eighteenth Century," *MP,* L (1952), 102-115; and Tave's more recent book, *The Amiable Humorist: A Study in the Comic Theory and Criticism of the Eighteenth and Early Nineteenth Centuries* (Chicago, 1960). The two works of Goldsmith figuring prominently in this chapter are the anonymous "An Essay on the Theatre; Or, A Comparison between Laughing and Sentimental Comedy," *Westminster Magazine,* I (1773), 4-6, and *Retaliation: A Poem . . . Including Epitaphs on the most Distinguished Wits of this Metropolis* (1774), both of which are included in Arthur Friedman's splendid edition, *The Collected Works of Oliver Goldsmith,* 5 vols. (Oxford, 1966). Goldsmith's letters provide some insight into the difficulties he encountered as a dramatist; see *The Collected Letters,* ed. Katharine Balderston (Cambridge, Eng., 1928), and her introductory section on the production of *She Stoops to Conquer.* Among modern studies, Robert B. Heilman offers a defense of Goldsmith's earlier play as a satire on sentimental comedy in "The Sentimentalism of Goldsmith's *Good-Natured Man,*" *Studies for William A. Read* (University, La., 1940), 237-253; also necessary to consult are Ricardo Quintana's two articles, "Oliver Goldsmith as a Critic of the Drama," *SEL,* v (1965), 435-454, and "Goldsmith's Achievement as a Dramatist," *UTQ,* XXXIV (1965), 159-177, as well as his more general critical appraisal, *Oliver Goldsmith: A Georgian Study* (New York and London, 1967). See also W. F. Gallaway, Jr., "The Sentimentalism of Goldsmith," *PMLA,* XLVIII (1933), 1167-81, and an interesting contemporary biographical and critical article, "Dr. Goldsmith," in the *European Magazine,* XXIV (1793), 170-171. A useful background article on Cumberland's *The West Indian* is Wylie Sypher's "The West-Indian as a 'Character' in the Eighteenth Century," *SP,* XXXVI (1939), 503-520.

CHAPTER VI. Sheridan's multifarious career inspired numerous biographies and memoirs, varying widely in trustworthiness; useful are John Watkins, *Memoirs of the Public and Private Life of the Right Honorable Richard Brinsley Sheridan* (1817); Thomas Moore, *Memoirs of the Life of . . . Sheridan* (1825); *Authentic Memoirs of the Life and Death of . . . Sheridan* (1816); *The Life of . . . Sheridan,* 2nd edn. [1816?]; and *Sheridaniana; or, Anecdotes of the Life of Richard Brinsley Sheridan; His Table-talk, and Bon Mots* (1826). Among the most interesting politically motivated attacks is William Cobbett's *The Political Proteus. A View of the Public Character and Conduct of R. B. Sheridan, Esq.* (January, 1804). Modern biographical studies include, importantly, Walter Sichel's *Sheridan,* 2 vols. (London, 1909) and R. Crompton Rhodes, *Harlequin Sheridan: The Man and the Legends* (Oxford, 1933); more biographical and other useful information is provided in Cecil Price's fine edition of the *Letters,* 3 vols. (Oxford, 1966). Contemporary studies focusing on *Pizarro* are John Britton's *Sheridan and Kotzebue* (1799); Thomas Dutton's *Pizarro in Peru; or, The Death of Rolla,* 2nd edn. ([1799]), a translation containing pointed general remarks on the performance at Drury Lane; and the satire on *Pizarro* by "Bam-ley Satiricon," *More Kotzebue! The Origin of My Own Pizarro* (1799). Modern scholarship on the play is limited but includes Myron Matlaw's two helpful articles, "English Versions of *Die Spanier in Peru,*" *MLQ,* XVI (1955), 63-67, and " 'This is Tragedy!!!' The History of *Pizarro,*" *QJS,* XLIII (1957), 288-294; Anthony Oliver and John Saunders, "De Loutherbourg and Pizarro, 1799," *TN,* XX (1965), 30-32 and Plate I; and Raymond Mander and Joe

Mitchenson, "De Loutherbourg and Pizarro, 1799," *TN*, xx (1966), 160 and Plate II. Studies of Kotzebue include W. Sellier's *Kotzbue in England* (Leipzig, 1901); L. F. Thompson, *Kotzebue: A Survey of His Progress in England and France* (Paris, 1928); and Grzegorz Sinko, *Sheridan and Kotzebue: A Comparative Essay* (Wroclaw, 1949).

CHAPTER VII. On the subject of closet drama, in addition to the references on the stage and the study gathered in footnote 5 in this chapter, see Stephen A. Larrabee, "The 'Closet' and the 'Stage' in 1759," *MLN*, LVI (1941), 282-284; Robert D. Williams, "Antiquarian Interest in Elizabethan Drama Before Lamb," *PMLA*, LIII (1938), 434-444; and Frank Paul Bowman, "Notes Towards the Definition of the Romantic Theatre," *ECr*, v (1965), 121-130, an article on French closet drama. On Byron's connection with the subject, see David V. Erdman, "Byron's Stage Fright: The History of His Ambition and Fear of Writing For the Stage," *ELH*, VI (1939), 219-243. For Shelley and *The Cenci*, Newman Ivey White's *Shelley*, 2 vols. (New York, 1940) provides detailed biographical background, as do the *Letters*, ed. Frederick L. Jones, 2 vols. (Oxford, 1964), containing also an appendix listing Shelley's reading; see also the valuable material in Shelley's *Note Books*, ed. H. Buxton Forman, 3 vols. (Boston, 1911); *Mary Shelley's Journal*, ed. Frederick L. Jones (Norman, Okla., 1947); and *Peacock's Memoirs of Shelley with Shelley's Letters to Peacock*, ed. H.F.B. Brett-Smith (London, 1909). A study of commentary on the play itself might properly begin with White's collection, *The Unextinguished Hearth: Shelley and His Contemporary Critics* (Durham, N.C., 1938). The source "Relation of the Death of the Family of the Cenci" may be found appended to an edition of the play with an intro. by Alfred Forman and H. Buxton Forman (London, 1886). The stage history has been examined by Kenneth N. Cameron and Horst Frenz in "The Stage History of Shelley's *The Cenci*," *PMLA*, LX (1945), 1080-1105, and Bert O. States, "Addendum: The Stage History of Shelley's *The Cenci*," *PMLA*, LXXII (1957), 633-644. Critical readings of the play are numerous; the reader should consult especially the following: Carlos Baker, *Shelley's Major Poetry: The Fabric of a Vision* (Princeton, 1948); Robert F. Whitman, "Beatrice's 'Pernicious Mistake' in *The Cenci*," *PMLA*, LXXIV (1959), 249-253; Paul Smith, "Restless Casuistry: Shelley's Composition of *The Cenci*," *KSJ*, XIII (1964), 77-85; and James Rieger, "Shelley's Paterin Beatrice," *SIR*, IV (1965), 169-184. Also of interest are Ernest Sutherland Bates, *A Study of Shelley's Drama The Cenci* (New York, 1908); Daniel Lee Clark, "Shelley and Shakespeare," *PMLA*, LIV (1939), 278-286; S. R. Watson, "*Othello* and *The Cenci*," *PMLA*, LV (1940), 611-614; Melvin

R. Watson, "Shelley and Tragedy: The Case of Beatrice Cenci," *KSJ*, VII (1958), 13-21; Marcel Kessel and Bert O. States, "*The Cenci* as a Stage Play," *PMLA*, LXXV (1960), 147-149; William H. Marshall, " 'Caleb Williams' and 'The Cenci,' " *N&Q*, n.s. VII (1960), 261; Joan Rees, "Shelley's Orsino: Evil in *The Cenci*," *KSMB*, No. 12 (1961), 3-8; Charles L. Adams, "The Structure of *The Cenci*," *DramS*, IV (1965), 139-148; and Terence J. Spencer, "Shelley's 'Alastor' and Romantic Drama," *TWA*, XLVIII (1959), 233-237. See also David S. Halliburton, "Shelley's 'Gothic' Novels," *KSJ*, XVI (1967), 39-49.

CHAPTER VIII. The reader concerned with materials relevant to this chapter should consult the sections on critical background, Shakespearean criticism, aesthetics, and philosophy and psychology above.

CHAPTER IX. On Garrick, in addition to works cited in the sections on the theater and on staging above, see Garrick's own anonymous *Essay on Acting* (1744) and other comments scattered through his *Private Correspondence*, ed. [James Boaden], 2 vols. (1831-32). An early description of his acting may be found in *Champion* No. 455, quoted in the *Gentleman's Magazine*, XII (1742), 527, and another, pertaining to his later career, in Andrew Erskine's "Ode to Fear," *Gentleman's Magazine*, XXXIII (1763), 196. See as well "Two Dialogues by Sir Joshua Reynolds In Imitation of Johnson's Style of Conversation," *Johnsonian Miscellanies*, ed. George Birckbeck Hill, 2 vols. (Oxford, 1897), II, 232-249. Other contemporary references include J. G. Cooper's praise in the anonymous *Letters Concerning Taste* (1755), p. 109; William Shirley, *Brief Remarks on the Original and Present State of the Drama* (1758), an attack on Garrick interesting for the satirical attempt to write down pauses and mannered speech; and David Williams, *A Letter to David Garrick, Esq.* (1770), 2nd edn. (1772). The work of George Winchester Stone, Jr. on Garrick is indispensable; relevant here are "The God of His Idolatry: Garrick's Theory of Acting and Dramatic Composition with Especial Reference to Shakespeare," *Joseph Quincy Adams Memorial Studies* (Washington, D.C., 1948), 115-128; "Garrick's Handling of *Macbeth*," *SP*, XXXVIII (1941), 609-628; and "Bloody, Cold, and Complex Richard: David Garrick's Interpretation," *On Stage and Off: Eight Essays in English Literature*, ed. John W. Ehrstine *et al.* (Pullman, Wash., 1968), 14-25, which appeared after this chapter had been written. See also Stone's edition of *The Journal of David Garrick Describing his visit to France and Italy in 1763* (New York, 1939), and K. A. Burnim, "The Significance of Garrick's Letters to Hayman," *ShQ*, IX (1958), 149-152.

CHAPTER X. In addition to works included in the section on drama and theater above, the reader with a special interest in Kemble may consult his "Memoranda," British Museum Add. MSS. 31,972-31,975 and the revealing titles and lists contained in *A Catalogue of the Valuable and Extensive Library, Choice Prints, and Theatrical Portraits, of John Philip Kemble, Esq.* (1821). Contemporary commentary on Kemble is, as one would suspect, rich in variety, ranging from such scurrilous pamphlets as *The Life of John Philip Kemble* ([1809?]), apparently occasioned by the O.P. riots, and *Broad Hints at Retirement, an Ode to a Tragedy King* ([1810?]), to such helpful essays as John Ambrose Williams, *Memoirs of John Philip Kemble, Esq. with an Original Critique of his Performance* (1817). Also of special interest are *Remarks on the Character of Richard the Third; as played by Cooke and Kemble* (1801; 2nd edn. rev. and enl., n.d.); [H. Martin], *Remarks on Mr. John Kemble's Performance of Hamlet and Richard the Third* (1802); *Kembliana: Being A Collection of The Jeu d'Esprits, Ec. That Have Appeared Respecting King John* (1804); and *An Authentic Narrative of Mr. Kemble's Retirement from the Stage* (1817). A modern work is Harold Child's *The Shakespearean Productions of John Philip Kemble* (1935); and see David Rostrom, "John Philip Kemble's *Coriolanus* and *Julius Caesar*: An Examination of the Prompt Copies," *TN*, XXIII (1968), 26-34. The most important study of Mrs. Siddons still remains Professor Bell's annotations of her performances, edited by H. C. Fleeming Jenkin in *Mrs. Siddons as Lady Macbeth and as Queen Katharine*, Pub. of the Dramatic Museum of Columbia University, 2nd ser.: Papers on Acting, III (New York, 1915).

CHAPTER XI. The primary works of Charles Lamb pertinent to this chapter are his *Specimens of English Dramatic Poets, who lived About the Time of Shakspeare: With Notes* (1808), and *Elia. Essays Which Have Appeared Under That Signature in the London Magazine* (1823), as well as other writings brought together in *The Works of Charles and Mary Lamb*, ed. E. V. Lucas, 5 vols. (New York and London, 1903-05); see also Lucas' edition, *The Letters of Charles Lamb to which are added those of his sister Mary Lamb*, 3 vols. (London, 1935). A helpful article is Sylvan Barnet, "Charles Lamb's Contribution to the Theory of Dramatic Illusion," *PMLA*, LXIX (1954), 1150-80. The basic works for the study of Coleridge on the drama are *Coleridge's Shakespearean Criticism*, ed. T. M. Raysor, 2 vols. (London, 1930), 2nd edn., 2 vols. (London, 1960), with some new material; and *Biographia Literaria*, ed. J. Shawcross, 2 vols. (Oxford, 1907). Other important collections include *Coleridge's Miscellaneous Criticism*, ed. Raysor (London, 1936); *Specimens of the Table Talk of the late Samuel Taylor Coleridge*, 2 vols. (London, 1835); *Collected Letters*, ed. Earl Leslie Griggs, 4 vols. (Oxford, 1956-59); and *The Notebooks*, ed. Kathleen Coburn, 4 vols. (New York, 1957-61). Modern scholarship and criticism on Coleridge is unusually full; the following works are cited for their special relevance to the subject of this chapter and for their indications of other useful secondary materials. The two early studies most helpful to me have been E. K. Chambers' *Samuel Taylor Coleridge: A Biographical Study* (Oxford, 1938), and John Livingston Lowes, *The Road to Xanadu* (Boston and New York, 1927). The best guides to modern editions and studies are to be found in the bibliographical essays by T. M. Raysor and René Wellek in *The English Romantic Poets: A Review of Research*, ed. Raysor, rev. edn. (New York, 1956), 75-109 and 110-137. Critical books and essays, in addition to those cited in the section on critical background above, include Howard Hall Creed, "Coleridge on 'Taste,'" *ELH*, XIII (1946), 143-155; W. J. Bate's valuable essay, "Coleridge on the Function of Art," *Perspectives of Criticism*, ed. Harry Levin (Cambridge, Mass., 1950), 125-159; Sylvan Barnet, "Coleridge on Shakespeare's Villains," *SQ*, VII (1956), 9-20; Barbara Hardy, "'I Have a Smack of Hamlet': Coleridge and Shakespeare's Characters," *EIC*, VIII (1958), 238-255; M. M. Badawi, "Coleridge's Formal Criticism of Shakespeare's Plays," *EIC*, X (1960), 148-162; J.R.deJ. Jackson's unpublished doctoral dissertation "The Influence of the Theatre on Coleridge's Shakespearean Criticism" (Princeton, 1961), as well as Jackson's two articles, "Coleridge on Dramatic Illusion and Spectacle in the Performance of Shakespeare's Plays," *MP*, LXII (1964), 13-21, and "Coleridge on Shakespeare's Preparation," *REL*, VII (1966), 53-62; Richard H. Fogle's indispensable study, *The Idea of Coleridge's Criticism* (Berkeley and Los Angeles, 1962); and George Watson, *Coleridge the Poet* (London, 1966). Among many essays on Coleridge in the context of the history of ideas, see especially A. O. Lovejoy, "Coleridge and Kant's Two Worlds," *Essays in the History of Ideas* (Baltimore, 1948), 254-276. Scholarship on *Remorse* begins as early as 1890 with J. Dykes Campbell's article on the early manuscripts, "Coleridge's *Osorio* and *Remorse*," *Athenaeum* (5 April 1890), 445-446; on the source of the play see Dora Jean Ashe, "Coleridge, Byron, and Schiller's 'Der Geisterseher,'" *N&Q*, CCI (1956), 436-438, and on stage history and revisions consult Carl R. Woodring, "Two Prompt Copies of Coleridge's *Remorse*," *BNYPL*, LXV (1961), 229-235; Charles S. Bouslog, "Coleridge's Marginalia in the Sara Hutchinson Copy of *Remorse*," *BNYPL*, LXV (1961), 333-338; and P. M. Zall, "Coleridge's Unpublished Revisions to 'Osorio,'" *BNYPL*, LXXI (1967), 516-523.

CHAPTER XII. With reference to the subject of this chapter, Leigh Hunt's most important writings are contained in his *Critical Essays on the Performers of the London Theatres* (1807); *Imagination and Fancy* (1844); and his theatrical reviews, chiefly in the *Examiner*, a selection of which has been edited by L. H. Houtchens and C. W. Houtchens as *Leigh Hunt's Dramatic Criticism 1808-1831* (New York, 1949); Hunt's *Autobiography* has appeared in a modern edition by J. E. Morpugo (London, 1949). One of the best examinations of periodical publication in the age is Edmund Blunden's *Leigh Hunt's "Examiner" Examined* (New York and London, [1928]). A more recent study of Hunt is Stephen F. Fogle, "Leigh Hunt and the End of Romantic Criticism," *Some British Romantics*, ed. James V. Logan *et al.* (Ohio State Univ. Press, 1966), pp. 117-139. Study of any aspect of Hazlitt requires the use of the splendid edition by P. P. Howe, *Complete Works*, 21 vols. (1930-34), nor can any student of the man and his works neglect Herschel Baker's admirable critical biography *William Hazlitt* (Cambridge, Mass., 1962). Modern criticism on Hazlitt has concentrated on his notions of imagination and tragedy, not on the theatrical reference of much of his writing; see J. M. Bullitt's assessment, "Hazlitt and the Romantic Conception of the Imagination," *PQ*, XXIV (1945), 343-361; W. P. Albrecht, "Hazlitt's Principles of Human Action and the Improvement of Society," *If by your art: Testament to Percival Hunt* (Pittsburgh, 1948), pp. 174-190, the first of numerous articles by this industrious Hazlitt scholar; Alvin Whitley, "Hazlitt and the Theater," *Studies in English* (Texas), XXXIV (1955), 67-100; G. D. Klingopulos, "Hazlitt as Critic," *EIC*, VI (1956), 386-403; Albrecht, "Hazlitt's Preference for Tragedy," *PMLA*, LXXI (1956), 1042-51; Sylvan Barnet and Albrecht, "More on Hazlitt's Preference for Tragedy," *PMLA*, LXXIII (1958), 443-445; Albrecht, "Liberalism and Hazlitt's Tragic View," *CE*, XXIII (1961), 112-118; Albrecht's book, *Hazlitt and the Creative Imagination* (Lawrence, Kan., 1965); my article, "Hazlitt's Sense of the Dramatic: Actor as Tragic Character," *SEL*, V (1965), 705-721, an earlier version of part of the present chapter; and Kathleen Coburn, "Hazlitt on the Disinterested Imagination," *Some British Romantics*, ed. Logan, pp. 167-188. The standard modern study of Kean is H. N. Hillebrand's biography, *Edmund Kean* (New York, 1933); see, in addition to works cited in the sections on theater, acting, and Shakespeare above, Carol J. Carlisle, "Edmund Kean on the Art of Acting," *TN*, XXII (1968), 119-120, and her reference to an important early study by Thomas Fitzgerald, "John Neagle, the Artist," *Lippincott's Magazine*, I (May 1868), 477-491.

INDEX